THE NEW CAMBRIDGE C
TO MEDIEVAL ROM

This New Companion provides a broad and
important vernacular literary genre of the Middle Ages.
original chapters from seventeen leading scholars introduce students and general readers to the form's poetics, narrative voice, and manuscript contexts, as well as its relationship to the Mediterranean world, race, gender, and the emotions, among many other topics. Providing fresh perspectives on the first pan-European literary movement, chapters range across a broad geographical area, including England, France, Italy, Germany, and the Iberian Peninsula, as well as a varied linguistic spectrum, including Arabic, Hebrew, and Yiddish. Exploring the celebration of chivalric ideals and courtly refinements, the volume excavates the tensions and traumas lying beneath decorous surface appearances. An introduction and a bibliography of texts and translations, as well as chapter-by-chapter reading lists, complete this essential guide.

Roberta L. Krueger is the author of *Women Readers and the Ideology of Gender in Old French Verse Romance* (1993), editor of *The Cambridge Companion to Medieval Romance* (2000), and coeditor of *Cultural Performances in Medieval France* (2007). She has published widely on medieval romance, conduct literature, Marie de France, and Christine de Pizan. With Jane H. M. Taylor, she translated *Jean de Saintré: A Medieval Education in Love and Chivalry* (2014). She is cofounder of the *Medieval Feminist Newsletter* (1985), now the journal *Medieval Feminist Forum*.

THE NEW CAMBRIDGE COMPANION TO
MEDIEVAL ROMANCE

EDITED BY
ROBERTA L. KRUEGER
Hamilton College

CAMBRIDGE
UNIVERSITY PRESS

CAMBRIDGE
UNIVERSITY PRESS

Shaftesbury Road, Cambridge CB2 8EA, United Kingdom

One Liberty Plaza, 20th Floor, New York, NY 10006, USA

477 Williamstown Road, Port Melbourne, VIC 3207, Australia

314–321, 3rd Floor, Plot 3, Splendor Forum, Jasola District Centre, New Delhi – 110025, India

103 Penang Road, #05–06/07, Visioncrest Commercial, Singapore 238467

Cambridge University Press is part of Cambridge University Press & Assessment, a department of the University of Cambridge.

We share the University's mission to contribute to society through the pursuit of education, learning and research at the highest international levels of excellence.

www.cambridge.org
Information on this title: www.cambridge.org/9781108479301

DOI: 10.1017/9781108783033

First published 2023

A catalogue record for this publication is available from the British Library.

A Cataloging-in-Publication data record for this book is available from the Library of Congress.

ISBN 978-1-108-47930-1 Hardback
ISBN 978-1-108-74958-9 Paperback

CONTENTS

FIGURES

CONTRIBUTORS

ELIZABETH ARCHIBALD is Emeritus Professor of English Studies at Durham University, and former Principal of St Cuthbert's Society. Her work focuses on the classical tradition in the Middle Ages, romance, and in particular the Arthurian legend. Her publications include *Apollonius of Tyre* (1991), *Incest and the Medieval Imagination* (2001), *A Companion to Malory*, coedited with A. S. G. Edwards (1996), and *The Cambridge Companion to the Arthurian Legend*, coedited with Ad Putter (2009). She is currently working on a study of bathing in the Middle Ages.

SUSAN ARONSTEIN is Professor of English and Honors at the University of Wyoming. She is the author of *Hollywood Knights: Arthurian Cinema and the Politics of Nostalgia* (2005), *British Arthurian Narrative* (2012), and *The Road to Wicked: The Marketing and Consumption of Oz from Baum to Broadway* (with Kent Drummond and Terri Rittenberg; 2018), as well as the coeditor (with Tison Pugh) of *Disney's Middle Ages: A Fairy Tale and Fantasy Past* (2012) and *The United States of Medievalism* (2021).

LAURA ASHE is Professor of English Literature at the University of Oxford and the author of *The Oxford English Literary History vol. 1: 1000–1350: Conquest and Transformation* (2017)and *Early Fiction in England: From Geoffrey of Monmouth to Chaucer* (2015). She is currently writing a book on Chaucer.

KEITH BUSBY is Douglas Kelly Professor of Medieval French Emeritus at the University of Wisconsin–Madison. He has worked extensively on Old French literature of the twelfth and thirteenth centuries. His major publications include *Gauvain in Old French Literature* (1980), a critical edition of Chrétien de Troyes's *Perceval* (1993), *Codex and Context* (2002), *French in Medieval Ireland, Ireland in Medieval French* (2017), and the first edition of the French works of the Irish Dominican, Jofroi de Waterford (2020). His edition and translation of *The Statute of Kilkenny* (1366) will be published by the Irish Manuscripts Commission.

LAURA CHUHAN CAMPBELL is Assistant Professor of Translation Studies and French at Durham University. She has worked on the movement of Arthurian Literature between France and Italy, particularly the Merlin stories. She is the author of *The Medieval Merlin Tradition in France and Italy* (2017) and coauthor of *The Bristol Merlin: Revealing the Secrets of a Medieval Fragment* (2021). Her current work focuses on medieval bible translation.

ALBRECHT CLASSEN is University Distinguished Professor at the University of Arizona.

JANE GILBERT is Professor of Medieval Literature and Critical Theory at University College London. She has published widely on medieval French and English literature and is at present especially interested in how literary form behaves in translation.

PATRICIA CLARE INGHAM is the Martha Biggerstaff Jones Professor of British Literature at Indiana University. Her current projects include a short book on reading Chaucer in our precarious age and a longer-term project on the uses of literary romance for imagining a better world.

SHARON KINOSHITA is Professor of Literature at the University of California, Santa Cruz. She specializes in twelfth-century French epic and romance, medieval Mediterranean studies, and Marco Polo and the Global Middle Ages.

KATHY M. KRAUSE is Emerita Professor Emerita Professor of French and Medieval and Early Modern Studies at the University of Missouri–Kansas City. Dr. Krause's research focuses primarily on Old French literature of the long thirteenth century. She is the editor, with Dr. Alison Stones, of *Gautier de Coinci: Miracles, Music, and Manuscripts* (2008) and the author of recent articles on female literary and manuscript patronage, including "From Mothers to Daughters: Literary Patronage as Political Work in Ponthieu," in *Elite Women and Power: Beyond the Exceptionalism Trope* (edited by Heather Tanner; 2019).

ROBERTA L. KRUEGER is Burgess Professor of French Emerita at Hamilton College. She published an earlier edition of *The Cambridge Companion to Medieval Romance* (2000) and *Women Readers and the Ideology of Gender in Old French Verse Romance* (1993). She has translated, with Jane H. M. Taylor, *Antoine de la Sale, Saintré: A Late Medieval Education in Love and Chivalry* (2104). She is currently writing a book that explores the intersection of courtly romance and conduct literature in medieval culture.

SYLVIE LEFÈVRE is Professor at Sorbonne Université in Paris. Past projects include critical editions of the *Roman de Renart* (coedited with Armand Strubel, Roger Bellon, and Dominique Boutet; 1998) and Marguerite de Navarre's *Heptaméron* (coedited with Nicole Cauzuron; 2000). She coedited, with Hedzer Uulders, *Lettres d'amour au Moyen Âge: Les saluts et complaintes* (2016). She is currently producing a monograph on Antoine de la Sale and critical editions of Eustache Deschamps's lyrics and Nicole Oresme's *Livre de divinacions*.

LEE MANION is Associate Professor of English in medieval and early modern British literature at the University of Missouri–Columbia. He is the author of *Narrating the Crusades: Loss and Recovery in Medieval and Early Modern English Literature* (Cambridge University Press, 2014) and is currently completing a monograph entitled *The Recognition of Sovereignty: Politics of Empire in Early Anglo-Scottish Literature*.

MEGAN MOORE is Associate Professor of French at the University of Missouri. Her work focuses on gender and community in the medieval Mediterranean. She has published *Exchanges in Exoticism: Cross-Cultural Marriage and the Making of the Mediterranean* (2013) and *The Erotics of Grief* (2021), as well as numerous articles about romance and courtly culture. Future projects include comparative work on medieval emotional communities and the posthuman, specifically in AI and cyborgs.

NAHIR I. OTAÑO GRACIA is Assistant Professor of English at the University of New Mexico. Her theoretical frameworks include critical race studies, translation theory and practice, and the Global North Atlantic – extending the North Atlantic to include the Iberian Peninsula and Africa. She has published several articles on literatures written in Middle English, Old Castilian, Old Catalan, Old Irish, and Old Norse-Icelandic. Her essay, "Towards a Decentered Global North Atlantic," won the 2022 MAA Article Prize in Critical Race Studies.

AD PUTTER is Professor of Medieval English at the University of Bristol and Fellow of the British Academy. He has published widely on medieval literatures and languages (English, French, Dutch, and Latin). His books include *Sir Gawain and the Green Knight and French Arthurian Romance* (1995), *Studies in the Metre of Alliterative Verse* (2007), and *North Sea Crossings* (2021). He is the editor, with Myra Stokes, of *The Works of the Gawain Poet* (Penguin, 2014). He is currently working on Anglo-Dutch relations in the medieval and early modern period.

CRAIG TAYLOR is Professor of Medieval History at the University of York and a Fellow of both the Royal Historical Society and the Société de l'Histoire de France. He has published widely on late medieval French and English History. His books include *Joan of Arc, La Pucelle* (2006), *Chivalry and the Ideals of Knighthood in France during the Hundred Years War* (2013), and *A Virtuous Knight: Defending Marshal Boucicaut, Jean II Le Meingre, 1366–1421* (2019). He is currently collaborating with Jane Taylor on fifteenth-century French chivalric biographies, is writing a book on the Nullification Trial of Joan of Arc, and continues to work on chivalric culture in France during the Hundred Years War.

JANE H. M. TAYLOR is Professor Emeritus at Durham University. Her research focuses on the literature of the late Middle Ages in France, lyric poetry and romance in particular. She has also translated the lives of Boucicaut and Jean de Bueil and is interested in medieval techniques of translation.

DAVID A. WACKS is Professor of Spanish at the University of Oregon. He is author of *Framing Iberia: Maqamat and Frametale Narratives in Medieval Spain* (Brill, 2007), *Double Diaspora in Sephardic Literature: Jewish Cultural Production Before and After 1492* (Indiana University Press, 2015), and *Medieval Iberian Crusade Fiction and the Mediterranean World* (University of Toronto Press, 2019). His current book project is tentatively titled People of the Book: Jewish, Muslim, and Christian Retellings of the Hebrew Bible in Medieval Iberia. He blogs on his current research at davidwacks.uoregon.edu.

ACKNOWLEDGMENTS

First and foremost, I would like to thank the authors who contributed chapters to this volume. During a time of unprecedented disruption to personal and scholarly life, contributors drew on their broad and deep knowledge of medieval romance and history to compose concise chapters for this book. It may have taken a bit longer than initially planned to finish our project but, with resilience and perseverance, everyone came through. For that, I am profoundly grateful. I like to think that our deadlines, even when extended several times over, provided structure and our writing a sense of purpose to a time that was otherwise amorphous.

Thanks are also due to a group of talented colleagues who commented on various parts of the manuscript, offering pertinent suggestions. Matilda Bruckner, Thelma Fenster, Elizabeth Robertson, and Helen Solterer intervened in just the right ways; any remaining errors or infelicities are of course my own. My students of French at Hamilton College continued to demonstrate over the years why medieval courtly romance, with its often unexpected complexity, ambiguity, comic interludes, and marvelous adventures, remains a perennial favorite.

The librarians of Hamilton College's Burke Library, in particular Margie D'Aprix of Interlibrary Loan, were immensely helpful in tracking down materials and making print and electronic resources accessible during the past few years. Jolanta Kormornicka expertly prepared the index, which was generously funded by the office of Academic Affairs and the Dean of Faculty at Hamilton. At Cambridge University Press, Emily Hockley provided wise counsel and showed infinite patience as our editor, while George Paul Laver managed the many details of production with efficiency and good humor.

Finally, I would like to thank my husband, Thomas Bass, and our far-flung children, Maude, Tristan, and Julian Bass-Krueger, for their unwavering love and encouragement during the many phases of this project.

CHRONOLOGY

It is often impossible to determine the precise date at which a romance was composed. Most dates given here are approximations. For French romance, we have followed the chronology suggested by ARLIMA (Archives de Littérature du Moyen Age), accessible online.

	Arabic
OF	Old French
	Italian
LG	Low German
	Castilian
	Catalan
	Medieval Dutch
ME	Middle English
MF	Middle French
MHG	Middle High German
	Greek
	Hebrew
	Latin
	Persian
	Welsh

1000s	Fakhraddin Gorgānī	*Vis and Ramin* [Persian]
c. 1135–60	Theodore Prodromus	*Rhodanthe and Dosikles* [Greek]
	Eumathios Makrembites	*Hysmne and Hysminian* [Greek]
	Constantine Manasses	*Aristandros and Kallithea* [Greek]
	Niketas Eugeniamos	*Drosilla and Charikles* [Greek]
c. 1136	Geoffrey of Monmouth	*Historia Regum Britanniae* [Latin]
c. 1140–70		*König Rother* [MHG]

c. 1150	Robert d'Orbigny	*Floire et Blancheflor*, "version aristocratique" [OF]
c. 1155	Wace	*Roman de Brut* [OF]
c. 1160		*Roman d'Eneas* [OF]
c. 1163–97	Nizami Ganjavi	*Khamsa* [Persian]
c. 1165	Benoît de Sainte-Maure	*Le Roman de Troie* [OF]
c. 1165–1200	Béroul	*Tristan* [OF]
c. 1165–70	Chrétien de Troyes	*Philomena* [OF]
c. 1170	Chrétien de Troyes	*Erec et Enide* [OF]
1170	Thomas	*Romance of Horn* [OF]
1170s	Thomas of Britain	*Tristan* [OF]
1170–90s	Marie de France	*Lais* [OF]
1156–7	Gautier d'Arras	*Ile et Galeran* [OF]
c. 1174–1200	Thomas of Kent	*Le Roman de Toute Chevalerie* [OF]
1170s	Heinrich von Veldeke	*Eneit* [MHG]
1190–1200		*Boeve de Haumtone* [OF]
c. 1176	Chrétien de Troyes	*Cligès* [OF]
c. 1178–81	Chrétien de Troyes	*Yvain ou le chevalier au lion* [OF]
c. 1178–81	Chrétien de Troyes	*Lancelot ou le chevalier de la charrette* [OF]
c. 1180		*Herzog Ernst* [MHG]
between 1182–90	Chrétien de Troyes	*Perceval ou le conte du graal* [OF]
1180–5	Hue de Rotelande	*Ipomedon* [OF]
1188	Aimon de Varennes	*Florimont* [OF]
1180–90	Hartmann von Aue	*Erec* [MHG]
1175–1200		*Partonopeu de Blois* [OF]
c. 1185–1200	Renaut de Beaujeu	*Le Bel Inconnu* [OF]
c. 1190	Hartmann von Aue	*Der arme Heinrich* [MHG]
before 1191	Hue de Rotelande	*Protheselaus* [OF]
late 1100s		First Continuation, *Le conte du Graal* (Gauvain continuation) [OF]
late 1100s, early 1200s	Wauchier de Denain	Second Continuation, *Le conte du Graal* [OF]
late 1100s	Ulrich von Zatzikoven	*Lanzelet* [MHG]
c. 1191–2(?)	Hartmann von Aue	*Iwein* [MHG]
c 1200–2	Jean Renart	*Le Roman de l'Escoufle* [OF]
between 1200–11	Jean Renart	*Le Roman de la rose ou de Guillaume de Dole* [OF]
early 1200s		*Perlesvaus (Le Haut Livre du Graal)* [OF]

c. 1215–35		*Lancelot en Prose* (from the *Lancelot-Graal* cycle, the Vulgate Cycle) [OF]
1225–35	Raoul de Houdenc	*Meraugis de Portlesguez* [OF]
c. 1220	Rudolf von Ems	*Der Guote Gêrhart* [MHG]
c. 1225–30		*La Queste del Saint Graal* (Vulgate Cycle) [OF]
c. 1230		*La mort le roi Artu* (Vulgate Cycle) [OF]
1200s		*Hadith Bayad wa-Riyad* [Arabic]
1200s		*Melekh Artus* [Hebrew]
c. 1200–50		*Gui de Warewic* (verse) [OF]
c. 1200–50		*Ziyad Ibn Amir al-Kinani* [Arabic]
c. 1200	Hartmann von Aue	*Gregorius* [MHG]
c. 1205	Wolfram von Eschenbach	*Parzival* [MHG]
c. 1210	Gottfried von Strassburg	*Tristan* [MHG]
c. 1218	Wolfram von Eschenbach	*Willehalm* [MHG]
c. 1220	Wolfram von Eschenbach	*Titurel* [MHG]
1200–10	Robert de Boron	*Joseph d'Arimathie (Le Roman de l'Estoire dou Graal); Merlin en prose* [OF]
1225	Guillaume de Lorris	*Le Roman de la Rose*, first part [OF]
c. 1220	"The Stricker"	*Daniel von dem Blühenden Tal* [MHG]
c. 1220	Wirt von Grafenberg	*Wigalois* [MHG]
c. 1220	Konrad Fleck	*Floris und Blanscheflur* [MHG]
c. 1220		*Perlesvaus (Le Haut Livre dou Graal)* [OF]
c. 1227–9	Gerbert de Montreuil	*Roman de la Violette ou de Gerart de Nevers* [OF]
c. 1230	Manessier	Third Continuation of *Le conte du Graal* [OF]
c. 1230		*Le Roman de Tristan en prose* [OF]
1230		*La Mort le Roi Artu* [OF]
1235	Gerbert de Montreuil	Fourth Continuation of *Le conte du Graal* [OF]

c. 1235–40		*Guiron le Courtois* (second continuation of the cycle of Guiron le Courtois) [OF]
c. 1280–90		*Mai und Beaflor* [MHG]
c. 1280–90		*Reinfried von Braunschweig* [MHG]
mid-1200s	Jacob ben Elazar	*Tale of Sahar and Kima* [Hebrew]
c. 1250–1300	Heldris de Cornuaille	*Le Roman de Silence* [OF]
c. 1250		*L'Âtre périlleux* [OF]
c. 1250		*La Châtelaine de Vergy* [OF]
c. 1270–1300		*Floriant et Florete* [OF]
1270	Jean de Meun	*Le Roman de la Rose*, continuation [OF]
mid-1200s	Alfonso X	*Estoria de España* [Castilian]
		"Primitive" *Amadís de Gaula* [Castilian]
before 1285	Adenet le Roi	*Cleomadés* [OF]
c. 1276		*Les Prophecies de Merlin* [OF in Italy]
c. 1285	Ramon Llull	*Blaquerna* [Catalan]
c. 1285	Jakemés	*Le roman du Chastelain de Coucy et de la dame de Fayel* [OF]
c. 1285–90	Konrad von Würzburg	*Partonopier und Melior* [MHG]
c. 1290		*Flores y Blancaflor* [Castilian]
late 1200s		"primitive" *Amadís de Gaula* [Castilian]
c. 1300		*Prosa Lancelot* [Medieval Dutch]
		Richard Cœur de Lion [ME]
		Culhwch and Olwen [Middle Welsh]
late 1200s	Rustichello of Pisa	Arthurian Compilation, *Roman de Roi Artus* [Franco-Italian]
late 1200s		*Tristano Riccardiano* [Italian]
early 1300s		*Tristano Panciatichiano* [Italian]
c. 1300		*Libro del Cavallero Zifar* [Castilian]
early 1300s		*Tristán de Leonís* [Castilian]
c. 1313	Juan Vivas	*Historia de la demanda del Santo Grial* [Castilian]
between 1313–44		*Perceforest* [MF]
1324–30		*Storia di Merlino*
c. 1325–50		*Peredur* [Middle Welsh]
before 1320		*Sir Isumbras* [ME]

c. 1330		*Guy of Warwick* [ME]
c. 1369	Jean Froissart	*Espinette amoureuse* [MF]
c. 1300–50		*Tavola Ritonda* [Italian]
late 1220s/early 1300s		*La Inchiesta del San Gradale* [Italian]
late 1300s		*Tristano Corsiniano* [Italian]
late 1300s		*Sir Gawain and the Green Knight* [ME]
1340–41	Boccaccio	*Teseida* [Italian]
1362–9; 1381–82	Jean Froissart	*Melyador* [MF]
1380s	Geoffrey Chaucer	*Troilus and Criseyde* [ME]
1390s	Geoffrey Chaucer	*Canterbury Tales* [ME]
c. 1350–1400		Stanzaic *Morte Arthur* [ME]
c. 1400		*Ysaïe le Triste* [MF]
c. 1400		*Ponthus et Sidoine* [MF]
1400s		*La Belle Hélène de Constantinople* (prose) [MF]
1403–5	Thomas III de Saluces	*Le livre du Chevalier errant* [MF]
c. 1430	Eleanor of Austria	*Pontus und Sidonia* [MHG]
c. 1430	Ulrich Fuetrer	prose *Lanzelet* [MHG]
c. 1432	Pierre de la Cépède	*Paris et Vienne* [MF]
1437	Elisabeth Von Nassau-Saarbrüken	*Königin Sibille* [MHG]
1440–60		*Malagis* [MHG]
1453		*Pierre de Provence* [MF], second version
mid-1400s		prose *Erec* [MF]
1454		prose *Cligès* [MF]
1453–67		*Roman du Comte d'Artois* [MF]
1456	Antoine de la Sale	*Jean de Saintré* [MF]
1457	René of Anjou	*Le Cuer d'amours espris* [MF]
1440–55		*Baudoin de Flandre* [MF]
c. 1450		Prose *Merlin* [MF]
1400s		*Istoire de la Chastelaine de Vergier et de Tristan le Chevalier* [MF]
1450		*Gillion de Trazegnies* [MF]
1453–67		*Roman du Comte d'Artois* [MF]
c.1450		*Curial et Güelfa* [Catalan]
1469–70	Sir Thomas Malory	*Le Morte Darthur* [ME]
1473–87	Ulrich Fuetrer	*Buch der Abenteuer* [MHG]
between 1475–89		*Valentin et Orson* [MF]
1481–3	Pulci	*Morgante* [Italian]

1483	Boiardo	*L'Inamoramento de Orlando* [Italian]
c. 1490		*Tirant lo Blanc* [Catalan]
1494–5		*Jean de Paris* [MF]
1501		*Tristán de Leonís* [Castilian]
1505–16	Maxmillian I	*Weisskunig* [MHG]
1507	Garci Rodríguez de Montalvo	*Amadís de Gaula* [print edition; Castilian]
1517	Maxmillian I	
1516–32	Ariosto	*Orlando Furioso* [Italian]
1525–9	Pierre Sala	*Tristan* [French]
1540		*Amadis de Gaule* [first French edition, in print]
1549	Jean Maugin	*Palmerin d'Olive* [FR]
1554	Jean Maugin	*Nouveau Tristan* [FR]
1556	Jean Maugin	*Melicello* [FR]
1496		*Ogier le Danois* [prose, FR]
		Robert le Diable [prose, FR]
		Huon de Bordeaux [prose, FR]
1581	Tasso	*Gerusalemme Liberata* [Italian]
1605	Cervantes	*Don Quixote* [Spanish]

ROBERTA L. KRUEGER

Introduction

To survey the field of medieval English and European romance is to witness the remarkable elasticity of a narrative genre that came from an irrepressible urge to tell and retell stories in new languages, with shifting themes, adapted into particular forms, and transmuted into new versions for different geographic, social, and political contexts. The term "romance" applies to a vast domain of texts, which were produced throughout Britain, Europe, and the Mediterranean world, as far west as Wales, as far east as Byzantium, from Scotland to Italy and Spain, from the twelfth century to the early modern period and even later.

From a brief verse idyll such as *Flore et Blanchefleur*, translated into many languages and adapted into a more "epic" framework, to the massive prose romances of the late Middle Ages and early modern period, romance appeared in a diversity of material contexts – from a single manuscript containing the only extant version of one story to lavishly illustrated multi-volume works on vellum or parchment, and later to books that are printed on paper instead of being handwritten. Audiences may have at first been limited to close members of an aristocratic family listening to a story read out loud,[1] but by the end of the Middle Ages, prosperous urban middle-class readers, reading silently in solitude, held printed copies in their hands.

What distinguishes this protean genre from other works in the rapidly changing landscape of medieval literature and culture? The thirteenth-century poet Jean Bodel addressed this question by placing medieval narratives into three categories: those telling the "matière de Rome" (matter of Rome), which included such classical subjects as the Trojan War and the exploits of Alexander the Great; those recounting the "matter of France," referring to stories about Charlemagne and other historical heroes; and, finally, the matter of Britain, which meant especially stories about King

Arthur, the knight Tristan, and the vast gallery of Arthurian characters and themes, such as the Holy Grail. Beyond these perennially popular "matters," there were other features common to romances: special attention to poetics, particularly rhyme and rhyming patterns (as Ad Putter and Jane Gilbert demonstrate in Chapter 3), and a heightened sense of authorship, of who is telling the story and how it is being told (as Sylvie Lefèvre examines for French romance). Romance authors' focus on their rhetorical and narrative strategies ensured that these tales would be told in a way worth remembering and would inspire future writers to be innovative in their composition. As they recounted stories of memorable feats of military strength, moving adventures of star-crossed lovers, and wondrous tales of marvelous encounters, romance authors in every language set a high bar for literary distinction. Romance was the most important secular, vernacular genre of the Middle Ages and the first great pan-European literary movement. Its legacy reached far into the Renaissance and early modern period, continuing even up to our day.

As the chapters in this volume will show, romances had a celebratory, self-congratulatory, and aspirational surface, replete with descriptions of luxury objects and characters wearing exotic costumes in beautiful fabrics shot through with silk and gold. Romance knights sometimes sported ceremonial armor, rode fine horses, and performed impressive feats of arms. But romances also had a darker underside that probed psychological and social tensions, violence, and family disturbances, which might be deeply obscured or buried just beneath the surface. And they vilified non-white and non-Christian peoples, furthering deeply held northern and Christian prejudices. The glories of the Arthurian court may be marred by Arthur's incestuous liaison with his sister, the bastard son they conceive, Lancelot's adulterous love for the Queen, or Gawain's flirtatious dalliance and his uncontrollable temper, all of which mean that King Arthur is never fully in command. Middle English crusading romances aspired to military victory at the price of dehumanizing the perceived enemies of Christianity, victims of violent racist and religious exclusion. Conversion to Christianity made to seem voluntary could be made worse by massacre of all who refused to convert.

Yet in many notable cases, romances conveyed the porous nature of social and religious identities, where Western and Eastern cultures intersected and Christian and Muslim identities crossed over, at nodes of overlap between Christian mores, Celtic fairytales, and Classical morality. Romance portrayed conflicting cultural values and combined them in playful or profound ways. It was perhaps this mutable quality of romances that made them so popular and useful to medieval societies as they migrated from elite courts to wealthy bourgeois households and urban settings from the twelfth to the fifteenth century, and beyond.

The more we read romances in their many manifestations throughout the major European languages, the more difficult it is to define the genre's stylistic or thematic parameters. Some romances celebrated the victories of illustrious families (as in the Anglo-Norman tales of Guy of Warwick and Bœve d'Haumtome). Others explored the history of renowned families with physical deformities or depraved morals (i.e. the offspring of the marvelous Mélusine of Lusignan). Still others probed the miracles and spiritual challenges associated with the Grail legend, which linked Arthurian adventures to Biblical history.

Chrétien de Troyes is often hailed as the founding father of Arthurian romance. His hallmark achievement lay in the conjoining of materials from oral and written sources by a narrator who often called attention to his artistry and distinction. Many of the chapters in this volume, whether devoted to texts written in French, German, Italian, English, or Spanish, make at least a passing reference to Chrétien's romances, as his stories spin out on so many narrative routes.

Recent critical studies remind us that Chrétien's earliest extant narrative poem was not the story of *Erec and Enide*, drawn from Celtic lore and set in King Arthur's court, but a translation of one of Ovid's *Metamorphoses*, the brutal tale of Philomela, abducted and raped by her brother-in-law, who cut out her tongue so she could not speak of his terrible crime. This disturbing tale does not resurface until the fourteenth century, in the anonymous *Ovide moralisé*, where it is attributed to Chrétien li Gois (perhaps signaling that the author of the *Ovide Moralisé* believed Chrétien to have been a Jewish convert to Christianity).[2] No authorial identification appears in *Philomena*, but many scholars today view Chrétien as its original adaptor. If this is so, then a tale about "deception, rape, incest, mutilation, infanticide and cannibalism" is close to the foundation of courtly romance.[3] Chrétien's *Philomena* shows how clever rhetorical flourishes – for example, Tereus's talk about love with the maiden he assaults – can be deployed to cover over primal violence. The tensions within *Philomena* forecast a troubling paradigm for future fictions. Romances may highlight and explore courtly language and celebrate the exploits of chivalric knights, but the threat – or memory – of physical violence or psychological trauma underlies the bright surface of so many tales.

The chapters in this volume provide fresh critical perspectives on myriad aspects of medieval romance, from its origins in translations from antiquity to some of its most ambitious and extraordinary later manifestations in multilingual contexts. The ensuing chapters of this new *Companion to*

Medieval Romance are intended to supplement, but not supplant, the literary and historical analyses of *The Cambridge Companion to Medieval Romance* published in 2000. In the more than twenty years since those chapters were published, the corpus of canonical romances has expanded. New editions and translations of canonical and lesser-known texts have not ceased to proliferate, as the endnotes to individual chapters and the final Bibliography of Editions and Translations will demonstrate. Even as earlier literary analyses remain insightful, recent criticism reflects new interest in the emotions, gender identities, the Crusades, the Mediterranean world, and the construction of race – subjects specifically examined in the pages that follow. Although the geographical features of the medieval West are constant, the origins and trajectory of romance have been decentered from Northern Christian Europe to encompass more porous and expansive boundaries that include the Mediterranean and its adjacent territories, and that extend to Arabic, Hebrew, and Welsh, among other languages. The chapters in this volume reflect a more fluid conception of linguistic and cultural boundaries and explore a more problematic set of values.

In Chapter 1 – "For Love and for Lovers: The Origins of Romance" – Laura Ashe describes how romance was created in twelfth-century England and France, in the French vernacular, "en romanz," for aristocratic patrons and audiences whose courtly lifestyle it idealized and celebrated.[4] Initially translating Latin sources, romance authors innovatively combined pre-existing genres – classical epic, Ovidian love poetry, and troubadour lyric – to create a new kind of narrative fiction. Writing for a mixed courtly audience, and often for aristocratic female patrons, authors of the earliest romances sought not only to celebrate chivalric battles and exploits, but also to write about true love, "fin'amor," and they created a complex psychological discourse of refined feeling, elaborated in chivalric adventures. Already in its origins we can see romance as an idealizing genre nonetheless deeply implicated in patriarchal and feudal social realities.

Keith Busby reminds us in Chapter 2, "The Manuscript Contexts of Medieval Romance," that we read medieval romances today in mass-produced print form that distorts their original literary format, overlooks their material qualities, and risks diminishing their complexity. Romance manuscripts were handwritten on parchment or velum (usually sheep or calf skin, more rarely, goat) by scribes or clerks; there are few copies of early romances that are contemporaneous with the stories' original composition. Instead, most extant manuscripts date from the thirteenth century and beyond, several generations after the moment when the romances they contain were composed, and it is not until the fourteenth century that we have manuscripts contemporaneous with the stories' composition.

Busby describes the many manuscript features that go beyond the story line – the way stories are laid out on the page and compiled in volumes and the special traits of medieval handwriting. Although modern editions may describe these features or attempt to reproduce some of them, many material qualities of handwritten copy cannot be reproduced; there is no substitute for reading the text in manuscript. Fortunately, many manuscripts can now be accessed through the digital libraries of the Bibliothèque nationale de France, the British Library, and others. Consulting the printed copy of a carefully edited manuscript alongside a digital image, students and other readers can begin to appreciate the codicological and cultural contexts of romance.

Ad Putter and Jane Gilbert describe the formal qualities of romance, focusing on French and Middle English romance, in Chapter 3, "Matters of Form: Experiments in Verse and Prose Romance." The earliest romances were composed in verse by authors who prided themselves on their artistic superiority. Chrétien de Troyes perfected the octosyllabic couplet, which became standard for the first generations of French romance. English-language romances also began in verse and displayed a surprising variety of verse forms, from tail-rhyme stanzas to alliterative verse, deployed in a variety of line length and rhyme schemes, including the rime royal longer stanzas popularized by Geoffrey Chaucer. French verse romancers later experimented by inserting lyric poetry within longer narratives, as we see in Chapter 4, "Authors, Narrators, and their Stories in Old French Romance," by Sylvie Lefèvre. Beginning in the thirteenth century, authors embarked on writing romances in vernacular prose, which, they claimed, conveyed historical veracity and spiritual truth without the distractions and embellishments of poetry. By the later Middle Ages, most romances throughout Europe were written in prose, sometimes adapted from verse originals, although verse romances could be copied in new manuscripts even up to the early modern period.

The Arthurian legend or "matter of Britain" was a dominant theme in medieval romance; Arthur's knights epitomize chivalric prowess and ideals. Romance writers introduced new characters and altered traditional roles; Arthur is sometimes passive and ineffective. Gawain is Top Knight in the English tradition, but in French narratives Lancelot becomes increasingly important, because of his valor and also his long affair with Arthur's queen. This affair creates one of the conflicts of loyalties which contribute to Camelot's collapse. Family relationships are very important; Arthur's sister Morgan plots against him, as does his nephew (and bastard son) Mordred. In the Grail quest, spiritual values challenge the ethos of secular chivalry and ennobling love. Does this quest glorify Arthur's Round Table, or critique it? Medieval romance offers important variations in approaches to the legend and its key characters, as Elizabeth Archibald describes in Chapter 5, "Arthurian Transformations."

In Chapter 6, "Romance and the Medieval Mediterranean," Sharon Kinoshita shifts the focus of romance criticism from Northern and Central Europe to the territories and domains adjacent to the Mediterranean. Rather than viewing medieval society through the lens of the modern nation state and focusing on the boundaries of contemporary Britain, France, Spain, Italy, and Germany, we can read a dynamic network of cultural relations throughout the territories that border the Mediterranean Sea, a central locus for transport and travel, trade, exchange, pilgrimage, and Crusade. Privileging "*routes* over roots and *acts* over identities" (p. 93) allows us to highlight new players beyond knights or crusaders: resourceful women, merchants, diplomats, translators, and go-betweens, as exemplified in the twelfth-century *Floire et Blanchefleur*. In this enormously popular tale, which circulated in most of the languages represented in this volume, a Christian slave girl and a "Saracen" prince fall in love, are separated, and overcome numerous obstacles before they are reunited and marry. Floire converts to Christianity and becomes King of Spain after his father's death, and pagans who do not convert are slaughtered in the end. Kinoshita emphasizes that, despite this violent conclusion, this courtly tale differs from Northern chivalric dramas in its emphasis on the mutability of identity and the "multiform complexity of Mediterranean-wide interactions," on clever ruses and mercantile transactions rather than on chivalric exploits, in this representation of the Mediterranean world.

Lee Manion explores a subset of Northern European romance in Chapter 7, "The Crusading Romance in Britain: Religious Violence and the Transformation of Popular Chivalric Narratives." He examines romances that directly promote the initiation or resumption of religious warfare in the Levant, after the demise of the First Kingdom of Jerusalem in 1187 and the final loss of Acre, the last mainland Christian territory in the Holy Land, in 1291. As powerful stories of loss and recovery that would prove immensely appealing throughout Europe, the chivalric "crusading romances" took hold in the thirteenth century. Manion studies both *Richard Coer de Lion* and *Guy de Warwick*, two fictional tales that presented themselves as "historical," to convey the justification for religious violence in different ways. Richard heads a large multinational army; Guy fights as an individual expiating his personal sin. Both stories attempt to foster crusading activity by fabricating "collective memories and narratives that can respond to ongoing concerns or can be intended to inspire action" (p. 106).

If Richard and Guy incarnate the upward path of English noble families in their fight against Saracens and others perceived as hostile, Nahir I. Otaño

Gracia in Chapter 8, "'Making Race' in Medieval Romance: A Premodern Critical Race Studies Perspective," shows how such struggles against demonized others create racism that romances often promote. Many romances construct a geography with a moral Christian center and demonized non-Christian, nonwhite, or dehumanized borderlands. Representation of people on the margins as outsiders, pagans, nonhumans, or giants allows the narrator and readers to dehumanize the others and thus to justify their oppression, exclusion, or death. Otaño Gracia shows how critical race theory can provide a powerful tool for analysis of racist ideologies and lay the groundwork for resistance and change. Medieval romance, with its fantastical representations and adventurous wanderings, allows contemporary readers to examine strategies of cultural appropriation and "race making" in early fictions that anticipate today's social and ideological conflicts.

Throughout the Middle Ages, romances proved a remarkably fluid genre within which social identities could be constructed, resisted, and transformed. Although chivalric knights and courtly ladies were frequently represented as heteronormative couples wherein men demonstrated "chivalric masculinity" and women were passive objects of male devotion, many romances explored an extraordinary range of social relationships: homosocial bonding and homosexual love between men; resourceful agency and female companionship and same-sex love between women. Romances not only promoted conventional gender identities but also explored alternate modes of perception and interaction, as Kathy M. Krause explores in Chapter 9, "The Construction and Interrogation of Gender in Old French Romance."

Drawing on ancient philosophy, modern psychology, and contemporary neurobiology, as well as on the first translations "en romanz" that expanded on the sentiments of characters, Megan Moore examines the primacy of emotions in medieval romance in Chapter 10, "Emotions as the Language of Romance." The first translations of Latin epics amplified descriptions of emotional states. The French-language stories that followed continued to explore sentimental relationships, using emotions as their building blocks to create communities of shared feelings among their elite readers. Beyond the "positive" feeling of love, romances examined negative emotions such as grief, rage, and sorrow. Often, as in the Tristan poems, love and suffering were intertwined and would intensify in the course of the story. "Noble suffering" became the very essence of what critics would call "courtly love"; the perception and misperception of emotions became key elements in a range of stories, from *Philomena* to the *Mort du roi Arthur*. As Moore demonstrates, following Barbara Rosenwein, romances promoted the expression of emotions, along with their misperformance and misperception, in a way that bolstered the social hierarchy and created community.

For years, literary history has viewed medieval French romance, and particular its Arthurian stories, as the wellspring for European avatars, but this was not the only source from which to spin a story. In Chapters 11 through 14, David Wacks, Laura Campbell, Albrecht Classen, and Patricia Ingham examine a range of literary translations, adaptations, and transformations as romances are retold and transmitted throughout England and the Continent.

In Chapter 11, "Medieval Iberian Romance," David Wacks expands our notions of literary history in medieval Spain, previously read largely as a backstory for Cervantes' *Don Quixote* (published in 1605), which parodies its Castilian predecessors. But long before the first Castilian translations of French prose romances, Hebrew and Arabic storytellers composed tales that blended Arthurian themes with their local cultures and literary traditions. A thirteenth-century Hebrew adaptation, *Melekh Artus*, was penned by a Italian Jewish scholar. In the same era, Jacob ben Elazar wrote original chivalric tales in Hebrew in Toledo, then a center of Jewish intellectual activity, transposing Arthurian motifs and incorporating Biblical allusions and Hebrew traditions into rhymed verse for Jewish audiences.

Around the same time, an anonymous Arabic writer wrote the tale of *Bayad and Riyad*, which blended conventions of French romance with the style of Arabic *maqama* (rhyming prose narrative). The tale of "Ziyad ibn Amir al-Qinani" also drew material from French romances while remaining firmly entrenched in Arabic culture. These Hebrew and Arabic textual cominglings all predate the Spanish and Portuguese translations of Arthurian romance. Wacks calls our attention to a series of stories that have been left out of mainstream Iberian literary history.

Arthurian translations into Castilian began in the early fourteenth century with retelling of stories of Joseph of Arimathea and the Grail. The monumental *Amadís of Gaula*, written in Castilian and considered the first "original" chivalric Iberian fiction, was published a century after Ben Elazar and the anonymous author of Arabic-Arthurian texts. Two later chivalric fictions, *Tirant lo Blanc* and *Curial et Güelfa*, reflect the dynamic geopolitical forces of the fifteenth century's Mediterranean world, as their subjects range from Northern Italy to Greece, the Middle East, and North Africa.

Italy, at a crossing point of Mediterranean voyages, was also a central locus of romance travel and transformation. Laura Chuhan Campbell examines three romances created at distinct moments in Italian history, representing different phases of the reproduction and transmission of French romance in Chapter 12, "Medieval and Early Modern Italian Romance." The *Prophesies de Merlin*, from the thirteenth century, retains French language, but reflects Italian politics in its recounting of Merlin's predictions. *La Tavolo Ritondo*, a century later, incorporates Tristan's story into Arthurian legend in a way that appeals to an audience of merchants, lawyers, and literate members of a new middle class. Despite his adulterous affair with Isolde, Tristan cultivates the personal, moral virtues of a good citizen.

Finally, a new genre emerges in the fifteenth century that combines features of Arthurian romance and epic tales of Charlemagne and Roland. In *L'Inamoramento de Rolando*, by Matteo Maria Boiardo, epic and romance values repeatedly come into conflict. Roland falls in love with Angelica, yet Charlemagne calls him away from her side to fight. The struggle between love and honor, according to Campbell, destabilizes the ethos of both epic and romance. Meanwhile, two female heroines, Bradamante and the Indian queen Marfisa, "challenge the monolithic masculinity of chivalry in both Arthurian romance and epic" (p. 190). As Campbell shows, Italian romances of this period play with shape-shifting paradigms of social identity and cross geographical boundaries in ways that "open a conversation" about gender, race, and political identity that will extend beyond the Middle Ages.

Albrecht Classen offers an overview of medieval romance in Germany in Chapter 13, "German Medieval Romance." Middle High German literature followed in the footsteps of French predecessors, from the first translation of the *Aeneid* through the adventures of Tristan and Perceval. The great classical romances of Hartman von Aue, Wolfram von Eschenbach, and Gottfried von Strassburg masterfully recast their French sources.

Later German romances, however, showed greater independence from French models, as they introduced important innovations and variations. Konrad Fleck intensified the sentimental travails of the lovers in his *Floris und Blancheflur* and expanded the global scope of their adventure. In *Daniel von der Bluhander*, the author known as The Stricker incorporated magical objects and creatures, and robots, and highlighted the protagonist's use of reason to handle his challenges, while the anonymous author of *Reinfried* looked toward Persia for inspiration. As romances transitioned from verse to prose, the figure of King Arthur faded away, often replaced by Charlemagne. The early modern period witnessed continued fascination with chivalry as romances reached new audiences, including some reading Yiddish readers.

Chivalric romance continued to be extremely popular, both for authors and their readers, as literacy expanded in the later Middle Ages and as printing gradually became more prevalent. How did late medieval writers breathe new life into a genre that had been so extensively deployed in previous centuries? The next two chapters survey the fate of romance in its final iterations in late Middle English and late medieval and early modern French respectively.

Two major Middle English writers deployed romance to very different ends, as Patricia Ingham shows in Chapter 14, "The Ends of Romance in Chaucer and Malory." In the *Canterbury Tales*, Geoffrey Chaucer explores and experiments with the ways that romances can represent marvels and fantasy, raise deeper philosophical questions (as in the *Knight's Tale*), and examine questions of gender and power (in the *Wife of Bath's Tale*). Chaucer's engagement with a variety of romance themes and structures in the *Canterbury Tales* allows him to show off his poetic skills, experiment with stylistic variations, and reflect more deeply on the role of tale-telling and moral education in a community of highly individualized pilgrims.

On the other hand, Thomas Malory's *Morte Darthur*, which draws largely from the Old French Vulgate Cycle and Tristan materials, takes a more conventional, conservative approach. A named author draws from disparate stories, sources, and languages to devise a single narrative structure and produce a unified story from multiple strands. Although the *Morte* exists today in a single extant manuscript, it was one of the earliest such romance compendia to be printed. Caxton's early modern printed edition (1485) was tremendously successful and, like many late medieval romance experiments, paved the way for the modern novel.

For years, late medieval French romances were dismissed as derivative or excessively fantastical or melodramatic; scholars took them less seriously than earlier "original" compositions in verse or prose and, as a result, many remained inaccessible, confined to manuscripts or early printed editions in library reserves. But thanks to a spate of new editions and translations (among them Gilles Roussineau's edition of the massive *Perceforest*, thirty years in the making), critics have focused more intently on later fictions for their complex recasting of romance conventions, their elaborate descriptions of chivalry, and their representations of late medieval morality and culture. Following Rosalind Brown-Grant's comprehensive study, in Chapter 15, "French Romance in the Late Middle Ages and the Renaissance," Jane H. M. Taylor explains that some late medieval romances often have a didactic, moralizing tenor that has much in common with contemporary didactic manuals and conduct books, as they offer advice on marriage and household governance.[5] Other romances follow the exploits and advancement of pseudohistorical figures, such as Jean de Saintré.

Arthurian fictions remained popular in the late Middle Ages and into the Renaissance. In addition to the *mises en prose* of *Cligés* and *Erec*, there were original fictions spun from Arthurian thread, such as Froissart's *Meliador*, considered the last Arthurian verse romance in French, and *Ysaie le Triste*, which provides a life of Tristan's son. One of the most notable late medieval romances in France was translated from Castilian. *Amadis de Gaule* appeared in twenty-four books and went quickly into print, becoming as popular in France as it was in Spain. What Jane H. M. Taylor calls *Amadis de Gaule*'s "rhetorical exhibitionism" seems to have inspired many more sentimental fictions. The taste for medieval "chivalry" and "romance" never completely disappeared, becoming source material for popular, mass-produced short fictions that traveled throughout France well into the nineteenth century, at which point medieval literature became the object of scholarly investigations such as those in this volume.

There is no single stylistic or thematic prototype that defines romance; no single authorial stance; no single moral teaching that emerges as the universal lesson to be learned. Romances can be recognized by their population of knights, courtly ladies, marvelous creatures, exotic landscapes, and spiritual challenges, but these features appear in such diverse configurations, differently motivated over four centuries of transition, that we cannot say what the relationship between romance and its social context will always be. Historian Craig Taylor addresses this question in Chapter 16, "Romance in Historical Context: Literature and the Changing Values and Norms of Aristocratic Society," where he ponders the social and historical contexts of romance. While earlier historians might have seen a pattern of chivalric glories in decline at the end of the Middle Ages, Taylor reminds us that chivalric ideals were always entangled with darker realities, principally the violence and misogyny that aristocratic elites inflicted upon less fortunate populations. (This observation brings us full circle to one of the founding fictions, *Philomena*, a tale of uncourtly villainy unleashed on helpless women by a powerful king.) Furthermore, from earliest texts, there is no one clear set of values to which all knights must aspire; the anonymous *Ordene de Chevalerie* and the works of Geoffrey de Charny and Ramon Lull each offer distinct visions of chivalry, with nuanced details according to time and place. Although many romances describe military exploits and feats on horseback with great energy and in detail, most fictions do not portray the significant changes in warfare that occurred from the twelfth to the fifteen centuries. By the end of the period, in England, men-at-arms fighting with longbows were more numerous than knights on horseback, yet most romances continued to glorify the activities of knights. Romances, Taylor reminds us, are "poor windows" of conditions on the ground (p. 244).

Romance's diversity and adaptability carry the genre through to new media in our contemporary age. As Susan Aronstein shows in Chapter 17, "Romance in Twentieth- and Twenty-First-Century Popular Culture," romance's "generic afterlife" recurs in an expanding universe of fiction, musical comedy, cartoons, films, and even opera throughout the twentieth century and up to the present. Focusing on Arthurian themes in what she calls "mass-market medievalism,"

Aronstein shows how artists, composers, and writers have remade iconic characters and themes so that they appeal to new audiences and adapt themselves to new technologies. If the early twentieth century, in the wake of T. H. White's *The Once and Future King*, portrayed the Arthurian court, idealized as Camelot, as a figure of benevolent patriarchy and American exceptionalism, later works submitted the model to parody and critique. *Monty Python and The Holy Grail* is a watershed moment which spoofs chivalry and the social institutions of male hegemony and supremacy that endure to the present. With John Boorman's *Excalibur*, even as the Arthurian legend becomes "popular" and accessible once again, the film critiques the idealization of chivalry and kingship. Marion Zimmer Bradley's *Mists of Avalon* presents a feminocentric retelling of the Arthurian legend, seen through the eyes of Morgan.

Finally, one of the most recent Arthurian recastings, *The Green Knight*, starring Dev Patel, explores the darker urges – masculine violence, underlying misogyny, neglect of family and community – that threaten the individual and the human community. Films, books, souvenirs, and artifacts in the twentieth and twenty-first centuries replay romance "matters" with as much innovative energy, diversity, and moral experimentation as did their medieval sources. Although rhetorical styles may have changed, and rhyme has been largely abandoned, the central marvels, mysteries, and paradoxes of romance continue to embody both the aesthetic aspirations and the deep social anxieties of our present moment, in ways that promise future explorations.

***

As varied and far-ranging as the chapters in this volume may be, they cannot tell the whole story of romance's evolution as a genre or provide a comprehensive account of even one language's history of courtly fiction. The multifaceted stories in so many languages, their intertextual connections and thematic echoes, and the questions they raise are innumerable. We hope to have touched upon some of the most compelling and significant features of this remarkable literary phenomenon, so that readers may be inspired to pursue their own further readings along directions not yet traveled.

Notes

1. Chrétien de Troyes depicts such a scene in *Yvain*, where a young noblewoman seated on a luxurious carpet reads a romance to her parents; *Yvain*, ed. Roques, ll. 5354–73.
2. Chrétien's status as a convert from Judaism is supported by the late Peter Haidu in his posthumous *The Philomena of Chrétien the Jew: The Semiotics of Evil*. Ed. Matilda Tomaryn Bruckner (Cambridge: Legenda, 2020).

3. Roberta L. Krueger, "*Philomena*: Brutal Transitions and Courtly Transformations in Chrétien's Old French Translation," in *A Companion to Chrétien de Troyes*, ed. Norris J. Lacy and Joan Tasker Grimbert (Cambridge: Boydell and Brewer, 2005), p. 89.
4. As Ashe reminds us, French became the elite vernacular in England after the Norman Conquest, and it continued to be used in aristocratic and urban society well into the fourteenth century. For more on Anglo-Norman romance, see Rosalind Field, "Romance in England, 1066–1400," in *The Cambridge History of Medieval English Literature*, ed. David Wallace (Cambridge: Cambridge University Press, 1999), pp. 152–76.
5. Rosalind Brown-Grant, *French Romances of the Later Middle Ages: Gender, Morality, and Desire* (Oxford: Oxford University Press, 2008).

1

LAURA ASHE

"For Love and For Lovers"
The Origins of Romance

Around 1155, a poet called Wace translated a long Latin history of Britain into French verse, and (we are told) presented it to Eleanor of Aquitaine, queen of England. His source, Geoffrey of Monmouth's *Historia Regum Britanniae* (*History of the Kings of Britain*, c. 1137), begins with the mythical arrival on the island of Brutus, a Trojan prince, and describes his foundation of Britain and the subsequent generations of British kings – their battles against enemies and invaders, and their own civil strife – culminating in the greatest of the Britons, King Arthur, who conquers almost all of western Europe before being plunged into a final, fatal civil war against his own nephew.[1] After Arthur's loss the British decline, ultimately losing their kingdom to the Saxons – those who later became the English. But by the twelfth century, when Geoffrey wrote his chronicle in a language that only clergy and the most highly educated could read, the English themselves had been conquered by the Normans. Wace's translation was written for the French-speaking aristocracy of the court of Henry II and Queen Eleanor, who between them held overlordship of lands stretching from Scotland to the Pyrenees.

All of this matters because it gives us a key example of the origins, in cultural, literary, and linguistic terms, of the romance. Geoffrey's history described the glories of King Arthur's court:

> Ad tantum etenim statum dignitatis Britannia tunc reducta erat quod copia diuitiarum, luxu ornamentorum, facetia incolarum cetera regna excellebat. Quicumque uero famosus probitate miles in eadem erat unius coloris uestibus atque armis utebatur. Facetae etiam mulieres, consimilia indumenta habentes, nullius amorem habere dignabantur nisi tercio in milicia probatus esset. Efficiebantur ergo castae et meliores et milites pro amore illarum probiores.
>
> (So noble was Britain then that it surpassed other kingdoms in its stores of wealth, the ostentation of its dress and the sophistication of its inhabitants.

> All its doughty knights wore clothes and armour of a single colour. Its elegant ladies, similarly dressed, spurned the love of any man who had not proved himself three times in battle. So the ladies were chaste and better women, whilst the knights conducted themselves more virtuously for the sake of their love.)[2]

Here is the seed ground for the romance: but this new genre has not yet appeared. Arthur's peacetime court is dead time for Geoffrey's history, because in historical terms, nothing happens. It is the chronicle's job, as it is King Arthur's and his knights', to move on to the next battle, the next conquest; and when ambassadors arrive from Rome threatening to make war on King Arthur, Sir Cador responds with enthusiasm, saying that too much indulgence in peacetime games and love affairs renders fighting men weak and cowardly (pp. 216–17). But when he translated this passage into French, writing for an aristocratic audience who would see themselves in the glittering court of noble knights and virtuous ladies, Wace added a response to Cador's speech, in which Sir Gawain disagrees with him:

> "Bone est la pais emprés la guerre,
> Plus bele e mieldre en est la terre;
> Mult sunt bones les gaberies
> E bones sunt les drueries.
> Pur amistié e pur amies
> Funt chevaliers chevaleries."

> ("Peace is good after war and the land is the better and lovelier for it. Jokes are excellent and so are love affairs. It's for love and for lovers that knights do knightly deeds.")[3]

This lighthearted intervention actually captures something revolutionary: it is the heart of the new genre of the romance.

The purpose of warriors, as celebrated in epics and in histories, had always been to make war: whether to defend their people or their faith, like Beowulf or Roland; to serve their king or their destiny, like Hector or Aeneas; or even in the sheer pursuit of martial glory, like Achilles. Ultimately, the warrior must die, gloriously and tragically, in the service of those ideals. Love plays no part in this picture. Aeneas must abandon Dido in order to fulfill his destiny; men's desire may spark war, as in Paris's abduction of Helen, but only by the war itself can men be measured. Geoffrey's ladies at King Arthur's court bestow their love only on those who have proved themselves in battle, and that makes them more virtuous – but the battle itself is the point. At this moment in Wace's poem, in contrast, an entirely different paradigm is advanced as an ideal of knighthood: the claim that a leisured, aristocratic life has value for its own sake, and that the purpose of chivalric endeavor, the purpose of knighthood itself, is to win love. With this shift, Wace opens up the whole vista of romance: a genre in which the knightly hero pursues his quest, battles his enemies, and overcomes all adversity in order to win the love of his lady and live happily ever after. And the lady's love is itself symbolic: it is what he wins, the marker of the hero's worth, as her body and her possessions are the material prize for his success. The turn is toward the individual protagonist and his inner life: no longer is he to be sacrificed to a higher ideal; rather, his fulfillment and success have *become* the ideal.

This new genre of the romance emerged out of those older, pre-existing genres: historical writing – and its influential proto-mythic relative, the epic – provided the framework of cultural capital and the authority of the heroic past. The term "romance" itself comes only from the language in which the genre appeared, first of all in translation from Latin: *en romanz*, "in French," written by a new class of courtly clerics, church-trained but embedded in secular life, for the French-speaking aristocracy of twelfth-century England and France. The Norman Conquest of 1066 had made French the language of England's royal court and highest aristocracy, and hence the language learned and used in elite society even when, as rapidly became the case, everyone's first language was English. The earliest patrons and dedicatees of romance were aristocrats and royalty – often women – on both sides of the Channel. Theirs was an aspirational world of courtly pastimes and leisure – feasting and hunting, tournaments, music and games – and the knights and ladies who were the romance's audience found in the genre an idealized version, and a pseudohistorical justification, of their own elite lives. Wace's own text was not (yet) a romance: he elaborates on, but does not fundamentally abandon, the shape of Geoffrey's Latin chronicle. But in his expanded description of the luxuries and joys of King Arthur's court, he speaks of the *chançuns, lais, contes e fables* (songs, lays, tales, and stories: ll. 10545–55) that one could hear there – and this is the cultural space that the romance came to occupy. There had always been songs and storytelling, a great deal of it lost to us, never written down. Now at this moment, when the French vernacular properly became a literary vehicle for the enjoyment of wealthy and leisured patrons, the romance emerged as the fictional idealization of its audience's own world.

The earliest works generally agreed to be romances (as opposed to histories with incipient "romance" characteristics) date from around 1150–60, and were themselves translations and adaptations from historical epics. Virgil's *Aeneid*, in which the Trojan prince Aeneas journeys and fights to establish what would become the Roman Empire, was rewritten in French verse as the *Roman d'Eneas*; Latin prose narratives of the Trojan and Theban wars became Benoît de Sainte-Maure's *Roman de Troie* and the anonymous *Roman de Thèbes*.[4] Collectively known as the "antique romances," these works rendered the classical past in distinctively medieval clothing, the warriors of Greece and Troy recast as chivalric knights; however, their transformation from Latin historical epic to French romance was not solely one of anachronism. Romance is a narrative mode, like the epic, and like history, but unlike those genres, and because it is focused on the individual, it also accommodates and represents kinds of experience that are purely fictional. "Fictional" does not only mean "invented"; it means, in an implicit contract between reader and (imagined or real) author, material which we understand need not be true, which indeed cannot be known to be true. The supreme category of things that must simply be believed, or have disbelief suspended while they are narrated, is the inner life of any other individual, for the most important aspect of the world to which we lack definitive, experiential access is what is going on in anyone else's mind. The romance, then, with its new focus on the individual and interiority, drew not only upon the epic, but also on its ever-present counterpart: the lyric. From the earliest literature, while epics were written of battles and kings, shoring up society's structures and values, lyrics – narratives of one voice, expressing interiority – were written to represent that impossible, absent experience: of access to the thoughts and feelings of another. The genre of romance came from the collision and combination of these pre-existing genres, as its first authors adapted their epic and historical sources with a new focus on the individual protagonist: the authoritative framework of epic history – which had never attended to emotional experience other than as cause or consequence of great and terrible actions – received an infusion of lyric expression, which insisted that emotional experience is a worthy subject of narrative for its own sake.

In the antique romances, tied to their epic sources but with this new commitment to a wholly different aesthetic, the effect is often to destabilize the narrative. When he came to the doomed love affair of Dido and Aeneas, the author of the *Roman d'Eneas* faced a particular problem: Virgil's equally influential classical contemporary, Ovid, had written a lyric addressed from Dido to Aeneas that provided an inescapable counternarrative. Where Virgil's Aeneas is commanded by the gods to abandon Dido's illicit love in order to fulfill his destiny, on which the whole fate of the Roman Empire hangs, Ovid in his lyrical *Heroides* had given Dido a heartbreaking lament: the sorrow and rage of a woman who has merely been cruelly and unjustifiably abandoned. In the *Aeneid*, the scale of the loss is correspondingly the measure of what Rome is worth, an ideal greater than any individual life; Ovid's lyric gives us only the searing anguish of the individual life, sacrificed to a meaningless ideal. The French poet is insufficient to the challenge of mediating these two visions, but perhaps they cannot be mediated; measuring our obligations to individual integrity and fulfillment against those we owe to a greater good, or the good of others, is one of the most intractable and vital difficulties of human existence. In *Eneas*, the poet resolves his problem by making Dido forgive Eneas on her deathbed (clearing him of Virgil's Aeneas's complicated betrayal), and then reintroduces the lyric love theme, for a second and successful time, by inventing a whole emotional (and notably histrionic) love affair between Eneas and his intended wife, Lavine. But if this author had to make some awkward adjustments to his sources, his difficulties nonetheless show us the true, astonishing scope of the romance, achieved in its melding of lyric and epic-historical sensibilities. Historical epic contained heroes, but it was never about the individual: it was about the greater forces they embodied, defended, or fought against; about the grand movements of history and the tragic scale of our own mortality. Lyric gave voice – literally, in song – to the other part of human existence, to the mind behind the eyes; it offered up that experience as all that really matters, to any individual in pain or in bliss. Romance, as a genre that places individual emotional experience into the historical narrative, and gives it equal weight and moral significance, is the kind of narrative that most closely answers to the business of actually living a human life.

Once the romance had been created, its energy and potential appeared limitless, and it flowered in multiple creative directions, in constant, self-conscious, intertextual interaction. The question for any literary text is what it *does* for its audience: How does it entertain, comfort, or affirm? Does it challenge, enchant, or provoke? What experience of *recognition* does it offer, in every sense? By the end of the twelfth century the romance had already taken several visibly different paths, which continued to develop and flourish throughout the Middle Ages and beyond.

In England, the romance's roots in history remained very visible; the early and virtuosic *Romance of Horn* (c. 1170) set a pattern for romances based on an "exile-and-return" plot, with a hero unjustly robbed of his inheritance in childhood who grows up to defeat his enemies and reclaim his rights.[5] The story of Havelok the Dane, set in the distant pre-Conquest past, sees the young Danish prince and an English princess both deprived of their rightful thrones by usurpers. It first appears as a lengthy interpolation in Geffrei Gaimar's *Estoire des Engleis* (*History of the English*, c. 1136–7), a verse translation of the Anglo-Saxon Chronicles and the oldest surviving history in French; by the end of the century the story of Havelok was in circulation as a standalone romance.[6] English heroes Guy of Warwick and Boeve (Bevis) of Hampton, later both hugely popular figures, were celebrated in early-thirteenth-century romances that combined their service of English kings with exploits undertaken across Europe and into the Holy Land.[7] Their adventures proliferate with exotic and varied locations and people, reflecting the ongoing legacy of the Crusades, the Latin west's uneasy relationship with the Byzantine Empire, and the wholly interconnected European and Mediterranean world.

In some contrast to the historical coloring of England's romances, it was with the work of Chrétien de Troyes, writing in the 1160s and 1170s for the court of Marie de Champagne, that the romance took something like its archetypal, fully fictional form. Chrétien wrote about the Arthurian world, cut loose from any historicity beyond its reflection of his own present time, and he put his own authorship center stage; at the opening of one romance, he tells us that "Crestïens de Troies ... trait d'un conte d'aventure / une mout bele conjunture" ("Chrétien de Troyes ... from a tale of adventure draws a beautifully ordered composition").[8] Each of his heroes is an individual knight driven to undertake quests and trials away from King Arthur's court, testing and proving his prowess and chivalry. His knights are spurred on their adventures by love, often personified and depicted as an irresistible force: "Cele plaie a mes sire Yvains, / dom il ne sera ja mes sains, / qu'Amors s'est tote a lui randue." ("My lord Yvain has suffered this wound from which he'll never be healed, for Love has completely overwhelmed him.")[9] In the course of their adventures they face sophisticated ethical questions, balancing the demands of love and fellowship, of chivalric performance and moral commitment. In *Erec and Enide* the eponymous hero wins his lady in an open contest of prowess, and she is hailed in Arthur's court as the most beautiful woman alive; but then he abandons chivalry in the pleasures of the marital bed, and it is Enide who must explain to him that knighthood is a constant duty. They set out on adventures once again, and although Erec intends his wife to be no more than the audience for his prowess, she saves his life on multiple occasions. This is a vision of courtly love and chivalry calculated to appeal to his mixed audience and female patrons. In *Yvain, or, The Knight with the Lion*, contrastingly, Chrétien has his hero abandon his wife in thoughtless commitment to winning a reputation on the tournament circuit; once he realizes he has broken his promises to her, he loses his mind and flees into exile. Eventually restored to his wits, he embarks on a new, anonymous quest with a lion as his faithful companion; now his exploits all involve coming to the rescue of the helpless and the oppressed, the lion comically portrayed both as a symbol of his goodness and as a fierce and furry animal that fights villains alongside him. With this new understanding of the moral purpose of chivalry fulfilled, he is finally able to win back his wife and return to court. Yet while Chrétien provides an overtly happy ending here, he also exposes some fractures in the complaisant structure of romance, for Yvain's wife is coerced into marrying him – after he has proved his worth by killing her first husband – and she is finally tricked into forgiving him. The assurance that love can be won with prowess is a fictional logic, an essential rule of the genre – but Chrétien is aware of its ideological dishonesty, its dependence on obfuscating the overwhelmingly patriarchal imbalance of power between the sexes.

These narratives, nonetheless, are devoted to the moral development of the hero and the corresponding establishing of chivalry as an ethical code, a virtuous and admirable way of life suited to the aristocracy and serving as a justification of their status and privilege. In this, the romance served a particular social and political purpose. The church insisted that a worldly life could barely be undertaken without sin, and that knighthood itself was irreparably marred by unjustified violence, greed, and pride. Conventional – and genuine – piety insisted on the constant need to confess and abandon sins that were an inherent part of aristocratic life. The romance, by contrast, gives us a window into an aristocratic culture of self-worth, a growing assumption that God's favor was demonstrated by the very fact of the social hierarchy. In its idealization of courtly life and codification of chivalry as a virtuous and noble vocation, the love plot became indispensably valuable, for it justified the knight's actions as being undertaken in service of a higher ideal. The hero undergoes extravagant psychological suffering for his love, which itself demonstrates his fineness of feeling and his capacity for humble service. He demonstrates his prowess and valor in a series of chivalric tests; ultimately, he is crowned with success: with wealth, social status, a marriage that combines both, and a glorious reputation. In these ways, by exploiting the new focus on psychological interiority encouraged by the church's own confessional culture and deploying the idea of love as a higher purpose for chivalric endeavor, the romance was able bombastically to idealize and ebulliently to celebrate the worldly lives of the twelfth-century aristocracy. Women, meanwhile – the frequent patrons and equally involved audience for these romances – were offered in this paradigm a superficially celebratory and elevating ideal of courtly love and happy marriage that served, above all, to control and direct female sexual desire in accordance with society's patriarchal demands.

It is ironic, then – or it is painfully instructive – that the twelfth century's new, revolutionary claim that *love* is the ultimate goal of life should retain its hold on our own, twenty-first-century culture. Deployed in the service of aristocratic ideology (and now, in its modern iterations, of capitalist ideology), this idea is not actually a rational one. Love in earlier literature had always been depicted as a source of potential tragedy, and besides that of humiliation, of the kind of suffering that is not ennobling but destructive; and in fact that narrative too makes its way into the romance. Chrétien de Troyes himself wrote the first romance of Lancelot, the greatest knight of Arthur's court who is doomed to love Queen Guinevere.

In later works their affair becomes a matter of tragedy, bringing about the destruction of the Round Table, but in Chrétien's playful poem Lancelot's subjection to the queen's every whim is extreme to the point of being comical. In one climactic scene it includes his being suddenly rendered incapable of movement during desperate single combat with a man intent on killing him:

> Molt est qui ainme obeïssanz,
> et molt fet tost et volontiers

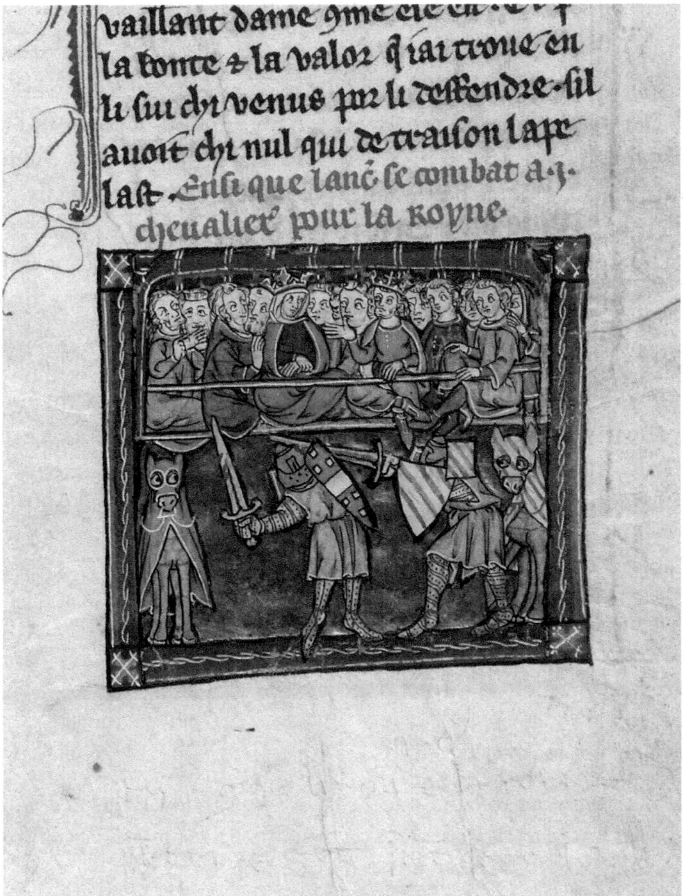

Figure 1.1 *La Mort le Roi Artu*: Lancelot fights for Guinevere. British Library, Additional MS 10294, fol. 68r.

la ou il est amis antiers
ce qu'a s'amie doie plaire. . . .
Ne puis que li darrïens moz
de la boche li fu colez,
puis qu'ele ot dit: "Quant vos volez
que il se taigne, jel voel bien."
puis Lanceloz por nule rien
nel tochast ne ne se meüst,
se il ocirre le deüst.

(One who loves totally is ever obedient, and willingly and completely does whatever might please his sweetheart. . . . No sooner had the last word flowed from her mouth – no sooner had she said, "Because it pleases you, I wish Lancelot to restrain himself" – then nothing could have made Lancelot touch Meleagant or make any move towards him, even if he had been about to kill him.)[10]

Lancelot's story cannot be fulfilled as those of Erec and Yvain were; it is the abjection of the best knight in the world to an impossible love, and Chrétien apparently lost patience with his theme: he tells us he wrote at the behest of his patron, Marie, and in the romance's epilogue we are suddenly informed that he did not finish it himself but gave it to another poet to confect a happy ending. The specter of misogyny grows darker over these narratives; of course, it is present in the patriarchal structures that shape all romances (perhaps all texts), but it appears openly expressed in narratives of infidelity or thwarted love: the *Roman de Troie* says of women that "Qui s'i atent ne qui s'i creit / Sei meisme vent e deceit" ("Whoever relies on them or trusts them pays dearly for it and deceives himself").[11] The same romance explicitly sets love in conflict with martial prowess, afflicting the Greek hero Achilles with a thoroughly twelfth-century romance-style love-longing for the Trojan princess Polixena, which prevents him from fighting and nearly destroys his reputation:

Aler i vueut, mais en poi d'ore
Li rest Amors si coruz sore
Qu'il n'i ose le pié porter.
Proëce e sen li tout amer
E hardement e vassalage. (ll. 20851–5)

(He wanted to go out to fight, but then Love quickly overwhelmed him once more so that he did not dare set foot on the battlefield. Love silenced Prowess's appeal, along with reason, boldness and valour; p. 297.)

The classical narrative of male desire – as a force that denigrates and humiliates the lover – appeared alongside the new romance narrative of ennobling love, where this suffering is a hard service eventually crowned with victory; yet neither of these paradigms sought to include the woman as any kind of real moral agent, or to reach beyond the solipsism of the hero-protagonist. Achilles, in the *Roman de Troie*, even compares his love of Polixena with Narcissus's love of his own reflection, on the grounds that both are hopeless (ll. 17691–746; p. 258). It is striking, then, that one of the earliest named female authors, Marie de France, writing (presumably in England) toward the end of the twelfth century, produced a series of lays – short romances – in which women characters are given (constrained) choices and (painfully explored) agency, within the bounds of the romance plot – and in which, very often, Marie is satirizing the paradigm as a whole.

En Bretaine a Nantes maneit
Une dame que mut valeit
De beauté e d'enseignement
E de tut bon affeitement. . . .
En Bretaine ot quatre baruns
    . . . de grant beauté
E chevalers pruz e vaillanz,
Larges, curteis e despendanz . . .
Icil quatres la dame amoënt
E de bien fere se penoënt:
Pur li e pur s'amur aveir
I meteit chescun sun poeir.
Chescun par sei la requereit
E tute sa peine i meteit;
N'i ot celui ki ne quidast
Que meuz d'autre n'i espleitast.
La dame fu de mut grant sens:
En respit mist e en purpens
Pur saver e pur demander
Li queils sereit meuz a amer.
Tant furent tuz de grant valur,
Ne pot eslire le meillur. . . .
Li uns de l'autre ne saveit;
Mes departir nul nes poeit.

(At Nantes in Brittany there lived a lady who was much praised for beauty and learning, and for her perfect manners. . . . There were four particular barons in Brittany . . . all very handsome, and brave and valiant knights, generous, courtly and extravagant. . . . These four loved the lady, and took pains to do noble deeds, each one doing everything he could to win her and have her love. Each one begged to have her for himself and took great pains about it; each one thought he could prove himself to be better than the others. The lady was

> extremely sensible: she took her time and carefully considered them, in order to decide which one would be the best to love. But they were all so valiant that she could not choose which was best. . . . They were each ignorant of the others, but no one could distinguish between them.)[12]

This is a straight-faced satire of the romance love plot in which the hero proves himself to be the best knight in order to win the most beautiful lady: for here there are four indistinguishable heroes, all striving for exactly the same accomplishments, and the lady is the only real protagonist despite her position as prize. Yet even so, a male voice succeeds in asserting itself by the end. The four are attacked in an unplanned skirmish (itself an understated condemnation of chivalry's real violence); three are killed and the last receives a wound that renders him impotent, incapable of marriage. As she mourns, the lady decides to compose a lay called "The Four Sorrows", to commemorate her losses, but the remaining knight insists that it should be called "The Sorrowful One", since the other three no longer suffer. In this dispute – which Marie leaves unresolved, but the lay is indeed known as *Chaitivel*, "wretched one" – the knight does not even acknowledge the lady's own emotional experience, referring only to his own and his fellows' suffering. But his assertion that the poem should memorialize the one who has suffered the most – separated from his unquestioning assumption that that can only mean himself – gives us the key to what Marie is doing in many of her short romances, which is to memorialize suffering itself. Tales of lost love, or love that ends in death, are offered up to their audience as sorrow made beautiful, pain rendered meaningful. By endowing suffering with the significance of art, Marie gives it value, and promises her reader that their own pain too is meaningful. It does not matter that her protagonists are ciphers, interchangeable ladies and indistinguishable knights; as she moves her lovers through different iterations of love, betrayal, loyalty, and loss, these poems illuminate how meaning itself is created, in literature and in our emotional lives.

One twelfth-century author produced an early romance that achieves the full status of tragedy: Chrétien de Troyes's contemporary, known to us only as Thomas of Britain, who wrote a long narrative of Tristan and Yseut around 1170. Thomas's *Tristan* survives only in manuscript fragments, but it was hugely well known and influential, rapidly translated into Old Norse and German (from which Thomas's full story can be speculatively reconstructed), and copied by many later authors. It is a story of tragic and impossible love between the knight Tristan and Queen Yseut, wife of King Mark, who is Tristan's own uncle. Tristan is banished from court, and they spend most of the romance separated from one another in anguished yearning; in his despair, Tristan marries another woman, also called Yseut, in a pitiful attempt to substitute what he can have for what he desires. It ends with the lovers' deaths. Thomas does something unprecedented with his narrative: he reaches beyond the perspectives of his two lovers in order to show us the inner lives, and the suffering, of the other characters, and he describes genuinely conflicting moral obligations, an ethical dilemma that cannot – ever – be resolved. He ignores the romance paradigm by which suffering is ennobling, and instead exposes it as the ugly, painful consequence of our own and others' actions – and when he compares different individuals' sorrows, we are made to understand that suffering is incommensurable. He describes the second Yseut's situation with great pity:

> Que que soit or de l'autre Ysodt,
> Hiceste sanz delit se deut:
> El n'a delit de son seignor
> N'envers autre nen a amor.
> Cestui desire, cestui ha,
> E nul delit de lui nen a.
> Hiceste est a Marque a contraire,
> Car il puet d'Ysod son bon faire,
> Tuit ne puisse il son cuer changier …
> … Ceste ne set ou deliter
> Fors Tristran sanz delit amer:
> De lui desire avoir deduit
> E rien n'en a ne li enuit.
> E l'acoler e le baisser
> De lui vousist plus asaier;
> Il ne li puet abandoner,
> N'ele nel volt pas demander.

> (Whatever comparison you make with the other Yseut, this one has all pain and no delight: she can get no pleasure from her lord, but nor can she love anyone but him. He is the one she wants, and he is the one she appears to have – but she has no happiness from him at all. Her situation is quite different from Mark's, for he can do what pleases him with Yseut, even though he cannot change her heart. But this Yseut does not know where to look for happiness, other than in loving Tristan joylessly: she longs to take pleasure with him, and has nothing from him but pain. She would love to experience more of his kisses, his embraces, but he cannot give them to her, and she does not want to beg.)[13]

This shift of perspective prevents the lovers from holding a special status within their own narrative; it demonstrates the moral limitations (and sheer loneliness) of subjectivity, and the essential impossibility of judging the rightness of any action which arises from the necessities of our own desires. In writing a love narrative so profoundly different from those of his contemporaries, Thomas reconstitutes the romance's representation of individuality and interiority as the grounds of moral agency, the whole ethical sphere of what we owe to others as well as to ourselves.

The romance is the Middle Ages' version of the novel: and like the novel, it was a form that didn't always exist, and had to be invented. In comparison with the writing that came before it, medieval romance represented reality in new ways: it was concerned with the individual, the hero's (and occasionally, within limits, the heroine's) movement through the world in a quest for success and fulfillment; it exploited the freedoms of fiction, toying with the marvelous and the monstrous, and seeing inside the minds of others; it focused on individual emotional experience, above all the travails and joys of heterosexual love (often in competition with homosocial, and sometimes homosexual, desire); and it celebrated, idealized, and justified the pursuit of worldly achievements and earthly happiness. Once that model had been established – with astonishing rapidity – it then immediately demonstrated its rapacious adaptability, in satirizing itself, in exploring its own moral dilemmas and tragedies, and in turning toward – and away from – the greatest questions of human existence. Romance is a structure within which all that is human can be explored; yet it is also, indelibly, the product of its time – and of all its times. Twelfth-century romance ideology underpinned patriarchy and misogyny; it celebrated and idealized an economic and social status founded on endemic violence, dispossession, and exploitation; it glorified the racist, imperialist, and colonialist idea of hegemonic Western European Christendom in conflict with its neighbors and its minority peoples. In its essentials the romance is still our most familiar literary model, as we are still wrestling with this cultural inheritance. We should remember that it was the invention and the servant of a particular time, place, and culture, and that all literature works to sustain, as well as to challenge and explore, the cultures that created it.

Notes

1. Geoffrey of Monmouth, *The History of the Kings of Britain*, ed. Reeve and trans. Wright.
2. Geoffrey of Monmouth, *The History of the Kings of Britain*, ed. Reeve and trans. Wright, pp. 212–13.
3. Wace, *Roman de Brut*, ed. and trans. Weiss, ll. 10767–72; translation slightly modified.

4. *Le roman d'Enéas*, ed. Petit; *Eneas*, trans. Yunck; Benoît de Sainte-Maure, *Le Roman de Troie*, ed. Constans; *The Roman de Troie*, trans. Burgess and Kelly; *Le roman de Thèbes*, ed. and trans. Mora; *Le Roman de Thèbes*, trans. Coley.
5. Thomas, *The Romance of Horn*, ed. Pope; trans. Weiss in *The Birth of Romance in England*.
6. Geffrei Gaimar, *Estoire des Engleis: History of the English*, ed. and trans. Short. *Le lai d'Haveloc* in *Le lai d'Haveloc and Gaimar's Haveloc Episode*, ed. Bell; trans. Weiss in *The Birth of Romance*. The later Middle English version is *Havelok the Dane*, in *Four Romances of England: King Horn, Havelok the Dane, Bevis of Hampton, Athelston*, ed. Herzman.
7. *Gui de Warewic: roman du XIIIe siècle*, ed. Ewert; *Beuve de Hamptone*, ed. and trans. Martin; *Boeve de Haumtone and Gui de Warewic*, trans. Weiss. On the medieval traditions of these heroes, see *Guy of Warwick: Icon and Ancestor*, ed. Rosalind Field and Alison Wiggins (Woodbridge: D. S. Brewer, 2007); *Sir Bevis of Hampton in Literary Tradition*, ed. Jennifer Fellows and Ivana Djordjević (Woodbridge: D. S. Brewer, 2008).
8. Chrétien de Troyes, *Erec et Enide*, ed. and trans. Fritz, ll. 13–14; trans. Carroll in *Arthurian Romances*, ed. and trans. Kibler and Carroll, p. 37.
9. Chrétien de Troyes, *Yvain, ou, Le chevalier au lion*, ed. Nelson, Carroll, and Kelly, ll. 1377–9; trans. Kibler in *Arthurian Romances*, ed. and trans. Kibler and Carroll, p. 312.
10. Chrétien de Troyes, *Lancelot, ou, Le chevalier de la Charrette*, ed. Aubailly, ll. 3798–812; trans. Kibler in *Arthurian Romances*, ed. and trans. Kibler and Carroll, p. 254.
11. Benoît de Sainte-Maure, *Le Roman de Troie*, ed. Constans, ll. 13455–6; *The Roman de Troie*, trans. Burgess and Kelly, p. 207.
12. Marie de France, *Chaitivel*, in *Lais*, Ewert, ll. 9–60; trans. Ashe in Laura Ashe, *Early Fiction in England: From Geoffrey of Monmouth to Chaucer* (London: Penguin, 2015), pp. 207–8.
13. Thomas of Britain, *Tristan*, ed. Gregory, in *Early French Tristan Poems: Vol. 2*, ed. Lacy, ll. 1068–84; trans. Ashe in *Early Fiction*, p. 119.

Suggestions for Further Reading

Ashe, Laura. *Early Fiction in England: From Geoffrey of Monmouth to Chaucer*. London: Penguin, 2015.

Ashe, Laura. *Fiction and History in England, 1066–1200*. Cambridge: Cambridge University Press, 2007.

Ashe, Laura. *The Oxford English Literary History vol. 1: 1000–1350. Conquest and Transformation*. Oxford: Oxford University Press, 2017.

Bridges, Venetia. "The *Romans Antiques* Across Time and Space." In *Medieval Romances Across European Borders*, ed. Miriam Edlich-Muth. Turnhout: Brepols, 2018, pp. 107–32.

Cooper, Helen. *The English Romance in Time: Transforming Motifs from Geoffrey of Monmouth to the Death of Shakespeare*. Oxford: Oxford University Press, 2004.

Gaunt, Simon. *Gender and Genre in Medieval French Literature*. Cambridge: Cambridge University Press, 1995.

Green, Dennis Howard. *The Beginnings of Medieval Romance: Fact and Fiction, 1150–1220*. Cambridge: Cambridge University Press, 2002.

Ingham, Patricia Clare. *Sovereign Fantasies: Arthurian Romance and the Making of Britain*. Philadelphia: University of Pennsylvania Press, 2001.

Jaeger, C. Stephen. *Ennobling Love: In Search of a Lost Sensibility*. Philadelphia: University of Pennsylvania Press, 1999.

Patterson, Lee. *Negotiating the Past: The Historical Understanding of Medieval Literature*. Madison: University of Wisconsin Press, 1987.

Rollo, David. *Historical Fabrication, Ethnic Fable, and French Romance in Twelfth-Century England*. Lexington, KY: French Forum, 1998.

Weiss, Judith. "Insular Beginnings: Anglo-Norman Romance." In *A Companion to Romance: From Classical to Contemporary*, ed. Corinne J. Saunders. Oxford: Blackwell, 2004, pp. 26–44.

Whitman, Jon. "Thinking Backward and Forward: Narrative Order and the Beginnings of Romance," *Partial Answers: Journal of Literature and the History of Ideas* 4.2 (2006), 131–50.

2

KEITH BUSBY

The Manuscript Contexts of Medieval Romance

It is doubtful whether any modern reader encounters medieval literature in manuscript before doing so in a printed book. [1] That printed book is likely to be a critical edition produced according to philological criteria developed over a period of nigh on two centuries, since the establishment of philology as an academic discipline.[2] Although there are variations in the way editions are prepared and in the kind of apparatus which accompanies the text, there is general agreement on the various editorial procedures and methods. Essentially, an editor may choose to produce a "best manuscript" edition or a critical edition accompanied by variants from all witnesses in which an attempt is made to move as close as possible to the author's original. The virtues and pitfalls of both types of edition are well-known and need not be rehearsed here.[3] Furthermore, the work of the scholar is presented through all the typographical conventions of the modern printed book, including choice of font, size, and layout of page, presence or absence of illustrations, binding, cover design, and much more besides. The modern publishing market has also made medieval literature accessible to a wider readership by means of texts accompanied by translations into a modern vernacular, or simply by translations alone.[4] As a means of accessing medieval literature and culture this is to be welcomed, but at the same time it should be stressed that neither the strictly scholarly edition nor the parallel-text version nor the translation bear a particularly close relationship to what was read or read aloud in the Middle Ages. This is true of romance and most forms of medieval literature, in both Latin and the vernaculars.

Even with the ongoing digitization of manuscripts for those who cannot visit repositories in person, approaching medieval romance initially through the medieval book alone is highly impractical as the tools required to do so are many and can only be acquired over a period of years. The mere act of reading a medieval text in manuscript requires palaeographical and codicological skills, not to mention an understanding of the syntax, morphology, phonology, and semantics of the medieval form of whatever language is at issue; linguistic concerns are crucial to the comprehension of any form of text, manuscript or printed.[5] All this, of course, constitutes the perfect argument for, and justification of, the modern critical edition and translation. Moreover, the readability of the modern edition with, say, a good linguistic introduction and glossary, does facilitate certain types of textual, stylistic, and literary analysis. The digitization of such an edition with search functions makes the generation of data for such analysis even easier, more efficient, and more reliable. There can be no denying, however, that the transformation of the medieval text into the form of a printed book is an anachronism which "demedievalizes" it to a degree and deprives it of much of its alterity. The medieval text is removed abruptly from its manuscript contexts and from its position and function as part of a codicological whole. Although carefully prepared critical editions can include a variant apparatus to reflect the readings of different manuscripts, the final critical text inevitably acquires a semidefinitive or semicanonical status, and it has to be asked how many readers, in all honesty, actually consult variants at the foot of the page or the notes following a text. The critical edition fixes the text in a way which denies its medieval mobility since each printed copy is identical.[6] Some of these deficiencies can be remedied in part in the critical apparatus, but only in part. Descriptions of manuscripts can contain full details of other contents which will restore some of the missing context, any illuminations can be described and some reproduced, and examples can be given of the *mise en texte* and *mise en page*,[7] but this cannot come close to reproducing "the real thing."

If medieval romance will of necessity continue to be approached principally through the medium of a critical edition, printed, digitized, or online, its manuscript contexts should be taken into account so as not to reinforce the transformation of the medieval into the modern. In a sense, this makes the process of reading romance simultaneously more complex and more rewarding. Precisely how to go about this will depend on the romance or romances in question as the transmission of each individual work is to a greater or less degree sui generis. In terms of scholarly research, direct or online access to manuscripts alongside a printed edition can provide most of the material required, but where neither manuscripts nor surrogates are available, full descriptions of all manuscripts and their contents are a necessity. The same would apply, perhaps on a more limited scale, for teaching purposes, where students should at the very least be introduced to the materiality of the medieval text. The rest of this chapter will essentially be devoted to considering what manuscript transmission and contexts can tell us about medieval romance and to establishing a number of topics which might cast light on texts, individually or collectively. The emphasis will be on medieval French romance, with some brief remarks on other vernaculars toward the end of the chapter. Although far from constituting a model or paradigm, some of these topics will nevertheless be of wide application. I move from the particular to the general, from the palaeographical to the codicological to the historical. It should be stressed here that the study of romance through manuscript is generally a study of its later reception rather than of any possible authorial intent and significance for first audiences. Before the mid- to late thirteenth century, only a few manuscripts survive from a romance's period of composition; even early-thirteenth-century copies are rare.[8] Intent and significance are therefore those attributed to manuscript planners and artisans of the book, their patrons, and extended communities of readers and listeners. Later prose romances from the fifteenth century are more likely to be preserved in manuscripts contemporaneous with their period of composition. Late copies of early verse romances and *mises en prose* are testimony to the enduring interest some texts hold for different audiences across the medieval centuries.[9]

Confronted for the first time by certain basic elements of the medieval *mise en texte*, such as abbreviations, lack of word spacing, lack of modern punctuation, lack of distinction between *i* and *j*, *u* and *v*, students often express irritation and impatience rather than wonder why a text is disposed in such a manner. The "problem" of minims is easily solved with a little reading practice, and when scribes do mark *i* with a faint stroke above the letter or distinguish *i/j* and *u/v*, this may even indicate the date or provenance of a manuscript. More significant, perhaps, are the other features mentioned here. Resolving abbreviations requires not only familiarity with the language but sometimes also familiarity with particular types of text or genres in which certain words occur most frequently, and sometimes uniquely. It has been argued that the writing of two or more words without modern spacing (clustering or agglutination) reflects the kind of rhythmic units which define oral presentation, even in prose, and that certain medieval punctuation marks act as a guide to the reading of verse, aloud in performance or silently by the inner voice. The *punctus elevatus* (resembling an inverted modern semi-colon) at the end of a line of verse often indicates *enjambement*, for example, and the raised *punctus* (simple dot) is frequently used to separate items in a list, guiding the reader.[10] Further study is required on this subject, but it may be possible to trace the evolution from performance to silent reading through changes over time in the *mise en texte*. The issue is not straightforward as manuscripts may preserve archaic features which do not reflect the reading and reception contexts at their time of production. Most of this palaeographical detail pertains to the corpus of romance manuscripts in medieval French. Germanists, Anglicists, Scandinavists, and others may find something similar in their own domains; comparison between the *mise en texte* of different vernaculars would likely prove informative.

Nothing is more familiar to anyone who has more than glanced at a medieval manuscript than the pen-flourished initial (French *lettrine*), often part of a hierarchy of decoration which can guide the reading of a text. The decoration may be as modest as a simple rubricated capital or as elaborate as a full-size miniature, with varying sizes of pen-flourished initial, *champie* (a painted initial, often red and blue, sometimes decorated with gold), or historiated capital (with an image inside or part of the letter) in between. All of these forms are decorative, while miniatures and historiated capitals, with or without rubrics, generate a text–image relationship which becomes an essential part of experiencing the romance in manuscript, and which will be discussed shortly. The simpler forms of decoration can appear as simply that, but their size and location were not chosen haphazardly by manuscript planners, and space had to be left for their execution after the principal text had been copied. It is clear that larger initials are often used to mark major divisions of a narrative, and it is possible to indicate this in a critical edition. Few (if any) editions specify the placement of the more frequent pen-flourished initials and rubricated capitals, yet their study can be instructive. In essence, such initials tend to occur on temporal conjunctions (such as "Lors," "Quant," "Atant," etc.), mark the appearance of characters in a scene ("Li chevaliers," "La roïne," "Mes sire Gauvains," etc.), and indicate the beginning of direct speech. In prose romance, initials also usually mark the transition from one narrative thread of *entrelacement* to another at the beginning of formulae such as "Or dist li contes" ("Now the tale says ..."). This both structures and manipulates the narrative, lending it rhythm and providing readers the opportunity to pause and reflect; it is not difficult to see how it can be used to accentuate the importance of events, figures, or themes. Particularly with verse romance, more likely to be read aloud to a listening audience than prose, rubricated capitals and pen-flourished initials may well have provided performers with cues for gestures and inflections or change of voice, moving romance toward the drama of a one-person show. To be sure, this suggestion is speculative, but it is hardly credible to imagine that romance (or any other narrative form, for that matter) was performed in an unrelieved monotone before an unresponsive audience.[11] Conclusions must be drawn cautiously, given the time-lag between text and manuscript. Depending on the manner of copying, the palaeographical features of a manuscript may represent a combination of the archaic and the contemporary.

We are on somewhat firmer ground when it comes to the matter of text–image relations. Although the best-known illuminated manuscripts of Old French romance are probably of Arthurian prose, most romance *matières* are illustrated in at least part of the corpus.[12] The *romans antiques* (particularly the *Roman de Troie*) and the *Roman d'Alexandre*, Chrétien de Troyes and his epigones, prose romances of different types, all survive in considerable numbers with accompanying miniatures and historiated initials, often accompanied by rubrics. This adds an extra dimension to the study of text and image since both rubric and illustration can tell us what manuscript planners and their readers considered important in a romance, and even whether planners, artists, and rubricators had actually read the texts they were producing.[13] The illustrated manuscripts of the *romans antiques*, for example, constitute a visualization of medievalized antiquity, wherein Greek and Roman figures from the *Iliad* and the *Aeneid* are depicted as knights and their ladies in medieval dress, the visible representation of their inner sensibilities. Some Arthurian romance manuscripts frequently illustrate scenes of the *merveilleux*, suggesting that readers at their time of composition regarded it as a defining and noteworthy characteristic of the genre. Most manuscripts include what may be regarded as "generic" scenes, such as encounters between lovers, single combats, and tournaments, which do little more than confirm that the text in question is in fact a romance. Others seem to offer a pictorial guide to a lengthy narrative, occasionally (when accompanied by rubrics) to the extent of providing a more manageable summary. Some of the run-of-the-mill Italian manuscripts of the Prose Tristan actually indicate the names of the characters next to their visual representation, perhaps suggesting that the readers for which they were intended (likely the merchant class in the north of the country) needed textual support in order to interpret the scene depicted. Other Italian copies are more luxurious and can be situated in a much more elevated social context.[14] Miniatures may also function as "bookmarks" to aid in the reading and orientation of the text. In addition to stressing certain aspects of a text, miniatures may also portray the "iconic" scenes of texts already well-known, such as Alexander's bathysphere or Renart preaching to the hens or Perceval leaving his mother's house. These are precisely the moments which are fixed in the memory, define the romance, and help the reader recall other episodes. The use of the word "reader" here is intentional: early romance manuscripts were likely intended as performance texts, but richness of illustration certainly points toward individual readers since an illustration cannot be read (although it can, of course, be described). In practice, of course, all manuscripts can be read in performance or individually, and the manner of reading early manuscripts will surely have changed with the spread of literacy. Manuscripts are precious objects and have a life long after their initial production and dissemination.

The earliest romance manuscripts, say, from the very end of the twelfth and first half of the thirteenth century, are modest, single-item codices with little decoration, and many seem to be from England and the western domains.

If their geographical provenance is significant in terms of the recent attention paid to medieval Francophonia, caution is to be recommended when interpreting them as many are fragments which give little indication of *mise en livre*. The *Tristan* romance of Thomas is perhaps the most prominent example of a major romance transmitted piecemeal in fragments. Nevertheless, it seems that the history of romance manuscripts is indeed one in which romances are first copied and circulate as individual texts, only later to be associated with other works in collective volumes. This is no doubt related to the evolving circumstances of commercial manuscript production. Patrons ordering a book will have wanted more than one text, and *libraires* either provided customers with what they wanted or assembled their own compilations, which were then put up for sale. In either event, texts were chosen for a particular reason and arranged purposefully in sequence. There are, of course, some romances which constitute their own context by virtue of length. Chrétien's *Perceval* and its continuations, the great prose cycles, the *Roman d'Alexandre*, and the *Roman de Renart*, for example, are usually transmitted in single-item codices, but even – perhaps especially – here, reading of what might appear to be a discreetly delineated text or section of text runs the risk of distorting its meaning. The process of cyclification, not to say simple intertextuality, anchors each part or "branch" of a longer text to the whole in some way. To read the Vulgate *La Queste del saint Graal* without the *Lancelot* before it and *La mort le roi Artu* following does the trilogy a disservice at the same time as it impoverishes each part.[15] Some branches of some manuscripts of the *Roman d'Alexandre* and the *Roman de Renart* pose particular problems, as their brevity lends them to detachment and isolated study outside of their codicological context, depriving them of their intertextuality with other branches. Certainly, the word "roman" or "romance" has to be understood differently in the cases of the Renart and Alexander texts, more in the sense of "a collection of episodes and adventures revolving around Renart or Alexander." Indeed, the textual boundaries of branches or other forms of unit are often either unclear or codicologically nonexistent. Many manuscripts of Chrétien's *Perceval* fail to mark the transition between the 9,234 lines of the "mother-romance" and

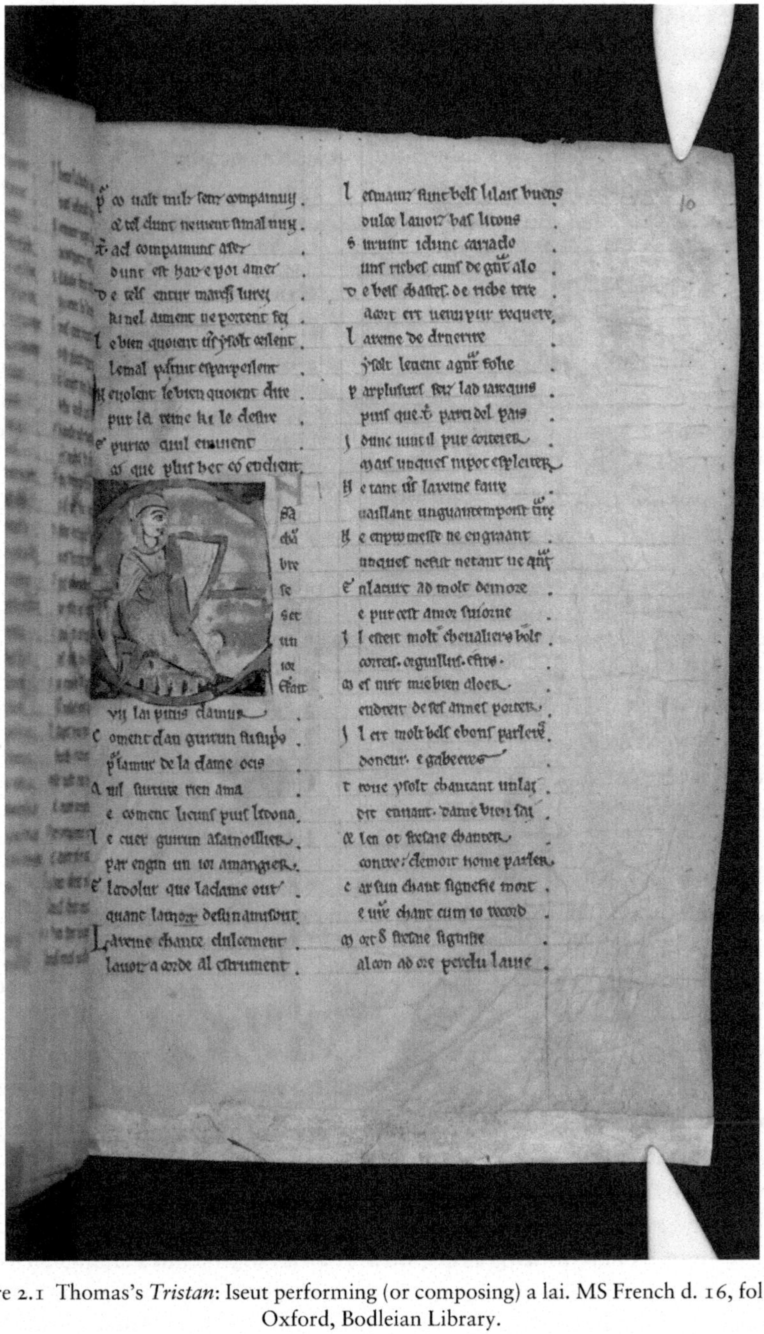

Figure 2.1 Thomas's *Tristan*: Iseut performing (or composing) a lai. MS French d. 16, fol. 10r. Oxford, Bodleian Library.

the First Continuation. Lack of prominent boundary markers leads the most complete manuscripts of the verse Grail texts to be seen in the Middle Ages as the Grail romance rather than a collection of texts by different authors (anonymous, Wauchier de Denain, Gerbert de Montreuil, Manessier).

It is difficult to generalize about the manuscript contexts of specific romances, but the inclusion of a romance in a multitext "recueil" at the very least demonstrates what could be termed "codicological compatibility."[16] Clearly, any number of considerations determined what was copied into a medieval book and how that book was disposed and ordered (*mise en recueil*, *mise en livre*). In the case of bespoke manuscripts, the wishes of the patron would have been paramount, but there is unfortunately no evidence of such transactions. We do, however, have some indications of individual orders from the highest social circles of manuscripts of the *Lancelot-Graal*, the Prose *Tristan*, the *Perceval*, and the *Roman de la Rose* in the records left by the Paris *libraires* in the early fourteenth century.[17] Some of the larger *recueils* containing romances are also multigenre manuscripts, such as Paris, BnF, fr. 19,152 (fabliaux ms. *D*) with *Partonopeu de Blois*, which is otherwise a collection of short tales, or Bern, Burgerbibliothek 354 (fabliaux ms. *B*), preserving Chrétien's *Perceval* and the prose *Sept sages de Rome*, again with many short texts of many different kinds. What is remarkable about these and many other manuscripts is the sheer variety of works they contain, from scurrilous fabliaux through pious and didactic pieces to full-length romances and even the occasional *chanson de geste*. This teaches us to be on our guard against developing too strict a model of genres or text-types, particularly with regard to intended audience and readership. There may have been clearer distinctions between courtly and noncourtly, between aristocratic and bourgeois, between *intra* and *extra muros*, in the very early periods of vernacular literature, but what defines the content of many large *recueils* is a leveling of text and intended public, an expansion of the canon, reflected in manuscripts that some have likened to small libraries.

Each romance has its own manuscript contexts, and some are many and various. The simplest cases are those romances preserved in a single manuscript (an editor's nightmare),[18] whose contents and ordering are quickly established. Reading a romance in such a manuscript is nevertheless a complex matter, and begins with consideration of the section of the book in which the romance appears. What precedes it and what follows it? If read in the light of its neighboring texts, how does its significance change? Does it provide a complement or contrast with these and other works bound between the same boards? Are there thematic or direct intertextual links between the romance and the other contents of the manuscript? If it stands at the head of the manuscript or closes it, does this accord it a particular status as introduction or conclusion? Answers to questions such as this do depend, of course, on whether medieval readers actually read the entire contents of a manuscript or at least scanned them. Readers might also have been familiar with the other texts from elsewhere and would not necessarily have needed to read the whole book before considering such matters. Readers and listeners might also have made associations as a matter of course with other works they knew. Assumptions concerning visual or aural reception figure largely among the variables when making assessments of this kind. In the case of romances preserved in multiple copies, this exercise can naturally be carried out for each manuscript in order to provide a complete picture. Commonalities and differences between the contexts of the various manuscripts can therefore offer insights into the dissemination of a romance and the ways it was viewed in the social strata in which it circulated at particular periods.

Shared and related subject matter is an evident principle behind the assembly and structure of some romance manuscripts.[19] The three *romans antiques*, for example, sometimes appear together in order (*Thèbes*, *Troie*, *Eneas*), either as a complete manuscript (Montpellier, Bibliothèque interuniversitaire H251, and Paris, BnF, fr. 60) or as a unit in a larger *recueil*. They should therefore be viewed as stages in that period of universal "history" seen as the beginning of the *translatio studii* which brought cultural authority from the ancient world to the then modern. In a number of manuscripts, such as Paris, BnF, fr. 1450, all or some of the *romans antiques* are followed by Wace's *Brut* as a continuation of the *translatio*, then by Arthurian romances which illustrate the adventures of Arthur's Britain. Genre (bearing all the necessary caveats about characterizing text-types) can also be a determining factor in the compilation and arrangement of manuscripts. Paris, BnF, nouv. acq. fr. 1104, for example, is a collection of *lais bretons*, which illustrates the expanding parameters of the *lai*, visible also in manuscripts such as BnF, fr. 2168, and Cologny-Geneva, Bodmer 82. Chantilly, Musée Condé 472 is a series of Arthurian verse romances, headed up by *Les merveilles de Rigomer*, from which all the other romances are seen as deriving. This turns the evolution of French Arthurian verse romance on its head, as the *Merveilles* is the last romance of its kind to have been composed (ca. 1275), while Chrétien de Troyes's and a number of epigonal romances are presented in a kind of codicological synchronicity. Only Chrétien has an œuvre large enough to constitute a book, although the two romances of Hue de Rotelande, *Ipomedon* and *Protheselaus*, are preserved together in London, BL, Egerton 2515 (Anglo-Norman); the two romances of Philippe de Rémi (*La manekine* and *Jehan et Blonde*) are preserved in Paris, BnF, fr. 1588, along with his other works, in what is clearly an author manuscript. The so-called "Annonay" fragments of Chrétien may have come from an early *œuvres complètes*, and other manuscripts, including the notorious Guiot copy (Paris, BnF, fr. 794), show awareness of an authorial identity with clusters of his romances. Romances may also be included in what appear to be regional collections which favor authors associated with a particular area of medieval Francophonia or texts associated with a region; the romances of Gauter d'Arras, for example, are preserved only in manuscripts from the Northeast (BnF, fr. 365 and Nottingham, UL, Mi LM 6), and BnF, fr. 1588 of Philippe de Rémi's romances is from Arras. Production and ownership of manuscripts of Old French romance in Italy, mainly in the fourteenth century, is a notable phenomenon demonstrating the long reach of the *langue d'oïl*.[20]

The "compare and contrast" method of reading romance in manuscript – that is, looking at thematic and structural similarities between texts in the same medieval book – has both pros and cons. Comparison need not be limited to two or more romances, as any text in the same manuscript might cast some kind of light on any other text or suggest an interpretation or approach which might otherwise have remained obscure. This has the virtue of breaking down barriers between types of text erected by literary historians in their desire to categorize and define unfamiliar and unruly material. The major criticism that can be leveled against sequential or comparative reading in general is that it can be done even when texts do not appear in the same manuscript or that the contents of a *recueil* can be rearranged in random order and produce similar results. There is, of course, nothing inherently misguided about the comparison of a romance with any other text or texts, but doing so within the bounds of a single manuscript at least has the advantage of medieval authenticity in that regard.

Mere numbers of manuscripts can also belie impressions resulting from a century and a half of scholarship. Literary histories and bibliographies suggest, for example, that of French verse texts of the late twelfth and early thirteenth centuries, the Tristan romances and those of Chrétien de Troyes enjoyed a prominent position, but manuscript transmission does not support this. Chrétien's works are each preserved in anywhere between eight and thirteen manuscripts (including fragments), with seventeen for *Perceval* (assuming all fragments of the Continuations once contained Chrétien's text). The *Tristan* of Béroul has survived in a single incomplete witness, and Thomas in mere fragments. The attraction of the Arthurian *merveilleux* and the paradigm of the courtly lovers are no doubt two of the principal reasons for the critical attention paid to Chrétien, Béroul, and Thomas, but the manuscripts tell another story: eleven copies of *Athis et Prophilias*, seventeen of Aimon de Varennes's *Florimont*, thirteen of *Partonopeu de Blois*, and so on; scholarship on these romances is nothing like as abundant as that on Chrétien and the verse Tristan texts. Although recent work has begun to reevaluate and reassess the Prose *Tristan* (surviving in over fifty manuscripts) and related works, scholarship is largely silent on the cycle of the prose *Sept Sages* (twenty-five copies). Scholarly progress on the *Tristan*, *Guiron le courtois*, and other prose cycles has been made largely possible by the careful and often laborious examination of their manuscript transmission.[21]

By and large, the reception of early verse romance in the fifteenth century is that of the *mise en prose*, but some are copied late in their original forms. There are Burgundian prose versions of Chrétien's *Erec et Enide* and *Cligès*, and a printed prose text of *Perceval* (1531). Romances such as *Floriant et Florete* and Gerbert de Montreuil's *Roman de la Violette* are also turned into prose,[22] but the fifteenth-century copies of *Athis et Prophilias*, *Florimont*, and *Galeran de Bretagne* (Jean Renart?), for example, appear as anachronisms or perhaps as the work of antiquarians without a desire to modernize. The enduring appeal of the *Roman de la Rose* is likewise reflected in numbers of fifteenth-century copies among its corpus of more than 250 manuscripts.

Marks of ownership, annotations, booklists, and documents such as wills and post-mortem inventories can give hints of circulation after the initial production and reception of a text.[23] We are ill-informed about the first owners of most manuscripts, although it may be reasonable to infer that patrons and dedicatees of romances (Marie de Champagne for Chrétien's *Lancelot* and Philippe de Flandre for *Perceval*, for example) would have received presentation copies. Even though no first-generation copies of these other romances have survived, it is clear that royal and aristocratic courts were where the very early manuscripts were to be found. Ample evidence for ownership only appears in the fourteenth century, and, when it does, it suggests that manuscripts of some romances which were already a century or more old (in what may have been contemporary or near-contemporary books) were valued enough to be preserved, inscribed, recorded as chattel, and passed on to heirs. Not surprisingly, much evidence comes from royal libraries and the records of the higher aristocracy, but book ownership soon moves down the social scale within the ranks of the nobility. The administrative classes acquired similar reading habits at about the same period, but their response to courtly romance may have been different to that of their masters. Counterintuitively, ecclesiastics and monastic institutions in France and England also owned numbers of secular works in the vernacular, including some classic romances. There is no proof, of course, that any owners actually read the manuscripts they possessed, but records suggest they may well have.[24] How they understood romances is harder to say. In the fourteenth and fifteenth centuries there is a clear movement toward individual (not necessarily silent) reading, and annotation by means of underlining and placement of *maniculae* (drawings of a small hand in the margin pointing at a passage of text) can give indications of what late readers found significant. Such annotations, however, are often notoriously difficult to date.

In a chapter such as this, it is not possible to give due consideration to the manuscript contexts of romances in other vernaculars, and, in any event, no one scholar can possess sufficient expertise in Germanic, English, Nordic, Celtic (principally Welsh), and other Romance philologies. French romance has the chronological priority over that in the other languages, and a comparison of manuscript contexts would complement the usual kind of textual analysis of relations between the originary tradition and its derivatives as well as revealing much about the derivatives themselves. Middle Dutch and Middle High German provide the most evident comparative codicological corpora in terms of kind and number, although the nonsurvival of first-generation French manuscripts creates more of a level playing field. Some of the many manuscripts of Wolfram von Eschenbach's *Parzival* and Gottfried von Straßburg's *Tristan* are illustrated and offer interesting potential when comparing the illuminated copies of Chrétien's *Perceval*, the meager fragments of Thomas's *Tristan*, and the richer transmission of the Prose *Tristan*, respectively. Special mention should be made of the Middle Dutch *Lancelot-Compilatie* manuscript (The Hague, KB 129 A 10), which inserts adaptations and original romances into the framework of the cycle; it preserves a large part of the Middle Dutch Arthurian corpus. Middle English romance develops late and in quite different social circumstances, largely due to the status of French in post-Conquest Britain, and this is reflected in its manuscripts, relatively few in number and all the more precious for what they preserve. Anglicists have examined in detail the so-called Thornton and Auchinleck manuscripts; the manuscripts of *Sir Gawain and the Green Knight* and Malory's *Morte Darthur* are both *unica*, study of which has proven rewarding. Thornton (Lincoln, Lincoln Cathedral 91, and London, BL, Add. 31042) and Auchinleck (Edinburgh, NLS, Advocates' 19. 2. 1) are closely linked to the merchant and landowning classes in both London and Yorkshire; London, BL, Cotton Nero A. X of *Gawain* is from northwest England (Cheshire?) and contains religious edifying texts alongside the romance; the Winchester Malory (London, BL, Add. 59678) offers a different reading experience to Caxton's 1485 printed text.[25]

However modern readers may choose to approach medieval romance, it has become clear from scholarship over recent decades that studying the modern printed text alone in a critical edition leaves much unsaid. The material objects which preserve and transmit the texts have more to tell us than can be deduced from a modern book. There is, of course, nothing inherently misguided about reading the text and nothing but the text, and although a manuscript cannot take us all the way back to the moment of the text's composition and first reception, it can take us much of the way and provide something resembling a medieval experience. The contexts of romance are many and various – as the contributions in this volume show – but consideration of its manuscript contexts enriches our understanding of the genre, its evolution, and its place in medieval culture.

Notes

1. Giving call nos. for all manuscripts of romances mentioned in this chapter would be unnecessarily cumbersome. Readers are referred to www.arlima.net and http://jonas.irht.cnrs.fr/, which list surviving manuscripts of all Old French texts; digitized reproductions may be found on numerous library websites, in particular Gallica: http://gallica.bnf.fr.
2. Beginning, say, ca. 1850.
3. See, for example, Pascale Bourgain and Françoise Vielliard, *Conseils pour l'édition des textes médiévaux, fascicule III: textes littéraires* (Paris: École nationale des Chartes, 2002).
4. The collections of "Lettres Gothiques" and "Champion Classiques" have been particularly successful in opening up medieval literature to a wider public. Bilingual editions can be problematic for teaching purposes, however, as students tend to rely on the translation and neglect the original Old French.
5. This makes the current decline in the teaching of the history of languages all the more regrettable.
6. It could be argued that all medievalists should attempt a critical edition, if only as an exercise, since the real nature of medieval textuality and scribal behavior is only revealed by painstaking comparison of several copies of the same text. On a microlevel, this is what Paul Zumthor famously termed "mouvance"; see, for example, his *Essai de poétique médiévale* (Paris: Seuil, 1972).
7. By *mise en texte*, I mean the palaeographical details of how a scribe writes (letter-forms, abbreviations, disposition of words and word-groups, punctuation, etc.), and by *mise en page*, the arrangement of all aspects of the manuscript page (columns of text, form, size, and location of initials, decorative elements such as capitals and miniatures, rubrics, *tituli*, and so on). *Mise en livre* or *mise en recueil* are of a higher order and refer mainly to the gathering and ordering of texts within a book.
8. For French manuscripts of the twelfth century, see Maria Careri, Christine Ruby, and Ian Short, *Livres et écritures en français au XIIe siècle* (Rome: Viella, 2011), and for the thirteenth, Maria Careri, Françoise Féry-Hue, Françoise Gasparri, et al., *Album de manuscrits français du XIIIe siècle: mise en page et mise en texte* (Rome: Viella, 2001). These indispensable works provide copious illustrated examples of the kind of palaeographical details discussed later in the chapter.
9. I treat here some of the same issues considered in my *Codex and Context: Reading Old French Verse Narrative in Manuscript*, 2 vols. (Amsterdam: Rodopi, 2002), but with perspectives gained with the passing of time, discussions with colleagues, and the pertinent observations of kind reviewers.

10. For abbreviation, punctuation, and word-clustering, see *Codex and Context*, I, ch. 3, pp. 127–82.
11. See *Codex and Context*, I, ch. 3, pp. 182–95.
12. For case studies of manuscripts illustrating the *Roman de Renart*, the Crusade Cycle, the Alexander romances, and Chrétien's *Perceval* with Continuations, see *Codex and Context*, I, ch. 4, pp. 225–365.
13. Manuscripts are often left unfinished, but even unexecuted miniatures can tell us a good deal. See, for example, my "Absence de l'image dans le ms. Montpellier, BIU, Sect. Méd. H 252," in *Mouvances et jointures: du manuscrit au texte médiéval*, ed. Miléna Mikhaïlova (Orléans: Paradigme, 2006), pp. 19–29, and "Filling in the Blanks: The Missing Miniatures in BnF, fr. 15101 of *Florimont*," in *"De sens rassis": Medieval Studies in Honor of Rupert T. Pickens*, ed. Keith Busby, Bernard Guidot, and Logan E. Whalen (Amsterdam: Rodopi, 2005), pp. 85–95. It is not out of the question that some unfinished manuscripts are workshop copies in which expensive decoration was redundant.
14. The range of Italian manuscripts of French romances can be seen in François Avril, Marie-Thérèse Gousset, and Yolanta Załuska, *Manuscrits enluminés d'origine italienne*, 2 vols. (Paris: Bibliothèque Nationale, 1984). See also *Codex and Context*, II, pp. 596–634 and 766–97.
15. The length and difficulty of access to the cyclical *Lancelot* prior to the edition of Micha, along with the handy format of Pauphilet's *Queste* and Frappier's *Mort*, essentially disassembled the *Lancelot-Graal* for many decades.
16. I use the French word "recueil" here as it is more current than the English "collection" in manuscript studies. English "miscellany" is problematic for a number of reasons.
17. See Mary and Richard Rouse, *"Illiterati et uxorati". Manuscripts and Their Makers: Commercial Book Producers in Paris, 1200–1500*, 2 vols. (London: Harvey Miller, 2000).
18. Insofar as there is no control manuscript in the event of scribal error or other difficult readings.
19. I treat this kind of contextual issue in *Codex and Context*, I, ch. 5, pp. 367–484.
20. For regional preferences, see *Codex and Context*, II, ch. 6, pp. 485–635.
21. See, for example, Patrick Moran, *Lectures cycliques: le réseau inter-romanesque dans les cycles du Graal du XIIIe siècle* (Paris: Champion, 2014).
22. See Chapter 15, by Jane H. M. Taylor (this volume), and the same author's *Rewriting Arthurian Romance in Renaissance France: From Manuscript to Printed Book* (Woodbridge: Boydell and Brewer, 2014).
23. See *Codex and Context*, II, ch. 7, pp. 637–813.
24. I am thinking here, for example, of the lending records of the Louvre library and the occasional informal note that a bookowner lent their precious volume to a friend.
25. For a brief discussion of Middle Dutch, Middle High German, and Middle English Arthurian romance manuscripts (and references to Nordic and Welsh), see Busby, "The Manuscript Context," pp. 105–14. Middle English romance manuscripts are surveyed by Maldwyn Mills and Gillian Rogers, "The Manuscripts of Popular Romance," in *A Companion to Popular Romance*, ed. Raluca Radulescu and Corey Rushton (Cambridge: D. S. Brewer, 2009), pp. 49–66. For Nordic, see

especially Stefka G. Eriksen, "New Philology/Manuscript Studies," in *Handbook of Arthurian Romance*, ed. Leah Tether and Johnny McFadyen (Berlin: De Gruyter, 2017), pp. 199–213, and for Welsh, Daniel Huws, *Medieval Welsh Manuscripts* (Cardiff: University of Wales Press, 2000). Manuscripts of romances in Nordic and Welsh are few in number when compared with those in Old French and Middle High German. For descriptions of Middle Dutch manuscripts of romances, see Hans Kienhorst, *De handschriften van de middelnederlandse ridder-epiek. Een codicologische beschrijving* (Deventer: Sub Rosa, 1988), and Bart Besamusca "The Manuscripts" in *The Arthur of the Low Countries: The Arthurian Legend in Dutch and Flemish Literatur* (Cardiff: University of Wales Press, 2021), pp. 45–62.

Suggestions for Further Reading

Besamusca, Bart. "The Manuscripts". In *The Arthur of the Low Countries: The Arthurian Legend in Dutch and Flemish Literature*. Ed. Bart Besamusca and Frank Brandsma. Cardiff: University of Wales Press, 2021, pp. 54–62.

Busby, Keith. *Codex and Context: Reading Old French Verse Narrative in Manuscript*. 2 vols. Amsterdam: Rodopi, 2002. French translation, *Codex et contexte: lire la littérature française médiévale dans les manuscrits*. Paris: Classiques Garnier, 2022.

Busby, Keith. "Codex, Context, Continuation". *Medioevo Romanzo*, 38, 1 (2014), 28–44.

Busby, Keith. "The Manuscript Context of Arthurian Romance". In *Handbook of Arthurian Romance: King Arthur's Court in Medieval European Literature*. Ed. Leah Tether and Johnny McFadyen, in Collaboration with Keith Busby and Ad Putter. Berlin: Walter de Gruyter, 2017, pp. 97–116.

Busby, Keith, Terry Nixon, Alison Stones, and Lori J. Walters. *Les Manuscrits de Chrétien de Troyes/The Manuscripts of Chrétien de Troyes*. 2 vols. Amsterdam: Rodopi, 1993.

Moran, Patrick. *Lectures cycliques: le réseau inter-romanesque dans les cycles du Graal du XIIIe siècle*. Paris: Champion, 2014.

Morato, Nicola. "Formation et fortune du cycle de *Guiron le Courtois*". In *Le Cycle de* Guiron le Courtois. Ed. Luca Cadioli and Sophie Lecomte. Paris: Classiques Garnier, 2018, pp. 180–247.

Rialfri: Repertorio Informatizzato Antica Letreratura Franco-Italiana Manuscripts – RIALFrI

3

JANE GILBERT AND AD PUTTER

Matters of Form
Experiments in Verse and Prose Romance

The earliest romances, written in a French that was thought of as "Roman" – the new Latin! – grew out of and responded to the many innovations in verse form, rhythm and rhyme (in both verse and prose), and style in earlier and contemporary Latin writings. At first imitating and further adapting French romances (in some cases, via German intermediaries), other western and central European vernaculars developed their own formal repertoires. The use of prose for storytelling is nowadays so normal that it requires some mental effort to imagine a time when audiences had different expectations, but when we travel back in time to the earliest medieval romances that leap of imagination is essential. For, except for a few languages (notably Welsh, Irish, and Old Norse) with well-established prose traditions that could absorb the new fashion for romance, medieval romance begins in verse. The first half of this chapter shows how that verse is often different from what we expect from poetry today, while its second explains why medieval prose, too, should surprise us.

Verse

A good place to start is with Chrétien de Troyes, the pioneer of Arthurian romance, who was active around the 1170s. A few lines from the prologue of his first romance, *Erec et Enide*, illustrate the quality of his contribution to the history of form:

> D'Erec, le fil Lac, est li contes
> que devant rois et devant contes
> depecier et corronpre suelent
> cil qui de conter vivre vuelent.
> Des or comencerai l'estoire

qui toz jors mes iert an mimoire
tant con durra crestïantez;
de ce s'est Crestïens vantez.[1]

(Erec, son of King Lac, is the subject of this tale [*contes*], which those who seek to make a living by storytelling habitually mangle and corrupt before kings and before counts [*contes*]. Now I will commence the story which will be in memory for as long as Christianity [*crestïantez*] endures. That is what Chrétien [*Crestiens*] asserts.)

False modesty was not for Chrétien and, unusually, the importance he claims for his story is based not on it being a *true* story but on its artistic superiority. Chrétien's formal choices push these claims very effectively, for what he did was to perfect what was becoming the staple meter for fiction, history, and didactic matter in French: the octosyllabic couplet. Chrétien's lines invariably consist of eight syllables, or nine if the line is feminine (ending on an unstressed syllable). The octosyllabic rhyming couplet had a long history before Chrétien and that history highlights the important innovations that Chrétien and, before him, the poets of the *romans d'antiquité* brought to it. The form goes back to Latin, where classical iambic dimeter gradually evolved into octosyllabic verse with rhyme. The formal characteristics of that early Latin rhymed verse – a mid-line caesura (break) after the fourth syllable, loose rhyme, sense units running in strict parallel with couplets – were transferred to the vernacular.

A generation before Chrétien de Troyes, poets associated with the Angevin court of Henry II of England and Eleanor of Aquitaine began the process of adapting the octosyllabic couplet from what was essentially a sung form to one that was suitable for long narrative. The earliest romances in French – the *Roman de Thèbes*, *Roman d'Enéas*, and Benoît de Sainte-Maure's *Roman de Troie* – are in this medium. Chrétien's business was to pick off the remaining eggshells of the older form. When you are writing long poems you need to avoid monotonous cadences, and Chrétien managed this by various means. He created a balance between masculine and feminine line endings that now seems "natural" but was in fact new. His verse flows because he frequently allowed the sense to spill over from one line to the next (enjambment). Moreover, contemporary audiences must have been struck by the richness of his rhymes. As the above-cited lines from *Erec* illustrate, his rhymes are often not just on the final stressed syllable but extend back to the syllable preceding it, as in *crestïantez*: *vantez*. In the octosyllabic romances that Chrétien knew, such *rimes riches* were still uncommon. Another feature that distinguishes the "high end" of romance composition in French (and English) is *rime équivoque*: when Chrétien rhymes *contes* ("story") with *contes* ("counts") in his prologue to *Erec*, he is not inanely repeating the same word but playing on different words with the same sound and spelling. This was a kind of verbal miracle that connoisseurs prized even more than *rime riche*.

Form, in other words, was a battleground for cultural capital, and educated readers and writers were more sensitive to the implications of formal choices than we may be today. Philippe de Beaumanoir shows that kind of sensitivity in his prologue to his early-thirteenth-century romance *La Manekine*, when he apologizes for the quality of his rhyming:

> Et se je ne sai leonime,
> Merveiller ne s'en doit on mie,
> Car molt petit sai de clergie.[2]

> (And if I don't know leonine rhyme, this should not come as a surprise, because I don't have much *clergie* ["learning, education"].)

'Leonine' was the term for what we now call *rime riche*[3] and Philippe de Beaumanoir, a nobleman rather than a cleric, associated this with educated poets – though, of course, poets who make declaimers of this sort are never as artless as they say, and the romance actually opens with an impressive volley of *rimes riches* (*ditier*: *delitier*, *l'orront*: *porront*, ll. 1–4) and *rimes équivoques* (*s'en*: *sen*, ll. 9–10; *dire*: *d'ire*, ll. 13–14).

Chrétien's romances were hugely influential not only on later romances in French but also on those in other languages. How did poets in other languages adjust to the octosyllabic rhymed couplet? The first vernacular romances in German were based on French models. Superficially, they look like their French sources. They employ end rhyme and are in couplets, but they clearly show less interest in syllabic regularity. Their poets counted *beats*, not *syllables*. The verse form they had inherited was the alliterative line, which required four beats (stressed syllables) and no fixed number of unstressed syllables. The new wine of romance was initially poured into these old prosodic bottles, now corked with end rhyme rather than alliteration.

With regard to rhyme, the similarities between Old French and Middle High German romances are closer, but here too there are some fascinating differences. The fundamental principle of rhyme is that it combines similarity with difference. In the case of *rime équivoque*, where the rhyme words (as in *contes*: *contes*, *fin*: *fin*) are phonologically identical, it is the semantic distinction between homophones that safeguards this principle. However, the fondness for *rime équivoque* was an acquired taste, and Middle High German poets did not share it. Rhymes on identical syllables were avoided. Where they occur, they are usually justified by subtle differences in degrees of stress. The master of this art was Gottfried von Strassburg, who rings the accentual changes on otherwise identical syllables. Here, for instance, is Isolde, explaining Tristan's alias, "Tantris," to her mother. We have marked the relevant rhymes for stress, using the *accent aigu* (´) for primary stress and the *accent grave* (`) for secondary stress:

> Nu muoter, nu scheide
> dise namen Tántrìs
> in ein tan und in ein trís
> und sprich daz tris vür daz tán
> so sprichestu Trístàn;
> sprich daz tan vür daz trís
> so sprichest aber Tántrìs.[4]

> (Now, mother, divide this name Tantris, into a "tan" and a "tris," and then say the "tris" before the "tan" and you will say "Tristan"; but if you say the "Tan" before the "Tris," then, however, you will say "Tantris.")

With the exception of a few romances written in the four-line strophe named after Wolfram von Eschenbach's *Titurel* (c. 1220), which first used it, all of Middle High German romance is in short couplets.

In Middle English romances, the rhymed couplet was also a popular vehicle. A good example of the English variation on the octosyllabic couplet is the fourteenth-century *Ywain and Gawain*, based on Chrétien's *Yvain.*[5] Most lines are iambic and octosyllabic (e.g. "Almyghty God that made mankyn," l. 1), but before Chaucer and Gower came along what mattered was the number of beats. An unstressed syllable could thus readily be omitted or added. In short, this was a rough-and-ready meter, and because poets liked alliteration (e.g. "Over ál the wérld wént the wórde," l. 46) the soundscape of alliterative meter is never far away. As in Middle High German poetry, *rime équivoque* was not part of most English poets' repertoire. The single example we were able to find in *Ywain and Gawain* – "Than went Ywain to his yn / His men he fand redy thareyn" (ll. 565–6) – suggests accident rather than design. Again it is Chaucer and Gower, who were deeply influenced by French (and in Chaucer's case also Italian) models, who developed an English taste for *rime équivoque.*[6]

What really sets English romance apart, however, is the amazing variety of verse forms that poets adopted. Alongside the couplet, the most popular form for Middle English romance was the tail-line stanza (known at the time as *rime couée*). The basis for this characteristically English stanza form is a rhyming couplet followed by a shorter "tail-line," which rhymes not with the couplet lines but with other tail-lines in the same stanza. Middle English poets played numerous variations on this basic form.[7] The rhythmical shape which tail-rhyme romances eventually gravitated toward was a four-beat couplet line plus a three-beat tail-line. This prosodic format is the one that Chaucer adopted in his parody of tail-rhyme romances, *Sir Thopas*, which begins:

> Listeth, lordes, in good entent,
> And I wol telle verrayment [truly]
> Of myrthe and of solas.
> Of a knyght that was fayr and gent [elegant]
> In bataille and in tourneyment;
> His name was sire Thopas. (ll. 1–6)[8]

The strengths of the form (an energetic rhythm, a colloquial directness – note, for example, plain *entent* rather than posh *entente*) – and its weaknesses (mechanical rhymes; monotonously end-stopped verses) are well illustrated here.

Chaucer did not capture, however, the enormous variety of tail-rhyme stanzas. In one of the earliest English tail-rhyme romances, *Sir Bevis of Hampton*, the tail-line is shorter (two beats).[9] And while *Sir Thopas* and *Bevis* are in six-line stanzas, some (e.g. *Emaré* and *Otuel and Roland*) are in twelve-line stanzas, while others (*Sir Perceval of Gales*, *Sir Degrevant*) are in sixteen-liners, with triplets instead of couplets between the tail-lines. The variety reveals the absence of an established norm for romance composition in Middle English. Apart from couplets and tail-rhyme, there existed an impressive range of alternative meters and stanza forms.[10] Thus, we have English romances in cross-rhyme, either in four-line stanzas (*abab*: e.g. *Sowdon of Babylon*, *Apollonius of Tyre* fragment) or eight-line ones (*abababab*: e.g. *Stanzaic Morte Arthur*); we have a romance in six-line *aaabab* stanzas (*Octavian*, Southern Version) and one in eleven-line stanzas (*ababababcbc*: *Sir Tristrem*). There exist romances (or should we say epics?) in unrhymed alliterative long lines (e.g. *Wars of Alexander*, *Alliterative Morte Arthure*), romances in rhymed alliterative stanzas (*ababababcdddc*: e.g. *Awntyrs of Arthure*), and one unique romance in stanzas of alliterative long lines followed by rhyming lines.

That unique romance is *Sir Gawain and the Green Knight*. It tells a wonderful story with a surprise at the end, and playing with expectations is also the essence of its verse form. Each stanza begins in alliterative meter:

> This **K**yng lay at **C**amylot upon **C**ristmasse
> With mony **l**uflych **l**ord, **l**edes of the beste. (ll. 37–8)[11]

> (This king was in Camelot at Christmas, with many a fine lord, men of the highest order.)

Unlike rhyme, where the sounds at the end matter, alliteration is essentially a rhyme on the beginning of stressed syllables. We have emboldened the alliterating sounds (always two in the first half-line and one in the second half) to illustrate this. Alliterative meter was popular in the poet's native region (Cheshire), but the original audience must have been very surprised when after the alliterative long lines they were treated to a bob, a one-beat verse (*On sille* in the example below), and a rhyming quatrain:

For all was this fayre folk in her first age
        On sille,
The hapnest under heven,
Kyng highest man of wille;
Hit were now grete nye to neven
So hardy a here on hille. (ll. 55–9)

(For these beautiful people were in the flush of youth, in the hall. The most blessed under heaven, their king a man of the highest mettle. It'd be very difficult to name a braver band of warriors existing today.)

The bob thus transports us from one type of verse (alliterative) to another (rhymed and iambic). Because there is no set number of alliterative long lines before the rhymed bob-and-wheel, that transition always takes us by surprise, just as the story does. But the biggest formal surprise comes at the end: despite the unregulated number of lines per stanza, the poem resolves itself into an exquisitely controlled cyclical shape. The first alliterative long line is repeated in the last, at line 2525 (encoding the number of the pentangle) and there are 101 stanzas, just as in the other famous poem by the same poet, *Pearl*.[12]

Last but not least, we should mention the seven-line rhyme-royal stanzas (*ababbcc*), which Chaucer pioneered for narrative. Chaucer got the stanza form from Middle French lyrics of love complaint, and first used it himself in a lyric complaint ("The Complaint unto Pity"). In Chaucer's finest romance, *Troilus and Criseyde*,[13] that association of the stanza form with lyric complaint repeatedly comes to the fore. An example is Troilus's song in book 1, the earliest translation of a Petrarch sonnet in English:

If no love is*, O God what fele I so? *If this isn't love
And if love is, what thing and which is he?
If love be good, from whennes cometh my woo?
If it be wikke, a wonder thynketh me,
When every torment and adversite
That cometh of hym may to me savory thinke* seem pleasant
For ay thurst I, the more that ich it drynke. (ll. 400–6)

Fifteenth-century poets so admired Chaucer's *Troilus* that many of them borrowed this stanza form for their own romances.

Why there was so much metrical diversity in English and so little in other languages is an interesting question. Romances in most European languages know only couplets and one or two other, local forms. Thus, Dutch and German poets wrote in couplets. The *Titurel* stanza provided a few German poets with an alternative, but the rhyme scheme of that strophe, *aabb* (followed by another strophe rhyming *ccdd*) is really no different from the couplet form. French had assonance and monorhyme in *chansons de geste*, with lines of different length: octosyllabic (in some early fragments), decasyllabic, and alexandrines (twelve syllables), so-called because it was the meter of versions of the legend of Alexander from the late twelfth century onward. Spanish had the *mester de juglaría*, similar in meter to French *chanson de geste*, and the *mester de clerecía* in *cuaderna vía*, four-line monorhymed stanzas of fourteen-syllable lines. However, keeping monorhyme or assonance going for any length of time is almost impossible in English or any other Germanic language, so Middle English poets, like Dutch and German poets, used the same verse forms for epics as they did for romance. This blurred the boundary between epic and romance, and the consequences for generic classification are with us to this day. For instance, texts that in French would be instantly recognizable and considered as *chansons de geste* are known in English as "Charlemagne romances" and in Dutch as "karelromans." Languages that made no formal distinction between epics and romances have thus ended up with a category of romance that is much baggier than that in languages where the distinction is formally obvious. Even so, generic diversity did not entail formal diversity in Dutch and German, which simply made do with rhymed couplets. Middle English poets, by contrast, co-opted for *narrative* verse what seem to have been originally *lyric* forms. Thus, the *abab* stanza that we find in various Middle English romances goes back to hymns, the tail-rhyme stanza to the Latin sequence, and Chaucer's rhyme-royal stanza to the French *complainte*. Perhaps it was the absence of a prestigious and established lyric tradition in the English vernacular that made it easier for Middle English poets to blur yet another formal boundary: that of narrative and lyric.

While in the French romance tradition, lyric and narrative maintained distinct verse forms, their formal segregation made possible some exciting experimentation of a very different kind: the inclusion of lyrics in the course of the story. The earliest example of a romance with inset lyrics is Jean Renart's early-thirteenth-century *Guillaume de Dole*. The story itself, told in octosyllabic couplets, is enhanced by the inclusion of forty-six *chansons*, some by named *trouvères* (lyric poets working in northern French), others anonymous dance songs. There is no better description of the colorful effect achieved by lyric insertion than that offered by the poet in his prologue. His romance is like a cloth colored with rich and expensive dye; it is "une novele chose," entirely different from other works, "brodez, par lieus, de biaus vers" (embroidered here and there with fine stanzas, l. 14).[14] It will be read and sung forevermore because the poet has given not just provided narrative but also "chans et sons" (songs and melodies, l. 10), and these songs are so well matched to the narrative that you would think that the person who made the romance ("cil qui a fet le romans," l. 27) also composed the lyrics.

The success of Jean Renart's experiment can be measured by the many romances that followed his example by inserting lyrics into verse narratives, from Gerbert de Montreuil's *Roman de la Violette* (c. 1228) to Jean Froissart's late-fourteenth-century *Meliador*. In English, Chaucer's *Troilus and Criseyde* owes something to this form, for in *Troilus*, too, lyrical insets, such as Antigone's song, are made to resonate with the mood of characters in the story, and Chaucer's remark that the romance may be read or sung – "red . . . or elles songe" (5.1797; cf. 4.799, 5.1059) – recognizes, as did Jean Renart ("chanter et lire l'orront," l. 22), that the mixing of forms also made possible a mixing of performance styles.

Prose

Modern readers, used to seeing prose virtually everywhere, may consider it to be a nonform: a minimalist intervention that allows the free and transparent transmission of content. We may even subscribe to the idea that prose is a kind of everyday plain-speaking, lacking literary artifice or rhetorical pretensions, and therefore somehow more natural, truthful, and authentic than verse – which, as something contrived for special occasions or purposes, may seem showy, artificial, and therefore hollow – or, at the other extreme, highly subjective and personal, in contrast to prose's greater objectivity. This set of ideas we may call "the myth of prose," which has been worked up by prose writers over many centuries as a way of promoting their product in a competitive literary market; claims like this on prose's behalf are akin to advertising that a particular laundry powder washes cleaner than others, and are not to be taken at face value. When we actually study any written (or declaimed) prose from any period and in any language, we see that the form has, of course, specific expectations of pattern, style, and register. No less than verse, prose is a form that intimately shapes and is shaped by its material, audience, and context. And formal experimentation in medieval romance writing did not happen only in verse: the appearance of prose romances in French around 1200 was a startling, radical development with Europe-wide impact.

European vernacular prose romance begins as part of a larger turn in French writing to prose narrative around 1200 CE, which produced histories of France, Normandy, the Crusades, and ancient Rome, sermons, and Bible translations alongside romances.[15] Prose narrative seems to have become rapidly fashionable: the long, elaborate works that form the backbone of the Arthurian tradition – the *Lancelot-Grail* Vulgate and Post-Vulgate cycles, the prose *Roman de Tristan*, *Guiron le Courtois*, and *Perlesvaus* – were all composed in the first half-century after 1200. The same period saw the start of a vogue for reworking verse texts into prose, with some verse romances being "prosified" (*dérimé*) multiple times. What was at stake in this early turn to prose? The answer is, necessarily, contextual, but we can draw a rough distinction between prose romances in the thirteenth century, when the form was new and experimental, and those in the fourteenth and, especially, fifteenth centuries, when prose narrative was considered normal usage.

Although the early prose romances in French do not have crusade settings – all are Arthurian – they resound with the renewal of the crusading movement which occurred after Salāh ad-Din reconquered the city and most of the Latin Kingdom of Jerusalem in 1187, capturing the relic of the Holy Cross. The politically and spiritually reformist tone of early French prose narratives pitches them as responses to these catastrophic losses, which were blamed on Christian moral and spiritual back-sliding and political deficiencies, particularly infighting and weak leadership. Writing in the international language that was French, the romancers addressed a wider and different audience from Latin, setting out new standards and a new vocation for European chivalry, calling upon the secular nobility to rise to the cosmic challenge posed by the Crusades, and according it a crucial role in cosmic history. The patrons of these early works were crusading families, whose home domains lay along the northern and eastern edges of the kingdom of France and adjoining parts of the empire. Robert de Boron, whose name is associated with perhaps the earliest prose romances, is thought to have written for one Gauthier of Montfaucon-Montbéliard in the western empire, who became regent of the Latin Kingdom of Cyprus (1205–10). Whether composed by Robert or prosified from his verse romances, *Joseph d'Arimathie* (also known as *Le Roman de l'estoire dou Graal*) and *Merlin* (both c. 1200–10) break new ground in the way that they weave together Arthurian and redemption history and prescribe a new spiritual and moral seriousness for chivalry and for romance. Bringing together for the first time the apocalyptic prophecies of Merlin with the personal and collective spiritual renewal promised by the Grail, these works would become the core of the great Vulgate and Post-Vulgate cycles and set the abiding themes of early prose romance.

To a new chivalric vocation, a new literary form. The pioneers of prose narrative in French, whether history or romance, repudiated the literary and formal playfulness that characterized verse romances and proclaimed that prose permitted new levels and kinds of historical and spiritual truthfulness. In prologues and epilogues, translators and authors claim that they avoid the formal constraints of meter and rhyme by choosing to write "en romanz sanz rime" (in Romance without *rime* [indicating both modern "rhyme" and "rhythmical" as distinct from "metrical" verse]). Axiomatically, "nus contes rimés n'est verais" (no account in *rime* is true), because "rime se velt afeitier de moz conqueilliz hors de l'estoire" (*rime* wants to adorn itself with words amassed outside the source [i.e., with extraneous matter]).[16] According to such claims, prose ensures greater fidelity to the *estoire* (story/source/history), whether that is (allegedly) historical events or a (posited) authoritative, ancient text. Prose supposedly affords better access to the wisdom or moral content conveyed by the source and, in particular, to its spiritual value. With these assertions, prose narratives aim to discredit their verse competitors in the struggle for dominance in the literary marketplace.

In the early period, a willful stylistic impoverishment supports these value- and truth-claims, with simple syntax, a restricted, commonplace vocabulary, and high levels of repetition. (Modern translators often introduce a variety and color that misrepresents this – to modern taste – excessive "prosaics.") This passage from the *Haut Livre du Graal (Perlesvaus)* illustrates the style:

> Atant es vos le chevalier ou descent tres par mi la sale, et estoit vestus d'une robe vermeille et corte, et estoit chains d'une riche chainture d'or et avoit un riche fermail a son col ou molt avoit riches pieres, et avoit un capel d'or en son chief. Et tenoit une grant hache a .ii. mains. Li chevaliers estoit de tres grant biauté et de jovene aé. Lancelot le voit venir, si le garde molt volentiers, car il le vit molt apert.[17]

> (Now see the knight, where he descends into the very middle of the hall, and he was clothed in a short scarlet robe, and was belted with a rich golden belt and had a rich brooch at his neck where there were many rich stones, and he had a golden hat on his head. And he was holding a great axe with both hands. The knight was of great beauty and of young age. Lancelot sees him come, and looks at him most willingly, for he saw him to be most adept.)

The simple grammatical articulations and coordinations create a weighty and mysterious sense of consequence.[18] Stripped-down literary form contrasts with luxurious trappings, so that the text reconciles spiritual and materialistic ambitions (just as crusading could make secular fortunes as well as redeeming the soul). For early-thirteenth-century prose romance writers, the form *en romanz sanz rime* allows "li contes" or "l'estoire" to unfurl its full moral, spiritual, historical, and social force. The purported rejection of formal frills, therefore, has great positive value.

Both the French prose romances themselves and the habit of prosification traveled widely, but which vernaculars were used, and how, depended on local conditions. Evidence that writing prose romances in French was a prestigious practice in other countries, and not one necessarily or primarily associated with the kingdom of France, is supplied by the late-thirteenth-century "Arthurian Compilation" of Rustichello of Pisa, in Franco-Italian (a regional variant now thought to be a written, rather than spoken, form of French). Scholars consider this to be an original work, though Rustichello asserts in his prologue that he copied it from a book in French provided to him by the future Edward I of England, an obvious authority on matters Arthurian, when on crusade (1270–74). At around the same time, Dante ring-fenced prestige in prose for French, limiting his own search for a properly Italian "illustrious vernacular" to verse:

> propter sui faciliorem ac delectabiliorem vulgaritatem quicquid redactum est sive inventum ad vulgare prosaycum, suum est: videlicet Biblia cum Troianorum Romanorumque gestibus compilata et Arturi regis ambages pulcerrime et quamplures alie ystorie ac doctrine.

> (because of the greater facility and pleasing quality of its vernacular style, everything that is recounted or invented in vernacular prose belongs to [French]: such as compilations from the Bible and the histories of Troy and Rome, and the beautiful tales of King Arthur, and many other works of history and doctrine.)[19]

Dante's comment dismisses from consideration the many translations of French narratives into Italian prose that were produced from the thirteenth century onwards by notaries, lawyers, and merchants in central and northern Italy: educated, multilingual writers, whose reputation as unlearned scribblers is preserved in the condescending modern designation of their productions as *volgarizzamenti* (popularizations).[20] Dante's preference for conducting his own groundbreaking efforts in vernacular verse reflects how verse writing had responded to prose's predations in the thirteenth century: by laying claim to a high ground of intellectual and courtly speculation and formal experimentation, exemplified by Jean Renart's *Guillaume de Dole* and by the internationally influential *Roman de la Rose* by Guillaume de Lorris and Jean de Meun (c. 1225 and 1270).[21] Since prose romances rejected ornament, formal complexity, and playfulness, verse seized these as the preserve of intellectual and social elites.

Things were different where local vernaculars enjoyed the sponsorship of a strong, centralizing regime. Prose romances were copied in the distinctive

French of England that was the vernacular of the country's elites (see, for instance, the early-fourteenth-century Cambridge, University Library, MS Additional 7071, which contains the Vulgate *Estoire del saint Graal* and *Merlin* and the Post-Vulgate *Suite du Merlin*), although there seem to have been few original compositions; romance writers in Anglo-Norman, as in English, preferred verse. Prose romance in English really took off only with printing. In contrast, chivalric prose writings (including, but not only, romances) in local vernaculars were tools of the well-oiled royalist machines of thirteenth- and fourteenth-century Castile and Aragon, and the reign of Hákon Hákonarson, king of Norway 1217–63, triggers an "avalanche"[22] of prose texts in Old Norse, including translations of French romances and *chansons de geste* alongside local sagas, hagiographies, and chronicles.

We have, then, a contrast in literary histories, and something of a puzzle: prose romance writing was embraced in some European vernaculars, but not in others Prose romances in French were read and copied internationally, adapting to very different local contexts. Vernacular prose romances were also widespread in southern Europe, the eastern Mediterranean, Wales, Ireland, and Norway–Iceland; but elsewhere in northern and central Europe, and in Sweden, verse was preferred until the fifteenth century (and even those areas that commonly used prose also wrote verse romances). Vernaculars where prose romances did not catch on did, nevertheless, employ prose for various practical or prestigious discursive functions: prose didactic, devotional, scientific, encyclopedic, and travel writings are all well represented. But, apart from what appear to be isolated experiments – for example, fragments of a Dutch prose *Lancelot* (c. 1300),[23] or the Middle High German *Prosa-Lancelot* (c. 1250) transmitted only in fragments until the fifteenth century – writers in some languages composed romances in verse, and translated French prose romances into verse. Thus, in Middle English, the prose romances of the Arthurian Vulgate Cycle were initially adapted from French into verse: into four-beat couplets (*Arthour and Merlin*, c. 1275), into alliterative meter (*Joseph of Arimathie*, c. 1350), and into *abababab* stanzas (*Stanzaic Morte Arthur*, c. 1400). The first adaptations into English prose come only in the middle of the fifteenth century, with the *Prose Merlin* (c. 1450) and Malory's *Morte Darthur* (c. 1460).

In spite of these varying times and rates of adoption, and in spite of the persistence of verse, prose unquestionably dominated European romance writing by the middle of the fifteenth century. Although it had lost its early strangeness and urgency, prose nevertheless still carried a distinctive freight. Its traditional truth-claims and aspirations evidently bestowed a luster of historicity and chivalric piety, whether in romanticized biographies (such as *Le livre des fais [de] Bouciquaut* [1409] or Antoine de la Sale's *Jean de*

Saintré [1460]) or in tales about an obviously legendary past, such as *Perceforest*, one of many examples of mid-fifteenth-century prose romances whose supposed authenticity is sustained not only by its prose form but also by the claim to rework an earlier product. These works also embody newly stringent devotional and moral tendencies.[24] The high courtly register of the *Istoire de la Chastelaine du Vergier et de Tristan le chevalier* (mid-fifteenth century) helps to establish its ideal of chaste and honorable love:

> "O," dist Tristan, "ma tres honoree dame et maistresse, je vous mercy de vostre gracieusse responce, pour laquelle je puis avoir grant esperance en vostre misericordieuse grace. Tres noble dame, vous plaise a savoir qu'y n'est riens plus impocible que mon cuer estre separé de vostre amour."[25]
>
> ("Oh," said Tristan, "my most honoured lady and mistress, I thank you for your gracious reply, by which I may have great expectation of your compassionate grace. Most noble lady, may it please you to know that nothing is more impossible than that my heart be separated from your love.")

Latinate polysyllabic vocabulary and complex syntax work to distinguish the text not only from the formal and stylistic plainness of early prose romances but also from its verse model, the early-thirteenth-century *Chatelaine de Vergy*, notorious for the moral ambiguities that it constructs around its lovers. Other styles were available: for example, *Baudouin de Flandre*, a midcentury prose romance version of a verse *chanson de geste* – for prosification overwrote the formal distinctions between genres that were obvious in verse – is briskly eventful. In any case, fifteenth-century prose continued to present itself as less ornamental than verse, although now time and profit are the main justifications.[26] Thus, Jehan Wauquelin in 1448 determines to "retrenchier et sincoper les prolongacions et motz inutiles qui souvent sont mis et boutez en telles rimes" (remove and cut the tardy augmentations and useless words which are often put and stuffed into such *rimes*).[27] Although often untrue, this rhetorical boast of relative brevity outlines a different set of social aspirations and obligations for its audience than those implied by the earlier claim to greater transparency and truthfulness.

Conclusion

The triumph of prose would be made complete by printing: the "myth of prose" joined forces with the Gutenberg revolution to produce the domination that we know today: in the novel, the short story, and even the prose poem. We should beware of oversimplifying: verse romance writing never died out and some old verse favorites made it into print. Elite circles (notably, the ducal court of Burgundy) continued to patronize manuscripts, and amidst the glut of prosifications of earlier verse romances we still find the odd instance of octosyllabic couplets, as in Pierre's Sala's modernization of *Yvain* (1520). Printing ensured, however, that the large-scale future of reading materials belonged to prose, and it clearly created a climate favorable to the preservation of earlier prose romances. Thus, the German *Prosa-Lancelot*, the Picard French *Perceforest*, and the Castilian *Amadís de Gaula* survive whole in fifteenth- and sixteenth-century copies, but only in fragments before then. The fact that Malory's *Morte Darthur* survives intact in manuscript (London, BL, Add. MS 59678, c. 1480), whereas, for instance, fourteenth-century manuscripts of the Dutch prose *Lancelot* were torn up to be used as binding waste, is a coincidence of historical circumstance. Malory was lucky enough to try his prose experiment at a time when printing made it the medium of choice. Were it not for Malory's timing and Caxton's decision to use the Winchester manuscript as the copy-text for his printed edition, Malory's experiment in prose might have been doomed to the same fate as the Dutch prose *Lancelot*.

Notes

1. *Erec et Enide*, ed. Roques, ll. 19–26.
2. Phillippe de Rémi, *Le Roman de la Manekine*, ed. and trans. Sargent-Baur, ll. 30–3. The translation is our own.
3. *Le Roman de la Manekine*, p. 99.
4. Gottfried von Strassburg, *Tristan*, ed. Utzmann and Hoffman, ll. 10616–22.
5. Cited from the edition by Friedman and Harrington.
6. See Ad Putter, "Metre and Versification," in Ian Johnson (ed.), *Geoffrey Chaucer in Context* (Cambridge: Cambridge University Press, 2019), pp. 72–82.
7. See Rhiannon Purdie, *Anglicising Romance: Tail-Rhyme and Genre in Medieval English Literature* (Cambridge: D. S. Brewer, 2008).
8. *Sir Thopas* is cited from *The Riverside Chaucer*, ed. Benson, pp. 213–17.
9. *Sir Bevis of Hampton*, ed. Fellows.
10. See Ad Putter, "The Metres and Stanza Forms of Popular Romance," in Raluca L. Radulescu and Cory James Rushton (eds.), *A Companion to Medieval Popular Romance* (Cambridge: D. S. Brewer, 2009), pp. 111–31.
11. *The Works of the Gawain Poet*, ed. Putter and Stokes.
12. On the verse form of *Sir Gawain*, see Howell Chickering, "Stanzaic Closure and Linkage in *Sir Gawain and the Green Knight*," *Chaucer Review*, 32 (1997), 1–31, and Ad Putter, "The Predictable and the Unpredictable: Sir Gawain and the Green Knight and the Metres of Middle English Romance," in Liliana Sikorska and Marcin Krygier (eds.), *Evur happie & glorious, ffor I hafe at will grete riches* (Frankfurt: Peter Lang, 2013), pp. 71–88.
13. Edited in the *Riverside Chaucer*, ed. Benson, pp. 473–585.

14. Jean Renart, *Le Roman de la Rose ou de Guillaume de Dole*, ed. and trans. Dufournet and Lecoy.
15. Lars Boje Mortensen analyses the significance of the "prose turn" (25) in different literatures: "The Sudden Success of Prose: A Comparative View of Greek Latin, Old French and Old Norse," *Medieval Worlds*, 5 (2017), 3–45.
16. Quotations, respectively, from Brian Woledge and H. P. Clive, *Répertoire des plus anciens textes en prose française: depuis 842 jusqu'aux premières années du XIII*[e] *siècle* (Geneva: Droz, 1964), p. 27, and Robert W. Hanning, "Arthurian Evangelists: The Language of Truth in Thirteenth-Century French Prose Romances," *Philological Quarterly*, 64 (1985), 347–65 (p. 352).
17. *Le Haut Livre du Graal (Perlesvaus)*, ed. Strubel, pp. 390–2. The punctuation is Strubel's.
18. For in-depth literary analysis of early prose style and its effects, see Wlad Godzich and Jeffrey Kittay, *The Emergence of Prose: An Essay in Prosaics* (Minneapolis: University of Minnesota Press, 1987).
19. Dante, *De vulgari eloquentia*, ed. and trans. Botterill.
20. For a recent reassessment with wide relevance for prose romance, see Alison Cornish, *Vernacular Translation in Dante's Italy: Illiterate Literature* (Cambridge: Cambridge University Press, 2013).
21. On verse's response to prose, see Adrian Armstrong and Sarah Kay, *Knowing Poetry: Verse in Medieval France from the "Rose" to the Rhétoriqueurs* (Ithaca: Cornell University Press, 2011). Ardis Butterfield shows how Chaucer's writings fit into this verse tradition: "Chaucer's French Inheritance," in Piero Boitani and Jill Mann (eds.), *The Cambridge Companion to Chaucer* (Cambridge: Cambridge University Press, 2004), pp. 20–35.
22. Mortensen, "Sudden Success," p. 35.
23. Orlanda S. H. Lie, *The Middle Dutch Prose Lancelot* (Amsterdam: Noord-Hollandsche Uitgeversmaatschappij, 1987).
24. Rosalind Brown-Grant, *French Romance of the Later Middle Ages: Gender, Morality, and Desire* (Oxford: Oxford University Press, 2008).
25. *L'Istoire de la Chastelaine du Vergier et de Tristan le chevalier*, ed. Stuip, p. 86.
26. Richard Trachsler, "From Verse to Prose, a Matter of Size? Length and Lacunae in French mises en prose," in Leah Tether and Keith Busby (eds.), *Rewriting Medieval French Literature: Studies in Honour of Jane H. M. Taylor* (Boston: De Gruyter, 2021), pp. 181–92.
27. Jehan Wauquelin, *La belle Hélène de Constantinople (1448)*, ed. de Crécy, p. 14.

Further Reading

Besamusca, Bart, "The Prevalence of Verse in Medieval Dutch and English Arthurian Fiction," *JEGP: Journal of English and Germanic Philology*, 112 (2013), 461–74.

Godzich, Wlad, and Jeffrey Kittay, *The Emergence of Prose: An Essay in Prosaics* (Minneapolis: University of Minnesota Press, 1987).

Lote, Georges, *Histoire du vers français*, 9 vols, part I, Le Moyen Âge: vol. 1 (Paris: Boivin, 1949), vol. 2 (Paris: Boivin, 1951), and vol. 3 (Paris: Hatier, 1955).

Mortensen, Lars Boje, "The Sudden Success of Prose: A Comparative View of Greek Latin, Old French and Old Norse," *Medieval Worlds*, 5 (2017), 3–45.

Purdie, Rhiannon, *Anglicising Romance: Tail-Rhyme and Genre in Medieval English Literature* (Cambridge: D. S. Brewer, 2008).

Putter, Ad, "The Metres and Stanza Forms of Popular Romance," in Raluca L. Radulescu and Cory James Rushton (eds.), *A Companion to Medieval Popular Romance* (Cambridge: D. S. Brewer, 2009), pp. 111–31.

Taylor, Jane H. M., *Rewriting Arthurian Romance in Renaissance France: From Manuscript to Printed Book* (Cambridge: D. S. Brewer, 2014).

4

SYLVIE LEFÈVRE

Authors, Narrators, and Their Stories in Old French Romance

Is the "narrator" an invention of modern theory? The word itself is recent; rather than the verb "narrer" (to narrate), Old and Middle French employ "conter" (to tell) or "dire" (to say, to speak). Moreover, we'll see the importance of the voice of the tale (*le conte*) itself in prose romances. However, the "narrator" is not simply a way to designate the author when he doesn't identify himself; there are indeed, from the Middle Ages onwards, voices of narrators detached from the personality of their authors; at the end of the medieval period, they can be designated by a term that's ambiguous for us today: the "actor" (*acteur*), the person or agent responsible for the progression of a text.

Medieval textuality remains notably different from that of later centuries: its existence in manuscripts means that the text is necessarily in motion; certain copyists take on the function of editor or *remanieur* (re-caster/adapter); the living voice remains present in the written language. French vernacular literature from the eleventh to the fifteenth centuries includes an enormous number of different kinds of texts, in many different forms. We must first consider how romance differs from other genres before we examine the differences between romances in verse and romances in prose; the complex relationships among authors, narrators, and characters; and, finally, the relationships between the space in the text and beyond the text to discern what could be early romance fiction.

Textual Voices and Authors' Names

At its inception, the epic or *chanson de geste*, devoid of prologue or author identification "n'a pas besoin de revendiquer son authenticité; il est, et cela suffit" (has no need to affirm its authenticity; it exists, and that alone is enough).[1]

The *Chanson de Roland* blends the voice of the author/narrator with that of the community to which it speaks: "Carles li reis, nostre emperere magnes" (Charles the king, our great emperor) (v. 1). The plural possessive adjective "nostre" (our) marks in a direct utterance an immediate ideological communality. Romance, on the other hand, comes into being as the result of a process: *mettre en roman* is "to set a text (typically from Latin) into the vernacular." From the start, romance needs to affirm not only its linguistic autonomy, but also its authority: that of a clerk able to "translater" (to translate, or to carry from one language to another) and to tell the story in writing better than simple storytellers and jongleurs do orally.

The narrative domain is not the only one shared between signed texts and anonymous ones. Lyric poetry has also left us hundreds of named troubadours (from the South) and trouvères (from the North), as well as numerous works for which there is no attribution. All the texts from the earliest centuries of the Middle Ages depend on the same enunciative context in a culture where communication with the public passes essentially through the voice of an interpreter. This explains why the *grand chant courtois*, a poem voiced by "je" (I), as well as a story where the narrator intervenes in the first person, would be preferably "signed" in the third person.[2] Chrétien de Troyes or Blondel de Nesle therefore remain identifiable – one as the author of a romance, the other as the author of a song – when in performance the story told aloud leads the role of the narrator as *je* ("I") to that of a speaker, and when sung with a melody, which manuscripts often conserve, the song makes the voice of the lover sound through and by the voice of the interpreter/singer.

In any case, three new developments profoundly transform the landscape of narrative in the thirteenth century: the advent of prose narrative; the *dit;* and the first-person romance.[3]

Verse and Prose: Fictive Authors and Real Authors

The prose romance (*Joseph-Merlin-Perceval* or the *Petit Saint-Graal*) appears at the same time as universalizing prose historiography (*Histoire ancienne jusqu'à César*) and it makes a claim for its story (*estoire*) in History (*Histoire*). With very different stylistic means than the *chanson de geste*, the new Arthurian romance, now focused on the Grail, makes truth-claims for history which had been reserved for epic poetry up to that point.

The thirteenth century also marks an important stage in the production of vernacular books, which are now created in a professional system within an urban setting. The *chanson de geste* will counterbalance the weight of writing in its phases of composition, reception, and diffusion by inscribing more imposing markers of orality and by the stronger presence of its narrator/*jongleur*. Romance texts, on the other hand, will reinforce their affinity with books as both source and as final product: romance takes off from one written book to create another book. The prose romance even presents as a physical space that is visual, shared with a public that is meant to *see* it and to read the writing: "Mais ci endroit ne parole plus li contes de Monseigneur Gauvain ne del roi, ainz retorne au chevalier dont li non est aportez a cort."[4] (But here [in this space] the tale speaks no longer about my lord Gauvain nor the king, but rather returns to the knight whose name is carried before the court.)

This kind of formula, which also signals the *entrelacement* (interlacing) of adventures typical of prose romances, has led to the observation that "le sujet d'énonciation de ce livre n'est pas une personne quelconque, c'est le récit lui-même, c'est le conte" (the enunciating subject of this text is not some kind of person, but is the narrative itself, it's the *conte* [*tale*]).[5] There remains right beside it, nonetheless, as in verse romance narratives, the "je" narrator. Marking its difference with the *Lancelot* cycle, *Tristan en prose* frequently employs "je." Indeed this romance opens with the following declaration by its purported author:[6]

> Je, Luces, chevaliers et sires del Chastel del Gat, voisin prochien de Salesbieres, cum chevaliers amoreus et envoisiez, enpreing a translater une partie de ceste estoire: non mie por ce que je saiche granment françois, enz apartient plus ma langue et ma parole a la maniere d'Angleterre que a cele de France, cum cil qui fui en Engleterre nez.
>
> (I, Luce, knight and lord of the Castle of Gat, very close to Salisbury, in my quality of amorous knight, full of joy, undertake to translate part of this story, not that I am expert in French, for my language comes more from the manner of speaking in England than in France, since I am a native of England.)

This legalistic formulation authorizes a name to enumerate titles possessed with the aim of producing a certain act: here, a linguistic act (translating from Latin to French), despite two apparent paradoxes. Luce is not a clerk, but a knight; he does not speak continental French, but the French of insular England. In fact, it is of course a question of particulars: Arthurian history has an essentially British geography with Salisbury as one of the reference points; besides being a knight, Luce announces himself as "amoreus et envoisiez" (in love and joyful), incarnating the essential quality of all medieval romances to be about "arms and love." The *Lancelot-Grail* cycle also creates an author figure: Walter (Gautier) Map. Known for having written in Latin under Henry II of England, Map became the pseudo-author of the *Lancelot*, dated a century later. At the same time that it extended Arthurian history over a long duration, prose writing invented its own genealogy of authors.

Verse romances also provide us with numerous names of authors. The development of encrypted signatures, beginning in the thirteenth century, attests in another way than in the prose romance to the gains made by the book and written composition: Jean Renart and Jakemés both hide behind anagrams or acrostics.[7]

Going forward, the split between verse and prose, particularly in Grail romances, will offer two different modes of writing and two different discursive systems. An author like Wauchier de Denain writes in verse the *Deuxième Continuation du Graal* of Chrétien de Troyes; he also writes in prose l'*Histoire ancienne jusqu'à César*, with no signature; and he signs translations of the *Vie des pères* and of the *Dialogues* of Gregory the Great. Thus, at the very beginning of the thirteenth century, so that his own voice can be discerned in the midst of his prose texts, Wauchier passes from prose to rhyme. When the subject says "je," whether "signed" by a name or not, the voice prefers verse.

Beyond the Arthurian tradition, the verse romance pursues its career into the fourteenth century, and certain verse romances are copied as late as the end of the fifteenth century. Readers at the end of the Middle Ages can therefore read romances from centuries earlier. In Jean Froissart's *Espinette amoureuse* (c. 1369), the narrator/hero falls in love with a young woman he comes upon as she reads Adenet le Roi's *Cleomadés* (v. 1280). From Adenet to Froissart, we move from a verse romance to another form of narrative in verse, but which takes on a subjectivity borrowed from lyric poetry: the *dit*. *Cleomadés*, like *L'Espinette*, inserts lyric poetry as did Jean Renart for the first time in *Le Roman de la rose ou de Guillaume de Dole*. The romance, with its heterodiegetic narrator (= a narrator speaking from outside the story), does it in the manner of a collage (the lyrics are performed and interpreted by the characters); the *dit*, with a homodiegetic narrator (=the narrator is himself a character in the story) does it in the manner of a montage (the inserted poems are created by the narrator as lover and poet). With the notable exception of the *Lancelot-Graal*, prose romances since the *Tristan* also transform some of their characters into poets and include lyric poems, indeed even epistles in verse or in prose. Such is the case in *Guiron le Courtois*, *Perceforest,* and *Ysaie le Triste*. In addition to the reported speech, these insertions reinforce the subjective voice of the characters over that of the external, distanciated narrator, in a narrative that continues to privilege the voice of the *conte*.

Froissart wrote *Meliador*, the last great Arthurian verse romance, in the late fourteenth century. The author places in the mouth of his characters the poetic production of one of his patrons, the Duke of Brabant. In order to include the work of someone other than himself, Froissart reworks the first version of the work with a heterodiegetic narrator, and the two authors' names are revealed elsewhere: in the *Dit du florin* and in the third volume of Froissart's *Chroniques*.[8] Even as he assumes the formal constraints that began with Jean Renart, Froissart writes in a new manner: rather than an "authentic" Breton romance, he creates a "collection of 'dits'," a romance of "sentimental situations."[9]

During the fifteenth century, there were even more diverse narrative experiments penned by princes: Thomas III of Saluces and René of Anjou. The *Livre du Chevalier Errant* (*Book of the Wandering Knight*) (1394–96) from Thomas and the *Livre du Coeur d'amour épris* (*Book of the Lovesmitten Heart*) from René can both be described as "des romans du moi issus du croisement du roman allégorique et du roman breton" (romances of the self produced at the crossroads of allegorical romance and Breton romance).[10] Both authors mix verse and prose: René makes the characters speak in verse, while the prose voice tells the story, but Thomas passes from verse to prose in a very free and seemingly unjustified manner, except at the first transition, "Car il m'ennuye de tant versifier" (because it pains me to write so many verses).[11] His tale plays with verse narrated in the first person, mixing the voice of the hero – the wandering Knight – with that of the narrator, free arbiter of formal choices, but also with an impersonal narration in prose according to the other great romance tradition. Besides this, the work also compiles an entire library that goes from extracts of Benoît de Saint-Maure's *Roman de Troie* and Aimon de Varennes's *Florimont* to the prose *Lancelot* and the *Tristan en prose*, along with the *Histoire ancienne jusqu'à César*, thus blurring the boundaries between fiction and historiography. At the end of this quest, the narrator reveals his genealogy and his name, transforming himself into an author (v. 10310 and 10319–20): "I, Thomas, third of that name .... I assuredly made and brought together this book, but Desire and Tribulation were its guarantors."

Desire, the companion of the knight Heart, is one of the main characters in the romance of René d'Anjou. More clearly than Thomas, René brings to life only the allegorical characters inherited from the other *Roman de la Rose*, that of Guillaume de Lorris, in a universe of chivalric quest. In René, we also find again the expected formula, "Or dit ly contes" (Now the tale says) but very quickly that tag is replaced by strange paired rubrics, such as[12] "Icy parle l'acteur et dit ainsi / Cy endroit dit ly contes" (Here the narrator speaks and says / In this place the story says).

This *acteur*, in fact, has taken the place of the historic author who has dedicated his work to John of Bourbon in a verse Prologue: "je, René"

(I, René) is going to tell John of Bourbon about a vision where Love has come to remove his heart from his chest in order to create an amorous knight launched in the pursuit of his lady, Lady Mercy. The author, who has retreated after this behind the authority of the *conte*, thus reappears transformed as a narrating force through this collaboration of the *acteur* and the tale.

In René's work, the use of these rubrics is an authorial choice. His contemporary and former servant, Antoine de La Sale, also has recourse to rubrics in his *Jean de Saintré*. In any case, before being adopted by authors, such announcements were a way for copyists and readers to distinguish the *acteur*/narrator from his characters, or even, as in the *Roman de la Rose*, the first thirteenth-century first-person romance, to distinguish *l'amant* from *l'acteur* (author). The written disposition of the text clearly reveals in the manuscript a literary expertise that scholarly circles displayed by other means, like glosses or commentary.

Author, Narrator, and Character

These subtle distinctions allow literature to exist as fiction: they open up, in particular, textual effects such as distancing and irony. In René's work, the character Desire leads an inexperienced Heart, but he does so in a way that is often impulsive, even though he has already completed this same voyage with other hearts. The allegory serves a general discourse under the cover of a singular, if not autobiographical, experience. From another perspective, the distance between the narrator and Heart can be completely erased, as when a couple of sirens interpret a song: the *acteur* claims that he cannot repeat their lyrics because Heart does not understand their language.

In Guillaume de Lorris's *Roman de la Rose*, the play of the gap between narrator and lover arises first from the five years that separate the dream from the time it is recounted. In the meantime, the author has been living his life and the narrator has gotten ahead of the Lover. The Lover can then be abandoned before the promised last stage in the amorous trajectory – the taking of Jealousy's chateau and the plucking of the rose. It remains to the public to accomplish what could not be achieved in the narrative, even as it has been promised or anticipated by the narrator.

In verse or prose romance, heterodiegetic narrators are often omniscient.[13] However, the narrator is likely to confess to his ignorance about the details. More significantly, the narrator can convey silence or reticence in speaking about a character. In *Jean de Saintré* (1456), Antoine de La Sale shows how the very young hero is called upon by a group of ladies of the court to announce that he has selected a woman to love, as he had promised to do:[14] "Lors elles lui dirent: 'N'est il pas vray, mon filz?' Le povre, tout esbahy et ainsy gehiné d'elles, force lui fut de dire oÿl." (Then the ladies replied to him: "Isn't that true, my son?" The poor boy, losing all composure before these ladies who were torturing him so, was obliged to say yes.)

Because the answer is provided by the narrator, we can imagine all the better the boy as terrorized and almost speechless. Marco Praloran has astutely analyzed such regulation of narrative information between the narrator and the characters in a chapter devoted to the prose *Lancelot* and the *Tristan en prose*.[15] So it is in the long scenes where Lancelot, who has become Galehaut's companion, continues to refuse to tell him who he is or to surrender himself to Arthur and the queen. Galehaut in the end persuades Lancelot to accompany him after these last words:[16]

> "Si m'aïst Dex, de ma dame ne voi ge mies commant vos an puissiez anpirier."
> "Certes, fait li chevaliers, assez i avra anui et joie."
> Lors s'aperçut auques Galehoz de son covine, si lo tien si cort que il li otroie ce qu'il li demande.

> ("God help me, I don't see what harm could befall you from going to see my lady." "Indeed," replied the knight, "I would have much sorrow and much joy." So Galehaut suspected something about the Lancelot's feelings. He pressed him so much that Lancelot agreed to what he had asked.)

Galehaut's tact here is equal to that of the narrator; even as it remains implicit, Lancelot's love for the queen becomes perceptible. The fluid convergence of narrative voices helps the reader to understand.

The relationships between the narrative voices ("narrative instance," in Genette's vocabulary) and the reader deploy more visible methods and, so to speak, more personal means in the verse romance. Thus, in the *Chevalier au lion*, the final combat between Yvain and Gawain is constructed on a well-known narrative motif: they do not recognize each other:[17]

> Coument? Velt dont Yvains occirre
> Monseigneur Gavain son ami?
> Oïl, et il lui autresi.
> Si voldroit mesire Gavains
> Yvain occirrë a ses mains,
> Ou faire pis que je ne di?
> Nenil, jel vous jur et affi.

> (How is this? Does Yvain want to kill Monseigneur Gauvain, his friend? Yes, and his opponent wants to do the same (to him). So Monseigneur Gauvain intends to kill Yvain with his own hands, or do worse than I say? Not at all, I swear to you and promise it.)

The paradox of this mortal confrontation between the two friends is enhanced in the rhetoric of the narrator who, by asking questions and providing answers, resembles Chrétien's amorous characters who debate contradictory feelings in their interior monologues[18]. Nonetheless, by introducing the *narrataire* and a public with the pronoun *vous* (you), the narrator seems to give them a voice through which to formulate the questions he answers with authority. The monologue becomes a dialogue between the narrator and the reader.

The *Chevalier au lion* also offers a perfect example of embedded narratives ("narrations enchâssées"). Beginning without a real Prologue, the text leaves no place for the figure of the author: better yet, the narrator quickly delegates the mission of "reconter / Chose qui faiche a escouter" (tell something that's worth listening to) to one of Arthur's knights. It is Calogrenant who, after intoning a Prologue (ll. 105–74), narrates his misadventure at the fountain in the forest of Brocéliande (ll. 175–578). This tale of failure elicits Yvain's reaction and incites his desire to venture forth in turn to attempt to avenge his cousin. The adventure that Calogrenant recounts in the first person provokes its repetition in the third person. This will also become an obligatory stepping-stone in other romances up to René d'Anjou, attesting to the lasting influence of Chrétien de Troyes, but also to the inventiveness of future authors in their retellings.

In his *Tournoiement Antéchrist*, Huon de Méry situates the literary fountain in its own geographic environment. Claiming to have followed the royal troops against the rebel barons, among them the Duke of Brittany, Pierre Mauclerc (1234–5), Huon transforms his historical testimony into a chivalric quest narrated, like Calogrenant's story, entirely in the first person:[19]

Le bacin, le perron de marbre
Trovai en itele maniere
Et le vert pin et la chaiere
Comme l'a descrit Crestïens.

(The basin, the marble slab, but also the green pine and the seat, I found them exactly as in Chrétien's description.)

Nonetheless, the episode of the fountain doesn't open the story, as it does in *Yvain*, to Laudine's kingdom, reminiscent of the Fairy world; it allows for an even more radical scene change, and it transitions to allegorical writing, with the confrontation between the army of the Antichrist and divine troops aided by Arthurian knights. The narrator who was at first a simple spectator of the combats becomes a victim.

At the same time period, the *Roman de la Rose* appears, also written in the first person but entirely allegorical. This text prefers not to name either the lover or the beloved lady. Of the latter, the reader knows only that she is worthy "d'estre rose clamee" ([worthy] of being called a rose) (v.44). Jean de Meun says nothing more but, on the other hand, he invents the name of the person whose work he continues: Guillaume de Lorris. The reader learns after a very significant delay (lines 10493–678), with respect to the end of the first text (at line 4058), that the narrator one thought was unique refers to two distinct identities. Up until that point, in fact, "il n'y a guère d'éléments troublants qui pourraient renvoyer à cette situation inédite d'expérience autobiographique 'partagée'" (there are hardly any disruptive elements that would refer us to the novel situation of a "shared" autobiographical experience). But then there appears a "divergence croissante des instances multiples que recouvre la première personne" (a growing divergence between the multiple voices to which the first person could correspond).[20] As an interloper, the author Jean de Meun distinguishes himself from the lover and the dreamer. The *Chevalier de la Charrete* proposes a similar situation – one narrator for two authors' names (Chrétien de Troyes and Godefroi de Lagny) – but very differently: these names don't intrude in the middle of the romance but appear in a more traditional position in the thresholds (Prologue, vv. 24–7; Epilogue, 7102–10), and the narrator is extradiegetic throughout the narrative.

Metaleptic Constructions: Closed or Porous Domains?

There is another essential difference in the two "doubled" works that we have just examined together: in one, the continuator Godefoi de Lagny remains unknown beyond this one appearance in the text; in the other, it's just the opposite. Jean de Meun, indeed, claims in the dedication to his translation of Boethius a list of works, among them the *Roman de la Rose*, which confers on him the full status of an author, a vernacular clerk. Chrétien, in his lifetime, also provided a catalog of his works at the beginning of his second romance (*Cligés*, ll. 1–8). Pride in his accomplishments confers an existence, if not a complete biography, on the signer of these lists.

The mention of two authors at the heart of the *Roman de la Rose* can in any case be analyzed in terms of narrative metalepsis, conferring an extra-diegetic reality to Guillaume de Lorris as well as to Jean de Meun.[21] In the heart of the reported dream, the God of Love speaks before his troops. He complains about the situation, because a number of his servants, lovers, and authors of works about love cannot bring him their aid: Tibullus, Catullus, and Ovid are dead; Bel Accueil is in prison; and Guillaume de Lorris is about to perish. And yet the latter will still serve Love by beginning the romance and writing it up to verse 4056: "Puis vendra Jehans Chopinel / Au cuer jolif, au cors isnel / Que naistra seur Laire a Meun" (ll. 10569–71) (And then will come Jean Chopinel / with a gay heart and a lively body / who will be born at Meung-sur-Loire). The speech of the prophet Love plays with anticipation to project into the world beyond the dream the disappearance of Guillaume and the birth, childhood, and youth of Jean. The different temporalities, like the different levels of narrative, find themselves thus short-circuited. The pact of the Prologue, which identifies the *je* of the narrator with that of the dreamer-lover, seems to be shattered once an unknown outsider slides not only into the discourse of the god of Love and thus into the dream, but also into the voice of the speaker and therefore into the telling of the dream.

However, in his Prologue the first author of the *Roman de la Rose* has undoubtedly set the foundations of the game within the extradiegetic framework, within the *hors-texte.* He asserts that he writes to obey Love, but also for his beloved, whom he hopes will receive his work favorably. Moreover, after the kiss and before the imprisonment of the rose, the narrator announces what is to transpire right up to taking of the castle of Jealousy, insisting on the reward he hopes to earn from the lady for his willingness to continue (telling the story) right up to the very end of his tale (vv. 3503–8). If the *Roman de la Rose* does not make its narrative direction or its conclusion directly dependent on the will of the *destinataire* (the beloved lady), called forth at the beginning and in the middle of the tale, other romances have actually set up such arrangements. The first is *Partonopeu de Blois*, from the twelfth century. The narrator begins with a long prologue wherein he presents himself as a lover. Later in the story, when the hero, Partonopeu, discovers the joys of love with Melior, the narrator compares their respective situations. After the protagonists' marriage, the romance could come to a definitive conclusion. But in the version that most frequently occurs in the manuscripts, a sort of false epilogue introduces a continuation (vv. 10607–12; 10618–24):[22]

> I leave Partonopeu to enjoy his happiness, not because I don't know more [about his story] but because of the lady I love. She makes me so distressed that I can't do anything more than cry and entreat her mercy, with warm tears. . . . All this, I do in vain; nonetheless, she inspires such fear in me, that I obey her and place myself humbly in her service, so that the smallest wink on her part will make me continue my story, I will be at her service.

And, indeed, at line 10657, the narrator, claiming to have received a favorable signal from his lady, returns to his story.

In *Le Bel Inconnu* by Renaut de Beaujeu (thirteenth century), once again the narrator inserts himself into his story: if the one he loves is not satisfied with an ending in which the hero marries the princess and if she prefers to see Guinglain reunited with the fairy lady, his true love, then she should "un biau semblant mostrer" (show him a favorable welcome) (v. 6255). If not, the narrator will avenge himself on the character by leaving him in his current unpleasant situation.

Should we see in these examples of narrative metalepsis effects comparable to those offered by the texts of *modernité* discussed by G. Genette? That is, a testing of the limits of illusion and reality, at the risk of sometimes disturbing the reader, who is placed before "L'hypothèse inacceptable et insistante, que ... le narrateur et ses narrataires, c'est-a-dire vous et moi, appartenons peut-être encore à quelque récit" (the powerful and inacceptable hypothesis that the narrators and narratees, that is, you and I, still perhaps belong to some story).[23] It seems, rather, that the medieval concept of fiction is radically different from that of the periods that followed. It is not until the mid-sixteenth century that the image of an "écrivain-démiurge" (writer-demigod) creates a novelistic discourse that constructs its own world, ready only much later to annex the real world, which includes the reader.[24] Medieval textuality belongs to another cultural and anthropological order; the reading contract (*pacte de lecture*) of these tales that we call fictional deploys metalepsis to reveal a natural porousness between the world of narration and the world beyond it.[25]

The examples that we have seen bear witness to that fluidity: the text engages its *destinataires* (implied readers), offering them a hermeneutic pathway to enter the text and act there, without creating a trap that an autonomous fiction might lay for its readers. Certain works from the late Middle Ages move, however, toward a reversal of this perspective. Thus, in a work of Antoine de la Sale, at the point of confrontation between the hero Jehan de Saintré and his companion Boucicaut against two Italian knights, the narration produces an *inssident* (an incident).[26] Rather than creating a digression, the text stages a moment of anticipation which claims to propel us beyond the temporality of the tale: since it is supposed to unfold during the reign of Jean le Bon (dead in 1364), the *inssident* tells us about a duel of 1395 and the murder in 1405 of the lord of Padua (that is, Francesco Novello da Carrara). Indeed, this last event marks the point of fracture between romance as historical fiction and real History, between inside and outside. The tale, which up until now has been a story of ideal optimism, lets a gust of tragic reality rush in. *Jean de Saintré* thus perhaps deserves the designation that some have given it of the first modern novel.

Notes

* This chapter was translated from the original French by Roberta L. Krueger.

1. D. Boutet, *La chanson de geste: Forme et signification d'une écriture épique au moyen âge* (Paris: Presses Universitaires de France, 1993), p. 253.
2. Sophie Marnette, *Narrateurs et points de vue dans la littérature française médiévale: une approche linguistique* (Bern: Peter Lang, 1998), pp. 36–8.

3. Michel Zink, *La subjectivité littéraire, autour du siècle de Saint Louis* (Paris: Presses Universitaires de France, 1985), passim.
4. *Lancelot en prose*, ed. Elspeth Kennedy, 1980, cited by Sophie Marnette, p. 98.
5. Tzvetan Todorov, *Poétique de la prose* (Paris: Seuil, 1971), pp. 129–50.
6. *Tristan en prose*, ed. Renee Curtis, vol. 1, p. 39.
7. Jean Renart, *Le Roman de la Rose ou de Guillaume de Dole*, éd. Félix Lecoy, Paris, Champion, 1979 (vv. 5653–5). Jakemés, *Le Roman du Châtelain de Coucy et de la Dame de Fayel*, ed. and trans. Catherine Gaullier-Bougassas, Paris, Champion, 2009 (vv. 8252–8).
8. Jean Froissart, *Dits et débats*, éd. Anthime Fourrier, Genève, Droz, 1979 (*Dit dou florin*, vv. 293–306). Froissart, *Chroniques*, éd. Siméon Luce, Gaston Raynaud et Léon Mirot, Paris, Société de l'Histoire de France, 1869–1975, vol. 12, p. 75.
9. Michel Zink, *Froissart et le temps* (Paris: Presses universitaires de France, 1998), pp. 123, 126.
10. Michel Zink, *Le roman*, in *Grundriss der romanischen Literaturen des Mittelalters*, vol. VIII/1, (1998), pp. 197–208, p. 206.
11. Thomas III de Saluces, *Le Livre du Chevalier Errant*, ed. Robert Fajen, vv. 4928–31.
12. René I d'Anjou, *Le livre du coeur d'Amour épris*, ed. and trans. Florence Bouchet, p. 98, p. 116.
13. See Marnette, *Narrateurs et points de vue; Erec et Enide*, p. 94; p. 109, an example from the *Lancelot en prose.*
14. Antoine de la Sale, *Jehan de Saintré*, ed. Joël Blanchard, trans. Michel Quereuil, pp. 58–9.
15. Marco Praloran and Nicola Morato, *L'orchestrazione del racconto: altri scritti cavallereschi* (Florence: Galuzzo, 2019), pp. 37–52.
16. *Lancelot du Lac*, ed. Kennedy, pp. 868–9.
17. Chrétien de Troyes, *Le Chevalier au Lion*, éd. and trad. David Hult, vv. 6066–72; citation by Marnette, *Narrateurs et points de vue*, p. 71.
18. See Chrétien de Troyes, *Cligès*, ed. Charles Méla, vv. 626–868.
19. Huon de Méry, *Li tornoiemenz Antecrit nach den Handschriften zu Paris, London und Oxford*, ed. G. Wimmer (Marburg: Elwert, 1888), vv. 100–3. See *Le Chevalier au Lion*, vv. 378–92, 411–27.
20. Pierre-Yves Badel, "Le Roman de la Rose de Guillaume de Lorris est-il achevé? Bilan et propositions," *Romania* 135 (2017), 285–312.
21. For an explanation of narrative metalepsis, which is the intrusion into the narrative of elements from outside the story, such as commentary by the author within a first-person narrative, see Gérard Genette, *Discours du récit, in Figures III* (Paris: Seuil, 1972), pp. 243–5.
22. *Le roman de Partonopeu de Blois*, ed. and trans. Olivier Collet and Pierre-Marie Joris.
23. Gérard Genette, *Figures III*, "Discours du récit", chap. 5 "Voix," Paris, Seuil (Poétique), 1972, p. 245.
24. Francesco Montorsi, "La métalepse de régie dans le roman du XVIe siècle," *Poétique* 181 (2017), pp. 53–65.
25. Marion Uhlig, "Métalepse et flux narratif au Moyen Âge: le récit à tiroirs, un Eden d'avant la transgression," *Fabula LHT*, dossier no. 20, "Le Moyen Âge pour laboratoire" (January 2018): www.fabula.org/lht/20/uhlig.html.

26. Sylvie Lefèvre, "Jean de Saintré et l'histoire, ou la valeur d'un inssident," in *De la pensée de l'histoire au jeu littéraire*, ed. S. Douchet, M.-P. Halary, S. Lefèvre, P. Moran, and J.-R. Valette (Paris: Champion, 2019), pp. 552–63.

Suggestions for Further Reading

Krueger, Roberta L. "The Author's Voice: Narrators, Audience, and the Problem of Interpretation." In *The Legacy of Chrétien de Troyes*. Ed. Norris J. Lacy and Keith Busby. Amsterdam: Rodopi, 1987, pp. 115–40.

Varvaro, Alberto. "Élaboration des textes et modalités du récit dans la littérature française médiévale." *Romania* 119 (2001), pp. 1–75.

Zink, Michel and Michel Stanesco. *Histoire européenne du roman médiéval. Esquisse et perspectives*. Paris: Presses Universitaires de France, 1992.

5

ELIZABETH ARCHIBALD

Arthurian Transformations

Part of the lasting popularity of the Arthurian legend can be attributed to its flexibility. As it evolved, Arthur did not always have to be active at the center of the stories, like James Bond or Robin Hood; most Arthurian romances focus instead on individual knights at his court, or on groups of knights, and over the centuries different ones come to the fore. Some are already present in the earliest surviving stories about Arthur in Welsh poems and pre-Conquest "histories" of Britain, notably Gawain, Kay, and Bedivere; but many more are added later. Some are only given one adventure, though it may be recounted in several languages; others may appear only in works in a single language, such as the Dutch knight Moriaen. The protagonist of a frequently retold quest may be altered: early on, Perceval is the Grail hero, but later he is replaced by Galahad. Relationships may alter too: Mordred is Arthur's nephew in the chronicle tradition, but in some romances he is also the king's illegitimate son by incest. From the beginning, Arthur's court is presented as a magnet for warriors from other lands, and characters from other legends can be incorporated into the Arthurian world – for instance Tristan and Merlin, or newcomers such as Lancelot. Arthurian writers in the Middle Ages had many choices to make: verse or prose; chronicle or romance; Arthur as protagonist, or another knight – and if another knight, familiar or new; Lancelot or Gawain as Top Knight; emphasis on war or on love (or both); significant role of magic, or of Christianity; criticism or praise of Camelot; happy or tragic ending. The choices may reflect larger sociopolitical contexts and concerns, both secular and religious.[1]

The range of possibilities is exemplified by the two twelfth-century writers who had an immense influence on the evolution of the legend: Geoffrey of Monmouth and Chrétien de Troyes. Geoffrey's *Historia regum Britanniae* (*History of the Kings of Britain*), written in Latin prose c. 1135, traces the royal line of Britain in great detail from Brutus the Trojan refugee to Cadwallader, the last British king before the Anglo-Saxons.[2] This "history" includes the first birth-to-death account of Arthur, and he is given a starring role as the supreme example of successful British kingship. He is presented as a great warrior and ruler who unites Britain, establishes a glamorous court, and conquers Western Europe; he reaches the gates of Rome before being recalled to Britain by the treachery of his nephew Mordred, who usurps the throne and also takes the queen. Civil war follows, and the fatally wounded Arthur departs to Avalon in search of healing; it is not clear whether he dies, but he is succeeded as king by Constantine, Duke of Cornwall. Britain declines after Arthur's time and is eventually conquered by the Saxons. Geoffrey came from the border of Wales and England and probably drew on a range of sources, written and oral, Latin and Welsh; but he also seems to have invented a good deal of his pseudohistory. Some scholars at the time questioned his book's reliability, but nevertheless it filled a gap, establishing the already well-known folk hero Arthur in an "historical" tradition as an important and successful British king in a country with a Trojan link; all this was flattering to the Norman conquerors to whom Geoffrey dedicated his book. It was very widely read (more than 250 manuscript copies still survive) and was rapidly translated into French and then English; until the sixteenth century it was generally accepted as the standard account of Arthur's birth, reign, and death.

From Chronicle to Romance

Geoffrey's portrayal of Arthur is closely followed in the chronicle tradition, both Latin and vernacular. But in the romance tradition which developed from the later twelfth century, Arthur is not always the protagonist, or particularly heroic.[3] Chrétien de Troyes is generally considered the first writer of Arthurian romance (c. 1160–80); he claims to have used written sources, but no trace of them survives, and he probably drew heavily on oral tradition in Wales and Brittany. His five long and witty poems in French octosyllabic couplets are not concerned with national politics or wars, but describe the fantastic adventures of some knights associated with Arthur during the years of peace, in a landscape full of marvels and magic.[4] Arthur and his court are presented as internationally renowned, but the king himself is a surprisingly passive figure, unable to rescue his abducted queen or avenge insults; he rarely goes on quests or fights himself. Usually the protagonist rides out from Arthur's court and proves himself in a complex series of adventures involving moral and martial challenges, and also amorous encounters; he may return to court at the end to general acclaim, or establish himself elsewhere with his bride. Chrétien's poems are set in a golden age where time seems to stop, and there is little sense of trouble in paradise; no explicit reference is made to the fall of Camelot or the eventual fate of the main characters. But the love affair of Lancelot and Guinevere, the central theme of Chrétien's *Lancelot* or *Le Chevalier de la Charrette* (*The Knight of the Cart*), and the challenges of the Grail Quest, the central theme of his *Perceval* or *Le Conte du Graal* (*The Story of the Grail*), foreground conflicts of loyalties, moral dilemmas, and a clash of spiritual and chivalric values. These themes were developed at great length by later writers: the French Vulgate and Post-Vulgate Cycles, long and elaborate prose romances written in the early thirteenth century and covering the whole history of Arthur and also the Grail, had a huge influence on writers across Western Europe, particularly in relation to the role of Lancelot, the impact of the Grail Quest, and the fall of Camelot.[5] In this chapter I shall look at some significant transformations in three main areas: new characters, changing characterizations, and conflicting values. The focus will be mainly on French and English texts, with some reference to Latin; Arthurian texts in other European languages are discussed elsewhere in this volume.

Arthur's Family

Medieval romance writers felt free to add to the traditional story, and one easy way to do this was to expand the families at the heart of the legend; this not only provided more characters, but also created complex relationships and potential conflicts of loyalties. Arthur's own family is a good example. In Geoffrey he has one half-sister, Anna, who is married to King Lot and has two sons: Gawain is a valiant warrior and features throughout Arthur's reign, but Mordred is only mentioned at the end, when he usurps the throne. Soon more sisters and nephews were added. I shall have more to say about the nephews later; first I want to discuss the sisters. One is Morgan, widely known as Morgan le Fay, who seems to have Celtic antecedents; elsewhere, Geoffrey describes her as one of nine sisters living in Avalon, a sort of white witch with healing powers, and Chrétien specifies that she is Arthur's sister.[6] Her character is greatly expanded in the Vulgate Cycle, where she is presented as a jealous and hostile figure who is constantly trying to damage her brother and his court. Lancelot rejects her advances and so she hates both him and Guinevere and is always looking for ways to attack them, including telling Arthur about their affair. In the Post-Vulgate Cycle composed a little later, she steals Excalibur and its magic scabbard for her lover Accolon, who is to fight a duel with Arthur, hoping to make him king; her plot fails and Accolon dies. It is a common folklore and mythology motif that a god or hero is undermined or betrayed by a family member, and no doubt medieval misogyny contributed to the increasingly negative presentation of Morgan as a sinister and promiscuous enchantress. English readers of *Sir Gawain and the Green Knight* who were familiar with the French romances would not have been surprised to find her revealed at the end as responsible for the plot, which was intended to dishonor Arthur and his court and to scare Guinevere to death. But a more positive side of Morgan, harking back to her white witch role, is shown at the end of the final part of the Vulgate Cycle, the *Mort Artu*, where she is one of the ladies on the ship which takes the fatally wounded king away after the final battle with Mordred (in Geoffrey he goes to Avalon, but there is no mention of a ship or ladies). In the *Mort Artu* scene Morgan says nothing, but in two English romances derived from it (the fourteenth-century verse Stanzaic *Morte Arthur* and Malory's prose *Morte Darthur*) she does speak: "'A, my dere brothir, why have ye taryed so longe from me? Alas, thys wounde on youre hede hath caught overmuch colde!'"[7] Her affectionate concern must have come as rather a shock to readers familiar with the Morgan of the hostile French prose tradition.

Another significant innovation of the French prose writers is that Geoffrey's Anna is renamed Morgause, and has five sons rather than two: Gawain and Mordred, plus Agravain, Gaheris, and Gareth.[8] In medieval accounts it is always Mordred who seizes the throne and precipitates the fall of Camelot. In Geoffrey and the chronicle tradition, and in some romances too, Mordred is Arthur's nephew, but in the Vulgate Cycle *Lancelot* he is told that the king is also his father, though without any further explanation. The story of his conception and birth is elaborated in the Post-Vulgate *Suite du Merlin*.[9] The newly crowned Arthur does not know his own parentage; he sleeps with the beautiful Queen Morgause, who is visiting his court, begetting Mordred. He then has a terrifying dream that he and the kingdom are attacked by a dragon; he manages to kill it but is mortally wounded in the process. Merlin reveals Arthur's true parentage and thus his relationship to Morgause, and explains the dream: the son he has begotten incestuously will destroy him and the kingdom. Incestuous birth does not make Mordred more of a villain, but the illicit liaison with his sister seems a black mark for Arthur, as is his subsequent attempt to get rid of the fatal infant. Merlin tells him that Mordred will be born about May Day, so Arthur has all male babies born then put to sea without a steersman in the hope of destroying his nemesis, in an episode disturbingly reminiscent of Herod and the Massacre of the Innocents (Malory 46.7–23; CI.25). Of course, Mordred survives to fulfill his destiny, like Oedipus; though he fails in his attempt to marry his stepmother, he does kill his father. Another probable influence on this episode was the legend of Judas, who according to medieval tradition was exposed at sea as a baby because of a prophecy that he would destroy his race; found and raised by an Egyptian princess, he comes to Jerusalem, where he unknowingly kills his father and marries his mother before betraying Christ.[10] It is not clear that Mordred knows his terrible destiny, but he betrays Arthur by knowingly trying to marry his stepmother, the queen, and knowingly killing his father in battle. In Geoffrey's account, Arthur and Mordred both fall at the battle of Camlann, but we are not told who killed either of them. In the Vulgate *Mort Artu* and its successors, they are aware of their relationship and quite deliberately kill each other; the simultaneous parricide and filicide increase the tragedy of the ending, as well as the villainy of the son. It seems curious that the medieval writers who decided to include the incest make so little of it; they do not comment on Arthur's culpability as one might have expected, nor does he acknowledge his sin or show any remorse. It is also striking that Malory chose to include the incest; as an English writer, he might be expected to want to make Arthur as admirable as possible. His Merlin is very frank with the king: "'[Y]e have done a thyng late that God ys displesed with you, for ye have lyene by youre syster and on hir ye have gotyn a childe that shall destroy you and all the knyghtes of youre realme . . . hit ys Goddis wylle that youre body sholde be punysshed for your fowle dedis'" (36.14–17, 22–3; CI. 20). Yet neither the sin of incest nor the punishment is mentioned again, by Merlin, Arthur, or anyone else.

In the romances, Mordred's role as the usurping villain is the same whether Arthur is his uncle or his father. The characterization of his brother Gawain, however, varies considerably over the centuries, and in different countries.[11] He seems to be identical with the Gwalchmai associated with Arthur in early Welsh tradition, but it is in Geoffrey's *Historia* that he appears as a key figure at court, a great warrior and an important counselor, and also the king's nephew. The sister's son relationship is a privileged one in myth and legend, probably because there can be no doubt about the kinship of brother and sister (for instance, Roland is Charlemagne's nephew). According to B. J. Whiting, "Gawain plays a larger role in the numerous branches of the Matter of Britain than any actor save Arthur, possibly a larger, and certainly a more varied role than Arthur himself."[12] In Chrétien's poems he often acts as a foil to the hero and is given parallel adventures (for instance, in the unfinished *Conte du Graal* or *Perceval*, where it is not clear that he will succeed in his quest for the mysterious Lance). He has a reputation for chivalric prowess and also as a lady's man; women tend to throw themselves at him, though he has no lasting love, and the young protagonists of Fair Unknown romances who come to Arthur's court to prove themselves and win their spurs very often turn out to be the result of his casual affairs.[13] The presentation of Gawain varies considerably in the French verse romances;

even where he is the main character, the tone can be somewhat irreverent or ironic. Busby comments: "[T]here is great reluctance to blacken his reputation completely. It is true, however, that as time passes authors treat the figure with more freedom and less respect..."[14] The writers of the French prose romances were less admiring; Gawain accidentally beheads a lady on his first quest as a knight and fails completely in the Grail quest, and his vendetta against Lancelot helps to bring about the final catastrophe.[15] In the Prose *Tristan*, composed a little later in the thirteenth century and also very influential, he is presented as a rapist and murderer.[16]

In England, however, Gawain is generally the star of the court and Arthur's right-hand man, famous for his courtesy; he is the protagonist of a number of romances, often stepping in to save Arthur from some embarrassment.[17] These two characterizations are intriguingly blended in the late-fourteenth-century alliterative poem *Sir Gawain and the Green Knight*, where both his reputations are cited, and challenged: the courteous hero of English tradition is combined with the unreliable French lady's man in an unsettling story with an enigmatic ending.[18] He is described early on in the poem as the epitome of chivalry and of *trauthe* (integrity; see the elaborate description of his arming at lines 619–69), and the court mourns when he sets out to defend Arthur's honor on a seemingly fatal quest for a green knight whom he has beheaded, after promising to allow his own head to be cut off in return a year later. When Gawain arrives at the castle of Hautdesert just in time for Christmas and the inhabitants discover his identity, they do not mention his prowess as a warrior, but are delighted that they will learn the art of "luf-talkyng" (l. 927); this comment comes to seem ironic as the lady of the castle flirts expertly with him over three days while her husband is out hunting, and he struggles to resist her. She says that if he were really Gawain, he would certainly kiss her (ll. 1297–1301); as he kneels nervously before the Green Knight to be beheaded, the giant says that if he were really Gawain, he would not flinch from an axe-blow (ll. 2270–3). At the end, when both Gawain and the reader receive revelations about what has really been going on, he blames himself fiercely for failures of chivalry (though he also unchivalrously blames women for deceiving great men through the ages). We cannot be sure whether he remains a paragon, as the Green Knight and the court think, or is indelibly stained by his mistakes and failures, as he himself believes. Much critical ink has been spilled over the question of whether this poem should be read as a critique of Arthurian chivalry or a celebration; both interpretations are plausible. It seems to have been written for an English audience familiar with French Arthurian texts, and intended to challenge, or subvert, the English characterization of Gawain and the standard motifs of Arthurian romance.

Conflicts of Loyalties

Though Malory seems to have known the English romance tradition well, he drew heavily on French prose sources for his *Morte Darthur*, and his Gawain is not the idealized English hero, but rather the impetuous, reckless, and sometimes violent figure of the later French tradition. His relationship with his brothers is key in the final tale, when the Round Table fellowship fragments and civil war becomes inevitable. Malory follows the French Vulgate line here, but with interesting additions which emphasize the conflict of loyalties between the ties of blood and of chivalric fellowship.[19] As in the Vulgate *Mort Artu*, Malory's Mordred and Agravain decide to tell Arthur about the queen's affair with Lancelot and to trap the lovers together. Gawain, with Gareth and Gaheris, tries to resist his brothers' plot and is more outspoken than his French equivalent in the *Mort Artu*, prophesying (correctly) that this "outing" will be disastrous for everyone: "'now is thys realme holy destroyed and myscheved, and the noble felyshyp of the Rounde Table shall be disparbeled [broken up]'" (872.1–3; C XX.1). The quarrel between the brothers mirrors the civil wars to come: Gawain against Lancelot and Arthur against Mordred. When Lancelot manages to fight his way out of the ambush in the queen's chamber, killing Agravain in the process, Gawain does not turn against him. But when Gareth and Gaheris are killed in Lancelot's rescue of Guinevere from burning, Gawain is devastated and his previous support for Lancelot turns to an implacable desire for vengeance. Lancelot is forced into exile in France, and Gawain makes Arthur pursue him there; this allows Mordred, the regent in Arthur's absence, to usurp the throne. In both the French and English versions, the dying Gawain does recognize his own faults. Malory has him repent of '"myn owne hastynes and my wylfulnesse'" and pride, apologize to Arthur, and also write to Lancelot urging him to come to the king's rescue, and to visit Gawain's tomb (918.5–919.18; C XXI.1–2). But overall there is little sense in Malory of the Gawain of the English tradition: the courteous and successful paragon admired by all.

Malory took this episode of complex relationships between brothers from his French sources; he would also have found it in the Middle English Stanzaic *Morte Arthur*, a fourteenth-century poem closely based on the Vulgate *Mort*, but he builds it up further to stress the conflict of loyalties between blood and fellowship. In the *Mort*, Gareth and Gaheris are part of the armed guard resisting Lancelot's attempt to rescue the queen; Gareth is killed by Lancelot, but Gaheris by Lancelot's cousin Bors. The Stanzaic *Morte* does not name their killers, though Gawain holds Lancelot responsible. Malory adds to the tragedy in several ways. Gareth and Gaheris refuse to fight against Lancelot, so are unarmed when he kills them both, having failed to recognize them. What makes this even worse is that Gareth is presented throughout the *Morte Darthur* as a good knight, unlike some of his brothers, and as particularly devoted to Lancelot, who knighted him; earlier in the *Morte* we are told that Gareth avoids his brother Gawain as much as possible, "for he was evir vengeable, and where he hated he wolde be avenged with murther, and that hated Sir Gareth" (285.31–2; C VII.35). This is in the Tale of Sir Gareth, when the young prince comes to court incognito to win his spurs (Gawain does not get a tale of his own in the *Morte*). This tale is an example of the Fair Unknown motif; here, the young unknown turns out to be not Gawain's son, but his youngest brother. There is no known source for Malory's version; whether or not it is his own invention, it seems clear that he adds it to make Gareth's later death at Lancelot's hands more tragic. The bond between fellow knights can be as strong as that between brothers, or stronger. This is one of the most striking examples of conflicts of loyalties at Camelot: the fellowship and camaraderie of the Round Table are set against the love between siblings, with Arthur caught in the crossfire.

The Introduction of Lancelot

In Geoffrey the only important family group is Arthur's, but as the romance tradition develops, other clans take on significant roles too. One of the major transformations of the legend is the introduction of Lancelot, the son of a French king, who was not part of the early Welsh tradition; as he becomes more important he too acquires a brother and cousins who will side with him against other Round Table knights, and he both experiences and causes conflicts of loyalties and of values.[20] The earliest known reference to him is in the first of Chrétien's romances, *Erec et Enide*, where he is listed as the third best knight at Arthur's court. He is the protagonist of a later work by Chrétien, *Lancelot* or *Le chevalier de la Charrette* (*The Knight of the Cart*), where he is presented from the beginning as obsessively devoted to the queen; he falls off his horse when thinking about her, performs heroic feats to rescue her from abduction, and enjoys a night of love with her described in terms of religious ecstasy. He is not named until well into the poem; it is not clear whether early audiences and readers would have known at once who he is, or have been aware of his passion for the queen, but he is certainly presented as one of the greatest knights. Chrétien claims in the prologue that his patroness, the Countess of Champagne, gave him the subject matter; there may have already been stories about Lancelot in circulation orally (this is also suggested by the reference in *Erec*). From the first, his devotion to the queen creates problems; she inspires him to great deeds, but he is also prepared to lose battles deliberately at her command, and of course there can be no happy ending to their love story since she is Arthur's wife. Lancelot's birth-to-death history is given in the Vulgate Cycle, including a detailed account of the beginning of the love affair; this became so well known that Dante has his tragic lovers Paolo and Francesca explain that reading about the first kiss of Lancelot and Guinevere was the catalyst for their own fatal affair.[21]

Lancelot is the hero of the Vulgate Cycle; his adventures dominate the story and he is the unquestioned leading knight in spite of cuckolding Arthur for many years. Though the final section is entitled the *Mort Artu*, it ends not with Arthur's death but with Lancelot's penitential retreat from the world and saintly demise, which indicates divine forgiveness for his sins. The contrast between the deaths of Arthur and of Lancelot is remarkable. In the Vulgate *Mort Artu* and in a number of derivative romances, including the Stanzaic *Morte Arthur* and Malory's *Morte Darthur*, Arthur's fatal wounding by Mordred is followed by his mysterious departure in a ship of ladies to seek healing, watched by his only surviving companion (Girflet in the Vulgate Cycle, Bedivere in the English tradition). There is no praise for the dying king, no assessment of his reign; no priest is present and he makes no confession or final prayer (this is also the case in Geoffrey's *Historia*). It is a curiously pagan and perfunctory ending, though subsequently a hermit describes how the body was brought to a chapel and buried there. In the Vulgate, the death of Lancelot is described in detail; he seems to eclipse Arthur in death, as he did in many ways in life. Again, it is surprising that several English writers follow this lead. The Stanzaic poet slightly reduces the admiring emphasis on Lancelot with the innovation of a very powerful final scene between him and Guinevere in her nunnery, where she regrets all the damage they have done and insists on devoting the rest of her life to saving her soul.[22] When Lancelot immediately says he too will leave the world for a religious life, the queen doubts his sincerity and refuses to give him a final kiss. Malory uses this scene from the poem almost word for word, though he turns it into prose. He adds one further innovation at the very end of the *Morte Darthur*: after Lancelot's death, his brother Ector arrives and makes the last speech in the book, praising Lancelot as "'hede of al Crysten knyghtes,'" courtly and brave, a faithful lover and a stern enemy (939.12–23; C XXI.12). Guinevere is not mentioned by name, but their relationship is strongly implied: Lancelot is described as "'the trewest lover, of a synful man, that ever loved woman.'" It is remarkable that an English writer would celebrate the foreign knight who cuckolds Arthur for so long by putting him at the center of the story and frequently adding to the sources used in order to praise or defend him.

At the beginning of his Tale of Sir Lancelot, Malory lays out very clearly the symbiotic relationship between love and chivalry central to medieval romance:

> ...for in alle turnementes, justys, and dedys of armys, both for lyff and deth, he passed all other knyghtes, and at no tyme was he ovircom but yf hit were by treson other [or] inchauntement.
>
> *So* this Sir Launcelot encresed so mervaylously in worship [reputation] and honoure, *therfore* he is the fyrste knyght that the Freynsh booke makyth mencion of aftir Kynge Arthure com frome Rome. *Wherfore* Quene Gwenyvere had hym in grete favoure aboven all other knyghtis, *and so* he loved the quene agayne aboven all other ladyes dayes of his lyff, and for hir he dud many dedys of armys and saved her frome the fyre thorow his noble chevalry. (190.8–18; C VI.1; emphasis added)

One of the main assumptions of chivalric romance is that prowess on the battlefield wins not only praise from fellow knights but also love from a lady, and that this love is ennobling and inspiring. Sometimes, however, the demands of love and chivalry clash. A knight who is too happy at home with his wife may be criticized for neglecting his chivalric duties, as in Chrétien's *Erec*; a knight who spends too much time on the tournament circuit may be rejected by his wife, as in Chrétien's *Yvain*. Love may make a knight behave contrary to chivalric ideals; Malory's Arthur makes all his knights swear an annual oath about behavior which includes the strict instruction "that no man take no batayles in a wrongefull quarell for no love ne for no worldis goodis" (97.34–5; C III.15; the multiple negatives are the equivalent of heavy underlining). Lancelot slides ever closer to the brink in the final tales, and eventually has to take a wrongful quarrel for love in order to defend the queen's honor. This is one of numerous conflicts of loyalties which come to a head as the Round Table disintegrates.

The Challenge of the Grail Quest

The fundamental assumptions of chivalry in relation to both fighting and love are called into question by the introduction into the Arthurian legend of the Grail Quest, which asserts a new set of Christian values incompatible with the world of chivalric adventure. In Chrétien's *Conte du Graal* everything about the Grail is enigmatic; it is not an explicitly Christian object, and as the poem is unfinished it is not clear what is required to achieve the quest, or what the outcome for the successful knight will be. Several continuations were produced within a few decades, but the version of the Grail legend and the quest which became the standard were developed by Robert de Boron in the early 1200s, and made famous in the Vulgate Cycle. The Grail is now the chalice of the Last Supper, used by Joseph of Arimathea to catch Jesus' blood during the Crucifixion, and brought to Britain by Joseph himself. The knight destined to achieve the quest is Galahad, illegitimate son of Lancelot; they are descended both from Joseph of Arimathea and from King David. Most of the knights at court set out on the quest, to Arthur's dismay, but are doomed to failure because the rules of the game have changed. Christian values are now paramount and there is a much more uncompromising position on sin. Knights cannot be accompanied by ladies, and only virgins will be successful; several knights encounter seductive ladies who turn out literally to be devils in disguise. The pride, competitiveness, and obsession with honor and status characteristic of chivalry are no longer acceptable. Black armor is now a sign of sin, not a fashion choice. Dreams and visions are frequent, and hermits and priests appear to interpret them. Gawain cannot find any adventures at all and is presented as a hopeless case, spiritually blind and too impatient to listen to a hermit's advice.

Even before they all set out, Lancelot is told explicitly that he is no longer the best knight in the world and will not achieve the quest. In Chrétien the Grail hero was Perceval, but in the Vulgate *Queste del Saint Graal* he has two companions: one is Bors, Lancelot's cousin, but the most important is a new character, Lancelot's illegitimate son Galahad, conceived through a magical but necessary trick, since he is destined for Grail greatness. When Galahad arrives at court, he is successful in drawing a sword from a stone (echoing Arthur's own arrival as a boy), and sits safely in the Siege Perilous, which is revealed to bear his name. Lancelot's sin in begetting Galahad out of wedlock seems to be cancelled out by his son's destiny; the affair with the queen, however, which had been tacitly accepted by all up to this point, prevents him from succeeding in the quest. He confesses the affair to a hermit and promises to stay away from Guinevere, but is not able to keep his promise. Like most of the other knights, Lancelot finds that the familiar chivalric values are no longer acceptable on the quest, though he does at least find some adventures, unlike Gawain.

Arthurian writers could choose whether or not to include the Grail Quest – but why was it introduced into the legend in the first place? Is it a compliment to Arthur that the quest occurs in his realm, and is achieved by his knights, or is it a criticism of chivalry in general and the Arthurian world in particular, since most of his knights fail in the quest, including Lancelot, his greatest champion? The Grail values seem incompatible with chivalric ones in most respects, and yet at the end of the quest the knights who have survived return to court and it is hardly mentioned again. Much has changed, however. There are no more random adventures and supernatural encounters, and the outing of Lancelot's affair with the queen draws inexorably closer. The Vulgate *Mort Artu* devotes much space to this, still focusing on Lancelot rather than Arthur, but the affair is not the only cause of the final catastrophe.

Destiny, Mutability, Responsibility

The prophecy about Mordred must be fulfilled, but Arthur's fall also exemplifies the mutability which was widely represented in medieval art and writing as Fortune's Wheel. In the Vulgate *Mort*, after the death of Gawain Arthur dreams that Fortune (as a beautiful lady) takes him to a mountain top and sits him in a chair on top of a rotating wheel. She tells him that, though he is the greatest king there has ever been, earthly pride means that even the greatest must inevitably fall, and she pushes him brutally to the ground.[23] In Malory's version Fortune does not appear herself, and Arthur falls from the wheel into "an hydeous depe blak watir" full of snakes and other creatures which seize his limbs (920.15–24; C XXI.3). These details recall his earlier nightmare after the conception of Mordred, in which a dragon attacked him and his realm, though no explicit link is made. Immediately after this episode Malory adds another factor, a random element of chance, borrowed from the English Stanzaic *Morte*. Arthur and Mordred agree a truce, but both sides are suspicious of treachery, and when a knight draws his sword to kill an adder it is taken as a sign that the truce is broken;[24] the final battle begins: what Malory's Sir Lucan calls "thys wycked day of desteny" (923.22–3; C XXI.4).

In Geoffrey, Mordred alone is responsible for ending Arthur's reign, out of a desire for power. Later writers introduce the prophecy of his fatal role, though Malory does not mention it when he attributes the fall of Camelot entirely to Mordred's and Agravain's jealousy and hatred of Lancelot (870.10–15; C XX.1); his Guinevere, Gawain, and Lancelot each claim that it was all their fault. What romance writers bring to the core plot of Arthur's rise and fall is a great interest in character and behavior, in exploring motivation and reaction. They describe battles, but also emotions and moral dilemmas. Magic can produce thrilling adventures, whether it offers challenges to Arthur's knights or saves them from disaster. Knights are bound by ties of fellowship, but also of blood; expanding the family relationships of key characters creates more opportunities for conflicts of loyalties. There is a tension between love and chivalry from Chrétien on, and to that is added the tension between secular chivalry and spiritual chivalry in the Grail Quest. Questions of responsibility become more complex as the legend evolves. Does illegitimate birth determine the moral status of the son, or stain the character of the father? Is Arthur responsible for his own downfall, and why is he often so passive? Guinevere always betrays him, either with Mordred (as in Geoffrey) or with Lancelot (as in Chrétien), but does she alone destroy Camelot? Lancelot is Arthur's main champion in many versions because of the prowess gained through his affair with the queen, so can that ennobling love be entirely wrong? If the Grail Quest can only be achieved by virgin knights who then die, what future can there be for knighthood? Is the Arthurian project doomed from the start?

Caxton summed up all that the legend has to offer very neatly in the prologue to his pioneering printed edition of Malory (1485):

> For herein may be seen noble shyvalrye, curtosye, humanyte, frendlynesse, hardynesse, love, frendshyp, cowardyse, murdre, hate, vertue and synne. Doo after the good and leve the evyl, and it shal brynge you to good fame and renommee [renown]. And for to passe the tyme thys book shal be plesaunte to rede in, but for to gyve fayth and byleve al is trewe that is conteyned herin, ye be at your lyberte.[25]

The many approaches to the legend in medieval romance have inspired later poets and novelists, as well as graphic artists and filmmakers, to offer their versions of what Dante called "Arturi regis ambages pulcerrimae" (the very beautiful stories of King Arthur).[26] Part of that beauty lies in the legend's infinite variety.

Notes

1. See, for example, Stephen Knight, *Arthurian Literature and Society* (London: Macmillan, 1983); Martin B. Shichtman and James P. Carley, eds., *Culture and the King: The Social Implications of the Arthurian Legend* (Albany, NY: SUNY Press, 1994); Richard Kaeuper, *Chivalry and Violence in Medieval Europe* (New York: Oxford University Press, 1999).
2. Geoffrey of Monmouth, *The History of the Kings of Britain*, VIII.137–XI.178, ed. M. Reeve, trans. N. Wright, pp. 182–253. See Ad Putter, "The Twelfth-Century Arthur," in *The Cambridge Companion to the Arthurian Legend*, ed. Elizabeth Archibald and Ad Putter (Cambridge: Cambridge University Press, 2009), pp. 36–52.
3. On the changing characterization of Arthur, see Rosemary Morris, *The Character of King Arthur in Medieval Literature*, Arthurian Studies 4 (Cambridge: D. S. Brewer, 1982), and *King Arthur: A Casebook*, ed. Edward Donald Kennedy, Arthurian Characters and Themes 1 (New York: Garland, 1996).
4. There are many editions and translations of the poems; see for instance *Arthurian Romances*, trans. W. W. Kibler; also Putter, "The Twelfth-Century Arthur," and *A Companion to Chrétien de Troyes*, ed. Norris J. Lacy and Joan Tasker Grimbert, Arthurian Studies 63 (Cambridge: D. S. Brewer, 2005).

5. These two cycles are translated as *Lancelot-Grail*, ed. Norris J. Lacy, 5 vols; reissued in 10 vols (Cambridge: D. S. Brewer, 2010); citations here are to the five-volume edition by page number, abbreviated as *L-G*. See also *A Companion to the* Lancelot-Grail *Cycle*, ed. Carol Dover, Arthurian Studies 54 (Cambridge: D. S. Brewer, 2003), and Jane H. M. Taylor, "The Thirteenth-Century Arthur," in Archibald and Putter, eds., *The Cambridge Companion to the Arthurian Legend*, pp. 53–68.
6. See Carolyne Larrington, *King Arthur's Enchantresses: Morgan and her Sisters in Arthurian Tradition* (London: I. B. Tauris, 2006).
7. Sir Thomas Malory, *Le Morte Darthur*, 926.31–3, CXXI.5, ed. P. J. C. Field. Page and line references to vol 1 of this edition will be given parenthetically in the main text, followed by the chapter and section reference in Caxton.
8. I use the English spellings familiar from Malory; in French Gareth is known as Gaheriet, and Gaheris as Guerrehet, though the spellings can vary.
9. For a full account of this episode see Elizabeth Archibald, *Incest and the Medieval Imagination* (Oxford: Clarendon Press, 2001), pp. 202–19.
10. See Archibald, *Incest and the Medieval Imagination*, pp. 107–10.
11. See the essays in *Gawain: A Casebook*, ed. Raymond H. Thompson and Keith Busby, Arthurian Characters and Themes 8 (New York: Routledge, 2006), and Keith Busby, *Gauvain in Old French Literature* (Amsterdam: Rodopi, 1980).
12. B. J. Whiting, "Gawain: His Reputation, His Courtesy, and His Appearance in Chaucer's *Squire's Tale*," *Medieval Studies* 9 (1947), 189–234; rp. in *Gawain: A Casebook*, ed. Thompson and Busby, pp. 45–94.
13. The best known is Renaut de Bâgé's *Bel Inconnu*, adapted in Middle English as *Lybeaus Desconus*. For an overview of the theme see Maldwyn Mills, "The Story of the Fair Unknown in Medieval Literature," in the introduction to his edition of *Lybeaus Desconus*, pp. 42–68.
14. Keith Busby, "Diverging Traditions of Gauvain in Some of the Later Old French Verse Romances," in *Gawain: A Casebook*, ed. Thompson and Busby, pp. 139–55 (p. 141).
15. The accidental beheading is described in the Post-Vulgate *Suite du Merlin*, by Paris and Ulrich as *Merlin: Roman en prose du XIII siècle*, vol 2 pp. 88–9 trans. as *The Merlin Continuation* in *L-G*, IV.230, I.89; Malory includes it too (84.30–3; C III.7).
16. See Fanni Bogdanow, "The Character of Gauvain in the Thirteenth-Century Prose Romances," in *Gawain: A Casebook*, ed. Thompson and Busby, pp. 173–81, and Busby, "The Character of Gauvain in the *Prose* Tristan," in the same volume, pp. 183–207.
17. See *Sir Gawain: Eleven Romances and Tales*, ed. Hahn, and Hahn; "Gawain and Popular Romance in England," in *The Cambridge Companion to Medieval Romance*, ed. Roberta L. Krueger (Cambridge: Cambridge University Press, 2000), pp. 218–34.
18. *Sir Gawain and the Green Knight*, ed. Ad Putter and Myra Stokes in *The Works of the Gawain Poet*, pp. 237–406. See also Ad Putter, *Sir Gawain and the Green Knight and French Arthurian Romance* (Oxford: Oxford University Press, 1995).
19. *La Mort le roi Artu*, chs. 85ff., ed. Jean Frappier, pp. 107ff.; *L-G* IV.118ff.
20. See *Lancelot and Guinevere: A Casebook*, ed. Lori J. Walters, Arthurian Characters and Themes 4 (New York: Garland, 1996).

21. Dante, *Inferno*, 5. 127–38, in *The Divine Comedy of Dante Alighieri*, 3 vols., ed. and trans. John D. Sinclair (Oxford: Oxford University Press, 1939; rp. 1978), 1. 78–9.
22. Stanzaic *Morte Arthur*, 3622–729, in *King Arthur's Death*, ed. L. D. Benson, rev. Edward Foster.
23. *Mort Artu*, ch. 176.56–79, ed. Frappier, pp. 226–7; *L-G* IV.149–50.
24. Stanzaic *Morte Arthur*, 3328–51; Malory 922.2–21; C XXI.4.
25. Malory, *Morte Darthur*, ed. Field, II.854–7 (p. 856).
26. Dante, *De vulgari eloquentia*, 1.x.2, ed. and trans. Botterill, pp. 22–3. The meaning of *ambages* here is much discussed; it can mean "riddles" or "puzzles," so it may refer to the interlace technique of the French prose romances, or the uncertainties of Arthur's own story, or the complexity of the adventures of Arthur's knights.

Suggestions for Further Reading

Archibald, Elizabeth, "Questioning Arthurian Ideals," in *The Cambridge Companion to the Arthurian Legend*, ed. Elizabeth Archibald and Ad Putter. Cambridge: Cambridge University Press, 2009, pp. 139–53.

Archibald, Elizabeth, and A. S. G. Edwards, eds., *A Companion to Malory*, Arthurian Studies 37, Cambridge: D. S. Brewer, 1996.

Barber, Richard, *The Holy Grail: Imagination and Belief*, London: Allen Lane, 2004.

Barron, W. R. J., ed., *The Arthur of the English*, Arthurian Literature in the Middle Ages 2, Cardiff: University of Wales Press, 1999.

Besamusca, Bart, ed., *Cyclification: The Development of Narrative Cycles in the Chansons de Geste and the Arthurian Romances*, Amsterdam: Royal Netherlands Academy of Arts and Sciences, 1994.

Burgess, Glyn S., and Karen Pratt, eds., *The Arthur of the French*, Arthurian Literature in the Middle Ages 4, Cardiff: University of Wales Press, 2006.

Fulton, Helen, ed., *A Companion to Arthurian Literature*, Oxford: Wiley-Blackwell, 2009.

Gilbert, Jane, "Arthurian Ethics," in *The Cambridge Companion to the Arthurian Legend*, ed. Elizabeth Archibald and Ad Putter. Cambridge: Cambridge University Press, pp. 154–70.

Grimbert, Joan Tasker, ed., *Tristan and Isolde: A Casebook*, Arthurian Characters and Themes 2, New York: Garland, 1995.

Leitch, Megan G., and Cory James Rushton, eds., *A New Companion to Malory*, Arthurian Studies 87, Cambridge: D. S. Brewer, 2019.

Mahoney, Dhira B, ed., *The Grail: A Casebook*, Arthurian Characters and Themes 5, New York: Garland, 2000.

Schmolke-Hasselman, Beate, *The Evolution of Arthurian Romance: The Verse Tradition from Chrétien to Froissart*, trans. Margaret and Roger Middleton. Cambridge: Cambridge University Press, 1998.

6

SHARON KINOSHITA

Romance and the Medieval Mediterranean

In a literary ecosystem in which romances are typically identified by language (French, German, Middle English, Italian, and so forth) or by thematic content (notably "Arthurian"), it is a challenge even to say what the designation "Mediterranean romance" might mean. On the one hand, there are romances produced in lands we might think of as "Mediterranean": the Iberian Peninsula, the Italian Peninsula, the Byzantine Empire; on the other, there are romances that take the Mediterranean as their setting, with protagonists who sail the sea in pursuit of adventures that take them to various port cities, kingdoms, and empires. Although the two may of course go together, this is not necessarily so: think of an Arthurian romance composed (including those copied, translated, compiled, or adapted) in Spain or Italy: does thinking of it as "Mediterranean" contribute new layers to the ways we read or understand it?[1]

The interest in "Mediterranean romance" goes hand-in-hand with the emergence, over the first two decades of the twenty-first century, of the new Mediterranean studies, a field of inquiry that cuts across such traditional disciplines as history, art history, religious studies, and anthropology as well as literature. In his now-classic work, *The Mediterranean and the Mediterranean World in the Age of Philip II*, French historian Fernand Braudel began by identifying the Mediterranean geographically, as a sea rimmed by mountains, at latitudes propitious to the cultivation of the olive and the vine; the new Mediterranean studies, in contrast, takes the Mediterranean as a "strategic regionalism" that allows us to displace or reshuffle the conceptual categories through which we typically see our objects of study.[2] For the Middle Ages, the most significant categories are the nation and religion: the former because, although nation-states would not appear on the historical stage for several centuries, we typically study the past under rubrics such as "medieval France" or "medieval Italy" despite the sometimes glaring anachronism (particularly egregious in the cases of Spain and Italy) this entails; and the latter because the Crusades (those papally sanctioned campaigns against Muslims and non-Latin Christians that punctuated the high and late Middle Ages) are sometimes treated as the default mode of interaction between Christians and Muslims in the medieval Mediterranean.[3] Displacing the nation as the default category of analysis decenters the tendency to read medieval phenomena as part of a historical or genealogical progression, with the Middle Ages supplying the origin point of subsequent national traditions. In literary studies, the significance of this shift is most visible in the case of epic, in which songs such as the *Chanson de Roland*, the *Nibelungenlied*, and the *Poema de mio Cid* have been privileged as precocious expressions of national origins or character. What about romance?

By displacing emphasis from questions shaped by the history of the nation or of the Crusades, the new Mediterranean studies clears a space for different kinds of questions, replacing a vocabulary of origins, development, and expansion with one of contact, interaction, and circulation. In this framework, which privileges *routes* over roots and *acts* over identities, new actors emerge: alongside, or sometimes instead of, the kings and popes who dominate standard histories (as well as "national" epics), merchants, diplomats, translators, and go-betweens of all sorts also appear, plying commercial and other networks of communication and exchange that, surprisingly often, survive world-historical changes of religion or empire. To see how this shift in perspective translates to our reading of medieval romance, let's consider *Floire and Blancheflor*, a pan-European textual tradition first attested in an Old French version dated to the middle of the twelfth century.[4]

Floire et Blancheflor tells the story of two adolescent lovers: one a Spanish Saracen prince, the other a Christian slave. Born the same day, they are nearly identical and all but inseparable – reared together at the court of Floire's father and learning the language of love from shared lessons poring over "livres paienors" (pagan books). Fearing that his son's obsession with the Christian slave will interfere with a proper political marriage, Floire's father, King Felix, fakes Blancheflor's death (erecting a false tomb recalling the funerary monuments of the Old French romances of antiquity) while selling her to some passing merchants who carry her overseas. Wringing the truth from his parents, a distraught Floire disguises himself as a merchant and tracks Blancheflor across the Mediterranean to far-off "Babylon" (medieval Europe's name for Cairo). On learning that she is about to be made the emir's wife, he sneaks into the Tower of Maidens where she is being kept. Reunited in a tender scene, the two lovers fall asleep in each other's arms; caught together in this position, they are condemned to death, until, softened by the pleas of his vassal-kings and moved by the young people's devotion to one another, the emir spares them and presides over their marriage. On learning his father has died, Floire returns home with his bride, converts to Christianity for her sake and, in a jarring finish, orders the conversion of all his subjects on pain of death. The two live happily ever after, becoming Charlemagne's maternal grandparents.

Floire, it is easy to see, falls outside the two categories of romance identified just before the turn of the thirteenth century by the Arrageois poet Jehan Bodel: the matter of Rome – stories of antiquity (on Aeneas, the Trojan War, Oedipus, and Alexander), translated from Latin; and the matter of Brittany – stories inspired by the Celtic tradition, including those of King Arthur. (His third category was the matter of France: the pseudohistorical legends, notably those of Charlemagne, told in Old French epics, or *chansons de geste*.[5]) Most notably, it takes interreligious contact between Christians and Saracens as central.[6] Unmarried and pregnant, Blancheflor's mother, the nameless daughter of an anonymous count, is on an expiatory pilgrimage to Santiago de Compostela in the far northwest corner of the Iberian Peninsula when she is captured (along with livestock and booty) in a Saracen raid.[7] Taken back to court, where she becomes the companion of King Felix's equally pregnant queen, her fate alerts us to the prevalence of slavery in the medieval Mediterranean, common on both sides of the Christian–Muslim divide.[8] And when the two women give birth on the same day and Floire's mother serves as wet nurse to both titular protagonists, the romance metaphorically casts Christianity and Islam as what the historian Richard Bulliet describes as "fraternal twins . . . almost indistinguishable in childhood," neither of which can be adequately understood without the other.[9] We are far from the Arthurian court elaborated by Chrétien de Troyes in the last third of the twelfth century in his canonical romances *Erec and Enide*, *Yvain or the Knight of the Lion* (*Le Chevalier au lion*), *Lancelot or the Knight of the Cart* (*Le Chevalier de la charrete*), and *Perceval or the Story of the Grail* (*Le conte du graal*), set in Wales or in hazily located forests and kingdoms.

Also indicative of *Floire*'s Mediterranean orientation is the small but significant role it allots to merchants. Like Old French epic, both the romances of antiquity and those inspired by the Celtic tradition typically idealize a culture of feudal warfare and chivalric refinement – an aristocratic culture shaped by lord–vassal relations, the feudal politics of lineage, and an ideal of courtly behavior in which merchants and other non-noble characters play little part. In the northern French context, framed by the ideology of the three orders (those who pray, those who fight, and those who work the land), merchant activity is cast as that which disrupts or threatens to supersede feudal and courtly cultures.[10] In the prologue of the *Roman de Thèbes*, the author addresses himself to clerics and knights; no others are capable even of proper listening, and his subject matter is of two royal brothers – not furriers, peasants, or shepherds.[11] In the *Roman de Toute Chevalerie*, Thomas of Kent's twelfth-century Anglo-Norman Alexander romance, as the protagonist is about to set off on his conquest of India, a vassal enjoins him: "let craftsmen come – along with valiant young knights, dukes, and counts – but not merchants, the low-born, or peasants" (ll. 3928–30). The campaign will be won, he continues, through the assertion of prowess, strength, vigor, and chivalry: "*We are not merchants*, to stop felons and traitors by buying them out" (ll. 3837–8; emphasis added).[12] In Chrétien de Troyes's *Perceval or the Story of the Grail*, a lord whom Sir Gawain encounters during his adventures opines, "He is a merchant; he is leading horses to sell and posing as a knight." The reaction of the lord's vassal registers the enormity of this insult: "What! This is too vulgar a charge I hear you speak!" (ll. 5200–1, 5202–3).[13]

In the medieval Mediterranean, on the other hand, merchants were "professional boundary crossers" who regularly negotiated linguistic, cultural, and confessional divides.[14] Romances we might consider "Mediterranean" feature them prominently; in *Floire*, "merchants of Babylon," as we have seen, play a key role in transporting our protagonists from their home in Saracen Spain to far-off Babylon. In the early-thirteenth-century French prose romance *La fille du comte du Pontieu*, a shipload of seaborne merchants of unspecified religion rescues the titular heroine at sea; sailing into the port of Almería, where they plan to offer her as a gift to its sultan, they proclaim "We are merchants" (*Marceant somes*), pointedly inverting the categorical denial –"N'eimes pas marchant" – issued by the anonymous vassal in the *Roman de Toute Chevalerie*.[15] So, it is not surprising that when Floire sets out in pursuit of his beloved Blancheflor, he does so disguised as one of these professional boundary crossers. Such a ruse is not unique to romance. In the late- twelfth-century parodic epic *Le Charroi de Nîmes*, the landless hero Guillaume Fierabrace gains entry to the Saracen city he hopes to conquer by posing as a merchant from Canterbury. And in novella 10.9 of Giovanni Boccaccio's *Decameron* (c. 1350), Saladin (a fictionalized version of the historical sultan of "Babylon"), wishing to assess the level of Latin Christian preparedness for the Third Crusade, comes through Pavia (in northern Italy) disguised as a Cypriot merchant on his way to Paris. In all these tales, "merchant" becomes a favored disguise for noblemen wishing to cross the Mediterranean incognito.[16]

In Chrétien de Troyes's *Perceval*, a shipload of merchants arrives just in time to relieve the siege of a castle that the titular protagonist is defending for a damsel named (like Floire's sweetheart) Blanchefleur. "We are merchants," they declare, "bringing food to market . . . bread and wine, bacon and ham, pork and beef" (ll. 2539–40, 2541–2).[17] The castle's besieged inhabitants welcome them jubilantly, promising to pay whatever they choose to ask for their wares. By contrast, in *Floire and Blancheflor*, the passage in which King Felix barters Blancheflor to the itinerant merchants of Babylon takes pains to detail the luxury commodities typical of long-distance maritime trade: "twenty Benevento silks, variegated eastern cloaks, and Indian purple tunics" (ll. 432–4), along with a golden goblet inscribed with scenes from the story of the Trojan War, but narrated in reverse chronological order – reversing the directionality of the legend of Aeneas's flight from Troy and founding of Rome that medieval writers (in the widespread topos of *translatio imperii*) took to be the first leg in the story of their own origins.[18] Interestingly, however, when a few scenes later Floire adopts the identity of a merchant to pursue Blancheflor across the Mediterranean, the baggage train he prepares – "seven pack animals . . . two loaded with gold and silver . . . the third loaded with deniers, which I'll need, and two with expensive textiles – the best you can find" (ll. 1143–4, 1148–9) – is stocked less with merchandise than with tributary gifts, echoing the opening scene of the *Chanson de Roland*.[19]

Nevertheless, Floire's recourse to disguise exemplifies another characteristic of the Mediterranean: the easy mutability of identities. In standard French romance, protagonists may grow up in ignorance of their identities, only later to discover or grow into them, like Perceval in Chrétien de Troyes's *Le Conte du grail* or Yonec in Marie de France's lai of the same name. In Mediterranean romance, on the other hand, identities are actively rescrambled: the high-born become slaves, slaves rise to positions of prominence, Saracens convert to Christianity, and even occasionally vice versa. In a world of such mutable identities, passing becomes a major plot device. In northern romances, in contrast, the most prominent "passer" is Tristan, who in various textual incarnations spends time as a fool, a madman, or a minstrel. More typical is the knight who conceals his identity under a carefully crafted pseudonym – the knight of the Cart, the knight of the Lion – or who intentionally or inadvertently sows confusion by switching or borrowing arms, like Chrétien de Troyes's titular protagonist Cligès at the tournament of Oxford. In comparison, Floire – besides disguising himself as a merchant – at various points in the romance poses as or is mistaken for an architect, a flower, and (thanks to his adolescent androgyny) a princess in the harem of the emir of Babylon. Meanwhile, Blancheflor, born a slave, traded as a commodity, and purchased by the emir of Babylon at "face value" for seven times her weight in gold, is by the end of the tale transformed into the queen of the court into which she had been born a captive, exemplifying the enormous power of routes over roots within the Mediterranean circuit of exchange.[20]

In *Corrupting Sea*, the book that did much to galvanize the current interest in Mediterranean studies, historians Peregrine Horden and Nicholas Purcell draw a useful distinction between "history *in* the region, contingently Mediterranean or best conceived under some other heading, and ... history *of* it – history either of the whole Mediterranean or of an aspect of it to which the whole is an indispensable framework."[21] Does a Mediterranean setting make a romance Mediterranean in this sense? One thing to remember is that the new Mediterranean studies does not seek to draw exclusionary lines defining what does or does not count as an object of study; rather, as a strategic regionalism, it seeks to stimulate new questions and new perspectives, drawing attention to lesser-studied texts. An interesting case is posed by the late-thirteenth-century French romance *Floriant et Florete*, its title so evocatively recalling that of *Floire and Blancheflor*.[22] The origins of the two titular protagonists – the dispossessed son of the ousted king of Sicily and the daughter of the emperor of Constantinople, respectively – situate us squarely in the Mediterranean; the overall arc of the plot has Floriant avenging his father and recovering his throne, falling in love with and eventually marrying Florete (whose father is originally an ally of the Sicilian usurper), and undertaking a new adventure to clear his name when his reputation is sullied. In other ways, however, the frame is distinctly Arthurian: abducted as an infant by Morgan le Fay, he is raised in ignorance of his identity. Setting out at the age of fifteen, he learns his name at Arthur's court and wins his battle in Sicily with Arthurian backing. After his second set of adventures, he and Florete return to Arthur's court; news arrives that Florete's father has died, and the couple succeeds him as the rulers of Constantinople. A final adventure takes Floriant back to Morgan le Fay at Mongibel, where he will have eternal life if he stays; Florete soon joins him, and the two are never heard from again. In the course of these episodic adventures, moreover, Floriant adopts two pseudonyms – "le chevalier qui la nef maine" and "Beau Savage," respectively – that mark him more as an Arthurian hero than a Mediterranean one. *Floriant et Florete* is shaped by intimate contact not with the Islamic world but with the Arthurian one.

An equally interesting example occurs in *Cligés*, the second of Chrétien de Troyes's five Arthurian romances. Its titular protagonist is a half-Arthurian prince: his mother, Soredamors, is the niece of Sir Gawain (Arthur's nephew); his father, Alexander, is the son of the emperor of Greece. After winning renown in a tourney at the Arthurian court in which he fights incognito, Cligès returns to Greece to avenge his father against the latter's usurping brother Alis; while there, he begins a Tristan-like adulterous affair with his uncle's wife, the German emperor's daughter Fénice, with whom he had earlier fallen in love. Eventually, Alis returns the throne to Alexander and Cligès marries Fénice (her marriage to Alis never having been consummated) and the two succeed as the rulers of Greece. Though set partly in "Greece" (in evocation of the Byzantine Empire of the twelfth century), the plot of *Cligés* displays relatively few traits that are distinctly Mediterranean.[23] On the other hand, the text is peppered with apparently gratuitous Mediterranean place names, as when the messengers King Arthur dispatches to seek out the mysterious black knight who has won the day at the Oxford tournament can find no trace of him, "any more than if he were in Caesaria, Toledo, or Candia."[24] Despite their apparent randomness, however, Chrétien's contemporaries would have recognized these sites as significant centers of translation (from Arabic to Latin), commerce (with both the Islamic and Byzantine worlds), and crusade.[25] Thus, while the main plot of *Cligés* may refer obliquely to the tangled politics of twelfth-century French–Byzantine relations, the text's proper names subtly evoke the multiform complexity of Mediterranean-wide interactions.

Alongside texts such as *Floriant* and *Cligés* are romances both composed and set north of the Mediterranean but which include distinctly Mediterranean episodes. One such work is Rudolf von Ems's *Der guote Gêrhart*, a Middle High German romance composed in the early thirteenth century, roughly contemporary with Hartmann von Aue's and Wolfram von Eschenbach's translations of the Arthurian romances of Chrétien de Troyes.[26] The titular protagonist is a merchant from Cologne who is held up to the German Emperor Otto as a model for doing good. During a commercial voyage in the eastern Mediterranean, Gêrhart is blown ashore in Morocco, where he discovers a Norwegian princess who had been taken captive on her way to marry the Crown Prince of England. Capitalizing on his skills as a merchant, he reconnoiters the market town near which he and his crew have landed and establishes friendly relations with the local ruler, speaking with him in French (their common language) and showing him his wares, including precious silks acquired in eastern Mediterranean sites such as Damascus and Nineveh (Mosul). The "heathen" prince, in turn, shows the merchant *his* treasure: the Norwegian princess and her entourage. The two agree to an exchange; Gêrhart ransoms the royal party and returns them safely to their respective homes. Put in a position to do "good" because of his "goods," he secures heavenly approval not for his act of ransom but for repeatedly refusing all the earthly rewards – monetary, political, and social – subsequently offered him. Where in the *Roman de Toute Chevalerie*, Alexander's vassal pointedly excludes merchants from a campaign designed around noble virtues like prowess and chivalry, here a merchant is promoted as an example, and a rebuke, to the reputation-conscious emperor himself.

Another such text is the twelfth-century Anglo-Norman *Boeve de Haumtone* – better known through its fourteenth-century Middle English translation/adaptation *Beues of Hamtoun* (Bevis of Hampton).[27] Metrically speaking, the Anglo-Norman *Boeve* is a *chanson de geste* (Old French epic), composed in the monorhymed *laisses* (stanzas) characteristic of the genre. The Middle English *Beues*, on the other hand, is a romance, prompting modern scholars to treat its Anglo-Norman predecessor as a romance as well:[28] a prime example of the generic drift of the word "romance" from its origins as a text translated (from Latin or Welsh/Breton) into octosyllabic rhyming couplets in the Romance-language vernacular to a thematically defined tale of adventure, often of an eponymous hero. And, in fact, *Boeve* turns on a plot twist that echoes that in *Floire and Blancheflor*. Targeted by his ambitious and unscrupulous stepmother, the titular protagonist, son of the count of Hampton, is sold to Saracen merchants for four times his weight in gold and transported to Egypt, where he wins the king's favor and falls in love with his daughter, Josiane. The action-packed plot spans many years and takes Boeve to multiple sites across the Mediterranean, as well as return stints to England: he refuses conversion but takes service under King Hermin of Egypt, spends seven years in captivity in Damascus, goes on crusade, eventually marries Josiane, suffers many changes of fortune, and ends up the ruler, with Josiane, of the kingdom of Munbraunt, near Carthage.

On the one hand, the fact that "Boeve . . . enters the romance the son of an English nobleman and exits it an African king" (Blurton, 466) means that the text partakes of a spirit of Latin Christian expansionism similar to that evinced at the end of *Floire and Blancheflor*, where Floire, on succeeding his father as king of Niebla, not only converts to Christianity but demands that his people, under pain of death, do the same. On the other hand, throughout the text:

> Boeve's foes are determined not by confessional identity, but largely by whether they threaten to come between him and his love for . . . Josiane, or his friendship with his tutor, Sabaoth, and Sabaoth's son Terri. From Egypt to Seville, Boeve is more likely to be found fighting alongside Muslim friends and allies than his Christian co-religionists. Boeve's alliances are based on affection rather than affiliation. (Blurton, 469)

The multiple examples in which personal relations trump religious identity allude to the complexity of medieval Mediterranean interactions, with an insistence that challenges the predominance of the protonational lens of

"Englishness" through which this text has typically been read (Blurton, 466–7). The significance its fourteenth-century translators attributed to the Mediterranean is attested by changes made to the geography of the Anglo-Norman text: Josiane's father is no longer king of Egypt but of Armenia, reflecting the importance assumed by Ayas, the main port of Cilician Armenia, following the fall of the crusader port of Acre in 1291; at the same time, the false itinerary the Anglo-Norman protagonist invents to chart his supposed adventures – Nubia, Carthage, Esclavia, Barbary, and Macedonia – is considerably expanded, enumerating several sites in the Holy Land (Jerusalem, Nazareth, Bethlehem) before widening the frame to include India, Europe, Asia and a hodgepodge of other places (Blurton, 473–4).

Finally, there is the extent to which *Floire and Blancheflor* itself becomes an object of circulation, through the translation and adaptation of the text across many languages. This dynamic of transmission is of course not unique to "Mediterranean" romance but is in many ways typical of medieval textuality.[29] Nevertheless, *Floire*'s reception history invites us to consider the extent to which the particularly Mediterranean interest that attaches to the oldest Old French aristocratic version in the mid-twelfth century is or is not sustained as the text moves across cultures, including some well north of the Mediterranean, through to the later Middle Ages, with its concomitant changes in political, cultural, and economic conditions. Does *Floire* remain "of" the Mediterranean or is it simply "in" it?

Floire and Blancheflor's juxtaposition of the names of its male and female protagonists sets it apart from other prominent twelfth-century French romances, which (with the exception of Chrétien de Troyes's *Erec et Enide*) tend to highlight their male heroes: from Aeneid (in the *Roman d'Enéas*) and Alexander to Yvain, Lancelot, and Perceval, and even to Tristan (despite the importance of Iseut). On the other hand, both the conjoined names and its plot fit seamlessly amidst four twelfth-century Byzantine romances composed in Greek c. 1135–60: *Rhodanthe and Dosikles* by Theodore Prodromos, *Hysmne and Hysminian* by Eumathios Makremblites, *Aristandros and Kallithea* by Constantine Manasses, and *Drosilla and Charikles* by Niketas Eugeniamos, all featuring "a pair of well-born lovers who are separated by dramatic misfortunes but eventually emerge unscathed to be united in marriage."[30] (In yet another example of the inconsistency of generic terminology across linguistic traditions, specialists in Byzantine literature conventionally refer to these twelfth-century works, composed under the Komnenan dynasty, as "novels," reserving "romance" for a set of texts composed in the fourteenth century, under the Palaiologoi.[31]) These romances, in turn, drew their inspiration from five surviving works of prose fiction, retrospectively dubbed "Greek novels" or

"Hellenistic romances," composed in Greek, probably in the first and second centuries CE. These tales, mixing love and adventure, feature a hero and heroine, "always young, wellborn, and handsome, [whose] marriage is disrupted or temporarily prevented by separation, travel in distant parts, and a series of misfortunes, usually spectacular."[32] The genre is marked by its expansive geography – "usually in three to five countries separated by seas" – along with descriptions of "specific features of countries, cities, structures of various kinds" and attention to "the habits and customs of the population, various exotic and wild animals and other wonders and rarities."[33]

For historians, taking the Mediterranean as a frame of analysis encourages the study of connections and parallels between the Latin, Islamic, and Byzantine worlds and beyond. In literature, this places the focus on translation, especially the translation of scientific and philosophical texts from Arabic to Latin (as alluded to in *Cligés*'s mentions of Toledo, Tudela, and Antioch). For romance, we have already noted the way texts such as *Floire* rapidly spread across the languages of Latin Europe and, in the later Middle Ages, to Byzantine Greek. In the Islamic world, there are few Arabic texts that we are tempted to call romance, though perhaps this is due in part to scholars' privileging of the Classical language and canonical genres of poetry over texts (perhaps some waiting to be "discovered") in the Middle Arabic vernacular. One notable exception is the *Hadīth Bayād wa Riyād*: the love story between a Damascene merchant and a courtly slave girl that survives in a single copiously illustrated manuscript from thirteenth-century Muslim Iberia and has been read for its similarities to *Floire and Blancheflor*.[34] In contrast, Persian, which was on its way to becoming a lingua franca, "a language of governance or learning in a region that stretched from China to the Balkans, and from Siberia to southern India," had a flourishing tradition of long romance-like narratives, often drawing on pre-Islamic Iranian history and culture.[35] The best known of these are, in the eleventh century, Fakhraddin Gorgānī's *Vis and Ramin* (possibly a distant influence on the Tristan legend) and, in the twelfth, Nizami Ganjavi's *Khamsa* (Quintet), including *Layli and Majnun* (inspiration for rock guitarist Eric Clapton's 1970 song "Layla") and *Haft Paykar* (Seven Beauties) – texts that were lavishly illustrated in luxury manuscripts produced over the centuries.[36] Recent English translations of texts such as these greatly expand our understanding of romance, broadly defined, as a genre widespread in the medieval Mediterranean and beyond. Alongside the classifications we inherit from Jehan Bodel of the Matter of Rome and the Matter of Brittany, imagining a "Matter of the Mediterranean" provides an optic to help expand our view of medieval romance in our current global age.

Notes

1. At its origin, the term "romance" designates texts in the Romance vernacular – Old French – in contradistinction to Latin: the so-called "romances of antiquity." I use the term for texts in the octosyllabic rhyming couplets associated with that subgenre, even in cases where the text themselves occasionally refer to themselves as "contes."
2. Braudel, *The Mediterranean and the Mediterranean World in the Age of Philip II*, trans. Siân Reynolds, 2 vols. (New York: Harper & Row, 1972); originally *La Méditerranée et le monde méditerranéen à l'époque de Philippe II* (Paris : Colin, 1949). For the new Mediterranean studies, see Brian A. Catlos and Sharon Kinoshita (eds.), *Can We Talk Mediterranean? Conversations on an Emerging Field in Medieval and Early Modern Studies*, Mediterranean Perspectives (New York: Palgrave Macmillan, 2017).
3. For romances on crusade-related themes, see Lee Manion, Chapter 7 (this volume).
4. This so-called "aristocratic" version has been edited, with a facing-page translation into modern French, in Robert d'Orbigny, *Le Conte de Floire et Blancheflor*, ed. and trans. Leclanche. The name of the author, Robert d'Orbigny, has been back-constructed from a mention in a subsequent German translation of the text. For an extended reading, see Sharon Kinoshita, *Medieval Boundaries: Rethinking Difference in Old French Literature* (Philadelphia: University of Pennsylvania Press, 2006), pp. 77–104 and 252–61.
5. Jehan Bodel, *La Chanson des Saisnes*, ed. Brasseur, l. 7. This quotation is from Ms A (Paris, Arsenal 3142).
6. "Saracen" was the general Latin Christian word for non-Christians: primarily (as here) Muslims, but occasionally for pagans, like the pre-Christian Danes.
7. Such raids were a regular part of life along the Christian–Muslim frontier, as memoralized at the eastern end of the Mediterranean by the Byzantine border epic *Digenis Akritis*. See *Digenis Akritis: The Grottaferrata and Escorial Versions*, ed. and trans. Jeffreys. Such raids, of course, were not unique to cross-confessional situations, as exemplified in the Irish epic *The Cattle Raid of Cooley* (*Táin Bó Cúailnge*).
8. On this common culture of slavery at a slightly later historical moment, see Hannah Barker, *That Most Precious Merchandise: The Mediterranean Trade in Black Sea Slaves, 1260–1500* (Philadelphia: University of Pennsylvania Press, 2019).
9. Richard W. Bulliet, *The Case for Islamo-Christian Civilization* (New York: Columbia University Press, 2004), pp. xvii, 10, 15.
10. Georges Duby, *The Three Orders: Feudal Society Imagined*, trans. Arthur Goldhammer (Chicago: University of Chicago Press, 1980).
11. *Le Roman de Thèbes*, ed. and trans. Mora-Lebrun, ll. 13–20. In English: *The Romance of Thebes (Roman de Thebes)*, trans. Ferrante.
12. (vienge li overur, / Li bacheler vayllant, li duc e li contur. / Ne vienge marchant, vilein ne laborur; *N'eimes pas marchant*, d'estre achatur, / D'estancher par avoir felon ne traitor.) Thomas of Kent, *Le Roman d'Alexandre ou le Roman de Toute Chevalerie*, ed. Foster and Short, trans. Gaullier-Bougassas and Harf-Lancner, ll 3927–38.
13. ("Marcheanz est, si maine vandre / Chevaus, et chevalier se fait."/ "Avoi! Ci a trop villain plait . . . que je vos oi dire.") Chrétien de Troyes, *Le Conte du graal*, ed. Méla.

14. Philip D. Curtin, *Cross-Cultural Trade in World History* (Cambridge: Cambridge University Press, 1984), 6. On merchants as Mediterranean figures, see David Abulafia, "Mediterranean History as Global History," *History and Theory* 50 (2011): 220–8 (at 223–7).
15. *La Fille du comte de Pontieu*, ed. Brunel, 254–64; see Kinoshita, *Medieval Boundaries*, 181.
16. *Le Charroi de Nîmes*, ed. and trans. Lachet. In English as "The Convoy to Nimes" in *An Old French Trilogy: Texts from the William of Orange Cycle*, trans. Jones, Kibler, and Whalen. Giovanni Boccaccio, *Decameron*, ed. Branca; there are numerous translations into English available.
17. See note 12.
18. ".xx. pailes de Bonivent, / et.xx. mantiax vairs osterins, / et.xx. bliaus indes porprins."
19. ".vii. somiers . . . les.ii. cargiés d'or et d'argent . . . le tiers de moneés deniers . . . et les.ii. de ciers dras, des millors que tu troveras." See Kinoshita, *Medieval Boundaries*, pp. 89–90.
20. See Kinoshita, *Medieval Boundaries*, pp. 93–94, 258n.63. On the privileging of "routes" over "roots," see James Clifford, *Routes: Travel and Translation in the Late Twentieth Century* (Cambridge: Harvard University Press, 1997).
21. Peregrine Horden and Nicholas Purcell. *The Corrupting Sea: A Study of Mediterranean History* (Oxford: Wiley-Blackwell, 2000), p. 2.
22. *Floriant et Florete*, ed. and trans. Trachsler and Combes.
23. On *Cligés* as a Mediterranean romance, see Megan Moore, *Exchanges in Exoticism: Cross-Cultural Marriage and the Making of the Mediterranean in Old French Romance* (Toronto: Toronto University Press, 2014).
24. "Ne plus que s'il fust a Cesaire / Ou a Tolete ou a Quandie." Chrétien de Troyes, *Cligés*, ed. Méla and Collet, ll. 4682–3.
25. Sharon Kinoshita, "Chrétien de Troyes's *Cligés* in the Medieval Mediterranean," *Arthuriana* 18.3 (2008): 48–61.
26. Rudolf von Ems, *Der guote Gêrhart*, ed. J. A. Asher. The following reading comes from William Crooke, "Der guote Gêrhart: The Power of Mobility in the Medieval Mediterranean." *postmedieval* 4 (2013): 163–76.
27. *Der anglonormannische Boeve de Haumtone*, ed. A. Stimming. In English, *"Boeve de Haumtone" and "Gui de Warewic": Two Anglo-Norman romances*, trans. Weiss. The following reading comes from Heather Blurton, "Jeo ai esté a Nubie": *Boeve de Haumtone* in the Medieval Mediterranean," *Neophilologus* 103 (2019): 465–77.
28. Blurton, "Jeo ai esté a Nubie," 465 n.1.
29. Patricia E. Grieve, *Floire and Blancheflor and the European Romance* (Cambridge: Cambridge University Press, 1997). For the wide transmission history of a later text with Mediterranean connections, see Lydia Zeldenrust, *The Mélusine Romance in Medieval Europe: Translation, Circulation, and Material Contexts*, Studies in Medieval Romance (Woodbridge: D. S. Brewer, 2020).
30. *Four Byzantine Novels*, trans. Elizabeth Jeffreys.
31. Elizabeth Jeffreys, "Introduction," *Four Byzantine Novels*, p. ix n.1.
32. B. P. Reardon, "General Introduction," in *Collected Ancient Greek Novels*, ed. B. P. Reardon (Berkeley: University of California Press, 1989), p. 2.

33. M. M. Bakhtin, "Time and Chronotope in the Novel," in *The Dialogic Imagination. Four Essays*, ed. Michael Holquist, trans. Caryl Emerson and Michael Holquist (Austin, Tex.: University of Texas Press, 1981), pp. 87–8. This comes from Bakhtin's extensive composite description of the "adventure novel of ordeal." Many of the features identified with the Hellenistic romance also appear in a subgenre of medieval romance termed the *roman idyllique*; see Myrrha Lot-Borodine, *Le Roman idyllique au Moyen Âge* (Paris: Auguste Picard, 1913).
34. Cynthia Robinson, *Medieval Andalusian Courtly Culture in the Mediterranean: Hadīth Bayād Wa Riyād* (New York: Routledge, 2007). See David Wacks, Chapter 11 (this volume).
35. Nile Green, "Introduction: The Frontiers of the Persianate World (c. 800–1900)," in *The Persianate World: The Frontiers of a Eurasian Lingua Franca*, ed. Nile Green (Berkeley: University of California Press, 2019), pp. 1–71 (at 1).
36. Fakhraddin Gorgānī, *Vis and Ramin*, trans. Davies; Nezami Ganjavi, *Layli and Majnun*, trans. Davies; Nizami, *Haft Paykar: A Medieval Persian Romance*, trans. Meisami.

Suggestions for Further Reading

Bakhtin, Mikhail M. "Time and Chronotope in the Novel," in *The Dialogic Imagination. Four Essays*, ed. Michael Holquist, trans. Caryl Emerson and Michael Holquist (Austin, Tex.: University of Texas Press, 1981).

Blurton, Heather. "Jeo ai esté a Nubie": *Boeve de Haumtone* in the Medieval Mediterranean," *Neophilologus* 103 (2019): 465–77.

Catlos, Brian A. and Sharon Kinoshita (eds.), *Can We Talk Mediterranean? Conversations on an Emerging Field in Medieval and Early Modern Studies*. New York: Palgrave Macmillan, 2017.

Crooke, William. "Der guote Gêrhart: The Power of Mobility in the Medieval Mediterranean." *postmedieval* 4 (2013): 163–76.

Kinoshita, Sharon. "Chrétien de Troyes's *Cligés* in the Medieval Mediterranean." *Arthuriana* 18.3 (2008): 48–61.

"Medieval Mediterranean Literature." *PMLA* 124:2 (2009): 600–8.

Lot-Borodine, Myrrha. *Le Roman idyllique au Moyen Âge*. Paris: Auguste Picard, 1913.

Manion, Lee. *Narrating the Crusades: Loss and Recovery in Medieval and Early Modern English Literature*. Cambridge Studies in Medieval Literature. Cambridge: Cambridge University Press, 2014.

7

LEE MANION

The Crusading Romance in Britain
Religious Violence and the Transformation of Popular Chivalric Narratives

Most premodern Europeans considered violence and war to be necessary aspects of existence. But until the eleventh century the majority of Catholics believed that the acts of fighting and killing themselves were sinful, so even combatants in a just cause required confession and penance to atone. However, that view changed through the development and spread of crusading practices in Europe from the eleventh century until their formal end in the seventeenth century.[1] In popular culture today, "the Crusades" often appear to be a unified (and embarrassing) historical phenomenon limited to the Middle Ages, imagined as armies of Christian knights marching to Jerusalem to fight against the forces of Islam. Yet in reality crusading was never unified; it was comprised of a loose set of devotional practices that changed over time, some of which fell outside or openly opposed ecclesiastical authority. Crusading practices could include large military campaigns to the Holy Land, but they also consisted of individual armed pilgrimages, seasonal raids against pagans, persecutions of Jewish people, popular "peasant" revolts, and wars against other European Christians who were deemed heretical. Other, less directly violent crusading practices include monetary contributions, women's memorializations of family crusading traditions, special masses and sermons, economic blockades, and short-term leagues among a few powers. To better understand the history and influence of European religious violence, then, we need to acknowledge its variable forms as well as its surprising longevity.

The most radical component of crusading practices was the notion that fighting itself could be spiritually meritorious. In other words, combat was so dangerous that it was thought to substitute for other kinds of penance or, as the idea evolved in the minds of the laity, it could even earn someone eternal salvation. Not everyone agreed with this sacralization of violence, but it marked a major shift in Christian thought that had a broad impact on culture and literature.[2] Crusading affected far more than warfare, causing alterations or innovations in the liturgy, preaching, taxation, trade, laws, family networks, visual art, propaganda, affective display, and medieval social orders while unleashing terrible violence on Jews, Muslims, pagans, and other people deemed heretical. Crusading eventually produced its own ecclesiastical ritual for "taking the cross" and developed a set of legal privileges, but despite the considerable reach of church authority it remained adaptable and subject to popular contestation, such that it also could serve as a tool of resistance against the aims of the elite.

For all its virulence and bigotry, crusading and crusading literature never established *consistent* religious or racial discrimination. Ethnic and religious terminology, though invariably biased in favor of European Christians, possessed a shifting range of meanings. Additionally, while crusaders committed many atrocities, they occurred mainly during instances of initial conquest and were not unusual in the period: outside of crusading conflicts, brutal massacres and enslavement were common among premodern Christians, Muslims, and other groups. Apart from such times, people of different faiths and backgrounds could and did live alongside one another for periods of relative peace; in some areas, Muslims, Jews, and Christians even served alongside one another in armies or garrisons. This coexistence, however, was not driven by increasing open-mindedness. Peaceful interdependence generally resulted from economic necessity, as when one minority group filled a crucial economic role, or from the solidarities of the aristocratic elite, whose wealthy status transcended religious difference and united them as distinct from commoners.[3] Such coexistence would eventually disappear in much of Western Europe in the early modern period when racial and religious ideologies hardened.[4]

People from the British Isles participated directly in crusading activity until the sixteenth century, beginning with their involvement in the large military campaigns known today as the First Crusade (1096–1102), Second Crusade (1147–9), and Third Crusade (1189–92), extending to the smaller group participation and financial support for later campaigns and the crusading leagues in the fourteenth and fifteenth centuries, and ending with a few participants in the crusading military orders in the 1560s.[5] This decline was caused not by disenchantment with religious violence but by the Protestant Reformation, which rejected papal authority and made cooperation with Catholic powers difficult. However, even after the Reformation resulted in Elizabeth I of England (ruled 1558–1603) becoming the target of crusade campaigns in Ireland in 1578 and 1579 and in England with the Spanish Armada in 1588–9, crusading still offered Renaissance Europeans a vocabulary and image of Christian cooperation that could be used to transcend confessional divisions. Many Protestants in Britain, including Elizabeth's successor, James VI and I of Scotland and England (ruled 1567–1625, 1603–25), found crusade rhetoric's emphasis on Christian unity appealing and adopted a more conciliatory attitude toward war against non-Christians.[6]

Above all, though, crusading's lasting impact on the British Isles and on Europe came through its salvific narrative that reached across social levels. That is, crusading offered medieval and early modern Christians a readily understandable *story* of loss and recovery, wherein the attempt to recover lands "lost" to Christianity or to convert people "lost" to a different faith correlated with the individual's effort to recover a spiritual purity "lost" to sin. It mattered little that this story elided hundreds of years of history: Jerusalem, for instance, had been under Muslim control since the Arab conquest in 638 from the Byzantine Empire. Nonetheless, it was only after the Seljuk Turks captured Jerusalem as one of their many conquests in the mid-eleventh century that the Byzantines appealed to the Western Church for aid and that Pope Urban II (reigned 1088–99) launched the preaching campaigns that would result in the First Crusade. Still, the call only received such a powerful response because it linked the fate of holy sites such as Jerusalem and the plight of Eastern Christians to the personal sanctification of the individual crusader, who could perform penance for sin without giving up his warrior status. This coordination of different forms of loss and recovery was a key part of what I have called crusading's narrative-generating power, something that enabled it to shape and reconfigure individual and collective action across places as disparate as the Eastern Mediterranean, Iberia, and North Africa to later European colonization in the Americas and in India.[7]

With such a wide reach and duration, it is unsurprising that crusading impacted several European literary genres, with some of the most prominent being the *chanson de geste* or epic, the chronicle, the love lyric, and the romance. In general, crusading literature tended to flatten the complexity of real-life relations among different peoples or distort them for its own purposes. Several popular chivalric romances adopted aspects of crusade discourse, especially its narrative pattern of loss and recovery, which resulted, in effect, in a subgenre that we might label the crusading romance. Common features of this genre include a proliferation of "Saracen" opponents – a generally derogatory name for Muslims or other non-Christians that was primarily a religious marker but that could conflate religion with race – as well as an increased focus on pilgrimage, personal reform or penance, religious conversion or vengeance, and political claims to holy places or relics.[8]

This chapter employs two popular Middle English romances, *Richard Coeur de Lion* (c. 1300) and *Guy of Warwick* (c. 1330), to illustrate the ways crusading affected and was affected by literary narratives. These poems possess several similarities: both are anonymous and exist in multiple versions; both draw from Anglo-Norman sources or material; both relate the story of powerful warriors who fight against enemies of the faith; both were widely read and later printed until at least the sixteenth century; and both were sometimes taken as "historical" texts. The last point is striking because while *Richard Coeur de Lion* is based on a real person, Richard I of England (ruled 1189–99), who did undertake a military campaign to the Holy Land known today as the Third Crusade, Guy of Warwick is a fictional character whose legend began in the thirteenth century, yet his tale influenced how the real history of Warwick was shaped, with the historical earls quickly claiming him as their ancestor.

Richard Coeur de Lion and *Guy of Warwick* differ, however, in how they present crusading. While Richard is portrayed as superhumanly strong, most of the narrative is about his leadership of a formal army of crusaders who have received papal indulgences (i.e., remissions of the penance assigned for confessed sins) to fight against non-Christian forces in the Holy Land in their attempt to recapture the cities of Acre and Jerusalem, which had been held by Western Christians since 1104 and 1099, respectively, and lost in 1187. Guy, by contrast, starts his career in tournaments and fights large armies of Christians and Muslims for the love of his lady, Felice, but later reflects on his sins and leaves her. Traveling alone, Guy goes to the East as a crusading pilgrim until he returns to save England from an African Saracen giant in single combat and later dies a saintly death, ascending directly to heaven. The two poems thus represent different kinds of crusading practices: the large army sponsored by ecclesiastical authorities, and the individual undertaking a personal vow without church involvement.

Furthermore, each romance offers critical commentary on crusading itself. In this respect they are part of intensified attention that crusading received after the final loss of Acre, the last Christian mainland stronghold in the Holy Land, in 1291. *Richard Coeur de Lion* echoes contemporary crusade discourse by highlighting Christian disunity as the main reason for crusading's military failures, but it articulates its own imagined solution of selecting a single leader and pursuing an aggressive policy of conquest and forced conversion. *Guy of Warwick*, by comparison, challenges the individual pursuit of love and fame over devotion to God, focusing on crusading's call to personal reform as part of broader expressions of lay piety, especially in relation to what Richard Kaeuper has labeled a "chivalric religious ideology."[9]

In what follows, I treat each romance in turn, offering a brief overview of its manuscript and print history before discussing its contributions to crusade discourse. But these texts are just two examples of the crusading romance's significant scope. Even if we consider only romances written in English that employ key aspects of crusade discourse, we are confronted with a wide-ranging group that includes some of the most popular romances of the period: *Richard Coeur de Lion* (c. 1300), *Sir Isumbras* (c. 1330), *Guy of Warwick* (c. 1330), *Octavian* (Southern version) (c. 1375), *The Siege of Jerusalem* (c. 1370–90), *Sir Gowther* (c. 1400), *The Sege of Melayne* (c. 1400), *Titus and Vespasian* (c. 1400), *The Sowdone of Babylone* (c. 1400), *Capystranus* (c. 1475), William Caxton's *Godeffroy of Boloyne* (1481) and *Charles the Grete* (1485), Lord Berners' *Huon of Bordeaux* (c. 1515), and Richard Johnson's *The Seven Champions of Christendom* (1596–7).[10] Judging by manuscript and print evidence, many of these texts had a substantial, lasting influence; *Sir Isumbras*, for example, survives in nine manuscripts and three printed editions, while Johnson's highly successful *Seven Champions* went through twenty-five editions between 1596 and 1700. For the sake of comparison, the chivalric romance most frequently taught to undergraduates today, the late-fourteenth-century *Sir Gawain and the Green Knight*, survives in only one manuscript and seems to have had little influence in the premodern period.

Importantly, then, these crusading romances and others like them situate the British Isles as part of a larger premodern world engaged in religious conflict and exchange. By recognizing the long relationship between the romance and holy warfare – one that lasted well into the early modern period, when crusading romances were grouped into a larger set of "heroic" narratives that included epics, drama, and other forms – we can better understand the interests of medieval and Renaissance audiences, as well as the foundational role of religious intolerance in modernity.[11]

Richard Coeur de Lion and Crusading Fellowship

The historical Third Crusade (1189–92) was prompted by the conquest of nearly all of the Christian Kingdom of Jerusalem in 1187 by the Sultan Salāh al-Dīn Yūsuf ibn Ayyūb (ruled 1174–93), known to Europeans as Saladin. In its reimagining of this event, *Richard Coeur de Lion*'s narrative sweep approaches the global, broadening the scope of the conflict to include groups stretching from the British Isles to Persia and India, while at the same time narrowing the focus to the exploits of its hero, Richard. In one sense, the romance reflects the influence of the *chanson de geste* and its tendency to portray religious conflict as a universal struggle between what the poem calls

"Christendom" and "Heathenness."[12] In another sense, though, *Richard Coeur de Lion* complicates that binary framework by gesturing toward the ethnic and religious diversity of the premodern world, as the romance is populated with various European Catholics, Orthodox Greeks, "renegade" Eastern Christians who have converted to Islam, and Muslims, as well as translators who enable all these groups to communicate. Only recently, however, has the poem begun to receive sustained critical attention that explores the significance of these contradictions, of its popularity and textual history, and of its engagement with contemporary crusade discourse.

In actuality, *Richard Coeur de Lion* is not one poem but several. It survives in seven manuscripts and one fragment from the fourteenth and fifteenth centuries, none of which is the direct source for any other, and in two early printings in 1509 and in 1528, with a possible additional printing, now lost, c. 1568. Though there is no extant source for the romance, it likely utilized an earlier, Anglo-Norman chronicle such as Ambroise's *L'Estoire de la Guerre Sainte* (*The History of the Holy War*) (c. 1194–9). In its different manuscript contexts, the poem can be found with historical items such as chronicles of Britain, sometimes being viewed as a supplement to them, as well as with other romances (in one case including *Guy of Warwick*), several of which feature crusading-type warriors. This mixed context helps to illustrate how the crusading romance does not simply derive from history, but instead fabricates collective memories and narratives that can respond to ongoing concerns or can be intended to inspire action.[13] Overall, though, the poem's high number of surviving witnesses is a measure of its long-lasting influence. Its relative obscurity today reminds us that our view of what literature mattered to the premodern world often is shaped by modern preferences.

Such preferences also affect the version we read. Five of *Richard Coeur de Lion*'s manuscripts present a shorter version that offers a romanticized history of the Third Crusade, while the other two add sensational episodes, such as the change of Richard's historical mother, the powerful Eleanor of Aquitaine (1122–1204), to a demon from the East who cannot witness the consecration of the host, Richard's eating a raw lion's heart (with salt) to earn his historical epithet, and two cannibalism scenes where Richard eats Saracen flesh in lieu of pork, dehumanizing and consuming his religious enemies.[14] These fantastical episodes have attracted a good deal of attention from scholars, who have discussed them in terms of medieval nationalism, premodern racial formations, masculinity, the borders between human and nonhuman animals, and emotions. Yet the earliest surviving version of the poem, found in the Auchinleck manuscript (c. 1330), contains none of these lurid details, and other manuscripts present Richard as being healed by God rather than by eating human flesh, raising questions about which text premodern audiences would have experienced and what they would have seen as its major interests.

In the modern era, it is notable that only the longer, fantastical version has been available in an edition for study. That trend continues in Peter Larkin's recent critical edition of the Middle English text as well as in Katherine Terrell's valuable modern English translation, which is the one cited here.[15] New readers of Terrell's translation should consider how the poem unfolds differently if they skip these grotesque sections; what is left may appear as a story more like *The Song of Roland*. The digital *Richard Coer de Lyon Multitext* project, currently in progress and codirected by Leila K. Norako and Bridget Whearty, seeks to remedy this situation by presenting editions of each of the surviving versions and will be a crucial resource for new explorations of the romance.[16] Such comparisons allow us to see, for example, how the mid-fifteenth-century British Library Additional 31042 manuscript counterintuitively contains a longer version of Richard's case for the crusade to his gathered nobles, clerics, and people that explains the papal indulgence, offers a mini-sermon on the transitory nature of this life ("Lords, consider in your mind / That this world's happiness lasts but a little while"), and calls the Holy Land "our rightful inheritance," all of which echo common historical elements of crusade discourse.[17] Comparative study would also give greater prominence to the four manuscripts that depict Eleanor of Aquitaine bringing Richard's real bride, Berengaria of Navarre (c. 1165–1230), to marry him while on crusade, thus highlighting the politics of the Angevin empire and of Richard's conquest of Greek-controlled Cyprus.[18]

Despite their differences, several common themes emerge across all versions of *Richard Coeur de Lion*. These themes address issues that occupied medieval Europeans almost from crusading's beginnings but that took on heightened significance after Acre's loss in 1291. A sizable body of writing began to coalesce just before this loss and continued to grow through the early fourteenth century – around the same time that *Richard Coeur de Lion* first was being composed. It was comprised of papal bulls, diplomatic letters, church decrees, preaching manuals, sermons, chronicles, and independent "recovery" treatises offering detailed crusading plans.[19] These crusade texts attempted to resolve critical problems that were seen as preventing successful campaigns, including questions of leadership, the stability of Christian alliances, violations of crusader protections, policies of conquest, and the threat of conversion to Islam.

Richard Coeur de Lion engages with these questions and offers its own imagined solutions through its narrative and the hyperbolic character of Richard himself. The romance repeatedly presents the destructive consequences of intra-Christian conflict in order to emphasize the benefits of crusading against nonbelievers. Traitorous, conniving Christian rulers are shown to learn the error of their ways through defeat and subsequent recompense to the crusading effort. By contrast, when united in a common purpose, the poem's Christian forces triumph over their opponents with divine support, resulting in ahistorical conquests of places such as Ninevah and Cairo. At the same time, any suggestion of coexistence with Muslims is viciously rejected. Richard adopts a ruthless policy of conquest that offers the choice of conversion or death for any captured Saracens. By comparison, offers of conversion to Islam serve to highlight the committed faith of the hero, who bluntly rebuffs them, as well as to explain the loss of the Holy Land, which, according to the poem, only occurred because of Christian converts to Islam.

As is evident, the romance's solutions are far from subtle or humane. They also are far from the typical reality of crusaders' negotiations with defeated populations, and far from the historical appeal of conversion to Islam for many poor, captured, or enslaved Christians throughout the premodern period – an appeal that, for the most part, was not reciprocal. However, in relation to contemporary crusade discourse, the poem's answers are not as extreme as one might imagine.[20] Several authors believed that European conversion to Islam or the forced conversion of Orthodox Greeks were major problems. For instance, in his 1290 recovery treatise, the Franciscan friar Fidenzio of Padua attributed this conversion to stereotypical representations of Eastern luxury, writing that it is an "exceedingly great evil" that "many Christians . . . who go across the sea go to the Saracens and, enticed by riches and carnal pleasure, become Saracens . . . and afterwards they fight armed against Christians."[21] In his treatise *How to Defeat the Saracens* (c. 1317), the Dominican missionary William of Adam blamed treacherous European Catholics for supplying Muslims with goods and slaves, suggesting that they had converted to become "Saracens," but also identified the forced conversion of Orthodox Greeks to Islam as a major problem, since the converts "forget all faith and Christianity and, more than those who were born Saracens, they persecute us, their brothers . . . even more sharply."[22] Such views parallel the treatment of Greeks in *Richard Coeur de Lion*, who are described disparagingly throughout as "Gryphons" (l. 1669) and are depicted as being of questionable loyalty. They also are analogous to the poem's representations of converts to Islam, who either are blamed for the loss of the Holy Land or are convinced of their error and restored to Christianity, as in the episode featuring an unnamed "apostate" (l. 4215) who "had been Christian in his youth" (l. 4077), attempts to destroy the crusaders through treachery, is caught, and re-converts.

In the romance, as with most crusade texts and medieval culture in general, notions of racial difference are largely unstable, being subsumed under or conflated with religious identities. This process is apparent in the poem's representations of the invented category of "Saracens." *Richard Coeur de Lion* contains hints of racializing discourse about Saracens' "dark" (l. 3211) complexion, marking their difference from and inferiority to the crusaders, but these occur only in the fantastical version when Richard is eating them. However, this brief mention of physical appearance is undercut by the poem's subsequent stress on the fluidity of its categories. Not only can Europeans become Saracens, as when Richard states that Conrad of Montferrat, a historical Italian nobleman, "has renounced his religion / And has become a Saracen" (ll. 3260–1), but Saracens can become Christians, as with the fantasy of mass conversion after the crusaders conquer Cairo, where "More than forty thousand / Were christened" (ll. 5881–2) and "had their idols destroyed" (l. 5884). Contradictions of this sort are inevitable because crusade discourse, like European Christianity in general, was split between the universalist desire to convert all nonbelievers and the need to assert Europeans' superiority to their enemies. Such ambivalences continue in the voluminous Renaissance humanist writings on the Ottoman Turks, which produced a racializing discourse that cast the Turks as uncultured barbarians while admiring their military achievements and often hoping for their conversion.[23]

Richard Coeur de Lion's imagined solutions to crusading's problems, while far-fetched, are built into the poem's larger narrative pattern of loss and recovery and serve to reinforce its thematic emphasis on crusading alliances and the need for a single, skilled leader. As a vernacular text, the romance relates a simplified history of the loss of the Holy Land and relics in an accessible manner. The romance's answer to this loss of Christian property is the launching of a crusade, but that expedition depends upon alliances made through mutual agreements to function. Richard and Philip II of France (ruled 1180–1223), for example, meet to become "sworn brothers" (l. 1674), reflecting a pact to participate in what is a temporary, collective enterprise. Moreover, when the ideal crusading army is assembled in the Holy Land, it is presented not as a series of national forces but as a "Christian fellowship" (l. 3161) comprised of fighters from a variety of regions. The poem celebrates Richard's multiregional leadership by listing England, France, Gascony, Provence, Apulia, Lombardy, Genoa, Sicily, Tuscany, Austria, and Germany, as well as the military orders of the Templars and Hospitallers (ll. 4977–86), as part of "the fairest host of gracious / Christian knights to the world's end" (ll. 4987–8). Richard's leadership of this fellowship is not decided from the start but results from his demonstrated skills and policies. In this respect, the poem responds to concerns in crusade discourse about the need for a single crusade leader to enable unified action.

Because it is based on actual events, *Richard Coeur de Lion* occupies a middle ground between history and fantasy. Readers must reconcile reconstructions of real people with entirely fictional ones, and must negotiate depictions of historical religious and cultural difference with misrepresentations of Muslims, all while being solicited to applaud the victories of a fellowship of "*Our* Christian men" (l. 4040, emphasis added). However, despite its propagandistic and chauvinistic attitudes, the poem remains riven with contradictions that provide a glimpse into the complexities of the premodern world as well as the role of the romance – especially the crusading romance – within it.

Guy of Warwick and Knightly Reform

Readers today are more likely to know Richard the Lionheart than Guy of Warwick, but adaptations of *Guy of Warwick* maintained lasting influence until the beginning of the twentieth century and beyond.[24] Unlike *Richard Coeur de Lion*, *Guy of Warwick* is not based on real events, nor does it describe a crusade army's campaign. Instead, it represents an alternative type of crusading romance, one that focuses on loss and recovery in relation to what I have called "individual crusading," and that deals mainly with the topics of knightly reform and penance through a different concept of conversion.[25] *Guy of Warwick* thus can be compared to other Middle English crusading romances such as *Sir Isumbras* (c. 1330) and *Sir Gowther* (c. 1400) that also feature solitary protagonists and that implicitly criticize the failures of crusade leaders by advocating personal action.

Technically, the story of Guy of Warwick is set in the reign of the historical King Athelstan (ruled 925–39), but this setting only is identified halfway through the tale, and its values are those of a post-Conquest, Norman knighthood. Excluding the ending portion that relates the exploits of Guy's son, the narrative can be divided into two main parts: first, Guy's adventures to become the best knight in the world in order to win the love of his lady, and second, his penitential pilgrimage fighting as a solitary Christian knight that ends with his pious death as a hermit. The tale begins with Guy, the son of the steward of the Earl of Warwick, falling in love with Felice, the earl's daughter. She refuses to accept him until he proves himself worthy, so he departs for the Continent, winning tournaments, fighting in wars among Christians, and eventually defending the emperor of Constantinople from an invading sultan. After returning to England, Guy presents himself to Athelstan before marrying Felice. They conceive a son, but Guy, looking at the heavens and reflecting on his sins, leaves her after two weeks to go on a penitential pilgrimage to the East. He defeats the Sultan of Egypt's giant, Amoraunt, in single combat, earning free passage for all Christians to the Holy Land, and, after some further adventures, Guy goes back to England and helps Athelstan to fend off a Danish invasion by killing their champion, the African Saracen giant Colbrond. He then visits Felice unrecognized before retiring to a hermitage in the forest, only sending for her as he is dying. A miraculous odor from his corpse marks his holy status, and eventually he is buried with Felice in Lorraine.

This brief summary illustrates how, as Velma Richmond puts it, "[t]ension between temporal and eternal is the heart of Guy's legend."[26] The original tale is the early-thirteenth-century Anglo-Norman romance *Gui de Warewic*, which blends elements from *chansons de geste*, other romances (especially the anonymous *Le Roman de Waldef* and Chrétien de Troyes's *Yvain*), hagiography, and folklore. *Gui de Warewic* survives in two versions across sixteen manuscripts with diverse contexts, with some incorporating Guy into collections about the history of Britain, some more focused on local history, and others placing him among various pious works or tales of holy warfare. The Middle English *Guy of Warwick* derives from the Anglo-Norman poem and exists in at least five different redactions. In its manuscript contexts it is sometimes paired with collections of romances, saints' lives, and didactic works. This romance was familiar to Geoffrey Chaucer, who imitated its phrasings and style for his *Tale of Sir Thopas* in *The Canterbury Tales* (c. 1386–1400), but there is another relatively well-known Middle English version surviving in seven manuscripts by the poet John Lydgate, who, drawing on chronicle sources, wrote *Guy of Warwyk* (c. 1420) in support of the family holding the earldom.

In the early modern period, Guy's story continued to flourish. A version of the Middle English romance was printed c. 1497, c. 1499, c. 1553, and c. 1565. Edmund Spenser drew on the story for the second book of his epic romance *The Faerie Queene* (1590/96) in the tale of Guyon, the Knight of Temperance. Samuel Rowlands adapted the story in 1609 as *The Famous History of Guy, Earl of Warwick*, which itself served as the basis for later adaptations in the seventeenth and eighteenth centuries, while John Lane created his own version in 1621 with *The Corrected Historie of Sir Guy, Earl of Warwick*. Guy also made appearances in other poems, as in Richard Lloyd's 1584 work on the Nine Worthies that replaces Godfrey of Bouillon, the crusader and first Christian ruler of the Kingdom of Jerusalem, with Guy himself. Lloyd's portrayal of Guy was the basis for an anonymous broadside ballad in 1592 that was frequently reprinted for about two centuries. Additionally, Guy was portrayed on stage in *The Tragical*

Figure 7.1 *Guy of Warwick*: Descents of the houses of Warwick and Essex, showing Guy standing over a defeated Colbrond with Felice and Reinbroun. Pierpont Morgan Library MS M.956 fol. 001v. The Morgan Library and Museum, New York.

History of Guy of Warwick (published 1661, composed c. 1593–4), which stresses his role as a crusader.

It may seem that Guy's story was meant to create an ancestral or national hero because of his connection to Warwick and his defense of England, but despite some later uses of the tale, there are problems with this assumption. One issue is that most of *Guy of Warwick* takes place outside of England, with the hero not even being buried there, so the focus of the narrative is on continental Europe and the East. Even Guy's celebrated defeat of Colbrond is not really about protecting the English "nation" but about upholding Athelstan's independence from Danish lordship. Another complication is that the Middle English versions, which one would expect to increase the emphasis on English identity, generally do not do so, but instead simply translate the Anglo-Norman romance's phrasings.[27] Moreover, the Middle English versions do not constitute one continuous poem but several discrete compositions.

What these romances present instead, as Ivana Djordjević explains, is the "frequent superficiality of Guy's attachment to England" and his "multiple and complex loyalties."[28] More recent scholarship thus has turned to crusading to understand the tale's interests. For instance, Rebecca Wilcox finds that *Guy of Warwick* engages with crusade history, particularly the Fourth Crusade's (1202–4) questionable capture of Orthodox Christian Constantinople, noting how "the hero's domination of Eastern empires, both Christian and Saracen" enables him to "re-evaluate his purpose as a knight" and "dedicate his life entirely to God."[29] Additionally, Leila K. Norako describes *Guy of Warwick* as comparable to *Sir Isumbras*, with the romances "contain[ing] episodes that reflect aspirations of recovery" and "confront[ing] contemporary fears and anxieties" related to crusading.[30]

Such approaches allow us to see how the story presents knightly reform through the practice of individual crusading. Certain episodes, such as its treatment of the Greeks and Saracens at Constantinople, Guy's disguise as a Saracen, and his conversion to the life of a crusading pilgrim, reveal the text's engagement with crusade discourse and its connections to "chivalric religious ideology."[31] Throughout this period, historical knights went on individual crusading journeys for a variety of reasons. For many, Guy's story could serve as a model for how one might transform a life of killing into something holy without clerical involvement by "recovering" a state free from sin.

Guy's early adventures to become the best knight involve intra-Christian conflict. But after Guy helps to make peace among warring Christians, he resolves to assist the emperor in Constantinople, who is besieged by a Saracen sultan. This episode marks the story's first use of the term "Saracen" (l. 2904), here meaning the traditional mischaracterization of Muslims as polytheistic idolaters, and its first clear engagement with crusade discourse.[32] Though not formally taking the cross or participating in a papally endorsed campaign, Guy is motivated in part by religious conflict, stating that the Saracens "have greatly destroyed Christendom" (l. 2854). Additionally, the story is notably positive in its portrayal of Orthodox Greeks. While initially labeling them "Griffins" (l. 3028), the derogatory name also found in *Richard Coeur de Lion*, it presents them as "good" (l. 3028) and "doughty" (l. 3602), eventually just calling them "Greeks" (ll. 3546, 3601). In this manner, *Guy of Warwick* differs from much crusade discourse that emphasized Greek treachery or that imagined the conquest of the Byzantine Empire as necessary for successful crusade campaigns.

By contrast, throughout this episode the romance portrays Saracens negatively, with a narratorial comment "May he have Christ's curse!" (l. 3882) about the sultan, and with Guy echoing this curse on the sultan and all the "misbelieving men" (l. 3898) with him before beheading him. When the sultan's forces are completely defeated, his head is put on a special pillar in Constantinople as a warning to enemies, thus characterizing Saracens as threatening, evil, and largely irredeemable.

Whereas Saracens were cursed religious opponents in Guy's defense of Constantinople but were not marked by physical difference, a later episode of racial impersonation reveals *Guy of Warwick*'s inconsistent sense of identity categories. In what today one would call an instance of blackface or Arabface, Guy adopts a disguise in order to enter Pavia in northern Italy to rescue his friend from a Christian duke. Guy purchases an "ointment" (l. 6105) that "made his coloring less fair: / His hair, that was yellow and bright, / Became black immediately" (ll. 6106–8), and when Guy presents himself to the duke, he claims that he is from a "distant land" (l. 6117), that his "kinsman" (l. 6122) is a "Saracen" (l. 6121), and that his name is "Yon" (l. 6178). Impersonating a Saracen, especially through a change in skin and hair color, is relatively rare in other romances, but significantly there is no indication in the text of discrimination against this identity apart from Guy's willingness to mimic it, since the duke easily accepts "Yon" into his service and trusts him. For this episode, Saracens and Christians are identifiably different but interact peaceably.

Guy's construction of the Saracen "Yon" is striking because in another version of the poem Guy will use this name again after he undertakes his penitential pilgrimage to the Holy Land. When preparing to fight the Sultan of Egypt's Saracen giant, Amoraunt, who is described as "huge," "ugly" (l. 737), and "As black ... as burnt nails" (l. 742), making him seem a "fiend ... out of hell" (l. 743–4), Guy conceals his identity, saying he is Yon from "England" (l. 974), a Christian knight. In the case of Amoraunt, physical difference, specifically blackness, is associated with monstrous otherness, yet these disparaging racial markers do not seem to apply to other Saracens, such as the Sultan of Egypt himself. Overall, Saracens can occupy a variety of roles in the story's world, sometimes being marked as different by skin color, sometimes being portrayed as monstrous and evil, and sometimes being accepted as valuable allies. Such complexities are evident in how, when fighting Amoraunt, Guy is helping one Saracen leader to defeat another's champion, and in so doing is earning the release of Christian prisoners as well as the free passage of all Christian pilgrims – two common crusading goals.

A final way that *Guy of Warwick* broadens our understanding of crusading romances is through Guy's conversion to the pious life of a crusading pilgrim. In crusade discourse, "conversion" had a dual meaning: it could refer to a change in religion, as it is commonly used today, but it also could describe a person's intensified commitment to a holier life, as when one took the cross to become a crusader.[33] Unlike *Richard Coeur de Lion*, *Guy of Warwick* is uninterested in converting non-Christians; instead, it emphasizes its hero's solitary reflection on his life and his desire to become a knight of God. After he seemingly has achieved everything a knight could want by marrying Felice and conceiving an heir, Guy goes to the castle tower and "beh[olds] the heavens / That stood thickly crowded with stars" (ll. 242–3). There he realizes that he "For the love of Jesus, our Savior, / Had never done any good deeds" (ll. 248–9) and "He had killed many men without just cause" (l. 250), so he resolves to go "Barefoot to [his] life's end / To atone for [his] sins" (ll. 305–6) in "pilgrimage" (l. 426). Felice is unable to convince Guy to stay with her or to engage in more traditional acts of aristocratic penance, such as the founding of churches, so Guy goes to the East "To seek out more shrines / In order to receive the rewards of heaven" (ll. 527–8). This combination of penance and a personal vow made outside of the ecclesiastical system reveals how lay piety could alter or resist clerical discourse about crusading and chivalry by adapting existing notions of conversion.

Through its episodic progression from Christian infighting to religious war to Guy's single combat with religious opponents and his sanctified death as a hermit, *Guy of Warwick* constructs its own crusading ideology that stresses individual salvation and knightly reform over assembling armies to recover holy places. Despite its fictional status, the story's real impact on the history of Warwick and the premodern literary tradition shows how crusading romances affected, not just reflected, cultural developments through their influential narratives.

Conclusion

Crusading maintained its prominence well into the beginnings of the modern world because it offered a broader vision of Christian unity with multiple methods for an individual to achieve redemption. The popular chivalric romance contributed to this longevity by presenting and reimagining the forms crusading could assume. *Richard Coeur de Lion* and *Guy of Warwick* are two crusading romances that survived in a wide array of manuscript and print contexts, attesting to the genre's adaptability, the appeal of its loss and recovery narrative, and its links with major cultural threads in the medieval and early modern periods. However, they represent only a fraction of the literary output in English and in other languages that took ideas of holy war or sanctifying pilgrimage seriously. Since crusading romances generally have been understudied, they offer several avenues for further exploration on topics such as collective memory, premodern biases against religious or racial difference, and the capacity of the romance to question or reinforce cultural norms. Studying such texts painfully reminds us of the power of narrative in shaping and sustaining religious violence.

Notes

1. Jonathan Riley-Smith, *The Crusades: A History*, 3rd ed. (New York: Bloomsbury, 2014), pp. 13–20.
2. James Turner Johnson, *The Holy War Idea in Western and Islamic Traditions* (University Park, PA: Pennsylvania State University Press, 1997), esp. pp. 50–6 and 84–9.
3. See, for instance, *Medieval Iberia*, ed. Constable.
4. See Brian Catlos, *Muslims of Medieval Latin Christendom, c. 1050–1614* (Cambridge: Cambridge University Press, 2014), and David Nirenberg, *Neighboring Faiths: Christianity, Islam, and Judaism in the Middle Ages and Today* (Chicago: University of Chicago Press, 2014).
5. See Kathryn Hurlock, *Britain, Ireland and the Crusades, c. 1000–1300* (New York: Palgrave Macmillan, 2012), and Norman Housley, *The Later Crusades, 1274–1580: From Lyons to Alcazar* (Oxford: Oxford University Press, 1992).
6. See William Brown Patterson, *King James VI and I and the Reunion of Christendom* (Cambridge: Cambridge University Press, 1997), Benedict S. Robinson, *Islam and Early Modern English Literature: The Politics of Romance from Spenser to Milton* (New York: Palgrave Macmillan, 2007), pp. 77–8, and Lee Manion, "Renaissance Crusading Literature: Memory, Translation, and Adaptation," *The Cambridge Companion to the Literature of the Crusades*, ed. Anthony Bale (Cambridge: Cambridge University Press, 2019), pp. 232–47.
7. See Lee Manion, *Narrating the Crusades: Loss and Recovery in Medieval and Early Modern English Literature* (Cambridge: Cambridge University Press, 2014), p. 2, and John France, *The Crusades and the Expansion of Catholic Christendom, 1000–1714* (New York: Routledge, 2005).
8. On the term Saracen, see John V. Tolan, *Saracens: Islam in the Medieval European Imagination* (New York: Columbia University Press, 2002), pp. 126–34. On the features of the crusading romance, see Manion, *Narrating the Crusades*, pp. 8–9.
9. Richard W. Kaeuper, *Holy Warriors: The Religious Ideology of Chivalry* (Philadelphia: University of Pennsylvania Press, 2009), p. 51.
10. See Manion, *Narrating the Crusades*, pp. 13–14, and Siobhain Bly Calkin, "Crusades Romance," *The Encyclopedia of Medieval Literature in Britain*, ed. Siân Echard and Robert Allen Rouse, 4 vols. (Chichester: Wiley-Blackwell, 2017).
11. Lee Manion, "The Crusading Romance in Early Modern England: Converting the Past in Berners's Huon of Bordeaux and Johnson's Seven Champions of Christendom," *Journal of Medieval and Early Modern Studies* 48.3 (2018): 491–517.

12. *Richard Coeur de Lion*, ed. and trans. Terrell, line 3250. All citations are from this edition by line number.
13. See Lee Manion, "'Perpetuel Memorye': Remembering History in the Crusading Romance," *Remembering the Crusades and Crusading*, ed. Megan Cassidy-Welch (New York: Routledge, 2016), pp. 114–28.
14. This division is complicated by the fact that one of the more historical versions – London, British Library MS Egerton 2862 – contains one of the cannibalism scenes. In fact, the relationship among the various manuscript versions is more complex than a separation into two groups, as there is much cross-influence.
15. *Richard Coer de Lyon*, ed. Larkin, and *Richard Coeur de Lion*, ed. and trans. Terrell.
16. *The Richard Coer de Lyon Multitext* project, dir. Leila K. Norako and Bridget Whearty, in progress at http://therclm.ds.lib.uw.edu/.
17. For the original text from the Additional 31042 manuscript, see Maria Cristina Figueredo, "*Richard Coeur de Lion*: An Edition from the London Thornton Manuscript," Diss., 2 vols. University of York, 2009, vol. 2, ll. 1367–71 and 1385; my translation.
18. See *Richard Coer de Lyon*, ed. Larkin, p. 207, note to line 2040.
19. Antony Leopold, *How to Recover the Holy Land: The Crusade Proposals of the Late Thirteenth and Early Fourteenth Centuries* (Burlington, VT: Ashgate, 2000).
20. In addition to the discussion in Leopold, *How to Recover the Holy Land*, see also Sylvia Schein, *Fideles Crucis: The Papacy, the West, and the Recovery of the Holy Land 1274–1314* (Oxford: Clarendon Press, 1991), and Torsello Sanudo, *The Book of the Secrets of the Faithful of the Cross*, trans. Lock.
21. Fidenzio of Padua, *Liber recuperationis Terrae Sanctae*, in *Biblioteca bio-bibliografica della Terra Santa e dell'Oriente francescano*, ed. G. Golubovich, 5 vols. (Quaracchi, 1906-27), vol. 2, pp. 9–60, p. 13; my translation.
22. William of Adam, *How to Defeat the Saracens*, ed. and trans. Constable, pp. 33 and 83.
23. See Nancy Bisaha, *Creating East and West: Renaissance Humanists and the Ottoman Turks* (Philadelphia: University of Pennsylvania Press, 2004).
24. See Velma Bourgeois Richmond, *The Legend of Guy of Warwick* (New York: Garland Publishing, Inc., 1996).
25. Manion, *Narrating the Crusades*, pp. 67–106.
26. Richmond, *The Legend of Guy of Warwick*, p. 115.
27. The limited evidence of Englishness being emphasized occurs only in the Auchinleck manuscript, mostly in the fight with Colbrond; see Ivana Djordjević, "Nation and Translation: *Guy of Warwick* between Languages," *Nottingham Medieval Studies* 57 (2013): 111–44.
28. Ibid., p. 121.
29. Rebecca Wilcox, "Romancing the East: Greeks and Saracens in *Guy of Warwick*," *Pulp Fictions of Medieval England: Essays in Popular Romance*, ed. Nicola McDonald (Manchester: Manchester University Press, 2004), pp. 217–40, 218–19.
30. Leila K. Norako, "*Sir Isumbras* and the Fantasy of Crusade," *The Chaucer Review* 48.2 (2013): 166–89, p. 167.
31. Kaeuper, *Holy Warriors*, p. 51.

32. Line numbers refer to the Auchinleck versions found in *The Romance of Guy of Warwick*, ed. Zupitza (couplet version) and *Stanzaic Guy of Warwick*, ed. Wiggins (stanzaic version). All translations are mine.
33. Manion, "The Crusading Romance in Early Modern England," pp. 493–4.

Suggestions for Further Reading

Bale, Anthony (ed.). *The Cambridge Companion to the Literature of the Crusades*. Cambridge: Cambridge University Press, 2019.

Manion, Lee. *Narrating the Crusades: Loss and Recovery in Medieval and Early Modern English Literature*. Cambridge: Cambridge University Press, 2014.

Riley-Smith, Jonathan. *The Crusades: A History*, 3rd ed. New York: Bloomsbury, 2014.

Robinson, Benedict S. *Islam and Early Modern English Literature: The Politics of Romance from Spenser to Milton*. New York: Palgrave Macmillan, 2007.

Wiggins, Alison, and Rosalind Field (eds.). *Guy of Warwick: Icon and Ancestor*. Cambridge: D. S. Brewer, 2007.

Yeager, Suzanne, *Jerusalem in Medieval Narrative*, Cambridge, Cambridge University Press, 2008.

8

NAHIR I. OTAÑO GRACIA

"Making Race" in Medieval Romance

A Premodern Critical Race Studies Perspective

The genre of medieval romance, from the perspective of critical race studies (CRS), justifies medieval imperial expansion. While medieval romances frame themselves as celebrating the culture of elite knights and ladies, they do so by imagining their borders as perilous spaces inhabited by dangerous people who must be defeated and eliminated while the enemy territories are subsumed into the territories of the elite knight. From this viewpoint, the margins are central to the depiction of an idealized European chivalry because medieval romances use chivalry to define who is accepted within the boundaries and who is left out of that formation.[1] Although European courts transformed romance to fit their own ideologies of expansion, the phenomenon of exclusion and dehumanization is apparent in most European medieval romances.

This chapter will discuss how different medieval romances make race through ideologies of exclusion by paying attention to fantastic scenarios such as giants and talking animals alongside other stories in which Jews, Muslims, and Welsh characters are dehumanized. This shows the similar patterns of dehumanization working in these texts. By introducing new research alongside my own on the topic of CRS in the Middle Ages, I will examine the process of race making in medieval romance. Because race is a social fabrication used by societies to establish and justify systems of power, privilege, disenfranchisement, and oppression, racism becomes a "system of advantage based on race" that benefits the dominant culture.[2] Geraldine Heng's definition of race as "*a structural relationship for the articulation and management of human differences*" in the construction of "a hierarchy of peoples" that are singled out "for differential treatment" helps to ground the way we discuss who is included and who is excluded within the borders created within romance literature.[3] Another important idea to consider is how systematic oppression functions within the historical contexts of texts analyzed. Oppression is an organized pattern of mistreatment that is woven into the culture, society, and laws – we find this in government, education, and culture.[4] By studying differing patters of dehumanization in medieval romance with a focus on Old French and Middle Welsh texts, I show some examples of the ways that the genre of romance makes race and of how the repercussions of making race further systems of oppression.

Romance tends to racialize the enemies of the chivalric heroes by dehumanizing them and normalizing violence in several ways, depending on the context and place of creation. Phillip Atiba Goff differentiates between dehumanization and prejudice: "Prejudice is a broad intergroup attitude whereas dehumanization is the route to moral exclusion." Dehumanization can lead to "the denial of basic human protections to a group or group member." While prejudice would lead to devaluing a person from a disliked group, dehumanization can lead to the "endorsement of genocide or extreme violence."[5] And this is one of the things that white supremacy does: it dehumanizes groups of people and normalizes exclusionary violence against them based on race. Dehumanization based on race is also about creating whiteness – those that are humanized are constructed as white. We can see how this structural injustice plays out in medieval romance. Because this is an introductory chapter, I will bring together several examples of dehumanizing tactics in both French and Welsh literature in order to show the patterns of dehumanization that emerge in romance and how they fit within larger patterns of creation.

Critical Race Studies and Romance

A CRS perspective on romance shows that romance normalized the violence enacted by the protagonists often by dehumanizing the enemies of the chivalric heroes. The texts dehumanize the enemies of the protagonists so that violence against them is celebrated instead of being understood as prohibitory violence. The study of the consequences of dehumanization on the basis of race is one of the ways that CRS advances analysis of the Middle Ages. Richard Delgado and Jean Stefancic note that CRS developed from both legal studies and radical feminism, and that it is an umbrella term that holds several theoretical frameworks that help to discuss different forms of oppressions.[6] I suggest that CRS is a theoretical and activist methodology that examines how race and racism are manifest in dominant cultural forms of expression. Although medievalists have been slow to use CRS as a tool of analysis, it is emerging as a key critical category for the study of the Middle

Ages because CRS is not concerned with determining whether or not the concept of race exists in the Middle Ages but with demonstrating how racism and oppression affected disenfranchised communities and how these communities responded to and resisted that subordination.

Margo Hendricks and Geraldine Heng, pioneers of the use of CRS in premodern literature (premodern roughly encompasses classical, medieval, and early modern literature), have defined premodern critical race studies (PCRS) as a theoretical framework that both analyzes race in the premodern world and that is critical of normative academic practices. At the 2019 "RaceB4Race: Race and Periodization" symposium, co-sponsored by the Folger Institute and the Arizona Center for Medieval and Renaissance Studies, Hendricks defined the parameters of PCRS:

> As part of the larger critical race theory practice and practices, PCRS actively pursues not only the study of race in the premodern, not only the way in which periods helped to define, demarcate, tear apart, and bring together the study of race in the premodern era, but the way that outcome, the way those studies can effect a transformation of the academy and its relationship to our world. PCRS is about being a public humanist. It's about being an activist. . . .
>
> PCRS also recognizes and acknowledges its genealogies. It celebrates that lineage – citation – and it uses it "to dismantle the master's house" since the master's tools are ineffective.[7]

Hendricks's call to action describes PCRS as a holistic approach that analyzes the making of race in the past, is critical of white-centric understandings of race and challenges those understandings, and celebrates previous scholarship. Therefore, PCRS both creates new scholarship of race and recuperates the work of previously marginalized scholars whose research is groundbreaking but has been rejected and/or erased by mainstream academia because the scholars are Black, Indigenous, or People of Color or they have prioritized methodologies and epistemologies that derive from marginalized communities.

Geraldine Heng, in conversation with Hendricks, defines PCRS as it applies specifically to Medieval Studies. She writes that

> Premodern critical race studies doesn't just concern itself with marshaling descriptions of race, or compiling taxonomies of race, or producing summations of race, but *sustains the critical analysis of race* in the European Middle Ages.
>
> Critical race scholarship on premodernity analyzes the sources, institutions, infrastructures, practices, technologies, and dynamics of race and racialization, in order *critically* to assess their ethical, political, and epistemological consequences and impacts.[8]

Heng highlights that it is not enough to list or compile instances of making race; instead, PCRS must examine the consequences of making race. Because PCRS celebrates previous scholarship that has influenced and built new scholarship, this introduction in itself is practicing a PCRS model of scholarship, as will the rest of the chapter. I do so by depicting how romance makes race, highlighting important work for the study of PCRS, and showing how scholarship on the topic of romance and race relies on the work of Black, Indigenous, and People of Color (BIPOC) and/or early career scholars. Indeed, the growth of research on the topic of critical race and the Middle Ages is the groundwork for understating my analysis on the dehumanization and the normalization of violence in medieval romance.[9]

French Medieval Romance

Giants have long fascinated critics for their role as fantastic literary creatures who reveal the fears and obsessions of medieval authors and readers. Giants become points of contradiction in which the knight must not only dehumanize and potentially kill the giant, but he must also show that he is not like the giant, on many occasions allowing the knight to claim the territories of the giant. The treatment of giants parallels ideologies of settler colonialism and racism because the giants are racialized to justify stealing their lands.[10] Geraldine Heng has shown the role of the giant in making race and creating medieval empire in her groundbreaking monograph *Empire of Magic: Medieval Romance and the Politics of Cultural Fantasy*.[11] The most recent study of medieval giants is Sylvia Huot's monograph *Outsiders: The Humanity and Inhumanity of Giants in Medieval French Prose Romance*, which gives a comprehensive account of giants in medieval French literature.[12] Although her array of primary sources varies and includes Chrétien de Troyes's *Erec et Enide* and *Le Chevalier au Lion*, *Perceforest*, *La Prise d'Orange*, *La Queste del Saint Graal*, and *La mort le roi*, the bulk of the book prioritizes French prose romances. From her many observations on giants, two of her key concepts become a priority for my study of race and race making: that the representation of giants is not uniform and tends to signify a "deformation of culture,"[13] and that their subject positionality is such that they cannot "make history" and instead, "history is made" by their humanization or dehumanization.[14]

Huot's most brilliant analyses rely on postcolonial theory and the work of BIPOC writers. She relies on Frantz Fanon and Edward Said, for example, to demonstrate that Romance denies the possibility of a "giant-centered, giant-driven history" similar to the ways that European powers portrayed colonized communities and individuals. Postcolonial theory calls for the critical study of the effects and the aftermath of colonization on the peoples affected by it. In medieval studies, postcolonial theory is helpful to understand how smaller cultures experienced and dealt with their medieval colonization and thus becomes an important component to understanding how medieval literature makes race. From this context, giants become a type of "fantasy race" that allows the text to create fantasies disguised as histories in order to dehumanize different groups of people and justify violence against them.[15] Huot's findings follow Heng's analysis on fantasy and romance by continuing to demonstrate that cultural fantasy "confronts history" and then helps to create discourses that create race and racism.[16] Giants become a race that helps produce historical fantasies within medieval romance.

Work on medieval French literature and race, however, goes beyond the consideration of giants. Jacqueline DeWeever's *Sheba's Daughters: Whitening and Demonizing the Saracen Woman in Medieval French Epic* combines CRS and postcolonial theory to investigate how Muslim women are categorized in medieval French epics, finding that they are described as either beautiful and white if they support the Franks and Christianity, or Black if they fight or reject the Franks and Christianity.[17] DeWeever has helped to pave the way for exciting scholarship such as that of Suzanne Akbari, Sharon Kinoshita, and Joseph Derosier, among others. As a group, these scholars have shown the importance of race, gender, postcolonial, and Mediterranean studies in understanding the French Middle Ages.[18] Drawing from DeWeever, Sharon Kinoshita and Suzanne Akbari show how this trope works in medieval romance: the white female Muslim who converts to Christianity brings cultural assimilation by producing offspring who are white and Christian, and who will rule the territories once controlled by Muslim kings. Joseph Derosier in particular discusses the grail romance *Li Hauz livres du Graal* (*The High Book of the Grail*), or *Perlesvaus*, as presaging Achille Mbembe's theories of necropolitics. Derosier argues that the poem creates a communal center through ideologies of exclusion and necropolitics. Certain communities are only "allowed to live on the periphery – under the conditions that the periphery is governed by the center."[19]

An early thirteenth-century text, *Perlesvaus* is a continuation of Chrétien de Troyes's *Conte del Graal* (ca. 1191), and follows Perlesvaus (a corruption or variant of "Perceval") on his adventures. Derosier reads *Perlesvaus* as a francophone text that helps to create an alternative center for Christendom by exploiting an anti-Jewish medieval Christian fantasy of biopolitics. Derosier embraces Mbembe's political act of provincializing France. Mbembe writes that:

> Both the homogeneity of the French and France's unity supposedly have been accomplished at three distinct dates: the battle of Poitiers in 732, which stopped the Arab invasion; the capture of Jerusalem in 1099, which bore witness to Christian Europe; and the revocation of the Edict of Nantes in 1685, which confirmed France's status as "the eldest daughter of the Church," demonstrating, symbolically, that France is exclusively Catholic and that its identity is forged on the exclusion of Arabs, Jews, and Protestants.[20]

Derosier's analysis of *Perlesvaus* demonstrates how the text participates in the symbolic homogenization of France through the exclusion of Muslims and Jews.

In one of the most complicated and hypersignified scenes in the poem, Perlesvaus enters the Forest Soutaine ("Solitary Forest") and witnesses an allegorical animal staging of the crucifixion of Christ in which a white animal, a *beste*, is killed by a litter of her own puppies that spring from within her. The puppies, who do not share her gentleness, tear her apart right next to a cross:

> La beste vit qu'ele n'avroit nul garant, si s'en vet vers la croiz. Li chael ne pourront plus estre dedenz li, si s'en issirent hors tuit vif autresi comme chien; n'estoient pas de sa douçor ne de sa debuenaireté. . . . Li chien l'orent avironnee, et li corent sus de toutes parz, et la depiecient tote as denz; mes n'orent onques pouoier que il manjassent de la char, ne que il l'esloniassent de la crois.[21]

> The beast saw that she had no protection, and she went to the cross. The litter could no longer stay inside her, and they came out alive and already like dogs; they had neither her sweetness nor her gentleness. . . . The dogs surrounded her, attacking from all sides, and they tore her apart with their teeth, but they were never able to eat the flesh, nor to pull her away from the cross.

In one of several glosses explaining the scene, the reader learns through Le Roi Hermite, Perlesvaus' uncle, that the *beste* signifies (*senefie*) God and that the twelve dogs signify "les Juïs de la Viez Loi" (the Jews of the Old Law).[22] The uncle says: "Beau niés, li xii chien sont li Juïs que Dex a norriz, e qui nasquirent en la loi que il establi, ne onques ne le voudrent croire ne amer; ainz le crucefierent e depechierent son cors au plus vilainement qu'il porent" (Sweet nephew, the twelve dogs are the Jews whom God nourished, and who were born into the Law that He established, but they never wanted to believe in nor love Him. And so they crucified him and cut up his body as cruelly as they possibly could).[23] Although the romance also has scenes in which pagans are either dismembered or converted, the scene quoted here uses signification to imagine "a figurative origin story of how Christians and Jews are subjugated to the law, how flesh and bodily dismemberment produce truth, and how allegory can make Arthurian motifs into Christian signifiers."[24] According to Derosier, *Perlesvaus* rewrites Chrétien's version through a systemic racist apparatus of anti-Jewishness that helps create a Christian center within the fantastical Arthurian kingdom.

Recent work by both Huot and Derosier moves medieval French literature into new areas of inquiry. While Huot adds to our knowledge of the way that giants are depicted and has compellingly continued to show how giants are represented as a fantasy race, Derosier exposes how *Perlesvaus* deploys medieval French anti-Jewish fantasies to form a "French" community through the exclusion of Jewish ones. This scholarship helps me corroborate how romance makes race through dehumanization.

Middle Welsh Romance

Welsh scholarship has done a great amount of work exposing Anglo-Norman oppression against the Welsh.[25] Indeed, since the creation of Offa's Dyke in the eighth century, the Welsh have been territorialized and essentialized, especially by the early English and the Anglo-Normans. The Welsh were in fact a large number of peoples, and the inhabitants of Wales neither called themselves by a single term nor understood themselves as a collectivity. The early English and the Anglo-Normans imagined the idea of a racialized Wales that helped justify their conquest. For example, the name "Wales," for the English, means "outsider." The early English and the Anglo-Normans created the image of the Welsh that is steeped in bias and stereotypes and was enforced systematically. As a form of response to Anglo-Norman oppression, Welsh Arthurian texts seem to counteract Welsh racialization by combining Welsh, Anglo-Norman, and chivalric ideologies to elevate Welshness through whiteness. The texts do so, however, by racializing other groups of people. Contextualizing the fraught position of the Welsh vis-à-vis the English, and demonstrating some of the ways that the Welsh were essentialized by the English, is key to introducing Welsh romance. As Coral Lumbley writes, it is "necessary to explore the role that the Welsh, who have been both outsiders and insiders in constructions of European whiteness, played as both objects and agents in the creation of medieval British racial structures."[26] The Welsh had many strategies to fight English oppression, including shifting racism away from themselves, which proved to be a very successful way to deflect racism. By way of an example, the text *Perlesvaus* (discussed earlier) was translated into Welsh and survives in three Welsh manuscripts. Known in Welsh as *Y Seint Greal*, the poem continues to express anti-Jewish and anti-Muslim fantasies and thus it continues to enact violence against both Jewish and Muslim communities.[27] The Middle Welsh romance *Peredur*, as well as the Arthurian text *Culhwch and*

Olwen, both found in the collection that is best known as the *Mabinogion*, are also case studies of how Welsh Arthuriana makes race to deflect against Welsh oppression.[28]

The *Mabinogion* is what we call the grouping of eleven medieval Welsh tales that are mainly found in the *White Book of Rhyderch* (c. 1350) and the *Red Book of Hergest* (1382–1410), manuscripts produced well after the Anglo-Normans gained control of Wales.[29] As a group these tales are a dynamic exploration of Welsh ideologies, including their anxiety about their own position within the rising European medieval nations, especially vis-à-vis Anglo-Norman England. Their inclusion in the *White Book of Rhyderch* and the *Red Book of Hergest* allow for these texts to become a Welsh respond to their positionality by arguing for their own humanization in opposition to Anglo-Norman dehumanization and violence. *Culhwch and Olwen* and *Peredur* in particular expose some of the ways the Welsh used Arthuriana to racialize giants and used anti-Blackness to argue for their inclusion within the borders of Europe, participating in medieval nation formation.

The giants in *Culhwch and Olwen* hold territories, have families, marry humans, and have children with them. Some giants are part of Arthur's retinue, and others are killed and dismembered throughout the story. They are dehumanized and the violence done against them is normalized. In this story, Culhwch is given a condition by his stepmother that he must marry Olwen, the daughter of the giant Yshbaddaden. Yshbaddaden will only allow Culhwch to marry Olwen if he brings Yshbaddaden several grooming items that the giant needs to be ready for the wedding and that require dangerous, deadly missions to attain. Culhwch is only able to fulfill the demands because of Arthur and Arthur's retinue (Culhwch is Arthur's cousin). Notable in the story is the degree of violence committed against giants. For example, Wrnach Gawr is decapitated; the hairs of Dillus the Horseman are tweezed out of him while he is alive, and he is killed right afterwards.[30] Finally, Ysbaddaden's skin, flesh, and ears are shaved off with the same grooming materials he asked for in the first place: "Ac yna yd ymauaelawd Gorau mab Custennin yndaw herwyd gwallt y penn, a'e lusgaw yn y ol y'r *dom*, a llad y penn a'e dodi ar bawl y gatlys. A goresgyn y gaer a oruc a'e gyuoeth" (and then Gorau son of Custennin grabbed him by the hair and dragged him to the *tom* and cut off his head and stuck it on the bailey post. And he took possession of his fort and territory)."[31] The meaning of the word *tom* ("dom" in Welsh) includes dung and excrement,[32] therefore Ysbaddaden is not only killed, he is also tortured, then beheaded in a pile of excrement, all while his territories are incorporated into the Arthurian milieu. This type of violence is only possible because Ysbaddaden has been dehumanized, in part by his status as a giant and by the earlier acts of violence against other characters who were giants.

Yet even characters such as Cai and Gorau, who are part of Arthur's retinue but who are also part giant, are dehumanized. The text demands that these giants and half-giants submit willingly to the dominant group by killing their family members who live in opposition to the Arthurian norm. Cai, Gorau, and Olwen, for example, function as what Sierra Lomuto calls exotic allies – that is, allies who are both feared and desired.[33] The text makes race by conditionally humanizing those that advance the Arthurian cause and by dehumanizing the giant who protects his own territory. Gorau, nephew to Ysbaddaden, cousin to Arthur, and half-giant, violently kills his giant uncle; and Olwen, daughter to Ysbaddaden, tells Culhwch how to beat and ultimately kill her own father.

Cai in particular is described as having monstrous undertones and gigantic attributes,[34] and although Cai is one of the men sent to find the dwelling of Ysbaddaden, decapitates Wrnach Gawr, and helps tweeze the hairs of Dillus the Horseman, Arthur mocks him for fulfilling his obligations:

> Ac yna y kanei Arthur yr eglyn hwnn:
> Kynnllyuan a oruc kei.
> O uaryf Dillus uab Eurei.
> Pei iach dy angheu uydei.
> Ac am hynny y sorres Kei hyt pan uu abreid y uilwyr yr Ynys honn tangneuedu y rwng Kei ac Arthur. Ac eissoes, nac yr anghyfnerth ar Arthur nac yr llad y wyr, nyt ymyrrwys Kei yn reit gyt ac ef o hynny allan.[35]

> And then Arthur sang this englyn:
> A leash was made by Cai
> From the beard of Dillus son of Efrai.
> Were he alive, he would kill you.
> And because of that Cai sulked, so that the warriors of this island could hardly make peace between Cai and Arthur. And yet neither Arthur's misfortune nor the killing of his men could induce Cai to have anything to do with him in his hour of need from then on.[36]

Arthur's poem scorns Cai for completing the demands that Arthur is honor-bound to accomplish. Although both Arthur and Cai seem to be depicted in the wrong – Arthur was rash and rude which ultimately means he makes rash and bad decisions, and Cai's moping and sulking ultimately lead him to abandon Arthur in his hour of need – Arthur and Cai do not carry the same power within the hierarchies presented in the story. This approach in storytelling, in which both Arthur and Cai are depicted in the wrong, seems to mark the text as measured and fair; however, the scene serves to reify Cai's status as a giant and an exotic ally. Arthur is king and Cai is still described as "a lionized figure of alterity characterized by the consolidation of fear, desire, and control."[37] Cai also "houses both negative and positive connotations that do not compete, but rather coincide and reinforce one another, capturing the ambivalence and contradictions that cohere within processes of racial formations."[38] By depicting Cai as an exotic ally, the scene both reaffirms and resists the human/giant hierarchy that the text as a whole promotes, but it ultimately fails to produce parity even as it seems to create it. At the end of the scene, Arthur continues to hold power and Cai continues to be dehumanized through his giant status. The scene, then, becomes an example of the ways that Welsh anxiety is projected in Welsh romance and how that anxiety is ultimately used in the service of elevating the Welsh to a closer proximity to power – what we call "whiteness."

Culhwch and Olwen tries to normalize violence against giants by portraying that violence as normal and nonviolent because the perpetrators of that violence are always seen as justified in using violence while the giants are seen as menacing and deserving of violence. The way that the giants are depicted in *Culhwch and Olwen* follows a similar logic to that of later medieval romances, including English, French, German, and Scandinavian romances, which enact violence against Africans, Muslims, and giants, among others.[39] These texts, under narrowly defined conditions, allow racialized characters to enter into Arthur's retinue.[40] In *Culhwch and Olwen* half-giants must enact violence against their own kin and societies, and, even then, Cai is mocked.

Beyond the representation of giants, several Welsh texts argue for Welsh humanization by using the language of the oppressor – resulting in anti-Blackness, anti-paganism, anti-Irishness, and the essentializing of Jews and Muslims. Lumbley's essay "The 'dark Welsh'" and Matthew Vernon's work on Gerald of Wales both describe how Welsh texts help make race and further complicate discussions of race in the context of Wales. The Welsh are described as primitive and barbarous, but they also share a common Christian and cultural inheritance with the English.[41] Daniel Armenti and I have briefly discussed how Gerald of Wales' *Topographia Hibernica* (*The Topography of Ireland*), *Itinerarium Cambriae* (*The Journey through Wales*), and *Descriptio Cambriae* (*The Description of Wales*) helped the Anglo-Normans justify expansion into Wales and Ireland. We explain that

> Because the men being conquered were Christian men, the ideologies of expansion evolved to distinguish those with the wrong kind of Christianity, in part, by drawing on the dichotomy of nature and nurture. . . . The description of the

> Irish draws a distinction between their nature (which Gerald implies is British and therefore excellent) and their Irish culture (their nurture), which is barbarous. Gerald continues to describe the Celts in dehumanizing terms in "The Description of Wales," where he uses the sexual depravities of the Welsh as reasons to support the Anglo-Norman conquest.[42]

Matthew X. Vernon uses Frantz Fanon's concept of the "colonized intellectual" in his analysis of Gerald of Wales' *Topographia Hibernica* to demonstrate how Gerald's work, similar to Welsh Arthuriana, creates a double discourse.[43] Gerard supports the colonization of Ireland as part of the medieval English nation by adopting the language that supported expansion into Wales. Vernon uses the concept of the "colonized intellectual" to show that Gerald of Wales "fails to realize he is using techniques and a language borrowed from the occupier."[44] The concept of the "colonized intellectual" is useful to discuss Welsh romance (as well as Scandinavian romance) because the concept helps to accentuate when Welsh agents and texts chose to enact dehumanization tactics against themselves and other minoritized groups.

Similarly, Lumbley shows that *Peredur*, which has been read as a postcolonial text,[45] uses anti-Blackness to support Welsh inclusion into whiteness. In fact, she builds on postcolonial readings of *Peredur* to show that "Middle Welsh romance deploys anti-blackness as an Othering mechanism which redirects negative attention away from the 'barbarian' Welsh toward the black African."[46] *Peredur* includes a "morwyn bengrych du" (black, curly-headed maiden) who is described in racist terms;[47] the lady, however, is transformed into Peredur's white and beautiful cousin. The lady is imbued with the motifs of the loathly lady and the Celtic sovereignty figure, but these motifs are now not just only Welsh but they have been imbedded in the Arthurian milieu. They become tools to argue for Welsh inclusion into Arthurian whiteness. The text combines Welsh and Anglo-Norman ideologies to elevate Welshness into whiteness and thus projects inclusion into medieval European ideologies of nation formation.

As a final note, it is important that the inclusion of the topic of race does not become a way to reiterate ideologies of white supremacy. We must continually remember that the ultimate goal of CRS is to affirm the lives of Black, Indigenous, and People of Color as well as other underrepresented communities. In this spirit of coalition, I have prioritized the work of scholars of color as well as early career scholars in order to show the vibrant work that can be done through a commitment to antiracist theory and pedagogy. As I have shown, using antiracist theory to engage with the Medieval past reveals structures of marginalization and dehumanization in medieval literature. Such analysis is necessary for the field of medieval studies and in our divided society today.

Notes

1. Nahir Otaño Gracia, "Towards a Decentered Global North Atlantic," *Literature Compass* 16.9,10 (2019): 4. See also Geraldine Heng, *The Invention of Race in the European Middle Ages* (New York: Cambridge University Press, 2018) and *Empire of Magic: Medieval Romance and the Politics of Cultural Fantasy* (New York: Columbia University Press, 2003).
2. David Wellman, *Portraits of White Racism* (New York: Cambridge University Press, 1977), cited in Beverly D. Tatum, "Talking About Race," *Harvard Educational Review* 62.1 (1992): 3.
3. Heng, *The Invention of Race*, 27.
4. In my opinion, the best way to understand how systematic oppression works in the Middle Ages is by reading Heng's second chapter, "State/Nation," in *The Invention of Race*, 55–109, wherein Heng's demonstrates how the English systemically essentialized and racialized its Jewish population, creating one of the first, if not the first, racial state in the European Middle Ages.
5. Philip A. Goff, Carmen M. Culotta, Natalie A. DiTomasso, et al., "The Essence of Innocence," *Journal of Personality and Social Psychology* 106.4 (2014): 527. See also Susan Opotow, "Moral Exclusion and Injustice," *Journal of Social Issues* 46.1 (1990); and Erwin Staub, *The Roots of Evil* (Cambridge: Cambridge University Press, 1989). For the application of dehumanization in the Middle Ages see Nahir Otaño Gracia and Daniel Armenti, "Constructing Prejudice in the Middle Ages and the Repercussions of Racism Today," *Medieval Feminist Forum* 53.1 (2017).
6. Richard Delgado and John Stefancic, *Critical Race Theory* (New York: New York University Press, 2017), 5, 4.
7. See Margo Hendricks, "Coloring the Past, Rewriting Our Future: RaceB4Race," Folgers Shakespeare Library, September 2019 (www.folger.edu/institute/scholarly-programs/race-periodization/margo-hendricks); Hendricks expands her definition of PCRS in the essay "Coloring the Past, Considerations on Our Future: RaceB4Race" (*New Literary History*, 52.3,4 [2021]). See also Dorothy Kim, "Critical Race and the Middle Ages," *Literature Compass* 16.9,10 (2019): 2–3.
8. G. Heng, "Why the Hate? The Invention of Race in the European Middle Ages, and Race, Racism, and Premodern Critical Race Studies Today," *In the Middle: Peace, Love, & the Middle Ages*, December 21, 2020, www.inthemedievalmiddle.com/2020/12/why-hate-invention-of-race-in-european.html.
9. In medieval studies in particular, several monographs and special journal clusters have been published relatively recently on the topic of race and the Middle Ages. As a group, these publications show a plethora of ways in which we can use critical race studies to study race, race making, and racism in the Middle Ages. The monographs include: Heng, *The Invention of Race*, Lynn Ramey, *Black Legacies: Race and the European Middle Ages* (Florida: University Press of Florida, 2014), Matthew Vernon, *The Black Middle Ages: Race*

and the Construction of the Middle Ages (Cham: Palgrave Macmillan, 2018), Lindsay Kaplan, *Figuring Racism in Medieval Christianity* (New York: Oxford University Press, 2018), Cord Whitaker, *Black Metaphors: How Modern Racism Emerged from Medieval Race Thinking* (Philadelphia: University of Pennsylvania Press, 2019), and Roland Betancourt, *Byzantine Intersectionality: Sexuality, Gender, and Race in the Middle Ages* (Princeton, NJ: Princeton University Press, 2020). Special journal clusters include: C. Whitaker, "Making Race Matter in the Middle Ages," *postmedieval* 6.1 (2015); Kim, "Critical Race and the Middle Ages," and "Race Before Race: Premodern Critical Race Studies," *Literature Compass* 18.10 (2021); T. Andrews and T. Beechy, "Indigenous Futures and Medieval Pasts," *English Language Notes* 58.2 (2020); A. Arvas, Afrodesia McCannon, and Kris Trujillo, "Critical Confessions Now," *postmedieval* 11.2 (2020); and Mary Rambaran-Olm, M. B. Leake, and Micah J. Goodrich, "Race, Revulsion, and Revolution," *postmedieval* 11.4 (2020).

10. For analyses on settler colonialism and the Middle Ages, see the special issue of *English Language Notes* edited by Tarren Andrews and Tiffany Beechy (2020). Describing the capacious work highlighted in the volume is beyond the scope of this chapter, but I would like to mention that Andrew's introduction combines Indigenous epistemologies with CRS as a call for scholarship to complicate "the difficulty of decolonization that includes both the actual act of returning land and the intellectual work required to navigate the complex structures of settler colonialism and racism that entangle us all" (Tarren Andrews, "Indigenous Futures and Medieval Pasts: An Introduction," *English Language Notes* 58.2 (2020): 1–17 at 9). There is nothing comfortable or easy about discussing settler colonialism and race.
11. See especially chapter 1 of Heng's *Empire of Magic: Medieval Romance and the Politics of Cultural Fantasy* (New York: Columbia University Press, 2003), 17–62.
12. Sylvia Huot, *Outsiders The Humanity and Inhumanity of Giants in Medieval French Prose Romance* (Notre Dame, IN: University of Notre Dame Press, 2016).
13. Huot, *Outsiders*, 41.
14. Huot, *Outsiders*, 38.
15. Huot, *Outsiders*, 38, 302. See Frantz Fanon, *Damnés de la terre* (Paris: Galliamard, 1991), 82, and *The Wretched of the Earth*, trans. Farrington (London: Penguin Classics, 2001), 40; E. Said, *Orientalism* (London: Penguin Books, 1985); and Huot, *Outsiders*, 38–9.
16. Heng, *Empire of Magic*, 15.
17. See Jacqueline DeWeever, *Sheba's Daughters: Whitening and Demonizing the Saracen Woman in Medieval French Epic* (New York: Garland Publishing, 1998).
18. Suzanne K. Akbari, *Idols of the East: European Representation of Islam and the Orient, 1100–1450* (Ithaca: Cornell University Press, 2009), 189; and Sharon Kinoshita, *Medieval Boundaries: Rethinking Difference in Old French Literature* (Philadelphia: University of Pennsylvania, 2006), 55.
19. See Joseph Derosier, "The forest and the heath," *Literature Compass* 16.9,10 (2019): 12. See also Achille Mbembe, "Necropolitics," *Public Culture* 15.1 (2003).
20. Achille Mbembe, "Provincializing France?" *Public Culture*, 23.1 [2011]: 106, cited in Derosier, "The forest," 3.

21. All translations cited of *Perlesvaus* are by Joseph Derosier, as provided in his article, and they are translated from *Le Haut Livre du Graal* (Chicago: University of Chicago Press, 1932–1937), ll. 5510–18. See Derosier "The forest," 5. An English version of the poem is available; see Nigel Bryant, *The High Book of the Grail: A Translation of the Thirteenth Century Romance of Perlesvaus* (Woodbridge: D.S. Brewer, 2007).
22. *Le Haut Livre*, l. 5986.
23. *Le Haut Livre du Graal*, ll. 5999–6002.
24. Derosier, "The forest," 7.
25. See, for example, Rees R. Davies, *The First English Empire* (Oxford: Oxford University Press, 2001). Davies shows how English expansion in the twelfth and the thirteenth centuries created an English medieval empire and identity in opposition to Ireland, Scotland, and Wales in which the English understood themselves as superior.
26. Coral Lumbley, "The 'Dark Welsh,'" *Literature Compass* 16.9–10 (2019): 2.
27. For details on the Welsh manuscripts, see C. Lloyd-Morgan, "A study of Y Seint Greal in relation to *La Queste del Saint Graal* and *Perlesvaus*" (unpublished DPhil dissertation, University of Oxford, 1978; available at https://ora.ox.ac.uk/objects/uuid:e32f2f44-16d5-40c1-b35a-14d238508c1f). See also A. B. Swanson, "A Study of the 1516 and the 1523 Editions of the *Perlesvaus*" (unpublished PhD Dissertation, University of Chicago, 1934), 3; and J. Derosier, "Imagining a New Britain" (PhD Dissertation, Northwestern University), 295–6. I would like to thank Joseph Derosier for bringing to my attention the translation of *Perlesvaus* into Middle Welsh (personal communication, December 8, 2020).
28. There are three texts known as the Welsh Romances: *Owain*, *Peredur*, and *Geraint and Enid*, which are counterparts to Chrétien de Troyes's *Yvain*, *Perceval*, and *Erec and Enide* respectively. As I have alluded, other romances such as *Perlesvaus* were available in Middle Welsh.
29. Sioned Davies, "Introduction," *Mabinogion* (Oxford: Oxford University Press, 2007), ix. Davies explains that the term "mabinogion" is a scribal error but has become a useful modern-day label for the eleven tales (ix–x).
30. Sarah Sheehan, "Giants, Boar-hunts, and Barbering," *Arthuriana* 15.3 (2005).
31. *Culhwch ac Olwen*, eds. Rachel Bromwich and D. Simon Evans (Cardiff: University of Wales Press, 2012), ll. 1238–41; and "Culhwch and Olwen," *Mabinogion*, trans. Sioned Davies (Oxford: Oxford University Press, 2007), 213; emphasis added.
32. According to the *Dictionary of the Welsh Language*, the range of meaning of the word *tom*, translated as mound, consists of "dung, excrement; heap of dung, dunghill; manure, compost; dirt, filth, mire, muck, mud; mound, head" (cited in Sheehan, "Giants," 17).
33. Sierra Lomuto, "The Mongol Princess of Tars," *Exemplaria* 31.3 (2019), 174.
34. Sheehan, "Giants," 10.
35. *Culhwch Ac Olwen*, ll. 977–84.
36. "Culhwch and Olwen," 207.
37. Lomuto, "The Mongol Princess," 174.
38. Lomuto, "The Mongol Princess," 174.
39. See, for example, Nahir Otaño Gracia, "Towards a Decentered," and "Imperial Ambitions and the Ethics of Power: Gender, Race, and the *Riddarasögur*,"

Arthurian Ethics, ed. Evelyn Meyer and Melissa Elmes (Suffolk: Boydell and Brewer, forthcoming 2023).

40. Heng writes that "the racing of the Islamic Saracen did not always require the production of difference as absolutely incommensurable. For instance: Under particular, narrowly defined conditions, Saracens can be allowed to resemble – and are praised for resembling – Christian Europeans, into whose company they might be imagined as inducted" (*The Invention of Race*, 55–6).
41. Heng, *The Invention of Race*, 37–42.
42. Otaño Gracia and Armenti, "Constructing Prejudice," 195–6. In *The History and Topography of Ireland*, Gerald of Wales describes the Irish as "barbarous," and in the *Description of Wales* he describes the Welsh as sexually devious. See *The History and Topography of Ireland*, trans. J. O'Meara (London: Penguin Books, 1982), 102–3, and *Description of Wales*, trans. L. Thorpe, (Harmondsworth: Penguin, 1978), bk. 2, chs. 6–9; see also Katherine Millersdaughter, "The Geopolitics of Incest: Sex, Gender, and Violence in the Fourth Branch of the Mabinogi," *Exemplaria* 14.2 (2002): 271–316 at 276.
43. Vernon, *The Black Middle Ages*, 171. See also D. S. Meecham-Jones, who explains that: "The discourse of peripherality drew attention to Wales's perceived status at the geographical margins of European civilization. The discourse of Britishness proclaimed the "natural" unity of the island(s) of Britain, inferring from physical continuity an inevitable political unity. The discourse of authority asserted the right of England to rule Wales, by virtue of tradition, God's favor, and England's greater civilization. Allied to this was the myth of the racial inferiority of the Welsh (and Irish)." Meecham-Jones, "Introduction," in *Authority and Subjugation in Writing of Medieval Wales*, ed. Ruth Kennedy and Simon Meecham-Jones (Basingstoke: Palgrave Macmillan, 2008), 2.
44. As Fanon explains: "L'intellectuel colonisé dans le moment même où il s'inquiète de faire œvre culturelle ne se rend pas compte qu'il utilize des techniques et une langue empruntées à l'occupant." See Frantz Fanon, *The Wretched of the Earth*, trans. Richard Philcox (New York: Grove Press, 2004): 160, and *Les damnés de la terre* (Paris: La Découverte/Poche, 2002), 212. Vernon, *The Black Middle Ages*, 171. A note here to point out that Huot and Vernon cite different translations of Fanon's work, and that Huot and I also have different editions of Fanon's work in the original French. For the sake of accessibility, I have cited all four versions.
45. Examples of academic analysis that rely on postcolonial theory in the study of Medieval Welsh literature and culture include: Susan Aronstein, "Becoming Welsh," *Exemplaria* 17.1 (2005): 135–68; Stephen Knight, "Resemblance and menace," *Canxhwyll marchogyon* 55.1 (2009): 128–47; A. Joseph McMullen, "The communication of culture," *Arthuriana* 23.3 (2013): 27–43; and K. L. Over, "Transcultural change: Romance to rhamant," in Helen Fulton, ed., *Medieval Celtic Literature* (Dublin: Four Court Press, 2005), 183–204.
46. Lumbley, "The "dark Welsh," 7.
47. Lumbley, "The "dark Welsh," 7–8; *Llyfr Gwyn Rhydderch*, ed. R. M. Jones (Cardiff: University of Wales Press, 1973), 83.

Suggestions for Further Reading

Delgado, Richard and Jean Stefancic. *Critical Race Theory: An Introduction*, 3rd ed. New York: New York University Press, 2017.

Derosier, Joseph. "The forest and the heath: Defining the human in medieval romance," Special Issue: Critical Race and the Middle Ages, Dorothy Kim (ed.) *Literature Compass* 16.9–10 (2019).

Hendricks, Margo. "Coloring the Past, Considerations on Our Future: RaceB4Race." *New Literary History*, 52.3,4 (2021): 365–84.

Heng, Geraldine. *Empire of Magic: Medieval Romance and the Politics of Cultural Fantasy*. New York: Columbia University Press, 2003.

The Invention of Race in the European Middle Ages. New York: Cambridge University Press, 2018.

Huot, Sylvia. *Outsiders: The Humanity and Inhumanity of Giants in Medieval French Prose Romance*. Notre Dame, IN: University of Notre Dame Press, 2016.

Lomuto, Sierra. "The Mongol Princess of Tars: Global Relations and Racial Formation in *The King of Tars* (c. 1330)," *Exemplaria* 31.3 (2019): 171–92.

Lumbley, Coral. "The 'dark Welsh': Color, race, and alterity in the matter of medieval Wales," Special Issue: Critical Race and the Middle Ages, Dorothy Kim (ed.) *Literature Compass* 16.9–10 (2019).

Otaño Gracia, Nahir. "Towards a Decentered Global North Atlantic: Blackness in *Saga af Tristram ok Ísodd*," Special Issue: Critical Race and the Middle Ages, Dorothy Kim (ed.) *Literature Compass* 16.9–10 (2019).

and Daniel Armenti. "Constructing Prejudice in the Middle Ages and the Repercussions of Racism Today," *Medieval Feminist Forum: A Journal of Gender and Sexuality* 53.1 (2017): 176–201.

Sheehan, Sarah. "Giants, Boar-hunts, and Barbering: Masculinity in 'Culhwch ac Olwen'," *Arthuriana* 15.3 (2005): 3–25.

Vernon, Matthew. *The Black Middle Ages: Race and the Construction of the Middle Ages*. Cham: Palgrave Macmillan, 2018.

Whitaker, Cord. J. (ed). "Making Race Matter in the Middle Ages," *postmedieval* (special issue) 6.1 (2015).

Black Metaphors: How Modern Racism Emerged from Medieval Race-Thinking. Philadelphia: University of Pennsylvania Press, 2019.

9

KATHY M. KRAUSE

The Construction and Interrogation of Gender in Old French Romance

Gender roles in medieval romance are often thought to be stereotypical, fixed, and easily categorized: a princess (probably in a tower) is rescued by a heroic knight. In other words, female characters are beautiful love objects won by the chivalric efforts of active male subjects. However, when we look at the romances themselves, beginning with the earliest known examples – whether the romances of antiquity retelling Classical narratives such as the fall of Troy, idyllic romances of star-crossed young lovers, or even the tales of Tristan and Isolde – and continuing throughout the medieval period, both the passive/active and the male/female binaries are complicated by deliberate strategies on the part of authors (and patrons). This chapter on gender and romance thus focuses on providing some representative glimpses of just how complicated, and fluid, the presentation of gender is in romance.

As the chapters in this volume demonstrate, romance was a very elastic genre, allowing for a multiplicity of subjects and forms; as a result, it would be impossible to discuss the topic of gender in all of medieval romance, or even in all of French or German romance, to mention only two linguistic categories. In what follows, I will focus on the so-called romances of adventure (*romans d'aventure*), which make up the largest, and most popular, category of romances. In addition, I will look primarily at romances written in French because they were the earliest to be written and served as the model for most of those we find in other western European languages. Even this subset displays quite a lot of variety (including of the basic form, as there are both verse and prose romances); nevertheless, we do find some relatively consistent elements, including some related to the question of gender.

Finally, although space precludes a discussion here, we need to recognize that questions of gender extend beyond the frame of the romance narrative proper. The system of production of medieval romance (and, indeed, almost all literary texts) depended upon wealthy patrons, many of whom were women. Patrons formed a privileged audience, whose tastes and interests could play an important role in the creation of a romance text: they might influence its subject matter, tone (e.g. comic or spiritual), setting, political message, etc. In addition, patronage could have an effect on a romance's distribution and diffusion within the manuscript culture of the Middle Ages.[1]

Romances reflect, in a stylized way, the world of their primary audience – the nobility – and its gender roles.[2] As a result, the actions of male protagonists in *romans d'aventure* primarily center around what was seen as a defining activity of (young) noblemen: fighting.[3] Knights in romance fight in formal, organized venues such as tournaments and judicial combats. Outside the formal court setting, they also battle enemies (both human and supernatural) encountered while traveling, or in (somewhat) more realistic combat situations, such as besieging a castle. Take, for example, the iconic figure of Lancelot in the first romance in which he appears, Chrétien de Troyes's *Le Chevalier de la Charrette* (*The Knight of the Cart*).[4] In the course of the romance, Lancelot fights in single combat against a giant knight defending a ford and (thrice) against the evil heir to a neighboring (and supernatural) land who has taken Arthur's queen prisoner; he fights in a major tournament on two separate days; he battles a group of men supposedly raping his hostess (the scenario is fake, designed to test his prowess); and he participates in a pitched battle against the evil heir's forces. Throughout the romance, although Lancelot does perform several noncombat-related feats and his love for Arthur's queen plays a major role in his identity, his worth, his status as the "best knight" and, as such, as an exemplary (noble)man, is predicated on his extraordinary fighting ability.

We might call this aspect of male gendered behavior in romance "chivalric masculinity,"[5] for in addition to their excellence in knightly combat, male protagonists generally behave according to the other tenets of the chivalric code as it was elaborated (but never truly codified) in the central Middle Ages: they defend those weaker than themselves, particularly women; they respect and defend the Church and its representatives (priests, monks, nuns, et al.); and they follow the rules of "chivalric" combat.[6]

Given the importance of combat in defining chivalric masculinity, the objects a knight utilizes for fighting – his arms and armor – are imbued with gendered significance. Indeed, they are so integral to knightly actions that they become extensions of a knight's masculine identity. For example, in Chrétien de Troye's *Conte du Graal* (*Story of the Grail*) the protagonist Perceval is a naïve adolescent whose mother has kept him far from all aspects of chivalry. He rides to Arthur's court to be knighted, clad only in his rustic tunic and carrying not a sword but the spears he uses for hunting game.

When Perceval kills (in a decidedly nonchivalric manner) a knight (who has come to defy Arthur) in order to obtain his vermillion armor, and thus, in his eyes, become a knight, he cannot get the armor off the corpse: "Qu'eles se tienent si au corps / que ce dedans et che defors / Est trestot un, . . ." (they adhered so well to his body that the interior and exterior are not separate but one . . .) (ll. 1139–42).[7] Although this passage is rhetorically designed to emphasize Perceval's naïveté and his lack of knowledge of knighthood, it simultaneously unveils a truth: the knight's armor is so much a part of his identity that there is almost no distinction between them. You cannot remove a knight's armor without removing his identity as knight. The converse is equally true: when Perceval puts on the Red Knight's armor, he metamorphoses, nearly instantaneously, into a knight. When he is first shown how to use his new arms, "il comencha a porter / Si a droit la alnce et l'escu / Com s'il eûst toz jors veschu / En tornoiemens et en guerres / Et alé par toutes les terres / Querant bataille et aventure" (he began to use the lance and the shield as skillfully as if he had always spent his days in tourneys and at war, and had traveled the world over seeking battle and adventure"; ll. 1474–9).[8]

As that last quote makes obvious, chivalric masculinity crystalizes around combat. Indeed, the structure of most romances is built upon the narration of a series of "adventures," which almost always involve knightly combat, sometimes against monstrous animals or demonic creatures (particularly in the romances narrating stories of the Holy Grail), but most often against other knights. (See, for example, the list of Lancelot's adventures cited earlier.) The omnipresence of masculine competition in romance has led a number of scholars to argue for a homosocial basis to romance depictions of chivalric masculinity. As William Burgwinkle puts it succinctly, "Gender is then inculcated not so much through opposition to femininity as through competition with other males."[9]

The negative implications of the omnipresence of competition between men, for both men and women, is explored in the serio-comic thirteenth-century Arthurian romance *Meraugis de Portlesguez*. In a scene reminiscent of a number of "customs" from Chrétien de Troyes's romances, each knight who arrives on an island must fight (to the death) the champion of the island's lady. Whoever wins becomes (or remains) the champion, fated to stay on the island and fight the next challenger. When Meraugis arrives, the lady's champion is none other than Gauvain, who laments that custom dictates that he and his friend fight to the death for a lady neither of them wants. Meraugis, however, proposes a stratagem that is as inventive (and successful) as it is anticourtly: he and Gauvain will pretend to fight, and when the Lady arrives, they will force her to let them don her clothes, thereby deceiving the boatmen into ferrying them off the island.

The episode exposes, in a comic mode, the essential paradox at the heart of the definition of courtly masculinity: if the "best" knight is defined by his ability to defeat all other knights, then he is always just one combat away from being dethroned. Meraugis (and Gauvain) escapes the never-ending spiral of competition only by changing (superficially, and temporarily) his gender.[10]

The narrative compounds the issue by first describing the cross-dressed Meraugis as "prettier than a doll" (*plus acesmez qu'une popine*; l. 3303) and then by having him threaten the boatmen with his sword when they ask where their lady is: "De souz le mantel a porfil / Tret Meraugis l'espee nue / E dit . . . Par m'ame / Cest espee, c'est vostre dame," ll. 3325–31 (Meraugis drew the naked sword under his cloak and said . . . By my soul, this sword is your lady).[11] The sexual play of a naked sword drawn by a man, but from under female dress, and identified as a lady sums up the pleasure this romance takes in playing with romance norms. It also makes bare what was implicit in earlier romances: the limits of the homosocial construction of chivalric masculinity.

On the other hand, it is the rare romance where the hero does not fall in love with a woman, and where that love is not a major motivating factor in the narrative. How, then, does heterosexual love fit into the depiction (and construction) of gender in romance? Lancelot again provides us with a superb example of how love could be intertwined with chivalric masculinity. In contradistinction to the other characters in Chrétien de Troyes's romance, who value Lancelot's fighting prowess, Guinevere prizes his love and dedication to her over all. This is particularly obvious in episode of the tournament of Noauz, where she first asks him to do his "worst" in the competition (and he complies) and then, only on the second day does she command him to do his "best" (ll. 5636–6056). We must note, however, that Lancelot fights anonymously in the tournament, wearing single-color arms that do not bear any identifying heraldry. As a result, his reputation as the best knight is not harmed by the queen's demands. Lancelot's excellence in love service is a private measure of masculine worth, only superficially in conflict with the public, chivalric definition.

Indeed, as the romance takes pains to demonstrate, Lancelot is worthy to be the queen's lover because he is the best knight, and he is the best knight because his love for her inspires him to ever-greater feats of chivalric prowess. The romance both creates this circular logic and complicates it, for Lancelot's chivalric service is also to King Arthur, and so he betrays his lord by loving his lord's queen, and yet it is his adulterous love for the queen that is the origin of his exemplary chivalric prowess, which he uses in service to the king.

The (potential) contradictions of chivalric masculinity due to the combination of knightly prowess and love lie at the very heart of the *roman d'aventures*. In two of Chrétien de Troyes's other romances (out of five in total), the conflict occurs between married love and chivalric prowess and reputation. In *Erec et Enide*, Erec leaves off knightly adventure because he has become so enamored of his new wife, Enide; the converse occurs in the *Chevalier au Lion*, where the hero, Yvain, forgets his promise to his new wife, Laudine, to return from the tourney circuit within a year. In both romances, the hero (and in *Erec et Enide*, the hero and heroine) spends the second half of the narrative working out the imbalance their behavior has created, although, as in the *Charrette*, the endings leave much room for ambiguity, particularly in Yvain's case where we hear Laudine's real reluctance to forgive him (ll. 6750–66).[12]

In another group of romances, romantic love comes into conflict with parental and familial expectations, which include masculine chivalric activities. For example, in Aimon de Varenne's *Florimont*, the young hero's love for the fairy of the "Île scellée" (the "sealed / closed island") threatens to separate him from his chivalric duty to his family and perhaps even from chivalry itself, as she desires to keep him to herself.[13] His parents succeed in separating Florimont from the fairy, but in doing so estrange their son, who first falls into a deep depression and then sails away to spite them. He travels incognito as "Povre Perdu," which literally translates as either "lost (male) pauper" or "poor lost one (male)": for Florimont, the loss of his fairy beloved entails a loss of identity. Like Erec (and others) before him, he has allowed love to overbalance chivalry. When, as Povre Perdu, Florimont comes to the aid of the besieged King Philip of Macedonia, thereby restoring "chivalry" to its right place in his life, he also falls in love with and wins the king's daughter. Crowning his reintegration into chivalric society via a proper conjunction of love and prowess, the romance ends with his being reunited with his parents after rescuing them from the Emir of Carthage.

The potential conflict between love and chivalry takes a very different turn in one of the most popular (in terms of the number of manuscript copies that have come down to us) medieval French romances: the *Lancelot-Grail* Cycle.[14] Composed in the early thirteenth century, this massive prose work brings together a wealth of different material in order to recount Lancelot's entire life, including the search for the Holy Grail and the eventual destruction of Arthur's kingdom.[15] Here, in a central episode, his exemplary knighthood and physical beauty engender love in another knight, Galehaut, who goes so far as to give up his successful fight against Arthur and become his vassal rather than an independent ruler in order to be with Lancelot. In a remarkable scene, Galehaut asks Arthur and Guinevere and other knights of Arthur's court what they would give in order to gain Lancelot (who has been fighting incognito as a knight in armor on Galehaut's side) as their knight. After they respond, Galehaut answers that "ien uaudroie auoir tournee ma grant honor a honte, par si que ie fuisse a tous iors aussi seurs de lui comme ie vaudroie que il fust de moi" (I would want to have my great honor turned to shame, if I could always be as sure of Lancelot as I want him to be sure of me, p. 254).[16] In other words, he is willing to give up one of the most important aspects of chivalric masculinity – his honor, his reputation – for love of Lancelot. Galehaut goes on to demonstrate the depths of his selfless love by facilitating the affair between Lancelot and the queen (in order to save Lancelot from despair). He ultimately dies of longing for Lancelot (he receives a false report of Lancelot's death), but the two are reunited in death: Lancelot is buried next to Galehaut in a sumptuous tomb constructed by Galehaut as a monument to their love.

Galehaut's intense love for Lancelot brings our attention back once again to the degree to which idealized male behavior in romance is homosocial in nature: chivalric masculinity not only defines men in competition with other men, it also does so in terms that appeal to other men.[17] The female witnesses to male–male competition, such as Guinevere watching Lancelot fight at the tournament of Noauz, or the various maidens rescued from a besiegers' designs on their person and their lands by a wandering hero (such as Yvain in Chrétien de Troye's *Chevalier au Lion* or Gerart in Gerbert de Montreuil's *Roman de la Violette*), serve to validate the masculinist hierarchy, even as the narratives (often) foreground, as we have seen, the conflicts between the homosocial character of chivalric masculinity and the needs and desires of women.

This brings me to the women themselves. We have been discussing romance as if its female characters function only as appendages to the male heroes. I have done so deliberately, in order to bring to the fore the degree to which masculinity in romance is constructed (i. e. not natural) and is "gendered" – it is not a neutral "norm" against which the feminine is defined. In order to highlight the complementary constructed, gendered, nature of femininity in romance, what follows will focus on female protagonists.[18]

In some ways, discussing female gender in romance is the harder subject, because romance heroines perform a broader range of actions than their male counterparts. Although initially this might seem somewhat counterintuitive, it arises, at least partially, from the focus on chivalric masculinity in romance, for while historically we have numerous examples of women participating in medieval warfare,[19] their participation did not involve knightly combat. Concomitantly, there is no such thing as a "domestic" medieval romance: romance protagonists always leave home, whether that is their actual home or what we might call their "home court," in order to provide the space for the adventures which form the narrative. As a result, a romance with a female protagonist (or co-protagonist) needs to motivate her departure from home in a manner that will allow for some sort of "adventure" even if it is not chivalric combat.

However, the norms for female characters, like those of their male romance counterparts, derive from medieval aristocratic social and cultural norms, and generally noblewomen did not ride off into the countryside on their own.[20] The ways in which medieval chivalric romances motivate their female protagonist's departure from home are a testament to narrative inventiveness. Some female protagonists leave home alone, against their will, often due to a traumatic situation – for example, a father's incestuous desire (e. g. the *Roman de la Manekine*, the *Roman du Comte d'Anjou*) or a false accusation of adultery (the *Roman de la Violette*), amongst others. In these romances, the heroine's status as victim from the beginning of the romance seems to color their behavior throughout the narrative: they tend to be (more) passive, and to be victimized by male characters several more times before finding a happy ending with a husband. They represent one pole of female protagonists' behavior in romance.[21]

Nonetheless, even these victimized heroines display character traits and behaviors that belie their passivity, and demonstrate female agency. For example, in the *Roman de la Violette*, the heroine, Euriaut, uses a variety of discursive modes, often in creative ways, in order to resist unwelcome male attention: she rewrites a song refrain to adapt it to her needs (ll. 440–50), spins a tale of being a grave-digger's thieving girlfriend (ll. 1191–1216), and offers a lengthy prayer adapting epic models (ll. 5182–331).[22] In a nonverbal mode, she wields a stone goblet to fight off an attacker, breaking his jaw with her strong blow. However, in the end, none of these demonstrations of her prowess, whether verbal or physical, allows Euriaut to rescue herself; that is left to the hero, Gerart, who fights two judicial battles for her innocence and her honor.[23]

Another group of female protagonists leave home more or less of their own will. Perhaps not surprisingly, they provide some of the most interesting and most active women in romance. For example, in the *Roman de Silence*, the protagonist, Silence, who has been raised as a boy for inheritance reasons, runs away from home to become a jongleur.[24] S/he later becomes a knight, finding such success in chivalric pursuits that s/he attracts the desire of the (evil) Queen. The narrative ends with Silence exposed as a woman (by Merlin), and her marriage to the king (the queen has been executed for adultery). Throughout, the romance highlights the debate between Nature and Nurture, going so far as to have the allegorical figures argue over who has primacy (for example, ll. 2500–656). This explicit questioning of gender determination appears to be shut down at the end, when Nature wins and returns Silence to her soft feminine body; however, it occurs only after Silence has repeatedly demonstrated her mastery of masculine pursuits, as well as her ability to pass undetected as male: the unmaking of Silence's masculine form cannot undo what the narrative has demonstrated so effectively.[25]

Although there are several other examples of female protagonists whose departure from home and adventures are well worth discussing,[26] I want to end by examining one romance in a bit more detail. The case of Aelis in Jean Renart's *Roman de l'Escoufle* (*Romance of the Hawk*[27]) is particularly interesting in our present context. Like other so-called idyllic romances, the romance features a very young couple of differing social status who leave home together when their union is opposed by the parents of the higher-class partner.[28] Here Aelis is the daughter, and heir, to the Emperor of Rome, while her beloved, Guillaume, is the son of the Count of Montivilliers, in Normandy, who has been serving the emperor. After fleeing Rome, the two are separated by misadventure, and have parallel sets of experiences as they try to find each other.

The narrative presents Aelis as the active agent of her fate from the moment she and Guillaume flee Rome, as she is the one who plans their flight. When they are separated (he leaves her sleeping while he tries to capture the bird of the title, which has stolen a silk purse and ring), she laments his betrayal, but quickly takes action: she walks to the nearest town, where we see her choose a poor young woman, Ysabel, to ask for shelter; she then initiates a friendship between them and convinces Ysabel to travel with her as she searches for Guillaume. After two years of fruitless searching, Aelis decides that they should stop traveling (before her money runs out), and they set up a business in Montpellier. They find financial and social success via a typically female activity: needlework (Ysabel sews wimples while Aelis, the aristocrat, does gold and silver embroidery). After their initial success, Aelis sets her sights on obtaining the custom of the most powerful woman in the city and she more than succeeds, as her gift to the lady leads to an even greater lady, the countess of St. Gilles, taking both Aelis and Ysabel into her household.

As even this very condensed narrative of events hints, Aelis not only takes control of her situation, she also creates a female-centric environment around and for herself. In fact, the romance strongly hints that her relationship with Ysabel is considerably closer than friendship. The first night, she insists the young woman join her in bed, despite Ysabel's reticence due to the difference in their social status. Although sharing a bed – for warmth, for lack of a sufficient number of beds, etc. – was not an unusual practice in the Middle Ages, Aelis uses the occasion to seduce Ysabel:

Lors li conte tot son couvine,
Ki ele est et dont ele vient,
Et se li dit que se ç'avient
K'ele vuelle estre sa compaigne,
Jamais, por chose qui aviegne,
N'avra ne richece ne bien
Ou el n'ait part, ce sache bien,
Ne a nul jor ne li faudra,
Ce sache bien, ains li fera
Tos les biens que li porra faire.
. . .
Ele se traist plus delés li,
Si la baise, estraint et acole.
Par la douçor de sa parole
La conquiert, . . . ll. 5274–93

"Then, Aelis recounts whole story, who she is and where she comes from, and she tells Ysabel that if she were to want to be her companion, she would always have a part of any riches or goods that Aelis might have; and she should know that she Aelis would never fail her, rather she will do for her all the good she can possibly do. . . . Aelis drew her closer to her, kissed her, embraced her. By the sweetness of her words, she conquered her . . ."[29]

The two are indeed inseparable from this point on; even when Guillaume and Aelis are reunited, Ysabel remains with Aelis. As with the love between Lancelot and Galehaut in the *Prose Lancelot*, the relationship between Aelis and Ysabel reveals the homosexual possibilities inherent in the medieval aristocratic social structure.[30]

On the masculine side of things, *L'Escoufle* is one of the rare romances where the hero performs no chivalric deeds. Even more, Guillaume suffers repeatedly during his time searching for Aelis: he is robbed and beaten while chasing the thieving hawk; he falls ill (for an entire year); he suffers poverty and ends up, like Aelis, turning to non-noble work: in his case he works at an inn. When he and Aelis are finally reunited at St. Gilles, the count knights Guillaume before they all ride to Normandy to claim Guillaume's paternal heritage. We might anticipate that this endeavor would provide the opportunity for Guillaume to display some chivalric prowess, but Jean Renart thwarts that expectation: all are overjoyed to welcome the rightful heir back, and no fighting occurs. The only hint we receive is the narrator's rather ironic assurance that, as count of Montivilliers, Guillaume holds his shield in front of him by its straps with more art than a woman holds her cloak with her nose in the fur lining (ll. 8481–5)! Humorous quips notwithstanding, the narrative presents Guillaume in a fundamentally positive light. He is beloved by every group with whom he interacts. When, for example, he and Aelis leave Normandy to become Emperor and Empress, the Norman knights bemoan their loss, saying, "Aimi! / Sire, com nous lais desconfis! / Or soit Mosterviler tous fis / que jamais tel seignour n'avra." (Alas, Lord, you leave us in such distress! For Montivilliers knows well that it will never have such a lord again, ll. 8695–7.)

In short, Jean Renart's depiction of both masculinity and femininity provide a notable counterpoint to the dominant chivalric model. Both Aelis and Guillaume are characterized by their adaptability, and by their willingness to earn their living in a decidedly non-noble manner, but Aelis's active self-determination in all matters contrasts with Guillaume's much more passive demeanor. Aelis not only rescues herself, she also chooses the object(s) of her affection and ensures that they become hers. She contrasts with the topos of the "beautiful noblewoman in need of rescuing" in every aspect – except for her exceptional physical beauty. She is the opposite of the victimized female protagonists, and yet she is also very different than Silence. Where Silence demonstrates her abilities and agency while passing as male, Aelis's acts of "prowess," if we may call them that (and the narrative does, in fact, call her "preux": ll. 5502–3[31]), are all very much in a feminine mode. Jean Renart's romance creates a female heroic example decoupled from male chivalric models.

As this chapter has demonstrated, medieval French romance both adheres to the model of heroic knights and maidens to be rescued – a model which the genre itself helped to create – and simultaneously (often in the same text) interrogates the contours of chivalric masculinity and the corresponding female gender conventions. Clad in the armor that can quite literally make them a knight, the masculine protagonists of romance confront not only fabulous antagonists but also the contradictions at the heart of chivalric masculinity between love and knightly combat, between the homosocial character of chivalry and the needs and desires of the beloved women who are (supposedly) the inspiration for chivalric excellence. For their part, female protagonists are less constrained by a heroic model, but the absence of such a model leads all too often – but not inexorably, as Silence and Aelis demonstrate – to victimization as the only way for female characters to experience the kind of "adventure" required by romance.

Notes

1. On the topic of female patronage see, in particular, Joan M. Ferrante, *To the Glory of her Sex: Women's Roles in the Composition of Medieval Texts* (Bloomington: Indiana

University Press, 1997), chp. 4, and June Hall McCash, "The Cultural Patronage of Medieval Women: An Overview," in June Hall McCash (ed.), *The Cultural Patronage of Medieval Women* (Athens: University of Georgia Press, 1996), pp. 1–49. The subject of patronage and manuscript culture is touched on in Chapter x of this volume. The classic work on women and book ownership in the Middle Ages remains Susan Groag Bell, "Medieval Women Book Owners: Arbiters of Lay Piety and Ambassadors of Culture." *Signs* 7, 4 (1982): 742–68.

2. One notable exception is Rudolf von Ems's eponymous romance *Good Gerhart* (*Der guote Gêrhart*), in which the protagonist is a virtuous merchant. In addition, some romances about separated young lovers of differing social status (often referred to as "idyllic romances") in which the classical origins of the tale are still very strong are not set within a chivalric context, and so, in these romances, there is little or no fighting, although there is much travel and searching for the beloved. It is perhaps telling that the best-known, and oldest, example of this type of tale in Old French, that of *Floire et Blanchefleur*, is usually referred to as a tale (*conte*) rather than as a romance (*roman*) in the manuscripts.
3. In reality, men of the nobility spent much of their time attending to nonmilitary responsibilities (see, for example, John W. Baldwin and William Chester Jordan, *Knights, Lords, and Ladies. In Search of Aristocrats in the Paris Region, 1180–1220* (Philadelphia: University of Pennsylvania Press, 2019). However, knighthood was defined in relationship to the bearing and using of arms (on horseback).
4. Chrétien de Troyes, *Arthurian Romances*, trans. Kibler; Chrétien de Troyes, *Le Chevalier de la Charrete*, ed. Roques.
5. An excellent discussion of chivalry that considers both historical and literary sources is provided by Constance Britain Bouchard, *Strong of Body, Brave and Noble: Chivalry and Society in Medieval France* (Ithaca, NY: Cornell University Press, 1998).
6. Vern L. Bullough, "On Being Male in the Middle Ages," in *Medieval Masculinities: Regarding Men in the Middle Ages*, ed. Clare E. Lees, Thelma Fenster, and JoAnn McNamara (Minneapolis: University of Minnesota Press, 1994), pp. 31–45.
7. All citations from the *Conte du Graal* are from Chrétien de Troyes, *Le Roman de Perceval ou Le Conte du Graal*, ed. Roach. Translations are my own with the help of: Chrétien de Troyes, *The Complete Romances of Chrétien de Troyes*, trans. Staines.
8. For a discussion of how clothing defines and creates courtly figures more generally in medieval French texts, see E. Jane Burns, *Courtly Love Undressed: Reading Through Clothes in Medieval French Culture* (Philadelphia: University of Pennsylvania Press, 2002). Perceval's knightly training also brings to the fore the importance of a horse to a knight's identity. The act of owning/riding a horse quite literally defines the word for "knight" in French (*un chevalier* being one who rides upon *un cheval*, a horse) and in German (*ein ritter* is a rider). The two are so synonymous, the existence of a knight's war horse (a *destrier* in Old French, *Roß* in Middle High German) often passes for given in romances, but Perceval's initial status as a country bumpkin brings the horse, as well as the armor, to the fore. He not only takes the Vermillion knight's armor, he also takes his horse, and his training (by an accomplished knight, Gornemant de Gohort) involves learning how to properly ride and guide the horse as a knight does (ll. 1416–38).

9. William E. Burgwinkle, *Sodomy, Masculinity, and Law in Medieval Literature: France and England, 1050–1230* (Cambridge: Cambridge University Press, 2004), 101. See also Ruth Mazo Karras, *From Boys to Men: Formations of Masculinity in Late Medieval Europe* (Philadelphia: University of Pennsylvania Press, 2002); Simon Gaunt, *Gender and Genre in Medieval French Literature* (Cambridge: Cambridge University Press, 1995).
10. My discussion of *Meraugis de Porlesguez* is indebted to Keith Busby, "'Plus acesmez qu'une popine": Male Cross-Dressing in Medieval French Narrative," in *Gender Transgressions: Crossing the Normative Barrier in Old French Literature*, ed. Karen J. Taylor (New York: Garland, 1998), pp. 46–8. Overall, the issue of female cross-dressing has received more attention than that of men. For an interesting analysis of both real and romance knights' cross-dressing that examines German and French examples, see Ad Putter, "Transvestite Knights in Medieval Life and Literature," in *Becoming Male in the Middle Ages*, ed. Jeffrey Jerome Cohen and Bonnie Wheeler (New York: Garland Publishing, 1997), pp. 279–302. On the topic of female cross-dressing fairly broadly in the Middle Ages, the standard study remains Valerie R. Hotchkiss, *Clothes Make the Man: Female Cross Dressing in Medieval Europe* (New York: Garland, 1990), chps. 6 & 7. More specific studies include Robert L. A. Clark, "A Heroine's Sexual Itinerary: Incest, Transvestism, and Same-Sex Marriage in Yde et Olive," in Taylor (ed.) *Gender Transgressions*, pp. 89–106; Michèle Perret, "Travesties et transsexuelles: Yde, Silence, Grisandole, Blanchadrine," *Romance Notes* 25, 3 (1985), 320–40.
11. Raoul de Houdenc, *Meraugis de Portlesguez*, ed. Szkilnik. All translations are those of Keith Busby.
12. Chrétien's ambiguity allowed ample room for later authors to adapt and rework his romances. For example, Hartmann von Aue's adaptations of *Erec et Enide* (*Erec*) and the *Chevalier au Lion* (*Iwein*) expand the narrator's presence significantly, lending a somewhat moralizing tone, and, as Rasmussen puts it, tend to "resolved deep conflicts, such as those based on gender dynamics, which are often left open in the Old French sources." Ann Marie Rasmussen, "Medieval German Romance," in *The Cambridge Companion to Medieval Romance*, ed. Roberta L. Krueger (Cambridge: Cambridge University Press, 2000), p. 188. See also Albrecht Classen on German romance (Chapter 13, this volume).
13. Unfortunately, there is no recent edition of *Florimont*. There is one scholarly edition available (n.b. the introduction and notes are in German): Aimon de Varennes, *Florimont*, ed. Hilka.
14. See also Chapter 5, by Elizabeth Archibald (this volume).
15. It was translated and adapted into several vernacular European languages, and served as the basis for Thomas Malory's Arthurian works (which in turn served as the basis for a majority of the modern retellings of the story of Arthur and the knights of the round table, such as T. H. White's *The Once and Future King*).
16. Sommer, ed., *The Vulgate Version of the Arthurian Romances*. My translation.
17. As the earlier quotations suggest, Galehaut's love can be read as homosexual as well as homosocial. The classic study is Christiane Marchello-Nizia, "Amour courtois, société masculine et figures du pouvoir," *Annales. Histoire, Sciences Sociales* 36, no. 6 (Nov.–Dec.) (1981), 969–82. Marchello-Nizia's analysis brings to the fore as well the conflation between the language of feudal vassalage

and the descriptions of courtly love in Old French romance; her arguments underlie much of the work done on the topic, including this chapter.

18. Secondary female characters of all types also offer insights for the study of gender norms. In particular, the contrast between the behaviors of the secondary characters and the female love interest can be quite significant. For example, in Chrétien de Troyes's *Chevalier de la Charrette*, several female characters travel on their own quests, including Meleagant's sister, who searches out Lancelot when he has been imprisoned by her brother.
19. Women led armies to battle, accompanied the crusaders to the Holy Land (onto the field of battle at the siege of Jerusalem, according to several accounts), defended their domains, etc. We even have several poetic accounts of tournaments of women (e.g. the *Tournoiement des Dames*), which, while fictional and presented as such, are also populated with real, historical female figures who are presented positively. The possibility of female chivalric action is explored in romance as well: cf. the discussion of the *Roman de Silence* in this chapter.
20. In fact, noblemen did not do so either, as a rule, but, given a knight's armor and horse, it was at least potentially possible.
21. The basic plotlines for the majority of these romances derive from folktale motifs. I have argued elsewhere that the closer a narrative remains to its folklore roots, the more passive the heroine. Kathy M. Krause, "Gender and Generic Paradigm Shift in Old French Narrative," in *Paradigm Shifts During the Global Middle Ages and Early Modern Age. Epochs, Epistemes, and Cultural-Historical Concepts*, ed. Albrecht Classen (Turnhout: Brepols, 2018), pp. 65–79.
22. Gerbert de Montreuil, *Le Roman de la Violette*, ed. Buffum. There is no English translation of the *Violette*; the modern French translation is now unfortunately out of print: Gerbert de Montreuil, *Le Roman de la Violette*, trans. Mireille Demaules (Paris: Stock, 1992).
23. Gerbert de Montreuil, *Roman de la Violette.*
24. Heldris de Cornuailles, *Silence*, ed. Roche-Mahdi. Roche-Mahdi provides a facing-page edition of the text and an English translation. For a scholarly edition of the Old French, see Heldris de Cornuailles, *Le Roman de Silence*, ed. Thorpe.
25. The ending leaves a bad taste for many modern readers: the narrative closure says nothing about Silence's own desires in the matter, only that the king's counselors recommend it and that her parents are delighted (ll. 6669–83). In becoming a woman again, she is effectively silenced, as her name indicates. Additionally, the narrator ends his tale with a notoriously slippery defense of his portrayal of women, claiming that one should praise good women more than blame bad ones because women have less opportunity (and, depending on how you read the text, less innate ability) to behave well (ll. 6686–702). Considerable recent scholarship explores issues of gender in the *Roman de Silence.* The two special issues of the journal *Arthuriana* devoted to the romance are perhaps the best introduction to the multiplicity of critical approaches: *Arthuriana* 7.1 (1997) and *Arthuriana* 12.1 (2002).
26. For example, to name just two, Liénor in Jean Renart's *Roman de la Rose*, and Andrivete in Girart d'Amiens's *Escanor*.

27. The Old French term "escoufle" refers to a bird of prey known in English as a kite. Given the possible confusion of the term "kite," I have translated the title as the *Romance of the Hawk*. Jean Renart, *L'Escoufle*, ed. Sweetser.
28. The only real constant in the "idyllic" romance is the youth of the couple and an obstacle to their union. Thus, in the earliest of the European versions, the *Conte de Floire et Blanchefleur*, the Christian heroine is sold into slavery by the hero's princely Muslim father, and she plays a very passive role in the narrative. In *Guillaume de Palerne*, the couple flee together and remain together throughout their adventures, while in others the hero departs to prove himself worthy of his higher-class beloved, and the heroine has to find a way to avoid a forced marriage (or at least consummation of the marriage) until the hero can return and they can flee together (e.g. *Jehan et Blonde*).
29. All citations are from Jean Renart, *L'Escoufle*. All translations from the *Roman de l'Escoufle* are my own.
30. In her analysis of Jean Renart's romance, Sahar Amer calls attention both to the lesbian and social implications of the relationship between Aelis and the other women, and to the cross-cultural resonances with medieval Arabic tales. Sahar Amer, *Crossing Borders: Love between Women in Medieval French and Arabic Literature* (Philadelphia: University of Pennsylvania Press, 2008), chap. 4. See also Anna Kłosowska, *Queer Love in the Middle Ages* (New York: Palgrave Macmillan, 2005).
31. "Sachiés que c'est une bons tresors / De bone feme, belle et preu" (Know that she is a true treasure of a good woman, beautiful and valiant); ll. 5502–3.

Suggestions for Further Reading

Amer, Sahar. *Crossing Borders: Love between Women in Medieval French and Arabic Literature*. Philadelphia: University of Pennsylvania Press, 2008.

Bouchard, Constance Britain. *Strong of Body, Brave and Noble: Chivalry and Society in Medieval France*. Ithaca, NY: Cornell University Press, 1998.

Bullough, Vern L. "On Being Male in the Middle Ages." In *Medieval Masculinities: Regarding Men in the Middle Ages*, ed. Clare E. Lees, Thelma Fenster, and JoAnn McNamara. Minneapolis: University of Minnesota Press, 1994, pp. 31–46.

Burgwinkle, William E. *Sodomy, Masculinity, and Law in Medieval Literature: France and England, 1050–1230*. Cambridge: Cambridge University Press, 2004.

Burns, E. Jane. *Courtly Love Undressed: Reading through Clothes in Medieval French Culture*. Philadelphia: University of Pennsylvania Press, 2002.

Busby, Keith. "'Plus Acesmez Qu'une Popine": Male Cross-Dressing in Medieval French Narrative." In *Gender Transgressions: Crossing the Normative Barrier in Old French Literature*, ed. Karen J. Taylor. New York: Garland, 1998, pp. 45–59.

Gaunt, Simon. *Gender and Genre in Medieval French Literature*. Cambridge: Cambridge University Press, 1995 (in particular, chapter 3: "The Knight Meets his Match: Romance").

Karras, Ruth Mazo. *From Boys to Men: Formations of Masculinity in Late Medieval Europe*. Philadelphia: University of Pennsylvania Press, 2002.
Krueger, Roberta L. *Women Readers and the Ideology of Gender in Old French Verse Romance*. Cambridge: Cambridge University Press, 1993.
Lees, Clare E., Thelma Fenster and JoAnn McNamara (eds.) *Medieval Masculinities: Regarding Men in the Middle Ages*. Minneapolis: University of Minnesota Press, 1994.
Marchello-Nizia, Christiane. "Amour courtois, société masculine et figures du pouvoir." *Annales. Histoire, Sciences Sociales* 36, 6 (Nov.–Dec.) (1981): 969–82.

10

MEGAN MOORE

Emotions as the Language of Romance

With the translations "en romanz" of Latin literature, vernacular fictions focused on amplifying emotional states, rendering emotion central to the emergent genre of romance. From Lavinia's love monologue in the *Roman d'Eneas*, to the explorations of psychological response in *Philomena*, to the ill-fated love triangle of Thomas's *Tristan*, early courtly fictions explored feelings, often in internal monologues that are added to the "translation" or adaptation or in authorial interventions. While positive feelings such as love and joy are integral to romance, grief, anger, and shame are also central to imagining the emotional world of the elite characters who inhabit their pages. In this chapter, I will explore how the writing of romance, with its new focus on courtliness, is intricately entwined with the language of emotions. I explore how medieval romance figures community through the ways it imagines, depicts, and narrates acceptable – and, crucially, unacceptable – practices of feeling. As I explain here, emotion is the very language of romance, and emotion emerges as a way of figuring noble identity in literature destined for the elite.

The Language of Emotions

Research on emotions spans fields as diverse as neurobiology and literary studies, inviting debate about the differences between feelings, emotions, and affect. Can feelings be controlled, or are they precognitive? Can feelings be trusted, and what determines their authenticity? Can language ever accurately negotiate and communicate what we feel for another person?

All of these questions had resonance for medieval people. They appear in sophisticated treatises written by medieval physicians (such as Aristotle via James of Venice, Avicenna via Dominicus Gundissalinus, Galen, Gentile), who expanded on Ancient Greeks' understanding of emotions as tied to four basic humors, or bodily fluids, sometimes naturalizing and pathologizing grief as "phlegmatic" and "feminine" or imagining cultural "others" as naturally "choleric" and prone to anger. Medieval literature resists such naturalizations, most famously in Charlemagne's extended, valorized weeping over the body of his dead nephew, Roland, reminding us that medieval discussions were as nuanced and contested across media as ours today. While medieval theologians (such as Aquinas and Gratian) explored how spirit produced feelings and were particularly concerned about how to regulate and prohibit the social and spiritual consequences of negative feelings, such as the illicit and unnatural appetites that structured extramarital and incestuous desire, philosophers and scientists (such as Duns Scotus and William of Ockham) pondered whether emotions such as love came in through the eye, like a beam, and how they provoked a bodily and psychological response.

Authors from texts as diverse as the *fabliaux* to *chansons de geste* to romance (most prominently, Chrétien de Troyes, Chaucer, Malory, and Marie de France) borrowed and improvised from Latin and Greek sources to translate old stories, revising and expanding to present them anew to their medieval audiences, now Christians who were most often elites.[1] These translations of Ancient Greek and Latinate feeling models offer insights into what constituted desirable emotional practices among medieval elites, sometimes articulated in resistance to the controls on noble behavior dictated by the medieval church. As Peggy McCracken has pointed out, for example, in medieval romance, elite adulterous desire is imagined as the norm, not the exception, in conflict with contemporary church strictures.[2]

Scholars of the history of emotions differentiate between three main words to describe the process of feeling: affect, feeling, and emotion. I find the specificity deployed by Stephanie Trigg to be particularly useful. "Affect" refers to the *precognitive neurobiology* of emotions, how neurotransmitters prompt chemical changes in the brain and the cascading chemical effects they produce on the body, such as the fight or flight response. "Feelings" refer to the *personal experience* of these affective states. A question such as "how are you feeling today?" invites introspection about one's mood, and it simultaneously admits a slippage: there may be a difference between internal psychological reality and outward appearance. Feelings can only be known by the feeler and explained through language to the outsider. Feelings become "emotions" when they are shared, as Trigg explains: "in contrast to the unconscious or pre-discursive emphasis of affect theory, 'emotion' emerges with a more specialized sense, referring to the way we experience, narrate, and perform what we feel."[3]

Emotions are *feelings in negotiation* between two or more people; they are feelings *as communication*, creating or disturbing community. Grief is an excellent example: in mourning, some cultures wail, while others are silent. If my performance of emotion is incongruous with your expectations, the mismatch may provoke discomfort, hostility, rejection, or fear. Emotions require an interpretive act, a negotiation of a set of bodily signs and language that creates agreement or disagreement, inclusion or exclusion, based on how my performance meets your expectations – emotions depend on and create community between people.

This chapter begins by foregrounding the centrality of *emotions* to medieval romance – that is, the expression of feelings within and as community. As historians of emotion Barbara Rosenwein and William Reddy each explain, emotions shape the boundaries of community.[4] In her landmark study *Emotional Communities in the Early Middle Ages*, Rosenwein posits the existence of "'emotional communities': groups in which people adhere to the same norms of emotional expression and value – or devalue – the same or related emotions."[5] Reddy extends the implications of thinking with emotional communities for the medieval elites we find in romance, and he identifies a relation between courtly love and elite reading communities that was at odds with and helped to differentiate elite practices from church doctrines.[6] That is, emotions had a profound influence on the normative boundaries of elite community, both within the text and, as Reddy claims, in the real medieval world.[7]

Sara Ahmed's work clarifies how emotions can negotiate community, how they can be a political practice:

> If good emotions are cultivated, and are worked on and towards, then they remain defined against uncultivated or unruly emotions, which frustrate the formation of the competent self. Those who are "other" to me or us, or those that threaten to make us other, remain the source of bad feeling in this model of emotional intelligence. It is not difficult to see how emotions are bound up with the securing of social hierarchy: emotions become attributes of bodies as a way of transforming what is "lower" or "higher" into bodily traits.[8]

In this vein, both romance and emotions are ways of "securing social hierarchy," or, as I frame it more broadly, negotiating communities of privilege, of medieval elites.

Scholars have suggested that romance was dependent on elites who could afford to sponsor a network of parchment makers, scribes, illuminators, and professional performers.[9] Romance's wealthy patrons also sometimes shaped its content.[10] In Chrétien de Troyes's prologue to *Le Chevalier de la charrette*, for example, he explains that he is responding to his patron

Marie de Champagne's "comandemanz" (commandment) (l. 22) for a "romans" (romance) (l. 4).[11] Considered together with the demands of a patronage system, the economics of medieval reading, court performance, and literacy suggest that romance is a genre that thematizes medieval privilege. That is, like the luxury objects in which romances are contained, the narratives themselves invite consideration of their subject matter – here, elite *emotions* – and elite community.[12]

Expressed as a negotiation of feeling between two or more people, emotions automatically provoke judgment. Partnership, friendship, family structures, and political allegiances depend on shared practices of emotion, on people exchanging common sets of signs in order to successfully broadcast and read the language of emotions in the same ways. In this way, as Sara Ahmed has pointed out, emotions are inherently a political practice, a delicate balancing act of power and communication in particular communities.[13] There is a kind of social contract created through emotional ties and, for all that emotions can bind people together, they can also tear them apart. There is much potential in possible disjunctures between what words about emotions *purport*, how they are understood, and what they actually *enact*.

In medieval romance, for example, one of the motivating questions is whether the performance of a lover's desire is authentic or merely an untrustworthy ruse. In Chrétien de Troyes's twelfth-century Old French romance, *Le Chevalier de la charrette*, Guinevere refuses to see her lover, Lancelot, because she believes his love to be inauthentic because he hesitated to get into a prisoner's cart in order to pursue her abductors (ll. 4484–90). Guinevere becomes uncertain about his commitment, and she demands that he prove his love for her by abasing himself; neither his words (his professions of love) nor his bodily signals (nearly dying of lovesickness when she scorns him) are sufficiently trustworthy signs of an internal emotional reality. The text imagines that emotions can enact (and disrupt) partnership by casting Guinevere's own true emotional motivations as suspect when she "*fet sanblant* de correciee, / Si s'anbruncha et ne dist mot" (*pretends* to be angry, / So she broods and does not say a word) (ll. 3940–41, emphasis mine).[14] Guinevere's seemingly flippant rejection of her lover reveals a deeper concern about the misapprehension of emotional signs: in the space between feeling-emitter and emotion-receiver lies danger.

This potential slippage is the stuff narrative is made of: misunderstanding, double-entendre, and reaction. The sites where language is inadequate makes for fruitful storyline potential. The possible slippages between "I love you" and the performance of perfect love are manifold; the potential mismatch between feeling-emitter and emotion-receiver situates emotions as performatives, what J. L. Austin has coined as "speech acts": words that *do* things, with the ensuing potential for *mis-doing* things.[15] When speech acts succeed in performing something, they are "felicitous," and when they fail, they become "infelicitous."

If felicitous, emotions have the power to bind people together, as in the happy endings wherein love strengthen the lovers' community; if infelicitous, they have the possibility of destroying the ties that bind, as in the cannibalistic infanticide of *Philomena*, the destructive, incestuous love of *Le Roman de la Manekine*, or the utter annihilation of Arthur's legacy in *La Mort le roi Artu*. Emotions are only felicitous when everyone can agree on how their expression should take form, when they function as a common language.

This common language of emotions entails some commonalities in community, and medieval authors are careful to describe their audiences in many of the prologues transmitted to us. In one manuscript version of *Floire et Blancheflor*, a late-twelfth-century Old French romance about a cross-confessional, Mediterranean love affair between a Christian girl and a Muslim boy, MS BnF Fr. 375, the narrator commands his audience:

Signor, oiiés, tot li amant,
Cil qui d'amors se vont penant,
Li chevalier et les puceles,
Li damoisel, les damoiseles!
Se mon conte volés entendre,
Molt i porrés d'amors aprendre[16] (ll. 1–6)

Lords, listen up, and all of the lovers,
Those who go along pained from love,
Knights and maidens,
Young men and young women!
If you want to listen to my tale,
You can learn a lot about love[17]

Here, the instruction is to learn about love if "young lords and ladies" or "knights and maidens" can be used to describe you. The audience for this romance is called into being by a narrator who identifies them by their social position and by their relation to love, linking elite community to both storytelling and emotion. The narrator suggests that, in gluing together community, emotions function as a sort of lingua franca: a common language of negotiation between elites, both internally within the text (between characters) and externally between text and audience (between elite medieval listeners). That is, for this narrator, the language of emotions creates community – it creates a compact between people about which expressions are welcome among "lords and ladies," and which are grounds for exclusion.

Words are required to transform private, interior sensations of *feeling* into spoken, public utterances of *emotion*, and they are not always reliable, even when shared among friends or lovers. To complicate things further, words for emotions vary by language and time. "Grief" connotes quite differently in modern English, Middle English, and Old French, for example. Old French texts more often use "dol," which connotes physical pain, to talk about grieving than "grief," which primarily connotes "heavy" or "burdensome" in some dialects. Likewise, in Middle English, "gref" connotes "hardship," "sickness," or "spite" before it connotes "sorrow," while "mŏrning" and "sorwe" more readily describe "sorrow, sadness."[18] Our languages about emotions may not match, as culture shapes the ways we describe and communicate about processing feelings within a community. As a result, we must be careful not to map our own modern expectations about words for emotions onto medieval texts.

In Chrétien de Troyes's exceedingly violent twelfth-century Old French *Philomena*, for example, the male protagonist, Tereus, unironically declares his *love* for the sister-in-law he intends to rape and torture:

> Mes de tant fait viaux que cortois
> Que s'amour li requiert ançois
> Qu'il li forface nulle rien.
> "Bele, fet il, or saciez bien
> Que je vous aim ..."[19] (ll. 763–7)

> But before [taking her by force] he tries to seem courtly
> [in] that he asks her for her love
> So that he doesn't transgress against her at all.
> "Beautiful one," he says, "now know well
> That I love you ..."

This version of love is unrecognizable both to us as modern readers and to Philomena as his medieval love object. Unsurprisingly, Philomena protests Tereus's performance of love by renaming it as violence, incest, and rape that transgress cultural norms, familial structures, and Christian law. Philomena's protests offer insight into the ways that at least one medieval author thought about emotions in relation to the structures that govern practices of courtly community: here, in terms of law, family, and religion, and, as I argue in *The Erotics of Grief*, in transforming the classical, Ovidian fable for a new, medieval context, *Philomena* explores a particularly medieval set of concerns about the relation between courtliness, law, and emotions.[20] Later, when her repetitive, anaphoric accusations qualify Tereus's love as "fel," Philomena castigates his misperformance of love as a misperformance of laws applicable to his *status*, thereby opening space for performances of emotions to test the boundaries of inclusion and exclusion within her courtly community (ll. 781–825).

Texts such as *Philomena* offer a caution to remember that words about emotions articulate the boundaries of communities – here, elite love – differently across time and language, and they invite us to pay particular attention to exactly what texts claim is at stake in exchanges of emotions between people, to identify what boundaries emotions are deployed to negotiate.

Emotions as the Narrative of Romance

As complex as the discussion *about* medieval emotions is – what they are, whether language can ever adequately represent feeling, how we can overcome differences in cultural semantics – emotions invariably *do* a lot within romance. Emotions create narrative structure, they are its very *language*, and the relation between their emission and reception often propels storylines. I consider the language of emotions to be the language of romance: the performances of a gamut of feelings – grief, love, shame, hate, and anger – are fundamental to how the genre narrates its community, both internally within a text and externally within its audience.

Perhaps counterintuitively, *negative* emotions such as grief, anger, shame, and hate are more prevalent than love itself. My research in a database of Old French literary texts, *TFA*, suggests that grief may be the most widespread of *all* the emotion words in Old French romance.[21] One of the most doleful and widely translated romances, *Tristan et Yseut*, focuses on a pair of star-crossed lovers who are bound by a love potion they were never meant to consume. The adaptation composed in Middle High German by Gottfried von Strassburg sees the eponymous protagonist Tristan born to a mother so bereaved that she predicts he will live a life full of sorrow and names him after sadness itself before dying with the newborn in her arms. The sadness not only calls Tristan into being, it also invites listeners to intuit dismay as attendant to Tristan's life story. Emotion becomes fundamentally interwoven with propelling the storyline: sadness structures the very core of the *Tristan* love story. Grief is at the very heart of noble love, according to Gottfried:

> wan ein dinc daz mir widerstât:
> swer inneclîche liebe hât,
> doch ez im wê von herzen tuo,
> daz herze stât doch ie dar zuo.
> Der inneclîche minnenmuot,
> sô der in sîner senegluot

ie mêre und mêre brinnet,
sô er ie sêrer minnet.
Diz leit is liebes alse vol,
daz ubel daz tuot sô herzewol,
daz es kein edel herze enbirt,
sît ez hie von geherzet wirt.
ich weiz ez wârez als den tôt
und erkenne ez bî der selben nôt:
der edele senedære
der minnet senedie mære.[22] (ll. 107–22)

though love and pain
Be intimately trussed, yet the heart must
Ever persist. For, as the lover's
Passion, so set to flame by its desire,
Must by this flame thrive, so in his passion's
Relentless gain does the fire ever rise.
This dear grief is the heart's most ardent will,
Which no noble heart may ever yield.
Of this I am certain as I am of death,
For I have learned it through the same dear distress:
All noble lovers love to read of love-tales.[23]

Gottfried describes love as interwoven (here, "trussed") with grief and suffering, and he concomitantly describes this particular mix of grief and love as particular to "noble lovers." Though many scholars have focused on this kind of romanticized suffering under the rubric of "courtly love," I recognize passages such as these as imagining a certain performance of love – love as grief – to be intimately entwined or "trussed" with creating *community* – *noble, courtly* lovers.

Here, Gottfried describes his courtly audience as constituted by what it desires: narratives describing the suffering of romantic love. What seem like oxymoronic juxtapositions constitute the very basis for narrative tension: "Love and pain [are] intimately trussed" and "grief [most commonly described as phlegmatic in medieval physiology] is the heart's most ardent will." The lovers are imagined to be both drowning in grief and consumed by the burning fire of their desire, and it is the suffering, rather than the resolution, that this *Tristan* poet seeks to amplify and reiterate and that his audience requests.

Gottfried's prologue not only foregrounds and explains the place of grief in narrating love, but it also interpellates a certain reading public: "noble lovers" who "love to read of love-tales." The community of the text is both announced by the prologue and ensured by the strictures of form: medieval literacies, the poet admits, proscribe this text for most, and so not only by nature, but also by class and education is love described as grief in ways that are reserved for and deployed to describe an elite audience. Wailing and suffering express love in texts as diverse as the *Bel inconnu* (ll. 2751–95), *Cligès* (ll. 1535–2199), *Floriant* (ll. 375–512), *Hunbaut* (ll. 1779–1889), *Yvain* (ll. 1144–1544), *Chaitivel* (ll. 71–143), and *Yder* (ll. 4967–5064), among many others.[24] In these romances, lovers sigh, moan, swoon, become emaciated, have fevers, and nearly die for their beloved; in some, such as *Erec et Enide*, a lover believes her beloved has died and begins actively mourning, ripping out her hair and scratching her face bloody as an expression of her love (ll. 2207–790). Good, noble lovers are good grievers, we are told by these romances.

Though nowhere as prevalent as grief, shame also influences community, for shame's power is fundamentally public. It is the public sharing of shame that degrades protagonists, expels them from their communities, and spurs revenge. In *La Mort le roi Artu*, for example, Guinevere is shamefully derided in front of the court; before storming off to avenge her, Lancelot demands to know why her shame was not averted by Arthur's knights (ll. 74.63–5). Shame is also a powerful motivator throughout Chrétien de Troyes's romances. *In Le Chevalier de la charrette*, Guinevere believes Lancelot has shamed himself (and her) by getting into a prisoner's cart in order to rescue her. Until he redeems himself, Lancelot is so shamed that he is no longer worthy of being included in her community. Another of his romances, *Le Chevalier au lion*, depends on the protagonist Yvain's determination to avenge his cousin Agravain's shameful defeat (ll. 745–46). The explicit moral of Chrétien's *Cligès* revolves around the resolution of the "honte" (shame; l. 6520) caused to the court by the deceptive, adulterous affair of Fénice and Cligès. And in *Erec et Enide*, Enide recounts that people are chiding her new husband for choosing to stay in bed over tending to his chivalric duties: "or se vont tuit de vos gabant," she recounts, "juesne et chenu, petit et grant; / recreant vos apelent tuit" (Now they all go around gossiping about you, / young and old, small and big; / "recreant" they are all calling you) (ll. 2549–51). Erec is so shamed by his wife's report of the gossip that he forbids her from talking to him and drags her off on a series of dangerous adventures in the forest, where her body often becomes the bait in contest after contest with other knights.

In these stories, shame drives the story of misperformed masculinity, of disproportionate love, of communal expectations about knighthood violated. And its power lies in its function for community: shame is only effective when it is known, shared, and gossiped about, and its force is to reject someone who is not conforming to communal expectations. Not only do emotions such as shame perform a relationship between individual people,

Figure 10.1 *La Queste del Saint Graal*: Arthur mourns the death of Erec. MS Français 112 (3) fol. 113v. Bibliothèque Nationale de France.

they also negotiate and narrate the borders of the acceptable within the broader communities in which the lovers belong. In these examples, shame frames the borders of acceptable noble masculinity – shame underscores that courtly knights must strike a healthy balance between their obligations to their lovers and to their community of warriors.

Like shame, other emotions, such as hate, may also delineate whom and what may be loved. In many medieval texts from diverse linguistic and geographic backgrounds, foreigners and class-transgressors are universally hated, mistrusted, and maligned until they can be recuperated by transformation, conversion, and incorporation into the dominant culture of the romance. Though hate can be directed internally to frame personal disputes within a courtly community, hate is often reserved for the abject of romance: gnomes, giants, enemies, foreigners, and the poor. Described in Old French through words such as "haine" and "het," often in tandem with "vil," which all seem to map straightforwardly onto modern French usage, hate appears an easy emotion to define – it is the opposite of love, it is detesting. But Old French usage suggests more: hate can figure the *liminality* of community, its borders and edges, delineating who cannot be loved and included.

Hatred shows us that medieval outsiders – foreigners, the poor, and religious others – are often reviled until they can be regularized into the feeling communities of the Christian, courtly west. In Chrétien's *Erec et Enide*, for example, the eponymous protagonist is an impoverished beauty bedecked in a "tant povre robe et si *vil*" (such a poor and *vile* robe) (l. 506) for whom popular revulsion is a function of her station – "d'un povre vavasor est fille: / povretez main prodome *aville*" (she is the daughter of a poor vassal: / poverty has *made vile* many a man) (ll. 1555–6) – until she can be bedecked in beautiful expensive clothing gifted to her by the queen and therefore become fit to marry Erec, no longer an object of revulsion, but one of love: "Por ce *l'ama*, et se li plot, / Qu'ele estoit bele et bien aprise" (for this, [the Queen] *loved* her, and so it pleased her / that [Enide] be well taken care of) (ll. 1672–73).

Looking abroad, one can identify similar transformations from reviled outsider to beloved community member at the heart of the *chantefable Aucassin et Nicolette* or variations of the romance of *Floire et Blancheflor*, both predicated on cross-confessional love that is imagined as transformative and recuperative in final scenes of religious conversion in the name of western, Christian, elite love. And elsewhere, the handless girl story told in *Le Roman de la Manekine* or *La Belle Hélène de Constantinople* transforms a mother-in-law's hate to communal acceptance of a foreign bride in a redemptive journey featuring elite maidens who flee their fathers' eastern incestuous desire in favor of redemptive, western exogamous love.

Such stories imagine hate for the "other" as a way of delineating the boundaries of the self within romance. The resolution of hate invites the possibility that certain identities can be subsumed, tamed, or transformed into acceptability. As these romances and their emotional trajectories show, hate not only names something as "other," it also helps perform and figure the boundaries of the elite self. We can discern the borders of welcomed, normalized elite, Christian identities as *the* community of western romances through the things they come together to hate.

Romance as the Misperformance of Emotions: The Case of Courtly Love

Finally, love: intuitive, fundamental, we think of it as *the* emotion of romance. This is in part because of a scholarly tradition devoted to the study of "courtly love" that elaborates on medieval treatises, most notably Andreas Capellanus' twelfth-century *De Amore*, which prescribes suffering for love as ennobling and beneficial.[25] Capellanus specifies "that love is suffering is easy to see, for before the love becomes equally balanced on both sides there is no torment greater, since the lover is always in fear."[26] Scholars have debated whether Capellanus' treatise represented *actual* noble practices or an imagined *ideal*.[27] Irrespective, lovers' suffering – remember here that the most often used emotive in Old French romance is "dol" and not "amor" – invites a crucial question: can romance ever depict *felicitous* love?

I argue that romance is predicated on the moments where emotions *misfire*: the plot depends on moments when emotions misperform human relationships, where they are misread by their sender or emitter. The case of the misreading of Lancelot's two steps in Chrétien's *Le chevalier de la charrette* is tell-tale, and worth returning to in detail:

Li chevaliers . . . n'i monte;
Mar le fist et mar en ot honte
Que maintenant sus ne sailli,
Qu'il s'an tendra por mal bailli;
Mes Reisons, qui d'Amors se part,
Li dit que del monter se gart,
Si le chastie et si l'anseigne
Que rien ne face ne anpreigne
Dont il ait honte ne reproche.
N'est pas el cuer, mes an la boche,
Reisons qui ce dire li ose;
Mes Amors est el cuer anclose
Qui li comandë et semont
Que tost an la charrete mont.
Amors le vialt et il i saut,
Que de la honte ne li chaut
Puis qu'Amors le comande et vialt. (ll. 365–81)

The knight . . . does not get in [to the cart];
To his detriment and to his great shame
Does he not jump in right away now,
For which he will consider himself mistreated;
But Reason, who departs from Love,
Tells him that he must refrain from mounting in it

So she chastises him and so she teaches him
That he never do nor undertake
Anything from which he may have shame or reproach.
It is not within the heart, but within the mouth,
That Reason dares to say this to him;
But Love is enclosed in the heart
Who commands and summons him
That he quickly mount into the cart.
Love wants it and he jumps in,
He does not care at all about the shame
Because Love commands and desires it.

Permeated with emotion, this passage reflects the complicated, tenuous relationship between the performance of emotions, the performance of chivalric masculinity, and their reception within the courtly community. Temporarily indecisive, Lancelot decides, in the end, to ride in the cart in order to save Guinevere, but his hesitation – fear of shame? concern for his reputation? hatred and mistrust of the gnome? – is later read as a *misperformance* of love by Guinevere. When she finally deigns to speak to him again, she demands:

"Comant? Don n'eüstes vos honte
De la charrete et si dotastes?
Molt a grant enviz i montastes,
Quant vos demorastes deus pas.
Por ce, voir, ne vos vos je pas
Ne aresnier ne esgarder." (ll. 4502–7)

"What? Did you not have shame
From the cart, and therefore doubt?
You must have been filled with great desire to get into it,
When you waited the time of two steps.
For this reason, truly, I did not want
To speak to or look at you."

Here, too, the queen's response is peppered with emotions, some explicit ("honte," "enviz") and some only audible to an attentive audience. Guinevere's hurt, derision, and sarcasm are moments of emotional disjuncture that are keys to understanding how emotions structure romance. The disappointment underlying her wry observation that "you must have been filled with great desire to get into [the cart] / when you waited the time of two steps" is most forceful if read as full of sarcasm; her pain underscores how emotional *misperformances* write the material of romance. The episode of Lancelot's two steps reminds us that it is not the successful performance of emotions but the ways that they *misfire*, are *misread*, and naturalize suffering that propels the material of romance.

Though ostensibly Lancelot's self-abasement in the cart should chiasmatically figure the extent of his love (that is, the depths of his shame should figure the heights of his love), instead its *misreading* by Guinevere becomes the basis for the emotional tension of the entire romance. Some might object that Guinevere is, in fact, an excellent reader of Lancelot's emotions, that one reading could claim that there is no misfiring: Lancelot *did* hesitate. Yet Lancelot's apology – in which he sidesteps whether or not Guinevere misread his emotions, and instead mollifies her by promising never to hesitate again – suggests it may not even matter whose assessment is accurate. More importantly, there has been an essential disjuncture between how one lover performs love and the other receives that performance, revealing its precarity in the very exchange through which it is constituted. The misperformance of love spurs Lancelot to try to win back Guinevere's esteem in encounter after encounter, becoming both a negotiation of the community of the couple and a building block of storytelling.

Such misfirings generate the very storyline of romance: moments of suffering created by misexchanged emotions, by the infelicity of trying – and failing – to connect. Thinking about love as a constant *mis*performance shifts the terms of the debate away from the "truth" of noble practices and toward the ways that emotions are imagined to test the limits of community in romance, from the negotiation of chivalric and amorous duties in *Erec et Enide* to the transformation of foreign, incestuous desire in *Le Roman de la Manekine* to the downfall of the court depicted through the rage and grief of *La mort le roi Artu*. Reading the constant misperformance of emotions as a fecund site of narrative potential invites recognition that emotions have the power to uphold, negotiate, or potentially even destroy the bonds of communities as small as the amorous couple and as large as the courtly milieu.

From shame and rage to love and despair, the translation – and mistranslation – of individual feelings into communal emotions remains a site rich with narrative potential in medieval romance. Attentiveness to the diction of emotions offers a new and potentially rich avenue of inquiry into how courtly readers imagined and represented connection. Emotion words function like a contract between people, similar to performatives: they negotiate, enact, and destroy relationships. And in romance, these utterances most frequently misfire, sowing confusion, misunderstanding, and, most of all, despair among the lovers and knights who are propelled to further the plot by repairing the damage of these misperformances to their relationships. Emotional misperformances are integral to storytelling, and they are the very building blocks through which romance negotiates and narrates elite communities.

Notes

1. See the excellent overview of emotion in Naama Cohen-Hanegbi, "A Moving Soul: Emotions in Late Medieval Medicine," *Osiris* 31.1 (July 1, 2016): 46–66.
2. Peggy McCracken, *The Romance of Adultery: Queenship and Sexual Transgression in Old French Literature* (Philadelphia: University of Pennsylvania Press, 1998), 2.
3. Stephanie Trigg, "Introduction: Emotional Histories – Beyond the Personalization of the Past and the Abstraction of Affect Theory," *Exemplaria* 26.1 (2014): 7.
4. See Barbara H. Rosenwein, "Thinking Historically about Medieval Emotions," *History Compass* 8.8 (August 1, 2010): 828.
5. *Emotional Communities in the Early Middle Ages* (Ithaca, NY: Cornell University Press, 2006), 2.
6. Reddy explains: "the 'courtly love' doctrine found expression in a shadowy space beyond clerical regulation, through vernacular literature, music, and the decorative arts. In these profane genres, carefully crafted to avoid direct challenge to priestly authority, the counterdoctrine of true love exercised a profound influence on gender norms and courtship practices"; William M. Reddy, *The Navigation of Feeling: A Framework for the History of Emotions* (Cambridge: Cambridge University Press, 2001), 4.
7. As Reddy points out, medieval elites deployed emotional practices as community, in order to articulate their power and differentiate themselves from the medieval Church: "longing for association was an experience that led European elites to push back against the Christian doctrine of desire-as-appetite ... they launched the extremely successful and enduring set of doctrines and practices that make up the romantic love tradition" (*The Making of Romantic Love: Longing and Sexuality in Europe, South Asia, and Japan, 900–1200 CE.* Chicago, IL: The University of Chicago Press, 2012, 35).
8. Sara Ahmed, *The Cultural Politics of Emotion*, 2nd ed. (New York: Routledge, 2014), 4.
9. June Hall McCash, *The Cultural Patronage of Medieval Women* (Athens: University of Georgia Press, 1996), XII–XIV.
10. In a gendered analysis of the patronage of romance, Joan Ferrante agrees that many of the patrons were nobles – noble women – whose influence is visible throughout the content of their work, but she does not identify a connection between noble patronage, the representation of emotions, and the depiction of elite community, as I suggest here. See Joan Ferrante, "Whose Voice? The Influence of Women Patrons on Courtly Romances," in *Literary Aspects of Courtly Culture*, ed. Donald Maddox and Sara Sturm-Maddox (Cambridge: D.S. Brewer, 1994), 3–18, 18.
11. Chrétien de Troyes, *Le Chevalier de la charrette*, ed. Méla.
12. Megan Moore, *The Erotics of Grief* (Ithaca: Cornell University Press, 2021).
13. Ahmed, *The Cultural Politics of Emotion*.
14. Chrétien de Troyes, *Le Chevalier de la charrette*, ed. Méla.
15. J. L. Austin, *How to Do Things with Words* (Oxford: Clarendon Press, 1975).
16. *Le Conte de Floire et Blancheflor*, ed. Leclanche.
17. Unless otherwise noted, all translations are mine.

18. See the Middle English dictionary at https://quod.lib.umich.edu/m/middle-english-dictionary/dictionary/MED19318/track?counter=1&search_id=5413572.
19. *Pyrame et Thisbé, Narcisse, Philomena*, ed. Baumgartner. English translations mine.
20. See in particular chapter 1, "*Philomena* and the Erotics of Privilege in the Middle Ages."
21. See the TFA database housed in the *Project for American and French Research on the Treasury of the French Language* at https://artfl-project.uchicago.edu. This database allows researchers to scan a large corpus of French-language texts by author, date, and word. A scan of their Old French database using base forms "dol.*" and "doul.*" reveals grief to be the most prevalent of all the emotions words. For more, see my work in the introduction to *The Erotics of Grief*, 15–17.
22. Gottfried von Strassburg, *Tristan*, ed. Marold.
23. Translation from Matthew Wildermuth at https://classicalpoets.org/2019/04/26/translation-of-gottfried-von-strassburgs-tristan-prologue/ Alternatively, from the Hatto translation: "The more a lover's passion burns in its furnace of desire, the more ardently will he love. This sorrow is so full of joy, this ill is so inspiriting that, having once been heartened by it, no noble heart will forgo it! I know as sure as death and have learned it from this same anguish: the noble lover loves love-tales," in Gottfried von Strassburg, *Tristan with the 'Tristran' of Thomas*, trans. Hatto, 42–3.
24. *Le Bel inconnu*, ed. Williams; *Les romans de Chrétien de Troyes. II: Cligès*, ed. Micha; *Floriant et Florete*, ed. Williams; *The Romance of Hunbaut*, ed. Winters; *Les romans de Chrétien de Troyes IV: Yvain*, ed. Roques; *Chaitivel*, ed. Rychner; *Der altfranzösische Yderroman*, ed. Gelzer.
25. Andreas Capellanus, *The Art of Courtly Love*, trans. Parry, 30.
26. Ibid., 4.
27. For an overview, see Douglas Kelly, "Courtly Love in Perspective: The Hierarchy of Love in Andreas Capellanus," *Traditio*, 1968, 119–147; Keith Nickolaus, *Marriage Fictions in Old French Secular Narratives, 1170–1250: A Critical Re-Evaluation of the Courtly Love Debate* (online edition; Routledge, 2013).

Suggestions for Further Reading

Ahmed, Sara. *Cultural Politics of Emotion*. 2nd ed. New York: Routledge, 2014.

Bataille, Georges. *Erotism: Death and Sensuality*. Translated by Mary Dalwood. San Francisco: City Lights Books, 1962.

Boquet, Damien and Piroska Nagy (eds.). *Medieval Sensibilities: A History of Emotions in the Middle Ages*. Translated by Robert Shaw. Cambridge: Polity Press, 2018.

Brandsma, Frank, Carolyne Larrington, and Corinne Saunders (eds.). *Emotions in Medieval Arthurian Literature: Body, Mind, Voice*. Cambridge: D. S. Brewer, 2015.

Burger, Glenn D. and Holly A. Crocker (eds.). *Medieval Affect, Feeling, and Emotion*. Cambridge: Cambridge University Press, 2019.

Derrida, Jacques. *The Work of Mourning*. Ed. Pascale-Anne Brault and Michael Naas. Chicago and London: The University of Chicago Press, 2001.

Dufallo, Basil and Peggy McCracken (eds.) *Dead Lovers: Erotic Bonds and the Study of Premodern Europe*. Ann Arbor, MI: The University Press of Michigan, 2006.
Jaeger, Stephen. *Ennobling Love: In Search of a Lost Sensibility*. Philadelphia: University of Pennsylvania Press, 1999.
Nussbaum, Martha. *Upheavals of Thought: The Intelligence of Emotions*. Cambridge: Cambridge University Press, 2001.
Reddy, William M. *The Making of Romantic Love: Longing and Sexuality in Europe, South Asia, and Japan, 900–1200 CE*. Chicago, IL: The University of Chicago Press, 2012.
Rosenwein, Barbara. *Emotional Communities in the Early Middle Ages*. Ithaca, NY: Cornell University Press, 2006.

11

DAVID A. WACKS

Medieval Iberian Romance

Literary histories of Spain and Iberia tell the story of how Iberian authors received (Arthurian) romance from French texts and, after the Grail cycle was translated into Castilian, proceeded to write their own romances, inaugurated by *Amadís de Gaula* (begun in manuscript in the late thirteenth or early fourteenth century and extended and brought into print in 1507 by Garci Rodríguez de Montalvo).[1] Occasionally there is mention of the Catalan works *Curial e Güelfa* (anonymous, ca. 1450)[2] and *Tirant Lo Blanch* (ca. 1490),[3] and the inevitable reference to the genre's savaging (or, as Harry Sieber writes, "reconciliation")[4] at the hands of Cervantes in *Don Quijote* (1605 and 1615). The story of medieval Iberian romance is in fact more complicated. Hebrew and Arabic authors also wrote texts that we might consider romances some years before the Castilian *Grail* and *Amadís* appeared. These authors adapted the motifs of Arthurian or chivalric romance, combining them with the literary tropes and conventions familiar to them from Hebrew and Arabic traditions. Others, such as the anonymous author of *Cavallero Zifar* (ca. 1300) and Ramon Llull in his ecclesiastical *Blaquerna*, transform the conventions of romance to suit their own ecclesiastical and spiritual purposes. In this way, if we imagine romance in Iberia less as a stable genre with a canon and more as a set of conventions and tropes that authors recombined in novel ways, we see it as a literary practice that crosses languages and religious groups that share chivalric and literary values across these differences. What is interesting to note is that the earliest significant production of Arthurian tropes in the Peninsula come not from Christian writers working in the Iberian romance languages, but from Jewish and Muslim writers working in Hebrew and Arabic. However, because Castilian went on to become the dominant language in the Peninsula and then the national language of what would become Spain, Spanish literary history tends to focus on Castilian.

Arthurian and other romances cultivated by French writers reached Iberian audiences in the twelfth century. The first references are by Catalan troubadours. In a composition dated to 1154, Bernart de Ventadorn mentions Tristan and Iseult, and around 1170 Guiraut de Cabrera follows suit, mentioning a whole string of French romances in one of his songs. Then follows a long silence until the end of the thirteenth century, when Alfonso X "The Learned" of Castile and Léon (1252–84) incorporates the *Floire and Blancheflor* story into his ambitious chronicle project, the *Estoria de España*. Elsewhere in his works, he makes mention of the Britannic legends of Brutus, Arthur, and Merlin in his hymns to Mary, the *Cantigas de Santa Maria*. At around the same time, we have fragments of the so-called "primitive" version of *Amadís de Gaula*, which would later be expanded and appear in print in the early sixteenth century. It was not until the fourteenth century, however, that specifically Arthurian romance took root and flourished in Castilian.

We know that Arthurian material circulated widely in the Crown of Aragon, especially in Catalonia, the Balearic Islands, and Valencia, and we have Catalan fragments of the Vulgate (*Stòria del Sant Graal*) and prose Lancelot (fourteenth century) and Tristan (fourteenth century). The Catalan and Valencian elites registered many copies of Arthurian texts, belying a popularity and circulation not borne out by the paucity of extant manuscripts. Likewise, the evidence from Portugal and Galicia is even slimmer: a fragment of the Portuguese *Livro de Josep Abaramatia* (earliest end of thirteenth century), and of the Prose Tristan in Galician (late fourteenth century).[5]

There is more (though not much more) extant Arthurian material from Castile. In addition to the lost *Libro de Don Tristán* copied in 1414, there is an extant full edition of *Tristán de Leonís* (Burgos, 1501). There is only a single manuscript of the Castilian translation of the *Post-Vulgate* cycle, and its books are "interspersed with various treatises of a religious nature."[6] The Castilian adaptation of Tristan and Iseult (*Tristán de Leonis*) dates from the early fourteenth century, roughly contemporary with the Castilian translation of Arthurian narratives (*Historia de la demanda del Santo Grial*, *Libro de Josep Abarimatia*, *Estoria de Merlín*, *Demanda del Santo Grial*) translated by Juan Bivas (or Vivas) around 1313.

Histories of Arthurian literature sometimes mention the anonymous thirteenth-century Hebrew adaptation of the Arthur cycle, the *Melekh Artus*, thought to have been written by an Italian Jewish scholar, which establishes that Hebrew-reading audiences in the region were interested in romance.[7] However, there are a number of medieval Iberian examples of Arthurian tropes and conventions that attest to Hebrew-reading audience's knowledge of and demand for chivalric narrative.

This should hardly surprise; in the thirteenth century, when Arthurian romance was likely well known to Iberians, a Hebrew poet such as Todros Abulafia wrote poems aping the *fin amors* of the troubadours, some of whom (Guiraut Riquier, Peire Cardenal) worked alongside him at the court of Alfonso X of Castile (ruled 1252–84), whose patronage attracted poets from Provence, Galicia, and elsewhere.[8] While perhaps Iberian Jews did not participate fully in chivalric culture (they rarely participated in armed combat or tournaments), they were, as native speakers of Castilian, Catalan, and other Ibero-Romance languages, familiar with the same songs and stories as their Christian neighbors, and it is natural that they should have included the fashionable literary tropes and motifs (and sometimes entire works) of the day into their literary practice in Hebrew.

One of the first examples of what we might call chivalric tropes in Hebrew writing from Iberia is found in a collection of stories by a writer named Jacob ben Elazar, who flourished in Toledo in the mid-thirteenth century. Ben Elazar's tale of Sahar and Kima is a very early example – perhaps the first example – of an autochthonous Iberian writer adapting Arthurian courtly discourse in an original narrative. His adaptation of courtly romance draws on the authority of Andalusi Hebrew literature, and as such is written in the rhyming prose interspersed with poetry in vogue with Hebrew and Arabic authors of the time. In some of the stories in this collection, Ben Elazar blends Andalusi- and French-style conventions and literary tropes, adapting the conventions of courtly romance to Jewish cultural sensibilities.[9]

Writing in a register of Biblical Hebrew sometimes peppered with Biblical allusions and direct quotations, Ben Elazar adapts the conventions of courtly romance to the sensibilities of an elite Jewish audience with enough formal training in Hebrew and Rabbinical traditions to understand the many references, quotations, and frequent wordplay. In one example, when Sahar attempts to kiss Kima, she scolds him, reminding him that noble lovers do not succumb to carnal desire, but rather follow a strict code of amorous behavior that leads their souls to join in spiritual love:

> Is kissing and embracing our desire?
> This is not done in our position.
> But our desire and the desire of nobility
> is to purify and whiten the hearts.
> Not like the ways of the sons of the mixed
> we shall sit together without kissing and embracing
> but the heart of the one adhering to the heart of the other
> The reason for the love of the sons of the precious
> is to receive the discipline of wisdom, justice, right, and equity[10]

Around the same time and to the south, probably in Granada, an anonymous writer working in Arabic gives us the tale of Bayad and Riyad (*Hadith Bayad wa-Riyad*). As with Ben Elazar's tale of Sahar and Kima, *Bayad wa-Riyad* blends features of the French romance and the Arabic *maqama*, tales written in a highly ornate mixture of poetry and prose. In this work, the author brings to life the wine-drenched poetic encounters described with such pride and enthusiasm by the Andalusi poets in Hebrew and Arabic verse, and introduces the figure of the go-between, the lady of a certain age who brings lovers together behind the scenes so familiar from Arabic tradition, into novelistic form.[11] Here again, as with the tales of Ben Elazar, the focus on rhetoric and poetics replaces the feats of arms, but the elevation of love to a code with spiritual value, and the sense that love is a game with rules to follow, coincide with the Arthurian tradition.

A third work from this period, also in Arabic, closes the loop between Arthurian and Arabic popular romance. An anonymous collection of tales written in Granada in the early to mid-thirteenth century features as its centerpiece the tale of Ziyad ibn Amir al-Kinani, a knight-hero who combines many of the features of the heroes of Arabic popular romance with those of the Arthurian tradition. "Ziyad" bends the tropes of Arthurian romance to the literary sensibilities of popular Arabic romance.[12] For example, the richly detailed descriptions of the material culture of the court that characterize romance also appear here in ways that distinguish the text from the Classical Arabic fiction of the times. Consider, for example, Ziyad's description of a castle as he approaches it:

> I saw a castle whiter than a dove, whose tall walls cast more shade than the clouds, built mostly of carved plaster and carved wood. It also had wrought stones, concave crystals, and rare marble; it was surrounded by gardens with a variety of trees. In the castle's peak were three towers of finest sandalwood, where maidens – endowed by God with beauty and grace and happiness – played ouds and zithers. The castle wall stood one hundred times the height of a man, and its circumference was eighty thousand arm's lengths.[13]

While the reference to the measurements of the castle is reminiscent of medieval Arabic travel literature, the description of the materials from which the castle is built and the clothing and musical instruments of the courtiers could be taken directly from the pages of Chrétien de Troyes. Both Ben Elazar and the author of *Ziyad* seem to pay homage to the vogue of the Peninsula's dominant literary culture without giving away the shop: they are very much examples of border literature in this sense, giving voice to a literary identity that draws on romance but with its roots planted firmly in Hebrew or Arabic tradition.

All of these works appeared well before the translation of French Arthurian romance into the vernacular languages of the Peninsula, and demonstrate the cultural importance of romance among religious minorities of the Christian kingdoms (Abulafia, Ben Elazar), and even in the Muslim-ruled kingdom of Granada, a client state of Castile during much of the thirteenth century.[14] These earlier examples of para-Arthurian production flew well under the radar of literary historians of "Spanish" literature, not only because they were not written in Castilian, but because they grew in part from literary traditions that have not always been considered part of Spain's national story.

In between these earlier glimmers of Arthurian romance sensibility and the appearance of the first surviving translation of Arthurian material into Castilian, there appear a series of works that we might describe as romances. Around 1300, three works appear that do not adhere to the stricter definition of chivalric romance developed on the basis of the French Arthurian corpus: The *Llibre de Evast e Blaquerna* or simply *Blaquerna* (Catalan, ca. 1285), *Flores y Blancaflor* (Castilian, composition ca. 1290, MS ca. 1390), and *Libro del Cavallero Zifar* (Castilian, ca. 1300). All three demonstrate very different formations of medieval romance that usually result in their omission from literary-historical accounts of the genre, and I would argue that all three respond specifically to the sociocultural conditions of Medieval Iberia, most importantly the question of *convivencia* or (relatively) peaceful coexistence of the dominant Christian population with significant numbers of Jews and Muslims whose existence shapes the nature of Iberian Christian culture and literary innovation itself.

Blaquerna, by the highly enigmatic and idiosyncratic polymath Ramon Llull, is a sort of ecclesiastical romance of an itinerant monk who undergoes a journey taking him on a series of ever-higher-stakes adventures, at the end of which he becomes Pope (much as heroes of certain romances end up as king or emperor). Like Ben Elazar and the author of *Ziyad ibn Amir*, Llull displays a knowledge of and deep appreciation for Arthurian romance while stretching and transforming the contours of the genre as traditionally understood. We know that Llull was immersed in chivalric culture as a young knight: he admits to having written "frivolous" troubadouresque verse in his youth (of which he later repents), before entering the Dominican and then Franciscan orders as a mature adult.[15]

As in the tales of Ben Elazar and the anonymous *Bayad and Riyad* that substitute feats of poetics and rhetoric in the service of love for those of arms, Blaquerna's heroics are spiritual. For example, he defeats a villainous knight by sermonizing to him about the damage to his soul caused by his deeds. Llull demonstrates an intimate knowledge of romance in his parody (in the most literal sense) of it: his hero is a spiritual knight errant whose lady is the Virgin Mary herself (he belongs to the order of *Benedicta tu in mulieribus*: "Blessed art thou among women"'; Luke 1:42). Just as the trajectory of some Arthurian knights land them in increasingly powerful positions at one court or another, culminating in their coronation as king or emperor,[16] Blaquerna occupies a series of increasingly powerful positions in the Church, eventually becoming Pope but ultimately renouncing the position in order to return to a life of contemplation as a monk (not unlike the Arthurian knights who retire from glorious military careers to spend their golden years as hermits).[17]

While *Blaquerna* is concerned with spiritual conquest (primarily in the form of conversion of Muslims), the Castilian *Flores and Blancaflor* resolves the Iberian "Muslim Question" through a love story. The tale of the two lovers was written originally in French, and was adapted by writers across Europe, with versions in Norwegian, English, German, Italian, and other languages.[18] Interestingly, the Castilian version of the text is woven into a chronicle of the struggle of the kings of Asturias against the Umayyad Caliphate in the ninth and tenth centuries, and so in a way is a fictional resolution of a historical problem: how to "convert" the Iberian Peninsula to Christianity. In history, this process occurred over hundreds of years, and was complete not with the military defeat of Muslim-ruled Granada and expulsion of the Jews in 1492, nor by the conversion of the Muslims of Castile (1502) and Aragon (1520), but rather with the much later expulsion of the Moriscos, the descendants of the Castilian and Aragonese Muslims, in 1613.[19] In the story, the Muslim Flores, Prince of Almería, falls in love with the Christian Blancaflor, daughter of a French Christian countess captured by Flores' father in a raid on the road to Santiago, where the then-pregnant countess was headed on pilgrimage. Blancaflor is born in the court of Almería and is raised alongside Flores. In adolescence the two fall in love, prompting Flores' parents, in an effort to avoid having their son marry a Christian, to sell Blancaflor into slavery. The ensuing goose chase around the Mediterranean ends in Flores' daring rescue of his beloved, and with his conversion to Christianity and the eventual conversion of the kingdom of Almería to Christianity.

If *Flores y Blancaflor* reimagines an al-Andalus made Christian through the power of love (the love of a romantic hero rather than the love of a Christian per se), then *Libro del Cavallero Zifar* (Castile, ca. 1300) imagines a Christian hero who is equal parts knight, religious, and philosopher-king. It is a sort of crusade-flavored fantasy of a Christian knight in "the Indies" who lived shortly after the time of the Apostle Bartholomew. *Zifar* blends elements of the Arthurian world with the rich intellectual and cultural stew of the Iberian Peninsula ca. 1300. The work is framed around a loose interpretation of the Life of St. Eustacius, grafted onto a Byzantine-esque romance of separation, shipwrecks, and eventual reunion, with a long section of wisdom literature – "The Counsel of King Mentón," when Zifar becomes king of the land of Mentón – inserted in the middle. The author was likely a cleric, which would explain the relentless spiritualism and critique of the nobility. The work is characterized by a pseudo-Arabism: character names are loosely based on Arabic equivalents, the work's "found manuscript" origin is in Arabic rather than Greek as in other Arthurian romances (prefiguring Cervantes' pseudo-author of *Don Quijote*, Cidi Hamete Benengeli), and the section on the "Counsel of King Mentón" is based on works of Arabic wisdom literature translated into Latin and Iberian Romance languages.

What all of this tells us is that, by the time the first translations of canonically Arthurian texts begin to appear in the Peninsula, Medieval Iberian authors were already practicing Arthurian romance, refracting it through the lens of their particular history and intellectual culture. Jewish authors had already adapted the sensibilities of trouabdouresque *fin amors*, blending it with the tropes and motifs of Arabic literature. Muslim authors living in Castilian-dominated Granada had worked elements of the Arthurian movement into tales set in the more familiar settings of the Andalusi *hortus conclusus* (*Bayad wa-Riyad*) and the Arabic popular epic (*Ziyad ibn Amir al-Kinani*). Christian authors, steeped in a culture of Andalusi translation, religious disputation, and domestic crusade, adapted various models of crusader-inflected Arthurian knights and set them to the task of converting Muslims and Jews, conquering al-Andalus, and turning the Andalusi intellectual legacy into an engine of conquest and crusade.

Only at this point do we see translations, rather than partial adaptations, of Arthurian romance in the peninsula. The Castilian translations of certain works of the Arthurian cycle appear in the first quarter of the fourteenth century with the *Libro de José Abarimatía* or *Libro del Santo Grial*, dated 1313. We can assume that there were others, perhaps earlier versions of Arthurian texts that did not survive, given (a) the density of allusions to and adaptations of various Arthurian traditions, and (b) Spain's extremely poor documentary record relative to that of France.[20] These translations inspire the first original Iberian work that fits more closely than its predecessors the definition of Arthurian romance: *Amadís de Gaula*. The "primitive" version of this text dates to ca. 1323, only a decade after the Castilian translations, but nearly a century after the experiments of Ben Elazar and the anonymous Granadan authors of *Bayad wa-Riyad* and *Ziyad ibn Amir al-Kinani.*

Amadís de Gaula is considered the first "original" chivalric romance composed on the Iberian Peninsula (or at least in Castilian) by most literary historians. It follows the conventions of the French Arthurian romance: an itinerant hero with an obscure origin who is nearly superhuman in battle, eloquent at court, and a compelling and passionate lover who puts into practice the spiritual *fin amors* of the troubadours. There is an evil wizard, a beautiful princess beloved, and a trusted sidekick. The storyworld of Amadís is a quasi-historical, quasi-fantastic geography. We have only fragments of this "primitive" Amadís, but it is mentioned by writers as early as the mid-fourteenth century, and is dated to the late thirteenth century, when court writers were active in adapting *chansons de geste* into Castilian prose works chronicling the feats of the heroes of epic songs. The "primitive" Amadís displays many of the characteristics of the medieval romance: the protagonist Amadís is of mysterious lineage, raised by adoptive parents in a distant land, defeats a dragon in battle, and is the subject of a prophecy in which he marries a princess and becomes King of England.[21] Subsequently, Amadís dies in a duel with his own son, Esplandían. His wife, Oriana, is overcome by grief and throws herself from a high tower, falling to her death. While the primitive *Amadís* follows the French model of courtly love in which the lovers consummate their relationship, sometimes legitimating it with the common practice of secret marriage to be later given the approval of the church, the sixteenth-century rewriting by Garci Rodríguez de Montalvo "marries off everyone in sight and drops the curtain on further chivalric service to the brides by their bridegrooms."[22]

During the long century between the Castilian translation of the Grail cycle (ca. 1320) and the publication of Montalvo's *Amadís* (1507), we see the emergence of a new sort of chivalric romance that reflects the historical engagement of the Crown of Aragon in the Mediterranean. The anonymous *Curial e Güelfa* (1445–8) and *Tirant lo Blanc* (Valencia, 1460 and 1490) blend features of the Arthurian romance with the contemporary Mediterranean world, shifting the narrative trajectory of Aragonese knights onto the broader canvas of the Mediterranean basin. These novels reflect the realities of Aragonese (Catalan and Valencian) conquest and trade in the Eastern Mediterranean, fusing the Arthurian storyworld with the contemporary worlds of the authors.

Curial e Güelfa is a fascinating product of Aragonese domination of Northern Italy, set at the court of Montferrat and ranging (like *Tirant lo Blanc*) from the Western Mediterranean to Greece, the Levant, and North Africa. The work is written in a Valencian-influenced Catalan prose with a high level of Italianisms owing to its imitation of Italian chivalric novels of the time. Like *Tirant lo Blanc*, it is characterized by its contemporary historical setting and its novelization of historical figures.[23] However, the contours of the hero's trajectory are not unlike the more canonical romances: Curial is a young knight of modest birth who rises to prominence at court under the protection of Güelfa, the widow of his lord, who throughout the novel acts as his muse and eventually becomes Curial's wife. Unlike the canonical Arthurian romances that take place in a dream-version of an insular and Western European geography, Curial's adventures map Aragonese conquests and ambitions across the Mediterranean, from the Levant to North Africa. The episodes in the Eastern Mediterranean belie a preoccupation with the increasing power of the Ottoman empire in that region, and we should remember that it was written less than a decade before the Ottoman conquest of Constantinople and the effective end of Christian political power in the Eastern Mediterranean.[24]

Tirant lo Blanc, like *Amadís*, was written in stages and as an asynchronous collaboration between two different authors. The Valencian knight Joanot de Martorell composed the first book in manuscript around 1460, and Joan de Galba added a further three books, publishing the first edition in Valencia (and in the Valencian language) in 1490. More than any other Iberian romance, including the paragonic *Amadís de Gaula*, *Tirant* goes to great lengths to legitimate itself as a specifically *Arthurian* romance. Arthur himself appears to the hero in a dream vision, and the first book of Tirant's adventures is a continuation of *Guy of Warwick* that begins with Tirant traveling to England to attend a wedding at court. The adventures shift from England to Valencia to the broader Mediterranean, and the settings are a wish-list of crusader nostalgia and aspirations circa 1490: Byzantium, Sicily, North Africa, the Levant. This is no coincidence: in addition to a strong culture of domestic crusade that would culminate in the conquest of Muslim-ruled Granada and the expulsion of the Jews in 1492, Ottoman power was expanding steadily in the Mediterranean from 1460 to 1480, by which time Ottoman forces briefly held the Italian port of Otranto.[25]

The age of print transformed the practice of romance on the Peninsula, and the early editions of medieval works of romance set the stage for the explosion of the genre's popularity that would begin with the publication of Garci Rodríguez de Montalvo's *Amadís de Gaula* and end only with the appearance of the first part of Cervantes' *Don Quijote*. The first works to be published in Castilian were elaborations of the early-fourteenth-century translations of the Post-Vulgate cycle: *Baladro del Sabio Merlín* (Burgos, 1498) followed by the *Demanda del Santo Grial* (1500), and the Castilian translation of *Tirant Lo Blanch* (*Tirante el Blanco*) (1501). During this period, the chivalric novel in Castilian took a decidedly imperial turn, and the heroes were cast as Catholic soldiers of empire. *Amadís* is laced with moralizing speeches and praise for the Virgin Mary. Just as there had been for centuries a significant feedback loop between the practice of chivalry and its literary representation,[26] in the sixteenth century this takes on a specifically Castilian sensibility with a focus on performance of Catholic piety, perpetual crusade at home and abroad, and an obsession with lineage that can only arise in a country full of baptized Jews and Muslims.[27] This feedback loop closes in the furthest Western reaches of the empire, California, so named after the fictional homeland of the Amazons in the very popular sequel to *Amadís de Gaula* titled *Sergas de Esplandían* (*Adventures of Esplandían*) (1510).[28]

Conclusion

The looming presence of *Don Quijote* has made the story of the medieval romance in Iberia into a back formation for the prehistory of the first novel, but the sources speak otherwise. Arthurian traditions reached the peninsula far before Christians translated the Grail cycle into Ibero-Romance languages, influencing Arabic and Hebrew literary traditions practiced on the peninsula. Later authors adapted the Arthurian storyworld under the pan-Mediterranean influence of the Crown of Aragon, transposing the insular dreamworld onto the contemporary Mediterranean and giving voice to Aragonese anxieties about waxing Ottoman power in the region. Finally, the Spanish Catholic imperialism that fueled Spain's global conquests gave rise to a new romance that recast the Arthurian hero in an imperial key and resulted in the boom of unimaginably popular Spanish chivalric romances, beginning with Garci Rodríguez de Montalvo's *Amadís de Gaula*, that would only end with the publication of Cervantes' *Don Quijote* in 1605. The takeaway is that it is impossible to tell the full story of Iberian literature without a broader consideration of the various linguistic traditions of the peninsula and how these interacted with and inspired each other to experiment and challenge tradition to give us new forms, influenced by French romance but reflecting Iberian experiences of multiculturalism and Mediterranean expansion.

Notes

1. Garci Rodríguez de Montalvo, *Amadís de Gaula*, ed. Cacho Blecua; Garci Rodríguez de Montalvo, Amadís of Gaul, *A Novel of Chivalry*, trans. Place and Behm.

2. Ramon Aramon i Serra, Joan Santanach, Amadeu Soberanas, and Jaume Torró, eds., *Curial e Güelfa*; Max Wheeler, *Curial and Guelfa: A Classic of the Crown of Aragon* (Amsterdam; Philadelphia: John Benjamins Pub. Co., 2011).
3. Joanot Martorell and Martí Joan de Galba, *Tirant lo Blanc*, ed. de Riquer; Joanot Martorell and Martí Joan de Galba, *Tirant Lo Blanch*, trans. Rosenthal.
4. Harry Sieber, "The Romance of Chivalry in Spain: From Rodríguez de Montalvo to Cervantes," in *Romance: Generic Transformation from Chrétien de Troyes to Cervantes*, ed. Kevin Brownlee and Marina Scordilis Brownlee (Hanover: University Press of New England, 1985), 204.
5. Paloma Gracia, "Arthurian Material in Iberia," in *The Arthur of the Iberians*, ed. David Hook (Cardiff: University of Wales Press, 2015), 11–32; here 12–15.
6. Ibid., 16–19.
7. Curt Leviant, ed. *King Artus: A Hebrew Arthurian Romance of 1279* (Assen: Van Gorcum & Co., 1969); Rella Kushelevsky, "Jews Reading Arthurian Romances from the Middle Ages: On the Reception of Chrétien de Troyes's *Yvain*, the Knight of the Lion, Based on Manuscript JTS Rab. 1164," *AJS Review* 42.2 (2018): 381–401; Caroline Gruenbaum, "Learning from the Vernacular: Non-Jewish Influence and Didacticism in Medieval Hebrew Narrative from Northern Europe" (unpublished doctoral dissertation, New York, New York University, 2019), 190–229.
8. Aviva Doron, *A Poet in the King's Court: Todros Halevi Abulafia, Hebrew Poetry in Christian Spain* [Hebrew] (Tel Aviv: Dvir, 1989); Judit Targarona Borrás, "Todros Ben Yehuda ha-Leví Abulafia, un poeta hebreo en la corte de Alfonso X el Sabio," *Helmantica* 36.110 (1985): 195–210; David A. Wacks, *Double Diaspora in Sephardic Literature: Jewish Cultural Production before and after 1492* (Bloomington: Indiana University Press, 2015), 64–92.
9. Jonathan P. Decter, *Jewish Iberian Literature: From al-Andalus to Christian Spain* (Bloomington: Indiana University Press, 2007), 138–56; Isabelle Levy and David Torollo, "Romance Literature in Hebrew Language with an Arabic Twist: The First Story of Jacob Ben El'Azar's *Sefer Ha-Meshalim*," *La Corónica* 45.2 (2017): 279–304; Tovi Bibring, "A Medieval Hebrew French Kiss: Courtly Ideals and the Love Story of Sahar and Kima by Ya'akov Ben El'azar," *Jewish Quarterly Review* 109.1 (2019): 24–37.
10. Jacob Ben Eleazar, *The Love Stories of Jacob Ben Eleazar (1170–1233?)*, ed. Yonah David (Tel Aviv: Ramot Publishing, 1992), 97, vv. 301–6; Tovi Bibring, "A Medieval Hebrew French Kiss: Courtly Ideals and the Love Story of Sahar and Kima by Ya'akov Ben El'azar," *Jewish Quarterly Review* 109.1 (2019): 26–7, https://doi.org/10.1353/jqr.2019.0001.
11. On the figure of the go-between in *Bayad wa-Riyad* and in medieval Iberian literature more generally, see Cynthia Robinson, *Medieval Andalusian Courtly Culture in the Mediterranean: Hadith Bayad wa-Riyad* (London: Routledge, 2007), 147–60; Leyla Rouhi, *Mediation and Love: A Study of the Medieval Go-between in Key Romance and Near Eastern Texts* (Leiden: Brill, 1999); Michelle M. Hamilton, *Representing Others in Medieval Iberia* (New York: Palgrave Macmillan, 2007).
12. Malcolm Lyons, *The Arabian Epic: Heroic and Oral Story-Telling* (Cambridge: Cambridge University Press, 1995); Peter Heath, *The Thirsty Sword: Sirat Antar and the Arabic Popular Epic* (Salt Lake City: University of Utah Press, 1996);

Dwight Reynolds, *Sīrat Bānī Hilāl*, *Arabic Literature in the Post-Classical Period* ed. Roger Allen and D. S. Richards (Cambridge: Cambridge University Press, 2006), 307–18; Peter Heath, "Other Sīras and Popular Narratives," in *Arabic Literature in the Post-Classical Period*, ed. Roger Allen and D. S. Richards (Cambridge: Cambridge University Press, 2008), 319–29.

13. Ali al-Gharib Muhammad Al-Shenawi, ed., *Kitab fihi hadith Ziyad ibn 'Amir al-Kinani* (Cairo: Maktabat al-Adaab, 2009), 76; Francisco Fernández y González, trans., *Zeyyad ben Amir el de Quinena* (Madrid: Museo Español de Antigüedades, 1882), 13; David A. Wacks, "Crusader Fiction for Muslim Readers: The Aljamiado Manuscript of Historia de Los Amores de Paris y Viana (Aragon, ca. 1560)," *David A. Wacks: Research and Teaching on Medieval Iberian and Sephardic Culture* (blog), March 16, 2014, 48, https://davidwacks.uoregon.edu/2014/03/16/crusader/.
14. María Jesús Viguera Molins, *El reino nazarí de granada (1232–1492): Política, instituciones, espacio y economía* (Madrid: Espasa Calpe, 2000), 87; Miguel Ángel Ladero Quesada, *Granada: Historia de un país islámico (1232–1571)*, 3rd ed. (Madrid: Gredos, 1989), 86–7, 217.
15. Ramon Llull, *A Contemporary Life*, ed. and trans. Bonner, 31–3.
16. David A. Wacks, *Medieval Iberian Crusade Fiction and the Mediterranean World* (Toronto: University of Toronto Press, 2019), 69–70.
17. In Ramon Llull's *Llibre de l'ordre de la cavalleria* (*Book of the Order of Chivalry*), such a retired knight instructs the young squire in the ways of chivalry. Ramon Llull, *The Book of the Order of Chivalry*, trans. Fallows, 35–6.
18. Patricia Grieve, *Floire and Blancheflor and the European Romance* (Cambridge: Cambridge University Press, 1997).
19. L. P. Harvey, *Islamic Spain 1250–1500* (Chicago: University of Chicago Press, 1990); L. P. Harvey, *Muslims in Spain, 1500 to 1614* (Chicago: University of Chicago Press, 2005); Matthew Carr, *Blood and Faith: The Purging of Muslim Spain* (New York: New Press, 2009); Brian A. Catlos, *Kingdoms of Faith: A New History of Islamic Spain* (New York: Basic Books, 2018).
20. Alan D. Deyermond, "The Lost Literature of Medieval Spain," *La Corónica* 5 (1976–7): 93–100; Maria Rosa Menocal, "Beginnings," in *The Cambridge History of Spanish Literature*, ed. David T. Gies (Cambridge: Cambridge University Press, 2004), 58–74, at 71–4.
21. Juan Avalle-Arce, *Amadís de Gaula: El primitivo y el de Montalvo* (Mexico: Fondo de Cultura Económica, 1990), 110–12.
22. Edwin B. Place, "Fictional Evolution: The Old French Romances and the Primitive Amadís Reworked by Montalvo," *PMLA* 71.3 (1956): 527, https://doi.org/10.2307/460718.
23. Montserrat Piera, *Curial e Güelfa y las novelas de caballerías españolas*, Pliegos de ensayo 140 (Madrid: Editorial Pliegos, 1998), 21–37.
24. Montserrat Piera, "Tirant Lo Blanc: Rehistoricizing the 'Other' Reconquista," in *Tirant Lo Blanc: New Approaches*, ed. Arthur Terry (London: Támesis, 1999), 45–58.
25. The Ottoman conquest of Otranto inspired Fernando of Aragon in 1480 to alert his Valencian governor to the possibility of Ottoman invasion. Mark D. Meyerson, *The Muslims of Valencia in the Age of Fernando and Isabel: Between Coexistence and Crusade* (Berkeley: University of California, 1991), 65.

26. Pedro Bohigas Balaguer, "La novela caballeresca, sentimental, y de aventuras," in *Historia general de las literaturas hispánicas*, ed. Guillermo Díaz-Plaja, vol. 2: Pre-renacimiento y renacimiento (Barcelona: Barna, 1951), 189.
27. Gregory B. Kaplan, "The Inception of *limpieza de sangre* (Purity of Blood) and its impact in Medieval and Golden Age Spain," in *Marginal Voices: Studies in Converso Literature of Medieval and Golden Age Spain*, ed. Gregory B. Kaplan and Amy Aronson-Friedman (Leiden: Brill, 2012), 19–42; Albert A Sicroff, *Los estatutos de limpieza de sangre: controversias entre los siglos XV Y XVII* (Newark, DE: Juan de la Cuesta, 2010); Barbara Fuchs, *Passing for Spain: Cervantes and the Fictions of Identity*, Hispanisms (Urbana: University of Illinois Press, 2003).
28. Ruth Putnam, *California: The Name* (Berkeley: University of California Press, 1917).

Suggestions for Further Reading

Brownlee, Kevin, and Marina Scordilis Brownlee, eds. *Romance: Generic Transformation from Chrétien de Troyes to Cervantes*. Hanover: University Press of New England, 1985.

González, Cristina. *El cavallero Zifar y el reino lejano. Madrid*, España: Editorial Gredos, 1984.

La tercera crónica de Alfonso X, La gran conquista de ultramar. London: Támesis, 1992.

Hook, David, ed. *The Arthur of the Iberians: The Arthurian Legends in the Spanish and Portuguese Worlds*. Cardiff: University of Wales Press, 2015.

Martorell, Joanot, and Martí Joan de Galba. *Tirant Lo Blanch*. Translated by David H. Rosenthal. Baltimore, MD: Johns Hopkins University Press, 1984.

Robinson, Cynthia. *Medieval Andalusian Courtly Culture in the Mediterranean: Hadith Bayad Wa-Riyad*. London: Routledge, 2007.

Rodríguez de Montalvo, Garci. *Amadis of Gaul: A Novel of Chivalry of the 14th Century Presumably First Written in Spanish*. Translated by Edwin B Place and Herbert C Behm. Lexington: University Press of Kentucky, 1974.

The Labors of the Very Brave Knight Esplandián. Translated by William Thomas Little. Binghamton, NY: Center for Medieval and Early Renaissance Studies, State University of New York at Binghamton, 1992.

Scordilis Brownlee, Marina. "Romance at the Crossroads: Medieval Spanish Paradigms and Cervantine Revisions." In *The Cambridge Companion to Medieval Romance*. Ed. Roberta l. Krueger. Cambridge: Cambridge University Press, 2000. pp. 253–66.

Terry, Arthur, ed. *Tirant lo Blanc: New Approaches*. London: Támesis, 1999.

Wacks, David. *Medieval Iberian Crusade Fiction and the Mediterranean World*. Toronto: University of Toronto Press, 2019.

Wheeler, Max, trans. *Curial and Guelfa: a classic of the Crown of Aragon*. Amsterdam; Philadelphia: John Benjamins Pub. Co., 2011.

12

LAURA CHUHAN CAMPBELL

Medieval and Early Modern Italian Romance

Romance literature was primarily imported into the medieval Italian world through contact with French literature, and it developed in Italy over several centuries through sustained exchanges with francophone cultures. Romance proved enormously popular on the Italian Peninsula and, although the genre itself became marked by associations of Frenchness, Italian readers and writers developed the romance genre in ways that incorporated the concerns and interests of a diverse audience. As the centuries went by, the format of romance narratives proved incredibly adaptable to changing tastes; from the popular songs that were sung in public squares to Boccaccio's *Filocolo*, and from Arthurian prose compilations produced in the Tuscan city states to the Renaissance Humanism of the princely courts. It is the intersection of these different circumstances of reception with the multiple possibilities of the fictional romance world that characterizes the Italian innovations in the genre.

Romance in Italy emerged as an essentially hybrid form that challenged the boundaries and values of the genre through its openness to creative combinations with other texts, genres, and ideologies. This hybridity is evident in the earliest Italian romances of the thirteenth century, which incorporated Italian perspectives into French Arthurian narratives and used the language of their sources. The late thirteenth and fourteenth centuries saw not only Italian dialect adaptations of prose romances, but also the distillation of romance narratives into *cantari*: short songs that pioneered a particular blend of materials from both romance and epic. This verse form and conflation of generic features would eventually develop into the epic romances of the fifteenth and sixteenth centuries.

In this chapter, I will examine the way in which several Italian writers exploited the formal and generic features of romance narrative – such as interlace structure, the magical Otherworld, and the Arthurian hero – in order to create a fictional space for incorporating the interests of a new readership. I will cover three texts that represent the different ways in which Italian cultures received and engaged with romance. Firstly, *Les Prophecies de Merlin*, a thirteenth-century Franco-Venetian adaptation of the Merlin stories which combines Arthurian romance with an interest in political and apocalyptic prophecy; secondly, the *Tavola Ritonda*, a fourteenth-century Arthurian cycle written in the dialect of Tuscany which foregrounds the character of Tristan as the perfect knight; and, finally, Matteo Maria Boiardo's *L'Inamoramento de Orlando*, a fifteenth-century epic romance written at the Estense court in Ferrara, which brings romance, epic, and classical narratives into a generic dialogue with each other. Whereas the *Prophecies* and the *Tavola* exploit the pre-existing motifs and structures of romance as a vehicle for cultural adaptation, *L'Inamoramento* uses the juxtaposition with other genres to destabilize and question the values of romance.

Les Prophecies De Merlin

Les Prophecies de Merlin is an Arthurian prose romance written in Venice around 1272–3. Although it was composed by an Italian author, it was written in French. The *Prophecies* belonged to a corpus of Italian texts from the thirteenth century onward that adopted the language of the French romances of Arthur and Alexander, *chansons de geste*, didactic and encyclopedic texts that were imported into Italy and read by literate Italians, apparently with little difficulty, in the original language.[1] Strong political and commercial connections between Italian- and French-speaking regions facilitated the transmission of manuscripts back and forth, while Italian workshops, notably in Pisa and Genoa, were also producing manuscripts in French. As a result, Italian readers came to perceive certain subject matters and genres as being associated with the French language itself, to the extent that it became the language of choice for authors composing romances and encyclopedic texts in prose and *chansons de geste* in verse, even after Italian vernacular romances began to appear. A major contribution to Italian romance in the thirteenth century was composed by Rustichello da Pisa, who is better known to modern readers as the coauthor of Marco Polo's *Travels* (*Le Devisement dou Monde*). Rustichello's Arthurian compilation, also known as the *Roman de Roi Artus*, is a long Franco-Italian prose romance that combined and rearranged material from various French Arthurian romances. Rustichello developed what would become a particularly Italian style of "compact compilation" while still using the same French language as its source material.[2] Romance in Italy, therefore, emerged early on as a hybrid genre that was strongly associated with French language and culture even when it was in the hands of Italian writers, copyists, and readers.

The anonymous *Prophecies de Merlin* is a clear example of that hybridity, not only in its use of French language and sources, but in its idiosyncratic combination of Arthurian romance with political prophecy. The link between the two is the character of Merlin, who appears in a number of French romances – most notably the Vulgate Cycle (the *Estoire de Merlin* and *Lancelot* branches) and the *Suite du Merlin* – as the son of a devil who can predict the future. But Italian readers would not only have known Merlin as a fictional prophet. His name also appeared in a number of political prophecies about the Holy Roman Emperor Frederick II (1194–1250), many of which were recorded by the Franciscan chronicler, Salimbene de Adam.[3] These two Merlins – the fictional Merlin of romance and the political Merlin of prophecy – were combined together in the *Prophecies de Merlin*, producing a highly unusual text in which political prophecies about medieval Venetian history and the apocalypse are inserted into an Arthurian romance which contains episodes from (among other sources) the *Suite du Merlin*, the Vulgate Cycle, the Tristan cycle, and the *Guiron le Courtois* cycle, which tells the story of the knights of Arthur's father's generation. The political orientation of the prophecies about medieval Venice are largely in opposition to the Holy Roman Emperor, Frederick, whom Merlin calls the "Dragon of Babylon," as well as a "felon seigneur" (malevolent lord) who has been identified with Ezzelino III da Romano (1194–1259), the tyrannical ruler of Padua, Verona, and Vicenza, and ally of Frederick. At the same time, Merlin also criticizes corruption among the highest levels of the Church, singling out the cardinals in Rome for particular critique. Of course, these are not real prophecies at all, because they were written about past events, but the romance setting of fifth-century Britain creates the illusion that Merlin was predicting the future.

The *Prophecies de Merlin*, then, is something of a chimera that does not fit easily into a generic box. Conventional romance episodes are juxtaposed with extended dialogues between Merlin and the scribes who write down his predictions, in which he prophesies in symbolic language about events that reach beyond the fictional world to incorporate material from contemporary Italian chronicles and religious and scientific texts. Indeed, the idiosyncrasy of this format has provoked the question of whether the *Prophecies* can even be classed as a romance at all,[4] but Nathalie Koble has more recently argued that the text can be identified structurally and thematically with the patterns of Arthurian romance.[5] Nevertheless, different manuscripts vary the amount of prophetic and romance material, with Bodmer ms.116 attesting to the most extensive romance redaction.[6] What is interesting about this combination of political and apocalyptic prophecy with Arthurian literature is that it draws on the pre-existing narrative spaces and structures of romance as a way to incorporate Merlin's political prophecies about Venice. The prophecies exist as a *merveille* (marvel) on the boundaries of the narrative, confining the information about the "real world" of medieval Italy and the apocalypse to the liminal space of the fictional Arthurian world.

Throughout the narrative, Merlin is associated with enclosed places that are removed from the main action of the romance.[7] Many of the prophecies are clustered at the beginning of the story, where Merlin discusses them in his room with one of his scribes, Maistre Antoine, who is collecting them together in a book. As the story moves toward a more conventional romance form, however, Merlin becomes increasingly inaccessible. He retires to a remote location in the Forest of D'Arnentes to live with the Lady of the Lake, an enchantress who learns his magic. She buries him alive in a tomb out of fear that Merlin's association with Claudas de la Deserte will jeopardize the life of her foster son, Lancelot, and his cousins (p. 94). Merlin's death is no obstacle to his continued ability to prophesy, however, and he declares that although his body has died, "mes esperit ne faurra de parler a tous chiaus ki chi venront encore.i. grant tans" (my spirit will not fail to speak to whoever comes here for a long time) (p. 95). Henceforth, Merlin's prophecies are only accessible to the Lady of the Lake's new lover (and Tristan's brother), Meliadus, who writes down his prophecies and conveys them to the "Sage Clerc de Galles" (the wise clerk of Wales), a scholar and magician who is attempting to compile a book of Merlin's prophecies. Any attempts by other characters to access this inaccessible space – "la roche ou Mierlins estoit en la croute, ensierres en la tombe meismes que il avoit faite" (the rock in whose cave Merlin was enclosed in the tomb that he had made himself) (p. 110) – are thwarted by supernatural deterrents. A delegation of enchantresses, led by the fairy Morgan, find that none of their spells are powerful enough to pass through the magic mountain that hides Merlin's tomb (p. 377), while the Sage Clerc instead attempts to find Merlin by climbing onto a rock in which the devil who fathered Merlin is trapped. Rather than taking the clerc to Merlin, the devil makes the rock fly all around the world (p. 134).

Merlin's prophecies are worked into the narrative through interlace, a conventional narrative structure in romance that switches the perspective between different, simultaneously occurring narrative strands. However, they are spatially confined to the margins of the action, in a liminal space that resonates with the romance convention of the Otherworld. In romance narratives, the Otherworld is a parallel dimension associated with the magic and the threshold between life and death. Time in the Otherworld becomes confused, and it can often only be accessed by characters who are chosen by a fairy. Meliadus is brought to Merlin's tomb – a space where prophecy distorts linear time – by a fairy figure, the Lady of the Lake, and the tomb of course reinforces the conventional link between the Otherworld and symbolic death. Prophecies and tombs seem to go hand in hand, as Dinadan also finds and transcribes prophecies written down by Merlin at the tomb of Uther Pendragon (pp. 235–6). Apart from Meliadus, the only other character capable of passing through the threshold between the romance episodes and the prophetic sections is Perceval, who is associated with the supernatural space of the Holy Grail in the romance intertext. In a situation that recalls the adventures of the French Vulgate *Queste del Saint Graal*, Perceval meets a hermit who reads to him from a book of prophecies and stories about Merlin that were compiled during Merlin's childhood.

The liminal space accorded to Merlin's prophecies about medieval Venice, the apocalypse, and other Arthurian texts, then, are superimposed onto pre-existing supernatural spaces that exist at the edges of Arthurian society in romance. The Otherworld, with its magical connotations and associations with the Grail, becomes a space to accommodate the similarly supernatural political prophecies that would have interested Italian readers. The result is a text that pushes against the formal and thematic limits of the romance genre itself.

La Tavola Ritonda

The *Tavola Ritonda*, written in Tuscany in the first half of the fourteenth century, is counted among the romances that began to be written in Italian vernaculars from the middle of the thirteenth century onward, most of which are based on Arthurian prose romances.[8] These include two versions of the *Prophecies de Merlin* in Venetian dialect, as well as the Tuscan *Storia di Merlino*, a Tuscan version of the *Queste del Saint Graal* (*La Inchiesta del San Gradale*), and a recently discovered fragment of a Tuscan *Lancelot*.[9] For Italian readers, however, the love story of Tristan and Isolde (or Tristano and Isotta) was undoubtedly the most well-loved romance tale. Including the *Tavola Ritonda*, five major versions of the Tristan story in Tuscan and Venetian dialects have survived, many of which are now available in modern editions with facing-page translations.[10] These Italian Tristan texts vary in terms of format; the *Tristano Riccardiano*, for example, is an abbreviated version of the life of Tristan, while the *Tristano Panciatichiano* is an anthology of disconnected episodes from the *Tristan en prose*. The *Tristano*

Corsiniano, on the other hand, isolates one episode from the Tristan cycle: the tournament at Louvezep. To say that these Italian versions were translations of the French Arthurian prose romances would be an oversimplification, because, as we have seen, the boundaries between French and Italian dialects, as well as between French and Italian cultural production, were largely fluid thanks to the circulation of French texts in Italy. The adaptation of the texts into Italian vernaculars also took many forms, from interlingual transcription, abbreviation, and editing to rewriting, compilation, and cyclification.[11] The *Tavola Ritonda* consists of a compact cycle that goes beyond the material from the *Tristan en prose* in an attempt to cover the Arthurian story from beginning to end.[12] It proved popular in the Tuscan city states and northern principalities alike, and has survived in ten manuscripts from around northern Italy, with three separate redactions.[13]

Just as the *Prophecies de Merlin* used the character of Merlin as a vehicle for incorporating its Italian readers' interest in prophecy into the fictional romance world, the *Tavola Ritonda* uses Tristano, the hero of romance, as a conduit for incorporating new cultural perspectives. There has already been much discussion of the *Tavola*'s ideological reinterpretations of love and chivalry for a new audience that included merchants, lawyers, and other educated middle classes of the Italian communes and *signorie*.[14] I will concentrate here, however, on the way in which the *Tavola Ritonda* imbues Tristano's status as a romance hero and the "best knight in the world" with the moral qualities that resonate with alternative political ideals, alongside those that are conventionally attributed to a knight. Ultimately, painting Tristano as a figure who is committed to upholding justice adds a new dimension to the mold of the romance hero.

As in the *Tristan en prose*, Tristano is both the ideal knight and the ideal lover; he exemplifies the balance between individual perfection and "concreto impegno civile incardinato intorno ai valori cristiani" (practical civic engagement based on Christian values).[15] In a narratorial interjection that claims to quote from a book by "Sir Peter, Count of Savoy," Tristano's perfection as a knight is framed in terms of personal virtue. The narrator explains that the world is sustained by four columns – loyalty, prowess, love, and courtesy – and that "queste quattro colonne furono nella persona di messer Tristano fermamente" (pp. 169–70) (These four columns were strong in the person of Sir Tristano) (p. 78). Loyalty, prowess, love, and chivalry are evidently chivalric virtues within the broader tradition of romance; here, however, they are embedded within a wider set of qualities that have a social and Christian dimension: love is interpreted as "carità" (charity) and "compassione" (compassion), courtesy as generosity in using his abilities, and we are told that his prowess came with moderation and humility. Tristano's loyalty, the narrator continues, is evident in the fact that the only deceit he committed was as a result of the love potion, "che gli fue uno legame lo quale gli costrinse lo cuore, la volontà e 'l pensiero" (p. 170) (a bind which constricts the heart, the will, the mind [p. 78]), thus absolving him of the moral ambiguity surrounding his affair with Isotta (who is married to his uncle, King Marco) that haunts him in most versions of the story. The fact that Tristano's chivalry is framed in terms of personal qualities that "sustain the world" recalls the way in which contemporary mirrors for princes – that is, political manuals for medieval rulers – conflate political responsibilities with personal virtues. Indeed, other virtues attributed to Tristan here intersect with those listed by the Florentine statesman Brunetto Latini in his encyclopedia, *Le Livre dou Trésor*, where he relates the qualities appropriate to the governor of a city; both Tristano and Brunetto's model governor should lack avarice and possess courage, a noble heart, and an ability to suppress anger. Nevertheless, we are told that Tristano never wanted to be a king so that he could be free to serve people as a knight.[16]

These virtues are reflected in Tristano's dedication to promoting justice and order in the Arthurian world. As he explains to his brother-in-law, Gheddino, "chè quando la contrada è più salvatica, tanto èe lo paese più dubbioso; e tanto quanto il cavaliere errante lo sae, tanto più l'assicura e lo addimestica" (p. 251) (the wilder a country is, the more likely it is to be lawless: when a knight errant knows this, the more he should try to make it secure and familiar) (p. 136). Despite the fact that virtually no one can defeat Tristano in single combat, he is merciful to his enemies in the besieged city of Gippa (p. 237) and convinces Arthur to end his siege of the Joyous Guard in his war with Lancelot (p. 230). In the earlier version of this episode in the *Mort Artu*, it is the Pope who convinces Arthur to end the siege; by giving this same peacemaking role to Tristan, the *Tavola Ritonda* makes his moral authority evident.

The personal and social dimensions of Tristano's virtues reflect the expanded notions of chivalry that are common to Italian romances. The qualities of nobility, courtliness, and chivalry are extended to both aristocratic and nonaristocratic characters, thus decoupling them from the social status that is usually a prerequisite of knighthood in chivalric romance. Ferragunze, a new character who embodies the *Tavola*'s definitions of courtliness, declares that "gentile può éssare ogni persona che à belli atti e costumi; et dolce parlare fa gentilezza" (p. 100) (any person can be noble who with fine customs, lovely manners, and sweet words behaves with courtesy) (p. 28). Tristano honors this expanded view of chivalry by awarding knighthoods to non-noble characters who have displayed skill or good character – for example, the son of an impoverished man who behaves selflessly in hosting Tristano and Lancilotto (p. 467), and a sculptor who makes a statue of Isotta for Tristano (p. 247). If knighthood comes with a civic responsibility and personal excellence, then personal excellence and civic responsibility can also make a knight.

It is Tristano's death, not the Grail quest, as in the French Arthurian Vulgate cycle, that triggers the collapse of Arthurian society. His commitment to upholding justice, it seems, is the centrifugal force holding it together:

> ciasuno barone che voleva vivere co' ragione, sì era da messer Tristano favoreggiato; e quello barone che pensava di volere isforzare altrui o di città o di castella, quella volontà sì tenea dentro dal cuore e nolla dimostrava, per la grande temenza ch'aviéno di Tristano, lo quale era campione e difenditore di ragione e di verità. (p. 511)

> [every nobleman who wanted to live according to justice was supported by Sir Tristano. Other knights who might have wanted to take someone or some city or castle by force, kept such desires to themselves and did not act on them for fear of Sir Tristano, for he was the champion and defender of justice and truth. (p. 323)]

After the tournament at Louvezep, Arthur has statues made of Tristano, Lancilotto, and several other knights to commemorate the event. After their deaths, their swords are hung from the statues. The narrator tells us that the Frankish King Charlemagne would later pass by the site, and he would remove the swords and give them to his twelve peers, keeping Tristano's sword for himself (pp. 413–14). The episode not only draws connections to *chanson de geste*, another genre of French origin enjoyed by Italian audiences which revolved around Charlemagne, but it also points to the *Tavola*'s interpretation of the romance hero as a moral example. The statue of Tristano is an artistic representation of the hero who serves as an inspiration for Charlemagne to take up his sword. Perhaps the literary representation of Tristano as a romance hero is also supposed to inspire moral commitments to peace and justice in the *Tavola*'s audiences.

L'inamoramento De Orlando

The brief appearance of Charlemagne and his twelve peers in the *Tavola Ritonda* may seem jarring from the perspective of conventional generic wisdom. In French literature, generally, Arthurian narratives took the form of prose or verse romance in octosyllabic rhyming couplets, while stories covering the Carolingian period usually took the form of *chansons de geste* or epic poems, which generally consisted of decasyllabic or dodecasyllabic *laisses* (that is, stanzas grouped by rhyme or assonance). That is not to say that the boundaries between genres in medieval French literature were not always fluid and open to influencing each other, but more extensive cross-fertilization between romance and *chanson de geste* is an increasingly significant feature of late medieval vernacular literature in both French and Italian. In northern Italy, this tendency to integrate themes, characters, and structures from the various genres broadly associated with "French" literature in a large-scale way began to take the form of the romance epic. Boccaccio's *Teseida* (1339–41) is thought to have been the earliest pioneer of epic romance in that it combines classical and romance material using the *ottava rima* meter that would become standard for the genre.[17] The best-known examples, however, appeared more than a hundred years later. The unfinished *L'Inamoramento de Orlando* (otherwise known as *Orlando Innamorato* [*Orlando in Love*], 1483) by Matteo Maria Boiardo (analyzed in more detail in the following paragraph) and its most prominent continuation, Ludovico Ariosto's *Orlando Furioso* (*The Frenzy of Orlando*) (1516–32) were both written in Ferrara for the court of the ruling Estense family. The story revolves around the heroes of the Carolingian cycles, including Charlemagne, Orlando (Roland), and Ranaldo (Renaud de Montauban), and inserts them into an epic narrative that uses interlace to weave together romance motifs, epic battles, and Greco-Roman material. Published in Florence contemporaneously to *L'Inamoramento*, Luigi Pulci's *Morgante* (1481–3) similarly brings together the epic characters of Orlando and Ranaldo with burlesque influences from the *cantari*. Torquato Tasso would later incorporate romance elements into his epic *Gerusalemme Liberata* (The Liberation of Jerusalem) (1580–1).

Just as the *Prophecies de Merlin* and the *Tavola Ritonda* imbue pre-existing romance conventions with new cultural and literary perspectives, *L'Inamoramento de Orlando* synthesizes the Otherworld of Arthurian romance with Classical mythology, in line with the humanist interests of Boiardo's Renaissance culture. While the magical world offers a space for the seamless integration of romance and Greco-Roman material, the juxtaposition of romance and *chansons de geste*, on the other hand, brings the two genres into a dialogue with each other that calls the values of both romance and epic into question. This destabilizes the ideological basis of both genres and creates multilayered perspectives on love, duty, chivalry, race, and gender. The love story at the heart of the *Inamoramento* interrogates the value and utility of the individual quest, a core narrative structure of romance, by bringing it into confrontation with the *chanson de geste*'s ideals of heroism in service of a collective. The heroes of Charlemagne's court, Orlando and Ranaldo, are torn away from their duties to pursue the affections of the beautiful Angelica, a princess from Cathay who represents a combination of the Muslim princess from *chansons de geste* and the fairy enchantress of Arthurian romance. She enters Charlemagne's court with her brother at Pentecost, in a scene that offers an erotic parallel to entrance of the holy grail in the Arthurian Vulgate Cycle.[18] Just as the grail sets in motion a mass exodus from Arthur's court, Angelica's entrance prompts the cousins Orlando and Ranaldo, among others, to fall in love with her and leave Charlemagne's court to find her. The love triangle becomes complicated when Angelica drinks from the "Fonte dell'Amore" (fountain of love), which causes her to fall in love with Ranaldo. Conversely, Ranaldo drinks from the "Fonte de Merlino" (fountain of Merlin), which causes the drinker to hate whoever they previously loved (I, iii, 31–50). Later in the narrative, both characters drink from the opposite fountain, leading Ranaldo to once again pursue Angelica who no longer loves him (II, xv, 59–63; xx, 44–6).

Meanwhile, Orlando is driven from adventure to adventure in search of Angelica. While Orlando and Ranaldo go continuously around in circles trying and failing to obtain the object of their affections, France is invaded by the African king Agramante. This pulls the knights away from the personal quests of romance and toward the collective duties of *chanson de geste*, especially the crusading narratives where knights fight in defense of Christendom. However, when Dudone conveys Charlemagne's request for Orlando and Ranaldo to return to France, Orlando is torn between the two competing forces that characterize this opposition between romance and epic: "L'amor, l'onor, il debito e 'l dileto / Facìan bataglia dentro dal suo peto" (II, ix, 46) (honor and love, delight and duty / strove and competed in his heart). Ultimately, he refuses to give up on his quest for Angelica to fight for Charlemagne:

> Ma quel che vince ogni om, io dico Amore,
> Gli avea di tal furor l'anima accesa
> Che stimava ogni cosa una vil fronda
> Fuorché veder Angelica la bionda (II, ix, 47)
>
> (But Love, which conquers every man,
> Had set such madness in his soul
> That he considered worthless all
> But seeing blond Angelica) (p. 326)

While the epic battle takes place, Ranaldo and Orlando instead duel with each other over Angelica, favoring the romance model of one-to-one combat over a lady to the defense of their kingdom (II, xx–xi). The romance quest, therefore, which is here represented by the individual quest for love, is brought into tension with the ethos of the *chanson de geste*. This would be especially evident to readers familiar with the legend of Roland, who famously dies defending Charlemagne in the early-twelfth-century epic *Chanson de Roland* and related stories, some of which were composed in Italy.[19]

If the heroic ideology of the *chansons de geste* destabilizes the value of the romance-style quests undertaken by Orlando and Ranaldo, then the introduction of romance alongside classical paradigms conversely undermines the conventional divisions of race, religion, and gender in the *chansons de geste*. Boiardo draws on the intertext of the virago figure from both classical literature and the *romans antiques*[20] to introduce two female knights: Ranaldo's sister, Bradamante, and the Indian queen Marfisa. Analogues to the classical Amazons and the *Roman de Troie*'s Penthesilea, these two characters challenge the monolithic masculinity of chivalry in both Arthurian romance and epic.[21] Not only do they decouple chivalry from the masculine body, but Bradamante – designated as the founding mother of the Estense line – introduces an alternative form of courtship that displaces the hierarchical and gendered modes of courtly love. Whereas ladies in Arthurian romance conventionally act as inspiration for chivalric deeds, Bradamante and Ruggiero inspire each other as they fight side by side:

> Già Bradamante non ne temerìa:
> Mostrar vòle a Ruger che cotanto ama
> Che sua prodecia è assai più che la fama.
> Né già Rugíero avìa voglia minore
> Di far veder a quella damigella
> Se ponto avìa di possa o di valore (III, V, 55–6)

> (The lady would have shown no fear
> But let her love Ruggiero see
> Her skill was greater than her fame
> Ruggiero had no less desire
> To make sure that the maiden saw
> That he was valorous and strong) (p. 543)

This generic confrontation challenges conceptions not only of gender, but also of race and religion. In the *Inamoramento*, the magical landscape of romance is mapped onto the world beyond Europe; Orlando's quest takes him to Cathay, India, and Tartary, where he encounters a number of pagan knights and ladies. While the vernacular crusading epics tend to depict the Muslim opponents as abject enemies, marked by religious and sometimes physical otherness, the imposition of the romance ethos of chivalric courtliness transcends and trivializes religious difference; knights encountered in

"Paganìa" (Pagany) (I, ix, 50), such as Brandimarte, Iroldo, and Prasildo, are defined more by their proximity to chivalric ideals than their religion. According to Jo Ann Cavallo, Boiardo's narrative "breaks out of the binary opposition of Christians and Saracens typical of Carolingian epic" because his characters are motivated by "a range of passions – primarily love, ambition, empathy, and the desire for glory or revenge," as opposed to the religious or ethnic differences between them.[22] These straightforward oppositions are undermined even in the epic-inspired battle between Christians and Muslims that takes place when France is invaded. King Rodomonte, a monstrous warrior with "a giant's build and strength" ("Persona ha de gigante e forte nerbo"; II, i, 56), who initially appears to embody the othered stereotype of crusading *epics*, is humanized by his romantic pursuit of Doralice of Granada (II, vii, 28–9), which resembles Orlando's own quest for Angelica.[23] Evil in the poem does not reside in the religious or racial other, but rather shifts and changes according to the context. In Book II, Canto x, Dudone fights the wizard Balisardo, who transforms himself into the shape of various monsters before taking the form of Dudone himself. Just like the shape-shifting wizard, the combination of various paradigms of conflict in the *Inamoramento* means that sometimes the antagonist is a monster, and other times he or she is the mirror image of the self.

Whether romance is brought into conflict with other ideals or harmonized with them, the Italian reception of the genre is characterized by an openness toward absorbing new perspectives, languages, forms, and ideologies. Emerging initially as a hybrid genre with French associations that Italians readily made their own, romance in Italy never calcified into a stable form with a fixed content. Instead, Italian romances such as *Les Prophecies de Merlin*, the *Tavola Ritonda*, and *L'Innamoramento di Orlando* were part of an ongoing and open-ended conversation that continued well into the Renaissance.

Notes

1. See Christopher Kleinhenz and Keith Busby (eds.), *Medieval Multilingualism: The Francophone World and its Neighbours* (Turnhout: Brepols, 2010), particularly pp. 145–218.
2. Fabrizio Cigni, "French redactions in Italy: Rustichello da Pisa" in *The Arthur of the Italians: The Arthurian Legend in Medieval Italian Literature and Culture*, ed. Gloria Allaire and F. Regina Psaki (Cardiff: University of Wales Press, 2014), pp. 21–40 (p. 26), and Marie-José Heijkant, "From France to Italy: The Tristan Texts" in *The Arthur of the Italians*, ed. Allaire and Psaki, pp. 41–68 (p. 47).
3. Donald L. Hoffman, "Merlin in Italian Literature" in *Merlin: A Casebook*, ed. Peter H. Goodrich and Raymond H. Thompson (London: Routledge, 2003), pp. 186–96 (p. 189).

4. Hoffman, "Merlin in Italian Literature," p. 191.
5. Nathalie Koble, *"Les Prophéties de Merlin" en prose: Le roman arthurien en éclats* (Paris: Honoré Champion, 2009), pp. 19–22.
6. Koble, *"Les Prophéties de Merlin" en prose*, p. 26.
7. On the broader connection between Merlin and enclosed spaces in the French romance tradition, see Miranda Griffin, "The Space of Transformation: Merlin Between Two Deaths," *Medium Aevum*, 80 (2011), 85–103.
8. Marie-José Heijkant, "From France to Italy: The Tristan Texts," pp. 41–69 (p. 47).
9. Luca Cadioli, "A New Arthurian Text: The Tuscan translation of the Lancelot en prose," *JIAS* 2 (2014), 63–9.
10. See the Further Reading section. For a complete list, see Heijkant, "From France to Italy," pp. 47–8.
11. Alison Cornish, *Vernacular Translation in Dante's Italy: Illiterate Literature* (Cambridge: Cambridge University Press, 2011).
12. Daniela Delcorno Branca, "The Italian Contribution: *La Tavola Ritonda*," in Allaire and Psaki (eds.), *The Arthur of the Italians*, pp. 69–90 (p. 69).
13. For a full list of manuscripts, see Delcorno Branca, "The Italian Contribution," p. 70.
14. See, for example, Franco Cardini, *L'acciar de' cavalieri: Studi sulla cavalleria nel mondo toscano e italico (secc.xii–xv)* (Florence: Le Lettere, 1997), p. 104; Joan Ferrante, *The Conflict of Love and Honour: The Medieval Tristan Legend in France, Germany, and Italy* (Paris: Mouton, 1973), pp. 27, 30–1.
15. Giulia Murgia, *La Tavola Ritonda tra intrattenimento ed enciclopedismo* (Rome: Sapienza, 2015), pp. 1, 4.
16. Brunetto Latini, *Livres dou Trésor*, ed. Pietro Beltrami, pp. 794–9; *Brunetto Latini: The Book of the Treasure*, trans. Paul Barrette and Spurgeon Baldwin, pp. 352–4.
17. Jane E. Everson, *The Italian Romance Epic In The Age Of Humanism The Matter Of Italy And The World Of Rome* (Oxford: Oxford University Press, 2001), p. 19.
18. Charles Stanley Ross, "Boiardo and the Derangement of Epic" in *Orlando Innamorato: Orlando in Love*, trans. Charles Stanley Ross (West Lafayette, IN: Parlor Press, 2004), pp. L–LXIV.
19. Everson, *The Italian Romance Epic*, pp. 27–36.
20. See Laura Ashe, Chapter 1 (this volume), pp. 14–28.
21. Gerry Milligan, *Moral Combat: Women, Gender, and War in Italian Renaissance Literature* (Toronto: University of Toronto Press, 2018).
22. Jo Ann Cavallo, *The World beyond Europe in the Romance Epics of Boiardo and Ariosto* (Toronto: University of Toronto Press, 2013), p. 4.
23. Tiziano Zanato, *Boiardo* (Rome: Salerno Editrice, 2015), p. 221.

Suggestions for Further Reading

Allaire, Gloria and Psaki, F. Regina, (eds.), *The Arthur of the Italians: The Arthurian Legend in Medieval Italian Literature and Culture*. Cardiff: University of Wales Press, 2014.

Cavallo, Jo Ann, *The Romance Epics of Boiardo, Ariosto, and Tasso From Public Duty to Private Pleasure*. Toronto: University of Toronto Press, 2016.

Delcorno Branca, Daniela, *Tristano e Lancilotto in Italia: Studi di Letteratura arturiana*. Ravenna: Longo, 2001.
Everson, Jane E., *The Italian Romance Epic In The Age Of Humanism The Matter Of Italy And The World Of Rome*. Oxford: Oxford University Press, 2001.
Koble, Nathalie, *Les Prophéties de Merlin en prose: Le roman arthurien en éclats*. Paris: Honoré Champion, 2009.
Zanato, Tiziano, *Boiardo*. Rome: Salerno Editrice, 2015.

13

ALBRECHT CLASSEN

German Medieval Romance

German medieval romance literature is well established as an important part of medieval world literature, deeply enjoyed also by the modern readership, and easily bears comparison with contemporary European romances.[1] However, the situation of German medieval romance is rather complex considering the literary situation which was in flux during the twelfth and thirteenth centuries.

Literary-Historical Outline

Before the rise of the "canonical" romances by Hartmann von Aue, Wolfram von Eschenbach, and Gottfried von Strassburg, several so-called precourtly poets created a number of romance-like texts, mostly bridal-quests, which borrow elements from the "emerging" romance and the contemporary heroic epic at the same time. The "post-classical" period in the thirteenth century witnessed the rise of numerous other romance-like texts, such as *Wigamur*, *Wigalois*, *Daniel von dem Blühenden Tal*, and *Partonopier und Meliur*, wherein "epigonal" elements seem to dominate and aspects of heroic epics also enter the picture, deliberately blurring the traditional concept of the courtly romance in response to many external factors. Moreover, we observe an increasing sentimentalization of romance, such as in the case of Konrad Fleck's *Florie und Blanscheflur* and *Mai und Beaflor* (both second half of the thirteenth century). This leads to the third puzzling piece: the strong dominance of heroic epics since the early thirteenth century, especially the *Nibelungenlied* and *The Lament*, not even considering the truly confounding *Kudrun* (late thirteenth century, but copied down in only one early-sixteenth-century manuscript). Each one of them contains romance elements and is yet clearly heroic in some respects. We could increase the complexity of the matter by also referring to the almost contemporary rise of short verse narratives (*mæren*), reflecting mostly the culture of the urban audiences, though their interest in the courtly values are certainly detectable as well (cf. the Old French *fabliaux*). Each of these genres finds direct parallels in contemporary European literature, which does not, however, minimize the uniqueness and significance of the Middle High German contributions.

Social-Historical Context

Medieval literature can only be fully understood if we keep in mind its central purpose for courtly audiences, which expanded considerably in the late Middle Ages to include urban listeners and readers. Courtly romances and poetry did not only serve as entertainment and aesthetic pleasure, but also assumed a critical significance for aristocratic society, above all in its efforts to come to terms with itself; to establish and practice social, ethical, moral, and legal principles and values; to reflect upon the courtly, chivalric, and knightly values and ideals; to learn about the relationship between self and other; and especially to explore the gender relationship. The courtly romance created a fictional platform for the exploration of knighthood, courtly love, personal honor, and dignity, and all that framed by the Christian faith, whether in Old French or Middle High German romances.[2]

Despite the considerable popularity of late medieval heroic epics, such as the many versions of the *Dietrich* cycle, courtly themes increasingly gained the upper hand, probably as a result of fundamental social-historical, economic, and climatic conditions since the early twelfth century. Moreover, the traditionally strong fervor to participate in crusades began to fade considerably, as indicated by the Fourth Crusade in 1204 which resulted in the conquest of Constantinople (a Christian, though Greek-Orthodox, city) instead of Jerusalem. We can thus speak globally of a paradigm shift from the early to the high Middle Ages, the reasons for and consequences of which remain fairly unclear to us. Most vividly, however, the Romanesque style was replaced by the Gothic and, from the twelfth century, massive Gothic cathedrals began to dot the European landscape. The worship of the Virgin Mary increased tremendously, and this might also have been associated with the discovery of the new topic: courtly love – that is, the new focus on the beloved courtly lady. In essence, we can document the development of the themes of courtly love, chivalry, and religious spirituality in the genre of the courtly romance, although the emphasis there tends to rest on chivalric adventures, individual challenges of ethical kinds, and the issue of the protagonist's social responsibilities.

Middle High German Literature

The Middle High German romance can be identified as a literary witness of many of those transformations, although it remains a matter of debate how to qualify this genre in specifics. All three compounds of the term "Middle High German" help us to comprehend the fundamental transition. Since the early and middle of the twelfth century, Old High German had given way to Middle High German, with the Limbourg poet Heinrich von Veldeke having been one of the first to embark on writing in the new courtly style. "High" refers to the geographical area of the German-speaking lands extending from the south (modern-day Switzerland) to the mid-northern region where Low German was the dominant tongue. "German" is self-evident here. Modern-day New High German is the chronological sequence.

In light of the survival of Middle High German literature in specific types of manuscripts, many of which were illuminated, considering the unique themes pursued and the language chosen, we can identify the emergence of the courtly romance at around 1160/1170. Veldeke was the first to render the Old French *Roman d'Eneas* into Middle High German as *Eneit* (or *Eneas*), combining much material from the classical *Aeneid* by Virgil (29–19 BCE) with a range of new courtly themes, one of which was, most centrally, the experience of erotic love. This early "romance" merges military operations concerning the fall of Troy with the protagonist's journey first to Carthage (encounter with Queen Dido), and then to the site of future Rome, existential battles, his falling in love with the local princess (Lavinia), and the happy outcome of all events for Eneas, leading to the founding of Rome. Classical themes, euhemerism, catabasis, chivalry and knighthood, and erotic love blend to create the basis of what we then would call courtly romances.[3]

The Precourtly World

While Veldeke took to the high road, so to speak, rendering the classical themes into Middle High German, various contemporary poets developed their own verse narratives, which are filled more with adventures, miracles, and wonders and tend to present the topic of a bridal quest. *Herzog Ernst*, *König Rother*, *Oswald*, *Salman und Morolf*, and *Orendel* have all been variously called *Spielmannsepen*, "goliardic verse narratives," "Byzantine narratives," or "minstrel epics" (all anonymous and composed sometime in the second half of the twelfth century). The first and last term refer to the idea that the anonymous poets belonged to the social group of minstrels, whereas the other terms reflect the common feature in all of these poems that the protagonist either travels to Byzantium/Constantinople or is bound to fight for a bride, the daughter of the Eastern Roman emperor. Religious (*Orendel*) and heroic elements (*König Rother*) tend to merge with aspects of the miraculous and wondrous, and at times magic is also at work (*Salman und Morolf*). In *Herzog Ernst*, the protagonist finds a friendly welcome in this famous Eastern Roman capital on his way to the Holy Land, whereas in *König Rother* the young king has to carry out a complicated operation to win his bride.[4]

Although these narratives certainly idealize an aristocratic protagonist and follow his actions with great sympathy, the main impetus always seems to be entertainment for a courtly audience. There tends to be considerable drama, and the political-military challenges associated with the king's future bride or wife are significant. Best known among the *Spielmannsepen* (plural), particularly because of its early development of courtly themes embedded in a heroic framework, is *Herzog Ernst*, wherein the young hero is badly maligned by an opponent who convinces his uncle, Emperor Otto, that the Duke of Bavaria is intent on usurping his throne – a common motif which was later copied especially in the fifteenth century in so-called romances (if not novels) focused on Charlemagne and his failure as a ruler, always trusting the wrong people (e.g., Elisabeth von Nassau-Saarbrücken, *Königin Sibille*, ca. 1437; *Malagis*). After years of bitter warfare, Ernst eventually can no longer resist the imperial forces, thus he has to leave Germany and goes on a crusade. But he becomes lost on his way once he has left Constantinople and enters the world of monsters by accident. The audience is invited to follow him on his many and varied adventures (including the dangerous Magnetic Mountain and the crossing of a mountain through a river tunnel), which at times take him to the brink of death, but he survives, of course, and can eventually return, bringing some "samples" of the monstrous races back to Germany, where he manages to overcome the emperor's enmity and regain his friendship.

Similarly, the other cases in this genre are determined by military prowess and existential conflicts, but then also by considerable humor and comedy (especially *Oswald*). The entertainment value is extensive, whereas the didactic intentions, which were then to become more fundamental in the courtly romances, are of less relevance. The minstrel poets intended primarily to offer literary entertainment and were not so much concerned with tragedy and existential conflicts.

'Classical' Middle High German Courtly Romances

Hartmann von Aue

Beginning around 1170, the Swabian poet Hartmann von Aue, mostly translating from Old French sources by Chrétien de Troyes, introduced the concept of the Arthurian romance to Middle High German literature. Most famously, he adapted/translated first *Erec* (*Erec*), and later, around 1200, *Iwein* (*Yvain*), the two of which have to be a considered a kind of pair because they are predicated on the same model, only that the latter romance represents the reverse of the former in its plot premise. In *Erec*, the protagonist's major problem consists of his excessive dedication to his new wife, Enite, spending all of his time in bed with her instead of taking care also of his courtly, military, and political tasks, falling victim to his uxuriousness.[5]

At some point, he realizes his failure and quickly rushes into a series of knightly adventures through which he eventually learns to accept not only his social obligations but also his wife as an equal partner. The outcome proves to be a well-balanced life in which the private and the public aspects match each other equally. For a long time, we could say, Erec is too self-absorbed, if not selfish, until he is eventually alerted to the extreme need to consider the demands placed by society on him as a knight. But in that long and painful process, during which he would have almost died several times in dangerous battles with hostile knights and mean-spirited giants, he also realizes how much he has to accept his wife Enite as his crucial helper. In essence, once Erec has learned his lessons in communication and social obligations, he emerges as a mature and responsible leader of his people. This romance can thus be identified as a literary mirror of pedagogical, ethical, political, and social ideals relevant for the members of the aristocratic court. Hartmann thus invited his audience to enjoy this romance and to utilize it as a public platform to explore the essential courtly values.[6]

In *Iwein*, which is even more closely modeled on Chrétien's romance, the opposite problem presents itself because the protagonist is too excessively committed to knighthood and thus forgets his duties regarding his wife, Laudine. When she realizes his failure, she rejects him as her husband in a public pronouncement, which makes him lose his mind. He recovers from this madness by means of a magical salve and also regains a new sense of responsibility and maturity through a long series of knightly accomplishments, in which he is constantly accompanied by an iconic lion friend who assists him loyally in many dangerous situations.

Hartmann also created other verse narratives, such as the religious tale of *Gregorius* (ca. 1200) and the spiritual-erotic *Der arme Heinrich* (ca. 1190), but those are not associated with King Arthur and the concept of knighthood, which characterizes the two romances. However, the role of Arthur never fully matters in medieval German literature, although he regularly constitutes the center of the world of chivalry and courtliness, being almost sidelined by the various protagonists who have to depart from the court and face critical challenges in the dangerous world outside, where evil knights, giants, and other threats await the protagonist.

If we consider subsequent "romances," we can clearly observe the problematic nature of that generic term since it is actually applicable to a variety of verse narratives determined by different themes. Nevertheless, as we will observe, the notion of the "romance" makes good sense if we recognize it more broadly as a term for longer verse narratives in which fundamental ethical and moral concerns relevant for courtly society at large are negotiated and where the protagonist emerges, after many internal and external struggles, as the future role model for his world.

Wolfram von Eschenbach

In Wolfram von Eschenbach's *Parzival* (ca. 1205), loosely predicated on Chrétien de Troyes's *Perceval* (ca. 1180/1190), we also encounter King Arthur, but only as a useful foil for the young protagonist who has to roam the world for a long time until he can accomplish his goal of redeeming the Grail kingdom and assuming the throne there. However, we first learn about Parzival's father, Gahmuret, whose life goals seem to be nothing but entertainment, knighthood, and personal glory, commonly disregarding the needs and desires of other individuals, especially of courtly ladies. Most unusually, however, he marries a black queen (Belacane), serves a mighty Muslim ruler (Balduc), and is killed in battle because someone had poured goat blood on his helmet made out of diamonds, thus making it completely soft without his knowledge. This death grieves his second wife, Herzeloyde, so much that she radically withdraws from courtly society into a forest (Soltane), where she tries to raise her son Parzival in utter social isolation from knighthood, the cause of her husband's death as she perceives it. Of course, she fails in this, as is to be expected, especially because the young man is almost instinctively driven to join King Arthur's court, where things do not turn out for him as expected, primarily because he is still too young to understand the consequences of his deeds and his impact on others. Having killed an opponent and taken on his armor, Parzival then leaves, which becomes the starting point for a long series of adventures through which he ultimately learns the highest ideals of courtliness and knighthood.

In light of these aspects, we might even call this romance a *Bildungsroman*, tracing the protagonist's years of training and education up to his adulthood. He also manages to reach the castle of Munsalvaesche where the Grail resides, but here as well he fails to ask the expected question, which forces him to go on a long quest until he has overcome his shortcomings and is granted a second chance to return to King Anfortas's mysterious court, to ask him what ails him and thus to heal his wound. This restores happiness and joy at the Grail castle, where Parzival is then enthroned as the successor king.

Especially because Parzival's friend Gawan appears in this romance in quite a significant manner, the world of King Arthur remains a steady narrative factor, though of no great significance for Parzival. Arthur matters as the central figure of worldly knighthood and chivalry, but the protagonist's destiny rests in a higher dimension. In contrast to the traditional Arthurian romance, the focus here shifts to the Grail, which is in dire need of redemption. Parzival is the predetermined successor, but due to his youth and wrong education, first by his mother, then by the old knight Gurnemanz, he is not prepared for the extraordinary and transformative challenges awaiting him in the world of the Grail. This means the utter collapse of all hopes for the members of King Anfortas's court, but eventually, after many knightly challenges, Parzival is allowed to return and ask the long-awaited question, which restores health to Anfortas and happiness to the Grail. In essence, we might call this romance a literary platform to explore the meaning and implications of constructive communication within the courtly world. Words and actions must come together to achieve the desired result, without which society cannot be maintained productively.

Wolfram integrates fascinating references to many social-historical and cultural issues. For instance, he has Parzival's father Gahmuret marry a black queen, which leads to a common child, Feirefiz, who is born as a motley colored person. Wolfram also mirrored new medical and scientific knowledge, as practiced by Gawan, and reflected some knowledge of Arabic and astronomy/astrology (Cundrie). Most importantly, however, his *Parzival* is predicated on a unique merging of the theme of marital love and the Grail myth, both of which, though, elude the protagonist, for a long time.

After he has departed from his wife Condwiramurs to visit his mother (by that time already dead, having passed away because of a broken heart when her son had left her without any consideration of her personal concerns), it takes him almost the entire rest of the romance to see her again and, at that time, also his two sons. In a way, he is granted that privilege only once he has been entitled to visit to the Grail castle a second time and thus to ask the decisive question. He thus achieves his personal happiness in private and public terms only after he has been able to live up to his social and spiritual obligations, and this strikingly parallels the situation in Hartmann von Aue's two romances. King Arthur's court, however, serves only as a catalyst to launch the protagonist onto his path into the world, though he revisits it at intervals as a rest stop on his long quest for the Grail.

But even there we observe political trouble which only Parzival can overcome by putting to shame the court steward, Kaye, who had mocked the young man in his foolish appearance early on and had encouraged Arthur to grant the stranger the right to fight against a member of his court, Ither. Like a new David pitted against Goliath, Parzival kills this "red knight" and then takes the armor for himself, not knowing that Ither was his own uncle. Subsequently, he fights on behalf of two female protagonists who are threatened by hostile princes who want to force the beleaguered lady to marry them. Having defeated his opponents, Parzival sends them to Arthur's court, where they have to admit their loss to this stranger knight and hence reveal their shame. One of those ladies, Condwiramurs, turns out to be Parzival's future wife, whom he loves deeply for the rest of his life, though he has to live without her for much of the romance, visualizing her when he sees three drops of blood in snow, which sets in motion a whole chain of ideas about epistemology.[7] Chivalry and marital love thus bond intimately here and underscore this unique romance. Parzival later has a chance to fight against Kaye himself and humiliates him in that process, which in a way redeems the protagonist and the Arthurian court as well, where Parzival is welcomed most hospitably and greeted with greatest honors. However, the protagonist cannot stay there and bask in that new-found glory, as would have been the case in traditional Arthurian romances. Instead, the Grail messenger Cundrie arrives and exposes Parzival's shameful neglect of having asked the crucial question during his visit on Castle Munsalvaesche. This embarrasses the protagonist to such an extent that he departs and embarks on a years-long quest to find the Grail once again.

Interwoven into this account of Parzival, Wolfram also integrated the story of the protagonist's friend, Gawan, who falls in love with Lady Orgeluse and has to undergo a long series of painful rejections and challenges which parallel those of Parzival but are focused "only" on love and knighthood. The protagonist, by contrast, faces the much greater task of redeeming the sorrowful Grail and thus restoring spiritual happiness to the world, whereupon he is entitled to encounter his family again.

Wolfram projected a highly complex universe in which knighthood, love, family, the court of King Arthur, and the society of the Grail matter centrally, all intricately interwoven with each other. In contrast to other courtly romances, we can follow the life of the young protagonist first as a child and then as a youth, until he reaches maturity, rises to the rank of a knight, and struggles for years to achieve his goals as a champion of women and, above all, as the redeemer of the Grail king, Anfortas. But, parallel to other courtly romances, the protagonist has to undergo a long series of challenges and needs to overcome both personal failures and the tragedy he incurs at the Grail court of Munsalvæsche. Wolfram created, with this literary masterpiece, a platform on which he could reflect on material and spiritual conflicts in his world, offering an intriguing biographical framework (Parzival), comments about friendship (Parzival and Gawan), magic (Clinschor), and medicine (Gawan), and projecting a story which, as he claims, had originally been discovered by the Syrian Jew Flegetanis, who had read it in the stars.[8] Wolfram the narrator then learned it from the Provencal Kyot (a converted Jew), and eventually cast it himself into his Middle High German account, not giving much credit at all to Chrétien, although in essence both *Parzival* and *Perceval* share many of the basic narrative motives. Although Kyot was clearly a fictional invention, this reference illustrates much of Wolfram's worldview, with its open perspective toward the Muslim and Jewish culture, superseding the world of King Arthur and introducing new spiritual ideals mysteriously represented by the society of the Grail.[9]

Gottfried von Strassburg

But how different romance could be at that time, when we consider Gottfried von Straßburg's almost contemporary *Tristan* (ca. 1210) wherein King Arthur is virtually absent and the focus rests on the love story involving Tristan and the Irish princess Isolde.[10] Although Tristan is presented as a kind of prodigal child and quickly grows into an ideal hero already in his youth, being a perfect master of virtually all musical instruments and languages, an artist and a knight, once he has fallen in love he increasingly faces difficulties in maintaining his identity and turns into a more passive character who carries out Isolde's requests (Ordeal episode) or sends her a gift in the form of a dog (Petitcreiu), which makes her feelings of longing for him abate because of music created by a bell hanging around its neck. Isolde realizes quickly the danger associated with this music and destroys it because she does not want to enjoy a false sense of happiness. Subsequently, after the two have spent some time in a mysterious love cave ("minnegrotte"), they deceive her husband, King Mark of Cornwall, one more time, who then allows them to return to his court. Although they enjoyed their love utopia in that enigmatic space far away from human society, they cannot continue to live in this esoteric environment where they lack all human contact. However, their passion continues to rage, and they cannot control themselves; Mark ultimately catches them *in flagrante*, which forces Tristan to leave for good.

While roaming the world, he encounters another Isolde (Whitehand), who hopes for his love, but Tristan only longs for the Irish princess and sings lamenting songs about Isolde, which greatly confuses the new lady. The romance breaks off at that point, maybe because the poet did not want to take the story to its bitter end, as Gottfried's predecessor Thomas de Bretagne and his successors Heinrich von Freiberg and Ulrich von Türheim did, leading to a tragic conclusion.[11] Instead, the fragmentary closure forces the audience to think about the profound implications of this love story, which does not really grant the protagonists the fulfillment of their most cherished desire.

A striking feature in this and other romances proves to be the poet's considerable interest in outlining the protagonist's family history. Already in *Herzog Ernst*, we are told much about young Ernst's history, with his mother being widowed and later wooed by Emperor Otto. Once the two have married, Ernst enjoys his father-in-law's strong liking, though that is then suddenly replaced by fear and suspicion because Heinrich, the Count of the Palatinate, another relative, maligns the protagonist, which triggers a long-term military conflict of national proportions. Hartmann von Aue imparts very little about his protagonists' family background, but both Wolfram von Eschenbach and Gottfried von Strassburg engage intensely with Parzival's and, respectively, Tristan's parents and outline how much they represented models according to which the young protagonists are codetermined and characterized. Both poets endeavored to show how particularly the father's impulsiveness, selfishness, and lack of rationality linger in the nature of Parzival and Tristan. In essence, these romances reveal the extent to which the individual has to learn how to come to terms with those shortcomings and to supersede them through their new values and ideals. These are such fundamental concerns that even modern audiences have richly responded to them, thus acknowledging the "classical" quality of these verse epics.[12]

Thirteenth-Century Middle High German Romances

The Stricker

The history of medieval German romance developed rapidly after Hartmann, Wolfram, and Gottfried had completed their works, and to some extent the concepts became rather repetitive, although a closer reading also indicates significant innovations and variations, addressing alternative social, ethical, and religious concerns. The best example would be the near-contemporary *Daniel von dem Blühenden Tal* by the poet known as "The Stricker" (ca. 1220), who is famous also for his collection of satirical tales about the Priest Amis, his fables and verse narratives, and a massive reworking of the famous *Rolandslied* by the Priest Conrad.[13] The Stricker proved to be highly versatile and was a master in various genres. In his *Daniel*, King Arthur's court is, once again, the starting point of the account, when Daniel arrives, a perfect knight. He never needs to grow or develop further since he is already a role model of knighthood and chivalry. But, in contrast to all other romances prior to The Stricker, here King Arthur is challenged and threatened by a robotic giant who operates on behalf of a hostile king, Matûr, demanding Arthur's immediate and complete submission. This robot has a brother who guards the passage to Matûr's kingdom, but Daniel quickly succeeds, against all odds, when he rescues various ladies who in turn secure magical instruments against the robots.

Once Arthur has arrived with his army, Daniel joins his forces and they achieve a major triumph, with Matûr being killed and Daniel marrying his widow. In the end, however, a new danger arises – one never before mentioned in any other courtly romance or heroic epic. The "father" (or creator) of the two robots appears and tries to avenge his "sons'" death. He commands much necromantic or magical powers and enormous strength, so he kidnaps Arthur and places him precariously on a mountain peak from which no one can rescue him. In his desperation, Parzival tries to attack the old man, but he is immediately captured as well and taken to another mountain peak. Daniel realizes that they must not kill their opponent because he would be the only one able to retrieve the two "prisoners" from their precipitous location. Again, he resorts to a magical object, a net from which there is no escape, which attracts the old man who is thus captured. They can finally illuminate the old man about the giants' misbehavior and threats against Arthur, which explains why Daniel killed them. The old man realizes that he was in the wrong, accepts the death of his two "children" as justified due to their own actions, and begs Arthur to welcome him as one of his vassals. He requests to be granted ownership over a mysterious land behind the mountains, access to which is only known to him. We can be certain that The Stricker somehow drew on the account of the mysterious ruler of the Assassins in modern-day Iran (The Old Man from the Mountain), who had launched a serious of murderous attacks against various crusader princes in the eleventh and twelfth centuries.[14]

The other innovative aspect in this romance is the protagonist's employment of *list* (smartness, rational handling of a situation), with which he succeeds in overcoming and defeating all the monstrous opponents and at times killing them with their own weapons. But on some occasions he is also at a loss about what to do in a situation that creates a dilemma for him, implying that the aspect of time has gained new meaning within the world of courtly romances. Moreover, the reference to the Assassins and the Old Man of the Mountain opens significant perspectives to the Middle East, although it remains unclear to what extent the poet was really aware of the history and culture of Muslim countries beyond the Mediterranean orbit.

Other Thirteenth-Century Romances

Subsequent poets such as Wirnt von Grafenberg (*Wigalois*, ca. 1220) or the anonymous poet of *Wigamur* (ca. middle of the thirteenth century) expanded on the traditional register of knightly motifs so well known from courtly romances; they did not innovate significantly, though they did expand the range of issues addressed in their works to include the quest for the self, the encounter with elves, and also demons. More interesting proves to be the variant of the traditional Arthurian romance, the sentimental romance, such as Konrad Fleck's *Floris und Blanscheflur* (also ca. 1220) or the anonymous *Mai und Beaflor* (ca. 1280/1290), in which knighthood certainly continues to matter significantly, but where the narrative focus increasingly turns toward emotional, if not sentimental, aspects, as best expressed through the passionate love of young people who face life-threatening obstacles and yet succeed because of their strong feelings for each other, their courtly values, and the male protagonists' knightly prowess. Despite their strong love, they tend to become separated and the male protagonist must endeavor for a long time to track down his beloved, to free her from imprisonment, or to avenge assassination attempts. In that process, the protagonists have to embark on nearly "global" travels (*Floris*), a narrative motif that subsequently became popular across late medieval Europe.

In this regard, most interesting proves to be the anonymous *Reinfried von Braunschweig* (ca. 1280/90), which allows us to probe this perspective to a greater extent. In the second half, the protagonist embarks on a crusade because he hopes that this would bestow God's grace on his wife to become pregnant. After a decisive battle against the Persian prince Arofels, who is modeled after the same character in Wolfram von Eschenbach's *Willehalm* (ca. 1218), Reinfried realizes that he cannot force the defeated opponent to convert to Christianity, so he grants him his life and the right to stick to his Muslim faith. Thereupon the two men strike up a friendship, and Arofels takes the Christian on an extensive touristic tour through his empire, delighting him with numerous wonders and monsters. Once the news has reached Reinfried about his wife's pregnancy, he decides to return home, but the romance concludes as a fragment.[15]

Again, we notice a number of narrative elements from a variety of genres merging here, though King Arthur is prominently missing from the picture. Nevertheless, the protagonist demonstrates the concepts of courtly manners, ideals, and values, and those are shared by his opponent, the Persian prince, which becomes the basis for an intercultural exchange. The poet obviously projected here, expanding the model already provided by Wolfram in his *Parzvival*, a new global perspective, even if only in fictional terms, signaling a considerable interest in Persia, above all.[16] In addition, *Reinfried* is clearly characterized by the fascination with the exotic, Oriental world, though fantasy dominates most of the account. Nevertheless, the poet has obviously drawn from contemporary *mappae mundi*, such as the *Ebstorf* map, taking his audience on a world tour of the Middle East in literary terms. Crusade aspects also play a major role, whereas there is never any question regarding the protagonist's personal qualifications as a courtly hero. Further, love and marriage matter critically, even though Reinfried departs from his wife for a long time to seek adventure and to gain God's favors. Wolfram's *Parzival* and also his *Willehalm*, as well as some of the precourtly romances (*Herzog Ernst*), seem to have served as important sources for *Reinfried*. We can thus conclude that the traditional concept of "romance" became increasingly diluted since so many different narrative elements were integrated to form a new whole. While older scholarship identified this phenomenon as an indication of the epigonal character of those works, modern research acknowledges that form of hybridity as a unique and significant element reflecting an innovative value system.[17]

Konrad von Würzburg

The same can be observed with regards to Konrad von Würzburg's *Partonopier und Meliur* (ca. 1285/90), which was based on the anonymous Old French *Partonopeus de Blois*, except that here the young protagonist encounters the Byzantine princess Meliur who can keep herself invisible by means of magic until her lover employs counter magic provided by his mother. This strategy, however, would have almost destroyed their love relationship, and Partonopier has to struggle for years until he can regain his beloved's esteem and eventually, as the result of his triumphs in a major tournament, her hand in marriage. Here, the protagonist also faces a Persian prince, this time as a competitor for Meliur's love, but Partonopier succeeds, of course, against all odds, which subsequently leads to the joyous union of these two young people, and hence also to the triumph of Christianity.[18]

Late Medieval Romances

The tradition of the Middle High German romance continued into the late Middle Ages, but it underwent considerable transformations. We could easily refer to numerous other versions by poets such as Rudolf von Ems (*Der guote Gêrhart*) and Ulrich von Zatzikhoven (*Lanzelet*), who either developed own narrative motifs and materials (Rudolf) or copied further Old French texts for their German audience (Ulrich). The romances included ever more adventures, but did not necessarily gain in thematic depth, such as

Konrad von Stoffeln's *Gauriel von Muntabel*. The fifteenth century witnessed the emergence of prose versions, perhaps comparable to the early novel, such as *Melusine* (Thüring von Ringoltingen, 1456) and the anonymous *Fortunatus* (printed in 1509). Numerous medieval verse romances were rendered into prose and then also entered the early modern book market in printed form, such as the novels by Elisabeth von Nassau-Saarbrücken (*Herpin*, *Loher und Maller*, *Königin Sibille*, and *Hug Schapler*, ca. 1437ff.) or the sole novel by the Archduchess Eleanor of Austria (*Pontus und Sidonia*, ca. 1430). Most remarkably, King Arthur almost vanishes from the literary horizon, whereas the near-mythical figure of Emperor Charlemagne gains in preponderance, often painted in rather dark colors.[19]

The thematic range expanded considerably, and ever new protagonists appear who display different interests and concerns than the "classical" courtly heroes. However, those poets who had set the "standards" of Middle High German romances had already displayed considerable interest in developing a variety of character types whose tasks and challenges were rather diverse.

Yet, the late medieval representatives of this genre demonstrated a much larger interest in exploring the world to the East, they were no longer concerned with the court of King Arthur, and they obviously felt forced to engage critically with social conflicts pitting the ruler against his subjects, such as in the anonymous *Malagis* (ca. 1440–60).[20] Nevertheless, the essential value system, the idealization of courtliness and chivalry, intimately combined with the theme of courtly love, did not disappear completely, even if it no longer mattered essentially in works such as *Melusine* or *Fortunatus*.

The late fifteenth century witnessed a new growth of chivalric romances by such poets as the Bavarian court painter Ulrich Fuetrer (ca. 1430–after 1493), who is famous for his prose *Lanzelot* and his *Buch der Abenteuer* (1473–87), in which he included, once again, the history of the Grail family and the story of the fall of Troy, but then also the romance of *Merlin* (no specific source is known), of *Ibein* (after Hartmann's *Iwein*), and a variety of other famous knights (*Wigoleis*, *Seifrid de Ardemont*, *Melerans*, *Persibein*, and *Poytislier und Flordimar*). The courtly romance had become a kind of library from which later poets freely drew inspiration and ideas, combining and experimenting with many different literary themes for the purpose of entertaining their urban and courtly audiences.[21]

Maximilian I

One of the last poets to compose a chivalric/courtly romance was Emperor Maximilian I (1459–1519), who penned, with the assistance of a staff of writers, the famous *Theuerdank*, which was first printed in 1517, richly illuminated by many extraordinary woodcuts. Maximilian revived the tradition of the chivalric romance, utilizing a strongly metaphorical autobiographical framework through which he could address the ideals of knighthood and courtly love once again. Adventures, challenges by hateful courtiers, attacks on his life, and the pursuit of his love highlight this work, which was then continued in his courtly romance *Weisskunig* (*The White King*; ca. 1505–16), which is also predicated on his own biography but focused on the political conflicts with foreign rulers.[22]

Conclusion

This brief outline of the genre of Middle High German courtly romances has only touched on some of the best-known examples; the full extent of other available texts associated with the court would have to be studied to a much greater depth. The basic concept emerged in the middle of the twelfth century (Heinrich von Veldeke), reached its peak around the turn of the century (Hartmann von Aue, Wolfram von Eschenbach, Gottfried von Strassburg), and then experienced a rich continuation throughout the following two centuries, with much copying and imitation, but also experimentation, to develop new knightly challenges and innovative configurations. On the one hand, we observe an intensification of emotions as essential motives (e.g., *Mai und Beaflor*); on the other, noncourtly elements gain in relevance, such as rationality (The Stricker), the pursuit of love in the Orient,[23] magic and necromancy (Konrad von Würzburg), the uncanny and ghostly (Thüring von Ringoltingen),[24] and endless money (*Fortunatus*). Nevertheless, even in the early sixteenth century, Emperor Maximilian demonstrated that interest in the courtly romance, in chivalry and knighthood, was still alive and well, at least among the high-ranking circles of aristocratic listeners and readers. In the early modern period, traditional courtly romances were often rendered into prose, and also translated into Yiddish, written down in Hebrew letters. Although the courtly framework and value system continued to be of critical importance, the genre obviously appealed, once adapted to modern tastes, to a growing audience, which makes it almost difficult to differentiate the Middle Ages from the early modern age.

Notes

1. Erika Wischer, ed. *Die mittelalterliche Welt 600–1400*. Propyläen Geschichte der Literatur, 2. (Berlin: Propyläen Verlag, 1982); Henning Krauss, ed. *Europäisches Hochmittelalter*. Neues Handbuch der Literaturwissenschaft, 7 (Wiesbaden: Akademische Verlagsgesellschaft Athenaion, 1981).

2. Marion E. Gibbs and Sidney M. Johnson, *Medieval German Literature: A Companion* (New York and London: Garland, 1997); Will Hasty, ed., *German Literature of the High Middle Ages*. The Camden House History of German Literature, 3. (Rochester, NY: Camden House, 2006).
3. Peter Andersen, Petrick Del Duca, and Delphine Pasques, ed., *De Troie en Thuringe: l'Eneas de Heinrich von Veldeke*. Collection "De l'allemand" (Paris: L'Harmattan, 2020).
4. Maria Dobozy, *Re-Membering the Present: The Medieval German Poet-Minstrel in Cultural Context*. Disputatio, 6 (Turnhout: Brepols, 2005).
5. James Rushing, "Erec's Uxuriousness," in *Discourses on Love, Marriage, and Transgression in Medieval and Early Modern Literature*, ed. Albrecht Classen. Medieval & Renaissance Texts & Studies, 278 (Tempe; Arizona Center for Medieval and Renaissance Studies, 2004), pp. 163–80.
6. Joachim Bumke, *Courtly Culture: Literature and Society in the High Middle Ages* (Berkeley: University of California Press, 1991).
7. Joachim Bumke, *Die Blutstropfen im Schnee: über Wahrnehmung und Erkenntnis im "Parzival" Wolframs von Eschenbach*. Hermaea, germanistische Forschungen, neue Folge, 94 (Tübingen: Max Niemeyer, 2001), pp. 59–64.
8. Heiko Hartmann, *Einführung in das Werk Wolframs von Eschenbach*. Einführungen Germanistik (Darmstadt: Wissenschaftliche Buchgesellschaft, 2015).
9. Albrecht Classen, "Noch einmal zu Wolframs 'spekulativer' Kyôt-Quelle im Licht jüdischer Kultur und Philosophie des zwölften Jahrhunderts," *Studi Medievali* XLVI (2005): 281–308.
10. William C. McDonald, *Arthur and Tristan: On the Intersection of Legends in German Medieval Literature*. (Lewiston, Queenston, and Lampeter: The Edwin Mellen Press, 1991); W. T. H. Jackson, "Tristan the Artist in Gottfried's Poem," in *Tristan and Isolde: A Casebook*, ed. Joan Tasker Grimbert (New York and London: Routledge, 2002), pp. 125–46 (orig. 1962).
11. Albrecht Classen, "Der Text der nie enden will. Poetologische Überlegungen zu fragmentarischen Strukturen in mittelalterlichen und modernen Texten," in *Zeitschrift für Literaturwissenschaft und Linguistik*, Heft 99: *Anfang und Ende*. Ed. Wolfgang Haubrichs (1995), pp. 83–113.
12. Mark Chinca, *Gottfried von Strassburg: Tristan*, Landmarks of World Literature. (Cambridge: Cambridge University Press, 1997).
13. Albrecht Classen, "Der Stricker," *The Literary Encyclopedia*, first published August 16, 2021: www.litencyc.com/php/speople.php?rec=true&UID=14777.
14. Albrecht Classen, "Assassins, the Crusades, and the Old Man from the Mountains in Medieval Literature: With an Emphasis on The Stricker's Daniel von dem Blühenden Tal," in *Marginal Figures in the Global Middle Ages and the Renaissance*, ed. Meg Lota Brown. Arizona Studies in the Middle Ages and the Renaissance, 45 (Turnhout: Brepols, 2021), pp. 123–40.
15. Werner Röcke, "Kulturelles Gedächtnis und Erfahrung der Fremde: Der Herzog von Braunschweig in der Literatur des Spätmittelalters und der Frühen Neuzeit," *Jahrbuch der Oswald von Wolkenstein-Gesellschaft* 10 (1998): 281–97.
16. Albrecht Classen, "The Topic of Persia in Medieval Literary Imagination, with a Focus on Middle High German Literature," *Ceræ: An Australasian Journal of*

Medieval and Early Modern Studies 8 (2021): 35–65. https://ceraejournal.com/wp-content/uploads/2022/07/Vol-8-FULL-VOLUME.pdf.

17. Wolfgang Achnitz, *Babylon und Jerusalem: Sinnkonstitutierung im "Reinfried von Braunschweig" und im "Apollonius von Tyrland" Heinrichs von Neustadt*. Hermaea. Germanistische Forschungen, Neue Folge, 98 (Tübingen: Max Niemeyer, 2002).
18. *Partonopeus in Europe: An Old French Romance and its Adaptations*, ed. and with an intro. by Catherine Hanley, Mario Longtin, and Penny Eley. *Mediaevalia* 25.2, Special Issue (2004).
19. Albrecht Classen, *Charlemagne in Medieval German and Dutch Literature*. Bristol Studies in Medieval Culture (Cambridge: D. S. Brewer, 2021).
20. Albrecht Classen, "Magic in Late Medieval German Literature: The Case of the Good Magician Malagis," in *Magic and Magicians in the Middle Ages and the Early Modern Time: The Occult in Pre-Modern Sciences, Medicine, Literature, Religion, and Astrology*, ed. Albrecht Classen. Fundamentals of Medieval and Early Modern Culture, 20 (Berlin and New York: Walter de Gruyter, 2017), 523–45.
21. Thomas Cramer, *Geschichte der deutschen Literatur im späten Mittelalter* (Munich: Deutscher Taschenbuch Verlag, 1990), pp. 27–33.
22. Jan-Dirk Müller, *Gedechtnus: Literatur und Hofgesellschaft um Maximilian I*. Forschungen zur Geschichte der älteren deutschen Literatur, 2 (Munich: Wilhelm Fink, 1982).
23. Konrad Fleck, *Flore und Blanscheflur*, ed. Putzo.
24. Contained in Jan-Dirk Müller, ed., *Romane des 15. und 16. Jahrhunderts*. Bibliothek der Frühen Neuzeit. Frankfurt: Deutscher Klassiker Verlag, 1990, 383–585; for critical comments, see pp. 1159–225.

Suggestions for Further Reading

Bumke, Joachim. *Geschichte der deutschen Literatur im hohen Mittelalter*. Munich: Deutscher Taschenbuch Verlag, 1990.

Classen, Albrecht. "Late Middle High German, Renaissance, and Reformation," in *A Concise History of German Literature to 1900*, ed. Kim Vivian. Columbia, SC: Camden House, 1992, pp. 58–90.

Hasty, Will ed., *A Companion to Gottfried von Strassburg's* Studies in German Literature, Linguistics, and Culture. Rochester, NY: Camden House, 2003.

A Companion to Wolfram's Parzival. Studies in German Literature, Linguistics, and Culture. Columbia, SC: Camden House, 1999.

Johnson, L. Peter, *Die höfische Literatur der Blütezeit (1160/70–1220/30)*. Geschichte der deutschen Literatur von den Anfängen bis zum Beginn der Neuzeit, II: Vom hohen zum späten Mittelalter. Tübingen: Max Niemeyer, 1999.

Tomasek, Tomas. *Gottfried von Straßburg*. Stuttgart: Philipp Reclam Jun., 2007.

Wehrli, Max. *Geschichte der deutschen Literatur im Mittelalter: Von den Anfängen bis zum Ende des 16. Jahrhunderts*. 3rd ed. Stuttgart: Philipp Reclam, 1997.

14

PATRICIA CLARE INGHAM

The Ends of Romance in Chaucer and Malory

Romances were widely popular in late Middle English contexts, often as vernacular versions of multilingual story traditions. Even when repeating the plots of well-known stories, the genre of romance constituted diversities of form and language, making it challenging to define in any exhaustive way. But in romance's versatility lies a key strength, a feature of the genre that would enable poetic and editorial experiments of lasting influence. This versatility would also, however, give rise to controversies about the genre. Is romance such a loose and baggy fictionalizing monster that it mostly rewards excesses, popularizing trivial tales and light fantasies? Alternatively, what might be made of the affordances of romance to prompt novel experimentation, or artistic flexibility?

Over the years, some critics have been skeptical of romance, precisely as a genre fraught with fantasy as falsehood and thus as more likely than other kinds of poetry to purvey ideologies or encourage idolatries.[1] There were certainly medieval thinkers who worried over the capacity of the genre to dazzle rather than edify. Yet much of what we now understand about the imaginative power and historical probity of medieval romance has been the result of efforts, over at least the last quarter of a century, to dismantle this kind of critical condescension toward the genre.[2] Examples from the late Middle English corpus suggest two points which I will pursue here. The first is that romances regularly probed serious matters of broad political, social, ethical, and aesthetic concern. Middle English romances are filled with divergent answers to compelling questions of social, political, and cultural import. Some romances did this by attending to specific geographies, or by placing historical figures in specific interpersonal or regional contexts. Such stories also regularly considered the power and limits of the imagination, of speculative thinking, or of prophetic futurism. Romances about the group known as the Nine Worthies (an heroic group that included King Arthur and Charlemagne) commented on real problems of wartime violence or imperial conquest. Others, like those examined by Lee Manion in Chapter 7, explored Crusader aggressions and interreligious conflict. Even those romances depicting magic and marvels, or those identified with prophets such as Merlin, had historical ambitions: exploring future possibilities or offering alternative accounts of historical events. Pointing to the truth-claims at stake even in fine fabling, such stories reflected on diverse kinds of social relations. As this suggests, romances were not (as has sometimes been argued) simply escapist fantasy necessarily at odds with history. The later Middle English period offers many examples of romance as a mechanism for analyzing some of the knottiest and most complex intellectual, social, artistic, and political issues confronting society, then and now.

A second point at issue here involves the range and versatility of the genre, and the ways that it offered opportunities for literary, translational, and editorial experimentation. Accordingly, I am interested in tracing late Middle English romance as a mode particularly suited to experiments in writing and editing. Experimentation is, I will suggest, one "end" of Middle English romance, and by end I mean both a capacity encouraged by certain features of the genre and an effect of the genre legible in the hands of some notable English authors. This chapter will pursue this question in a somewhat circumscribed way. What did the romance genre make possible, I ask, in the hands of two well-known late medieval English authors? What poetic or narrative experiments did the power of romance render in the works of Geoffrey Chaucer, in the fourteenth century, and Thomas Malory, in the fifteenth? To what ends has romance been put by Chaucer and Malory, and what place do the Middle English romances penned by these two writers hold in a larger and longer literary history?

The Ends of Romance, 1: Geoffrey Chaucer (c. 1342/3–1400)

Geoffrey Chaucer exploited romance conventions in a range of settings, experimenting with voice, poetic pacing, form, and aesthetics. Many of Chaucer's early narrative poems (including *the Book of the Duchess*, *Anelida and Arcite*, and *Troilus and Criseyde*) engage romance conventions wholly or in part. A diverse range of romances, moreover, feature in Chaucer's *Canterbury Tales* project, texts that include *The Knight's Tale* (*KnT*), *the Squire's Tale* (*SqT*), *Sir Thopas* (*Thopas*), and *The Wife of Bath's Tale* (*WBT*). These poems demonstrate Chaucer's knack for rendering old traditions in fresh, often metacritical, ways.[3]

The romances included as part of his *Canterbury Tales* frame-story, moreover, offered the poet special opportunities for experimentation with narrative plot as well as with voice. They are told via a diverse array of tale-telling voices: Chaucer's Knight (a war-weary crusader), tells a lengthy, tragic, philosophical tale of unexpected death, a text into which his own distinctive voice regularly intrudes. His son, the Squire, offers a romance replete with exotic marvels but one so overburdened with the Squire's own rhetorical flourishes that it is much less successful than the tale told by his illustrious father. The Wife of Bath, a particularly memorable Chaucerian figure, tells a romance with magical features, even as her story fittingly emphasizes issues of gender and power from her own social location, imagining possibilities for recuperative justice in the rehabilitation of a rapist knight. Gesturing to his own metacritical interest, Chaucer, the poet, assigns a romance to his fictional persona in the Canterbury pilgrimage. Geoffrey, the Canterbury pilgrim, tells a "native" Middle English poetic romance (the *Tale of Syr Thopas*) in a way that satirizes familiar adventure tales with a boy-knight as its hero.

As these examples suggest, the diversity of romances in the *Canterbury Tales* comment more generally on the flexibility of the genre even as they demonstrate Chaucer's poetic range. *The KnT*, which inaugurates the entire tale-telling performance in the Canterbury frame-story, bridges the poet's earlier, "courtly" period, and likely originated as a self-standing poem before being assigned to the Knight. It belongs to a subcategory of romances known as *romans d'antiquité* (romances about antiquity), and is rendered in an elevated poetic style appropriate to an aristocratic knight. It is a free adaptation of Boccaccio's *Teseida*,[4] a story of war and tournament, of the limitations of human willing, of intimate rivalries and unanticipated deaths, recounted in the voice of the Knight. Throughout, Chaucer's Knight invites readers to think complexly about fate and catastrophe, war and tyranny, and the traumatic precarity of those (ladies or warriors) too easily sacrificed to a ruler's pursuit of "necessity." The tale takes a somber tone, even despite the fact that story culminates in joy when the infinite sorrows of Thebes (*KnT*, l. 2827) turn into the perfect joy (*KnT*, l. 3072) of Emily and Palamon's marriage bond. Loss and death dominate from the beginning. Only thirty-five lines in, a group of widows plead with the victorious Athenian Duke Theseus, who rides through the city "in his mooste pride" (in greatest pride; *KnT*, I 895). They seek to be allowed to bury their dead. The problems of war surface immediately, and critics have pointed out the subtle critique of a leader prideful in the midst of destruction, the winner, Theseus, perhaps more similar to the Theban tyrant, Creon, than he recognizes. About 200 lines later we are introduced to the poem's two young heroes, Palamon and Arcite, in a heap of battlefield dead, "liggynge by and by" (lying side by side; *KnT*, I. 1011). War's cruel violence is starkly rendered here, as it will be throughout the romance. Indeed, when Arcite dies from an accidental wound caused by the actions of jealous pagan gods, the poetry emphasizes both the ruler Duke Theseus' inability to stop this injustice and the gruesomeness of the wound's suppurating infection. There is, it seems, a corruption at the heart of wartime rivalries, and this is made clear to us throughout Chaucer's Theban romance.

Furthermore, the passage understood as key for interpreting the *KnT* – Duke Theseus's philosophical "Prime Mover" speech, borrowing themes from Boethius's *Consolation of Philosophy* – calls on all to make a virtue of necessity. Yet in the context of Chaucer's revisions to his source, and as critics have long pointed out, this somber advice does not satisfy.[5] Loss overshadows any apparently happier end. Both Chaucer as poet and the Knight as tale-teller offer plenty of evidence that we are meant to doubt the apparently heroic picture that the philosophical Duke Theseus adduced.

If much of this sounds more like tragedy than romance, we should recall that many late Middle English romances involve just such crossings of mood and feeling. The Arthurian alliterative *Morte Arthure*, for instance, takes a determinedly tragic mode in its critique of the excesses of King Arthur's imperial conquests. Furthermore, precisely as a tragic romance, the *KnT* assesses the social and political complications of loss as a gendered arrangement, a point noted by critics.[6] Widows suffer; knights are sacrificed to masculine militarism; ladies submit to marriage even when they don't much want to do so. In this case, we are also offered digressions in the tale-telling Knight's own voice, as when he overlays what is ostensibly a description of the Temple of Mars that Arcite visits with a gruesome scene evoking the fog of war, a moment that has been read as a poignant recollection of the Knight's own experience of unforgettable battlefield horrors.[7] Or, again, when the Knight's himself responds to the problem of Arcite's unexpected, unexpectedly gruesome, death. Here is the Knight's stunning disclaimer, in language stilted and difficult to parse:

> [Arcite's] spirit chaunged hous and wente ther,
> As I cam nevere, I kan nat tellen wher.
> Therfore I stynte; I nam no divinistre;
> Of soules fynde I nat in this registre,
> Ne me ne list thilke opinions to telle
> Of hem, though that they writen wher they dwelle.
> Arcite is coold, ther Mars his soule gye! (I. 2809–15)

His spirit changed house and went where / Since I came never (there), I can not tell where. / Therefore I stop; I am no theologian; / I find nothing about souls in this register, / Nor do I wish to tell such opinions / Of them, though they write of where they (the souls) dwell. / Arcite is cold, may Mars guide his soul!

The speech refuses consolation and records the tale-telling Knight's inability to know, or say, what Arcite's death portends. The Knight speaks in a staccato style, and his speech comes close to halting entirely at its midpoint: "therefore, I stop," the Knight proclaims. His voice carries on, but mainly to circle around his own linguistic incapacity. He cannot, at this crucial juncture, say anything that really matters. This is the kind of masterful technique that critics have come to expect from Chaucerian romance; in this case, it renders a fictional Knight's inarticulate response to his own tale's most tragic moments. This is, moreover, one way that Chaucer's poem makes room for resistances to Duke Theseus's explanatory power: it offers an account of the ineluctable trauma that even the Duke can neither contain nor explain.

As with *The Knight's Tale*, *The Wife of Bath's Tale* aims at a social problem of enormous consequence. But unlike the blending of violent human tyranny with the cosmological jealousies of the ancient gods motivating the former tragedy, victimization in *WBT* is a more quotidian and local affair: an errant knight's rape of an innocent maid he happens upon in the countryside. The tale is set, moreover, not far away in Thebes or Athens, but localized in Britain, a place denominated as *this land* (*WBT*, III 859). As romance, the *WBT* tale belongs to a different subgenre entirely, that of Arthurian Romance: the wide-ranging, international set of stories about the legendary British King Arthur and his knights, including texts surviving in Latin, Welsh, French, German, Icelandic, Old Norse, and Hebrew, to name a few. As Chaucer's lone intervention into the Arthurian subgenre, the *WBT* reworks its topic in ways suitable for his character of the Wife: this version of Arthurian romances explicitly addresses issues of power, gender, sovereignty, and sexuality – many of the same issues emerging in the Wife's autobiographical prologue. As with the *KnT*, Chaucer seems to have made a very deliberate choice in assigning this tale to its teller. Surviving textual evidence demonstrates that he had, at one point, planned to assign the fabliau now known as the *Shipman's Tale* to the obstreperous Wife. Such facts suggest that this Arthurian story, specifically positioned as the Wife's Tale, might enable a larger reflection upon women as consumers, as well as producers, of romance tales, as we shall see.

The sources behind *The Wife of Bath's Tale* are more proximate, too, as the tale's major plot turn depends upon a romance motif familiar from Irish and Welsh textual traditions: the figure of the loathly lady. The lady's transformation is crucial to the tale's major redemption plot, whereby the rapist knight is rehabilitated by submitting to the demands of an old, haggard lady who magically rewards his submission to her by changing into a young beauty. This is, to be sure, a fantasy of recuperation: imagining a rapist newly transformed into a sensitive husband via a dream of turning back the clock on an aging female body. Like the *KnT*, the *WBT* ends with a happy marriage, but here too readers are not allowed to rest too easily on such reconciliations, no matter how desired they may be.

These two tales share other romance features, too. Both the *KnT* and *WBT* look to an imagined past to tell tales useful in their present. Temporal dislocation is a feature of the *KnT*'s place in the *Canterbury* frame-story, signaled in the Knight's "once upon a time" opening: "Whilom as olde stories tellen us" (Once, as old stories tell us; *KnT*, I, 859). Ushered into another time and place, readers are suspended in a world where events happen, but without compelling reference to the passage of time. Years are stipulated more than experienced (and, as details, they are easy to miss, often rendered in a single line, as "after a year or two"). The temporal span from the tale's start to its end is long, but it has no narrative duration; instead, the movement of plot keeps catching on the tragic eruption of violence and loss. The Wife also opens her tale by way of a chronological distancing: "In th'olde dayes of the Kyng Arthure" (In the old days of King Arthur; *WBT*, III, 857). Yet this account of time distinguishes past from present, evoking time passing in a gorgeous meditation on "then" versus "now." The Wife's historical moment (legible to us from her autobiographical prologue wherein she meditates on her own aging) is the "now" when, as she puts it, "kan no man se none elves mo" (no man can see any elves; *WBT*, III, 864); this is juxtaposed against the "manye hundred yeres ago" (many hundred years ago; *WBT*, III, 863) when elf queens still danced in English meadows.

These are arguably historiographical moves, pointing to the power of romance to make claims about history even as it narrates magical events. Here and elsewhere, the Wife voices a set of imaginary enchantments with an eye toward those features of time passing that have long been identified with realist narratives, and with the novel. Chaucer's use of romance seems, in this regard, self-consciously metacritical, raising issues about authorship and audience; the voice of the teller assigned to their particular romance tale regularly gives Chaucer's romance experiments their metacritical edge. This is pointedly the case at the end of the *WBT*, as the Wife's own voice intrudes into the narrative. She curses husbands like those she has had, husbands who, unlike the rehabilitated rapist knight in her tale, resist the sovereignty of their wives: May God give such stingy men the plague, she avers. Breaking out of his own fictionalizing romance space, Chaucer has the Wife bring us back into the unidealized world of gender politics in her own day, fourteenth-century England. At such a moment readers can see an outline of Chaucer's account of women as readers of romance, who relish romance fancies so as to imagine a different world than the one they inhabit. Yet this is not wish fulfillment or in any way naïve: the Wife is capable of dreaming up the possibility of justice and recuperation in her tale, even as she remembers the politics of her own historical moment. And so, too, readers are invited to attend to these gender politics, rendered in Chaucer's historical moment by way of a female persona, the Wife.

If the *KnT* and the *WBT* remind us of Chaucer's fascination with the serious ethical, political, and moral issues addressed by the genre, two other romances from the Canterbury project reflect on the limitations and liabilities of romance patternings, although here, too, these questions are addressed in complex, metacritical ways. *Sir Thopas* gently parodies popular insular versions of romances involving youthful knights, narratives also known as stories of boyhood or "enfances." Sir Thopas is a handsome young knight, "a doghty swayn" whose face is white "as payndemayn" (that is, as white bread), with "lippes rede as rose" (*Thopas* VII, 724–6). He was a boy with a "semely" (handsome) nose (*Thopas* VII, 729), a cringe-worthy rhyme to "rose" from line 726. As these lines may already imply, the tale is, in the first instance, meant as a gentle takedown of the jingle-jangle of some popular adventure tales of English heroes, such as Bevis of Hampton or Guy of Warwick. Sir Thopas, our hero, is all boyishness and clever charm, a young adventurer seeking his beloved Fairy Queen by vanquishing his adversary, Sir Olifaunt (that is, Sir Elephant). Thopas is fully equipped for the task, from his sweet nose to his nifty spear. Here, overly regular meter, short stanzas, stereotypical rhymes, and unsophisticated poetic diction suggest that this is the stuff of children's stories, as they are meant to do in this case.

This is a failed tale in many ways. It is also one, as noted previously, that Chaucer the poet assigns to his fictional self, the pilgrim Geoffrey, one among the Canterbury band. Inspired by texts reputed to be entertaining but not particularly edifying, the romance's notoriously inelegant features come in for gentle satire. These are likely the kinds of narratives, ballads, or shorter poems that Chaucer heard as a boy. That is, in fact, part of the joke. *Thopas* may be a case of Chaucer ventriloquizing his own imagined juvenilia: Geoffrey the pilgrim notes that the romance he will tell is "a rym I lerned longe agoon" (a rhyme I learned long ago; *Thopas*, VII, 709). To be sure, this parodic romance shares little with Chaucer's quite sophisticated forays into the romance form, both within the Canterbury project and beyond it, but that is precisely why it resonates with the most whimsical examples of the genre.

If *Thopas* stands at the vanishing point of romance scale – as the lightest of light entertainments – the *Squire's Tale* (*SqT*) sits at the other extreme, threatening an impossibly grandiose expansiveness. Yet it, too, is less than successful as a performance. A putatively exotic romance set in the court of Genghis Khan, the *SqT* has long been identified as a composite romance – that is, a romance story incorporating diverse motifs traceable to French, Arabic, and classical Greek sources and analogues. Set at the court of Genghis Khan (Cambryskan), the *SqT* relates the story of a series of marvels (a flying, mechanical horse, a magical mirror, a ring that provides communication between men and birds, and a sword with special powers) given to that court and tested by local courtiers as well as by Cambryskan's daughter, Canacee. It is an engrossing and fabulous tale, typical of international romance traditions in its topic as well as its meandering style.

Throughout its lines, the tale alludes to the matter of romance poetry as both dependent on international sources and analogues and attentive to a locally situated audience. It opens with an overly long excursus on rhetoric in the Squire's voice, reflecting on diverse romance sources pertinent to the tale about to be told. Since at least the sixteenth century, readers have often judged *SqT* to be one of the *least* successful texts in the *Canterbury Tales* collection, but this may be precisely what Chaucer the poet had in mind. After modestly confessing his own limited rhetorical skills (*SqT* v, 7, 34–41), the Squire outlines his narrative plan for a lengthy romance (*SqT* v, 661–70). Notably, the tale could not possibly have been completed under the plan that the Squire initially outlines in his Prologue (*SqT* v, 661–70): by some estimates, and considering the length of the tale's first two parts, the completed tale would have exceeded the scale of the entire *Canterbury Tales* collection. Some readers have, accordingly, viewed the tale as one of Chaucer's experiments in poetic composition and rhetoric, a satire of the Squire's volubility and testimony to his lack of rhetorical control. In that context, the tale has been read as a failed attempt by a son (the Squire) to imitate the grandeur of his father's (the Knight's) epic romance.[8] In more recent decades, moreover, *SqT* has become increasingly important for its consideration of scientific knowledge and technical gadgetry, and as evidence of Chaucer's interest in stories about the East and in Arabic sources and intellectual traditions.[9]

Positioned within the Canterbury tale-telling competition, these two romances also serve to heighten Chaucer's metacritical consideration of romance artistry. They do so by attending to the dissatisfied reactions of the assembled audience of Canterbury pilgrims to these tales. Both of them, for one thing, yield to audience objections, with the details of audience reaction described in the interlinking head notes and end notes that connect particular tales to the story of the larger Canterbury pilgrimage. Before the tale of *Thopas* has really got going (and only about 200 lines into the romance proper), the Canterbury host, Harry Bailley, interrupts the speaker in exasperation: no more of this, he exclaims, noting that the "lewedness" (ignorance) of the romance makes his ears ache (*Thopas*, VII, 919–23). The rhyme is doggerel, "drasty rymyng ... nat worth a toord!" (worthless rhyming . . . not worth a turd) (*Thopas*, VII, 930).

This is clearly broad humor, but also a metacritical reflection on the art of tale-telling. And the failure of authorship is doubly emphasized since, remarkably enough, the poet assigns what Harry Bailley proclaims to be doggerel to his fictional self, his doppelgänger in the frame-story, Geoffrey, member of the Canterbury pilgrim band. Earlier, this same Harry Bailley has invited pilgrim Chaucer to tell the kind of light tale that he now deplores: a tale of mirth (*Thopas*, VII, 706), some dainty thing (*Thopas*, VII, 711). Such instructions emphasize the lightness of the story to come, and the tale that Chaucer the poet assigns to Chaucer the pilgrim clearly plays with and against Bailly's prompting as well as his reactions. Offering a sweet adventure tale of a child knight, Chaucer the poet uses this romance to unsettle questions of the relation of textual instruction (as in the Middle English word "sentence") to textual pleasure (the Middle English "solaas"). How much pleasure is too much, and how little edifying meaning is too little? The performance of Thopas, then, and as a tale interrupted, puts pressure on issues long associated with the condescension toward the romance genre: are such tales mere entertainment that will never matter except as a meaningless diversion? The charming figure of Thopas as boy-knight goes a good way to suggest that Chaucer's game here is in earnest: this parody of romance lightness is fond rather than harsh. In its larger contexts, moreover, *Thopas* reaffirms the importance of pleasure for story, and the story that Chaucer the pilgrim tells next is a moral treatise in prose that is long and heavy, full of meaning but a hard-going read. We are left, Bailly's rejections notwithstanding, with a sense that too little pleasure in the text is as disabling as too much. Pleasure seems a romance necessity here, and simple tales with adventure plots, jangly rhythms, and predictable rhymes (in other words, romances) can evoke fond pleasures even if judged trivial by some particular audience.

When the Squire takes his turn at the Canterbury pilgrims' storytelling game, his romance will also be interrupted, though in that case the problem sits at the opposite extreme: the *SqT* of romance marvels impresses the audience not as too little, but as very much too *much*. It will be cut off preemptively, too. At the start of its third section, the impatient Franklin interrupts, anxious to tell his tale (also a romance, not incidentally). Like the *Tale of Syr Thopas*, the Squire's performance wearies his audience (the Franklin, the Host, and presumably the other pilgrims): it is excessive in its sources and overbearing in length. Here, however, the Franklin is all courtesy, respecting the Squire's status (as the Knight's son and a member of the aristocracy) and damning him with faint praise: a noble effort, the Franklin asserts, at least considering the Squire's youth.

In both the *SqT* and *Thopas*, we see authorial performance as embedded in a local audience, an audience actively dissatisfied and ready to judge the romancer. Chaucer's reflection on the power of an audience's judgment is not limited to these two examples; nevertheless, it is undeniable that his romance tales raise such questions in a particularly focused manner, and in terms of textual pleasure and questions of textual scale. These moments imply a reflection on the power and limits of romance: stories too short or too long; tales weighted down with unnecessary rhetorical commentary, on the one hand, or so flighty as to seem meaningless, on the other. In these romances, moreover, Chaucer raises questions about the prestige (or lack of prestige) afforded to the role of the romancer or the fabulist, a problem that he casts here as measured by the judgments of an audience.

If romance affords Chaucer such metacritical experiments in fictionalizing failures, it is nonetheless important to remember that he also deploys the genre in some of his most admired *Canterbury Tales*. The joke of tale-telling excess aimed at Chaucer's Squire might just as well have been directed to the Squire's father, the Knight. His tale, too, takes up a great deal of space, more than any other tale in the collection. Yet in that case, Chaucer's modifications to his source suggest instead the capacity of romance to accommodate imaginative recastings on grave topics of cosmological consequence.

The Ends of Romance, 2: Thomas Malory's *Morte Darthur*

If Geoffrey Chaucer's forays into romance demonstrate an interest in thinking analytically about the power and limits of this fabulist genre, Thomas Malory's experiments in the romance form work in a more conservative mode, so as to consolidate diverse story traditions. And if Chaucer's use of romance is notable for its poetic range and breadth, Malory's romance, the *Morte Darthur*, offers a deep dive in a prose narrative and an exhaustive recrafting of the long narrative arc of the story of King Arthur and his court.

Thomas Malory is, it must be said, an author of dubious personal reputation. It is clear, for one thing, that he finished his masterpiece while in prison, the culmination of a murky career as a (likely criminal) knight, imprisoned for all manner of thievery and abductions during that series of wars over dynastic rule from rival branches of the Plantagenets known as The Wars of the Roses (1455–87). Malory's great work interlaces and regularizes diverse stories from French, Middle English, and Latin sources, from prose and from poetry, into a coordinated narrative of the birth, rise, flourishing, downfall, and death of the legendary British king, Arthur. Malory's integrated prose account maps the entire arc of the Arthurian story, from Arthur's conception and birth through his accession to the throne, the flourishing of his community to the Grail Quest, and on down to the fracturing of Arthur's Round Table fellowship and the king's death. The stories included are taken from chronicles as well as from romances: from Geoffrey of Monmouth's Latin history, from John Hardyng's fifteenth-century, rhyming *Chronicle of England*, and from both French and Middle English vernacular poems and prose narratives. In 1485, the work was published by England's first commercially successful printer, William Caxton. It was Caxton who gave the work the title it bears today: the *Morte Darthur*, or *The Death of Arthur*. Malory's *Morte* was part of a series that Caxton would publish within a relatively short period: books aimed at a gentry audience and dedicated to highlighting the scope of "British" history. This series proved to be crucial to the eventual financial success of Caxton's press.[10]

Malory's *Morte Darthur* is, accordingly, more a compendium of already existing romances than a radically new work; nevertheless, the editing and translating that Malory pursued resulted in an innovative version of the story, one that would cast a very long shadow, having an authoritative effect upon nearly all future versions. The text is organized into eight separate books, and the sources from which those books are drawn give a sense of the achievement of Malory's art of design. Book I, *Merlin*, tells the story of Arthur's conception and birth and is a translation of the French Prose *Merlin* and taken from a story originating in Geoffrey of Monmouth's *Historia regum Britanniae*. Book II, *Arthur the Emperor*, tells of Emperor Arthur's war with the Roman ruler Lucius and is a prose adaptation of the Middle English alliterative poem, *Morte Arthure*, the latter a masterpiece of alliterative poetry and regularly read as a pacifist poem, one that locates the roots of Arthur's tragic fall in Emperor Arthur's overweening imperial ambitions. Although Malory remains attentive to the critiques of disastrous violence in his source, his relocation of this story to an early moment in his larger narrative, along with his rewriting of the episode's usual tragic ending, de-emphasizes imperial overreach as the key factor in the downfall of Arthurian rule.

The next three books focalize around particularly famous figures in the story tradition. Book III, *Lancelot*, tells the story of this most famous Arthurian knight and is taken primarily from the French Prose romance of the same name. The source for Book IV, *Gareth*, is the least clear: it may be somewhat original, though likely based on the folktale tradition of the *bel inconnu*, or "Fair Unknown" knight: a youth who comes to court without name or lineage and distinguishes himself by his deeds rather than his renown. Book V, *Tristram*, is the longest of these books (originally two separate books) and is based on a French prose romance that is itself based on earlier verse retellings of the adulterous affair between the knight, Tristan, and his lord's queen, Iseult. In Book VI readers encounter the story of the pursuit of the Holy Grail, and this book closely follows the religious mysticism of the French *Queste del Saint Graal*, with a tale of the grail quest focusing on knights, Bors, Perceval, and Galahad.

The last two books, mirroring the first two, return us to the longer narrative arc, focusing on the splintering and downfall of the Round Table fellowship and of Arthur's death. Book VII, *Lancelot and Guinevere*, recounts the infamous adultery of Lancelot with Arthur's queen, Guinevere; it interlinks several sources, and is thought by some critics to be Malory's most original section. The story is based on *La mort Artu*, the final romance in the French vulgate romances, and on the English Stanzaic *Morte Arthur*, which is itself indebted to the vulgate version of the same story. It details the well-known plot regarding Lancelot and Guinevere's disastrous love affair, affording this event primacy of place in the lead-up to King Arthur's downfall. Book VIII, the *Morte d'Arthur*, is indebted to these same sources, given in somber, elegiac tones.

As this suggests, Malory's *Morte* is structured at its largest as a combined episodic and sequential history. This is itself an artistic achievement, coordinating features of sweeping Arthurian chronicle tradition interspersed with episodic forms taken from shorter romance tales. This means that, at key moments, Malory's *Morte* shares the repetitive, meandering features of the adventure tale familiar from other kinds of romances. Throughout the *Morte*, readers find numerous detours devoted to the story of the pursuit of the Grail or the particular fortunes of one or another of Arthur's Round Table knights. Such episodes owe debts to a series of minor French and English romances that circulated in earlier centuries. These include numerous French romances highlighting the fortunes of particular knights: *Erec et Enide*; a French romance featuring Gawain (*L'âtre périlleux* or *The Perelous Cemetery*); *Perlesvaus*; *Yvain* (along with its Middle English analogue, *Ywain and Gawain*); and the late Middle English poem, *The Weddynge of Syr Gawain*. Malory regularly positions the action of key figures (Lancelot, Galahad, Bors, Gawain, Perceval) in the particular quests of individual knights; yet, he uses repetition and coordination of these stories to excellent effect, giving the middle books in the *Morte* a kind of simultaneous timing, transitioning, for instance, from the story of one knight's pursuit of the Holy Grail to the adventures of another on the same quest, all via a kind of temporal suspension rendered through the repetition of "meanwhile." This structure enables a diffusion of particular episodes while sustaining a coherent unifying structure – Knights have their own particular adventures, with only the most honorable (Galahad, Percival, and Bors) coming near to the Grail. Other knights errant from the Round Table fellowship journey from court, responding to challenges posed to Arthurian sovereignty by enemy knights or pursuing quests to aid someone in distress (often ladies named Elaine), whom they have happened upon. Throughout, female figures prove crucial to the development of the narrative momentum, and not only as love objects or victims. In general, Malory regularly emphasizes the crucial role of female figures: by foregrounding the Arthurian chivalric oath to protect women, drawing Guinevere into episodes from his sources that do not feature her, and granting Morgan le Fay (an infamous villainess in the larger tradition) an explicitly consoling role in ferrying Arthur's dead body to the island of Avalon. Such details prompted a critic named Dorsey Armstrong to argue that the depictions of gender in community in the *Morte Darthur* are crucial to the larger narrative emplotment.[11]

Knightly adventures are subsumed under the larger structure that balances variation with coherence, with central sections focalized around the Grail quest or a particular knight's response to challenges posed to Arthur's kingship. This structure resulted from Malory's dual roles: editor as well as writer, he consolidates available motifs, drafting transitions from one to the other and adding in regular commentary of his own. Far from inert copying of source material, this is a complex act of narrative arrangement, as are his translations of materials originally in French or Latin into a new kind of Middle English prose. Such shifts (from poetry to prose; from diverse languages to late Middle English) demonstrate Malory's artistry as an exploration of how writing might bridge tradition with innovation, the old with the new. Moreover, at least since the 1970s, most critics would agree that Malory's great acts of arrangement, of editing, of translation, and of commentary made a strongly coherent story tradition much greater than the sum of its parts.[12]

In this lies his experimental originality. Whether linking wide-ranging episodes about this or that knight together in the overarching Grail story or accommodating divergent Middle English versions of Arthur's downfall, Malory consolidates competing stories and competing meanings of Arthur's kingship. Does Arthur's fellowship represent the height of chivalric honor, or community that fails to achieve its greatest possibilities? Praise for Round Table glory is placed side by side with critique of chivalric frailties, and Malory manages his narrative structure so that these two alternatives augment rather than undermine one another.

Like Chaucer, Malory's use of romance had a broadly cultural aim in mind. A traditionalist at heart, Malory prepared his Arthurian masterpiece for a future audience that, he worried, might be too flighty to appreciate this legacy. In one of his most famous asides, Malory tellingly comments on what he would have his readers see as the incapacity of English readers to honor the Arthurian past:

> Lo, ye all Englishmen, see ye not what mischief here was? For [Arthur] . . . was the most [greatest] king and noblest knight of the world, and most loved the fellowship of noble knights, . . . and yet might not these Englishmen hold them content with them. Lo thus was the old custom and usages of this land, and men say that we of this land have not yet lost that custom. Alas! this is a great default of us Englishmen, for they may no thing please us no term.
>
> (Book 21, chapter 1)

There is no small amount of nostalgia here – a sense of romance as a genre that glories in the past, but not perhaps in the self-conscious, metacritical manner of Chaucer in his *Wife of Bath*. And with regard to figures like Chaucer or the Wife, hailing from the middling classes, we should not forget that Malory's narrative makes the royal trappings of Arthurian honor pertinent for the gentry classes – a group on the increase at the time his work first appeared from Caxton's press.

Malory had little need to fear for his or Arthur's perpetuity. William Caxton, Malory's own eventual editor, would ensure a wider readership than Malory himself likely envisioned. And Malory's work will imprint an authoritative narrative version of Arthur's story. A long train of poets, novelists, dramaturges, and filmmakers would follow his lead, from Alfred Lloyd Tennyson to Sidney Lanier; from T. H. White to Donald Barthelme; from Mary Stewart to Marion Zimmer Bradley. Malory's legacy is well represented in the Anglo-American corpus.

The power of romance, as the cases of Malory and Chaucer each suggest, has to do with the capacity of fictionalizing to render the conflicts and affections of human community in complex ways. Middle English romance regularly does so, sometimes by detailing critiques of King Arthur by way of specific, regional geographies across the English realm. At other times, Middle English romances render the complexities of gender and sexuality, of class and power, by outlining the vicissitudes of relations – pleasurable or agonizing, violent or peaceful, political or sexual – giving readers accounts of the poignant complications of living and loving in community.

Furthermore, from the long line of literary history, these kinds of romances set a few of the terms important to the future of the novel. Examples from

Geoffrey Chaucer and Thomas Malory offered here demonstrate some of the ways that Middle English romances – whether in poetry or in prose – feature as ancestors to the novel. When Chaucer has his Wife of Bath fantasize a bedroom rehabilitation of a dishonorable knight, he anticipates what would come to be known as the novel's marriage plot. When Malory coordinates the story of Arthur's history, he gives later writers, British and American, fodder for versions of Arthur's story suited to their own political moment. Romance enabled this kind of flexibility and experimentation. There were those who worried that romance's popularity could be dangerous, aimed primarily at providing distraction rather than wisdom for its readers. But this worry, too, sounds familiar. And that is because it will re-emerge, in later centuries, in popular concerns about the imaginative excesses prompted by a dialogic form we might consider the progeny of medieval romance: the novel itself.

Notes

1. Stephen Knight, for instance, has interrogated the ideological force of Arthurian romance, aiming sustained critique at "idealist" readings and stressing the important "social function" of romance. This important work, however, can be condescending insofar as it duplicates rather than interrogates the understanding of romance as "escapist" fantasy. See "The Social Function of the Middle English Romance." In *Medieval Literature: Criticism, Ideology, and History*. Edited by David Aers, 99–122. New York: St. Martin's, 1986.
2. The bibliography is long. For a critique of romance so-called "escapism," see many of the essays in Roberta L. Krueger, ed., *Cambridge Companion to Medieval Romance* (Cambridge: Cambridge University Press, 2000). L. O. Fradenburg has identified the genre's capacity to harness revolutionary potential, as in her early essay on "The Wife of Bath's Passing Fancy," *Studies in the Age of Chaucer* (1986): 31–58. Susan Crane reads romance as crucial to Chaucer's sophisticated analyses of gender dynamics: *Gender and Romance in Chaucer's Canterbury Tales*. Princeton, NJ: Princeton University Press, 1994. The volume edited by Nicola McDonald offers multiple accounts of cultural sophistication of the most infamous Middle English stories Nicola McDonald, ed. *Pulp Fictions of Medieval England: Essays in Popular Romance*. Manchester: Manchester University Press, 2004. Lee Manion (Chapter 7, this volume) emphasizes crucial cultural analyses raised in Crusader romances.
3. All references to Chaucer's poetry are taken from *The Riverside Chaucer*, ed. Benson.
4. The *Thebiad* by Statius is another likely source. Chaucer's version stands behind Shakespeare's play, *Two Noble Kinsmen*.
5. For a recent summary of the history of these critical accounts, see Elizabeth Scala, *Desire in the Canterbury Tales*. Columbus: Ohio State University Press, 2015.

6. Crane argues that Chaucer highlights the victimization of women, Theseus's Amazonian captives, Hippolyta and Emily, in particular. *Gender and Romance in Chaucer's Canterbury Tales*. Princeton, NJ: Princeton University Press, 1994. Aranye Fradenburg analyzes "sacrificial knighthood" in *The Knight's Tale* as making legible the way that chivalric culture produces suffering male bodies: "Sacrificial desire in Chaucer's Knight's Tale." *Journal of Medieval and Early Modern Studies* (1996): 47–75. For an account of the Tale's identification of futurity with masculinity, see Patricia Clare Ingham, "Homosociality and Creative Masculinity in the Knight's Tale." In *Masculinities in Chaucer: Approaches to Maleness in the Canterbury Tales and Troilus and Criseyde*. Ed. Peter G. Beidler. Cambridge: D.S. Brewer, 1998, 23–35.
7. On the Knight's recollections as a brand of wartime PTSD, see Brooke Hunter, "Remenants of Things Past: Memory and the Knight's Tale." *Exemplaria* 23.2 (2011, Summer): 126–46.
8. Craig Barry, "Flying Sources: Classical Authority in Chaucer's Squire's Tale," *ELH* 68.2 (2001), 287–313.
9. The gadgets in the *Squire's Tale* have been usefully analyzed by John Fyler, "Domesticating the exotic in the Squire's Tale," *ELH*, 55 (1998): 1–26; Scott Lightsey, "Chaucer's Secular Marvels and the medieval economy of Wonder," *Studies in the Age of Chaucer*, 23 (2001): 289–316; and Patricia C. Ingham, "Little Nothings: *The Squire's Tale* and the Ambition of Gadgets," *Studies in the Age of Chaucer*, 31 (2009): 53–80.
10. On this point, see William Kushkin, "Caxton's Worthies Series: The Production of Literary Culture." *ELH* 66.3 (1999): 511–51; and his edited collection, *Caxton's Trace: Studies in the History of English Printing* (Notre Dame: University of Notre Dame Press, 2006)
11. Dorsey Armstrong, *Gender and Chivalric Community in Malory's Morte Darthur*. Gainsville: University of Florida Press, 2003. See especially, pp. 19–24. For a different account of the association of female figures with loss, death, and fragmentation in Malory see Patricia C Ingham, *Sovereign Fantasies : Arthurian Romance and the Making of Britain*. Philadelphia: University of Pennsylvania Press, 2001, chp. 6.
12. On this point, see Bonnie Wheeler, "'As the French Book Seyeth': Malory's *Morte Darthur* and Acts of Reading," in *L'Héritage de Chrétien de Troyes, Cahiers de Recherches Médiévales* 14, ed. William B. Kibler and Bernard Ribémont (Paris: Honoré Champion, 2007).

Suggestions for Further Reading

Armstrong, Dorsey. *Gender and Chivalric Community in Malory's Morte Darthur*. Gainsville: University of Florida Press, 2003.

Benson, Larry, ed. *The Riverside Chaucer*. New York: Houghton Mifflin, 1986.

Crane, Susan. *Gender and Romance in Chaucer's Canterbury Tales*. Princeton, NJ: Princeton University Press, 1994.

Cooper, Helen. *The English Romance in Time: Transforming Motifs from Geoffrey of Monmouth to the Death of Shakespeare*. Oxford: Oxford University Press, 2004.

Field, P. J. C., ed. *Sir Thomas Malory: The Morte Darthur, 2 vols*. London: D. S. Brewer, 2013.

Finke, Laurie, and Martin Schichtman. *King Arthur and the Myth of History*. Gainsville: University Press of Florida, 2004.

Fradenburg, L. O. Aranye. "Sacrificial desire in Chaucer's Knight's Tale." *Journal of Medieval and Early Modern Studies* (1996): 47–75.

Leitch, Megan G. and Corey James Rushton, eds., *A New Companion to Malory*. London: Boydell and Brewer, 2019.

Ingham, Patricia Clare. "Pastoral Histories: Utopia and Conquest in the Wife of Bath's Tale," *Texas Studies in Language and Literature*, 44.1, 2002: 34–46.

Saunders, Corinne. "Middle English Romance and Malory's Morte Darthur." In *The Cambridge Companion to Medieval English Law and Literature*, ed. Candace Barrington and Sebastian Sobecki, pp. 188–201. Cambridge Companions to Literature. Cambridge: Cambridge University Press, 2019.

Scala, Elizabeth. *Desire in the Canterbury Tales*. Columbus: Ohio State University Press, 2015.

Schiff, Randy. *Revivalist Fantasy: Alliterative Verse and Nationalist Literary History*. Columbus: Ohio State University Press, 2011.

Warren, Michelle R., "Good History, Bad Romance, and the Making of Literature," in *Thinking Medieval Romance*, ed. Katherine Little and Nicola MacDonald. Oxford: Oxford University Press, 2018, pp. 205–22.

15

JANE H. M. TAYLOR

French Romance in the Late Middle Ages and the Renaissance

Until relatively recently, critical consensus on late French romances – those, that is, composed, rewritten, or adapted in the fourteenth and fifteenth centuries – was dismissive: they were derivative, "sprawling," and either insipid or melodramatic. They suffered badly, again until recently, from comparison with the earlier romances of the twelfth and thirteenth centuries, which were felt to be more authentic and, if sometimes fantastical, at least discreetly so: tales in octosyllabic couplets deriving from classical sources and which retold the "respectable," documented, histories of Troy, or Aeneas, or Thebes; other tales, also in octosyllabic verse and this time deriving, distantly, from Celtic or other sources, which, in the hands of poets such as Chrétien de Troyes and Béroul, told stories of Arthur, his knights and their ladies, Tristan and Iseult, with subtlety and, it was felt, offered real insights into a chivalric world; tales again, epics, *chansons de geste* in decasyllabic *laisses* (stanzas), which were translated into prose and, with some embroidery and a pleasing patriotism, were exciting versions of a heroic French past. In that context, what to make, for instance, of a huge romance such as *Perceforest*, to which I return later, which purports to tell a fantastic history of Britain from Alexander the Great to Arthur, in no fewer than twelve sizable quarto volumes?[1] Or, to take another example, of *Valentin et Orson*, a stirring tale of twins separated in childhood, one becoming a knight of high renown at the French court, the other raised in a cave by bears, and who rescue their mother from an evil giant: the romance had fourteen early editions before 1600, and eight between 1600 and 1853.[2] Both of them, in other words, enjoyed considerable popularity in their own times but, like the vast majority of these romances, were until very recently inaccessible: Gilles Roussineau has just completed the masterly edition of *Perceforest* on which he has been working for more than thirty years;

Valentin et Orson acquired a modern edition only in 2011.[3] The late romances, accordingly, were unread or read only by the most dedicated specialists.[4] Over the last half-century, however, more of them have been edited (or perhaps, more importantly, become readable online, if only in early editions): *Perceforest* does indeed "sprawl" – but it offers fascinating insights, for instance, into how the later Middle Ages addresses issues of kingship; *Valentin et Orson* is indeed melodramatic (absurdly so, in all honesty), but Orson, brought up wild and language-less in the forest, is an interesting study in late medieval "otherness." These stereotypical, innocuous love stories, in other words, can tell us much about social contexts, emotional norms, and changes in mentality across the centuries.[5]

As witness, again, a whole class of romances in prose usually labeled "bourgeois" or "idyllic," the publication history of which, in the fifteenth and sixteenth centuries, is further testament to an enthusiastic readership: *Ponthus et Sidoine* (c. 1400), for instance, exists in thirty-one manuscripts and thirteen early editions;[6] *Pierre de Provence* (1453) in only two manuscripts, admittedly, but no fewer than thirty-two early editions.[7] *Ponthus et Sidoine* is the story of a young knight winning by his prowess the hand of his lady; *Pierre de Provence* the story of young lovers' elopement. Rosalind Brown-Grant's important study of these late romances[8] has done much to reframe analysis: she calls them "historico-realist" and argues that they are the products of a late medieval "moralizing culture," thus having much in common with more sober writings such as moral treatises.

Take, for instance, a romance like Pierre de la Cépède's highly popular *Paris et Vienne*, translated, we are told, from the Provençal and composed in c. 1432; a first version is preserved in nine manuscripts; another, somewhat abridged, was later adopted for no fewer than sixteen early printed editions.[9] To read this romance, in either version, is to understand the flexibility of romance and the seriousness underlying romantic comedy. *Paris et Vienne*, for instance, is the story of a hero's development from untried squire to acknowledged expert in chivalry, and of his lady's determined efforts to control her own destiny. Paris is of lesser birth, and earns Vienne's love by jousting in her honor; her father, however, insists she make a highly advantageous marriage with the son of the Duke of Burgundy. Paris is thrown into a state of theatrical despair, exiles himself disguised as a "Saracen," and achieves renown and fortune by rescuing the Dauphin of France; Vienne, with remarkable ingenuity, fends off the unwelcome suitor with her clever eloquence, and in particular by concealing slices of rotten chicken in her armpits. The romance is, on the surface, a charming little love story – but, says Brown-Grant, it also serves as an acute illustration of the importance to late medieval readers of what she calls "the problems created when a young couple's desire for marital self-determination comes in conflict with parental authority."[10] She argues that whereas the first, manuscript version concentrates principally on the comic means by which the lovers are able ultimately to achieve social respectability, the second, printed, version seems adapted to respond to late medieval and Renaissance disquiets focusing on troubled relations between parents and adolescents, and interrogates social anxieties and norms. Interestingly, again following Brown-Grant, it seems to show the lovers initially, certainly, as carefree adolescents, but, as the romance develops, as more thoughtful, more engaged with key pressures of duty and love: more understanding – indeed, more respectful – of the father's reservations. By contrast, the anonymous (1453–67)[11] focuses on the problem of childless marriage; another, *Gillion de Trazegnies*, on the duties of the husband. As Brown-Grant shows,[12] these and other "matrimonial" romances interrogate the conventions and the very nature of marriage, addressing a range of questions to do with the roles of husband and wife, and the importance of dynasty and family; each may be seen as exemplary of a particular marital dilemma, and again, as Brown-Grant suggests in her conclusion, as informed by and reflecting "ideas about gender which circulated in contemporary works such as manuals of chivalry, moral treatises, and marriage sermons."[13] These fifteenth-century "bourgeois" or "idyllic" romances are thus far from uncomplicated entertainment; they embody and debate ethical and moral questions to do with chivalry and its relation to personal and amatory dilemmas.

But as concerns modern readership and critical attention, the "bourgeois" romances have long been eclipsed by other romances seemingly more documentary, more rooted in historical circumstance: *Jean de Paris*,[14] for instance, written seemingly in the 1490s, which seems to hint at political relations between France and Spain, or, far more widely known, Antoine de La Sale's pseudohistorical *Le Petit Jehan de Saintré* (1456).[15] This latter tells the story of an unpromising young page singled out at court by an older lady of royal blood known only as Madame des Belles Cousines, who undertakes to make him a champion of chivalry. Under her instruction – and armed, usefully, with her purse – he makes an outstanding name for himself in the most splendid of tournaments and *pas d'armes*.[16] His career culminates in a triumphant crusade, and in his reclaiming autonomy with a chivalric enterprise of his own devising; alas, when he returns successful, his lady has taken up with a libidinous Abbé. Saintré punishes the latter for his impudence and Belles Cousines for her treachery; he lives on in memory, we are told, as an exemplar of ideal knighthood. The author – veteran of some of the great military campaigns of the period, courtier, tutor, author of moralizing treatises, and writer of a comprehensive guide to the art of the tournament – shows us in forensic and authentic detail how his hero deals victoriously with his opponents in tournament and *pas d'armes*; he revels in knightly techniques and elegant accoutrements, and in the exotic vocabulary of heraldry. This aesthetic of glorious detail lends the romance a tempting semblance of reality, and may explains why *Saintré* is today valued far above the sentimental "bourgeois" romances – but it has masked a caricature which exposes the social realities underlying "courtliness." The young Saintré is of necessity grovelingly subservient; Belles Cousines is not only his inspiration but, in a domain where women have no rightful place, his "manager" and, crucially, his banker; the Abbé's vulgar sensuality lays bare the lady's own underlying vulgarity. What in other words has seemed a poignant, a courtly, even a pedagogic portrait has a dark underbelly: that chivalric success depends not just on innate athleticism and nobility of soul, but on patronage, and funding.

But if late medieval romance in general has been much neglected by modern critics, then even greater neglect has met late medieval and Renaissance Arthurian romance in particular. That it was popular in the period is clear: the great royal and ducal libraries held multiple copies of Arthurian romances, often gloriously illuminated, and the early stationers, seeing promising commercial opportunities, published an abundance of canonical romances, often in luxurious editions.[17] Burgundian circles of the fifteenth century even commissioned prose versions of two of Chrétien de Troyes's romances, *Érec et Énide* and *Cligès*, the former seemingly dating from 1454, the latter undated. It is unclear if both were composed by the same *prosateur*, but they share, interestingly, particular strategies of updating to reflect the culture and ideologies of the Burgundian court:[18] in *Cligès*, the cultural ambitions of the dukes; in *Érec et Énide*, their conceptions of governance and royal authority.

Given this, it is unsurprising that the late medieval and early Renaissance world saw opportunistic attempts by new writers to capitalize on the popularity of Arthurian romance – opportunistic because the fifteenth-century authors, familiar with the Arthurian canon, seek to plug the gaps of pseudo-history: Jean Froissart's *Melyador*, the very last Arthurian verse romance, by addressing the unknown history of Arthurian Scotland and Ireland; the *Roman de Perceforest* by giving Arthur, and his Round Table knights, an implausibly illustrious ancestry; *Ysaïe le Triste* by having Tristan's previously unsuspected son by Iseut become ancestor to Pepin the Short, first Carolingian King of the Franks; the *Chevalier du Papegau* by devising for Arthur himself a series of unsuspected, and burlesque, early adventures.[19] All these romances were once thought to be arch-examples of what *The Gentleman's Magazine* of January 1839 calls the "maudlin book-doctrine of chivalry" (p. 55), but recent years have seen the appearance of new editions[20] and extensive studies that have thrown new light on these much-maligned fictions, their sheer inventiveness, and their occasional comedy: they highlight the bad-tempered parrot of the *Papegau* and the libidinous monkeys of the *Perceforest*; they invent the rumbustious toddlers Passelion in *Perceforest* and Marc in *Ysaïe*;[21] they linger, lovingly, on every technical detail of the colorful tournaments in *Melyador* and *Perceforest*.

A reader may easily be left, however, with the impression that these are romances specializing in the exotic and the absurd – but this would be an incomplete reading. Take, for instance, the *Roman de Perceforest*, an astonishingly ambitious attempt, in six books now housed, in the only complete manuscript, in twelve large quarto volumes, to link two of the great monarchs of medieval myth and "history." Its starting point is a violent storm at sea which, fortuitously, drives Alexander the Great's ship out beyond the Straits of Gibraltar to the shores of Britain where, he finds, the king, Pir, has just died without heirs and left his kingdom in chaos, under attack by a race of robber enchanters infesting the forests. Alexander provides the country with a new dynasty from among his followers:[22] Betis (later known as Perceforest) is to become king of England, his brother Gadifer king of Scotland. Over the next few centuries, they, their successors, and their followers will take part in strings of bizarre and marvelous adventures, survive the incursion of Julius Caesar, adopt Christianity, succumb to Danish and "Sicambrian" (Frankish) invaders, and become, ultimately and directly, ancestors to Arthur and to all the most renowned of his Round Table knights.

Absurd, of course, historically speaking – and certainly sprawling – but this is by no means a mere string of outlandish quests and exploits. On the contrary: beneath a welter of adventures, *Perceforest* exemplifies a remarkable seriousness of intent. First, for the attention it pays to the ethics and politics of kingship and authority. Arthur emerges not, as he does in Geoffrey of Monmouth's pseudo-history and indeed in the Vulgate and Post-Vulgate cycles of Arthurian romance, from a line of ineffectual and sometimes unscrupulous prior monarchs, but with pleasing genetic determinism from the heroic patronage of Alexander the Great himself – whose nominees as kings make it their business to restore peace and prosperity to a lawless Britain. Their weapon in this endeavor is chivalry: their first gesture therefore, incongruously, is to invent the tournament as a way of instilling in their subjects the crafts of warfare and, more importantly, the virtues of loyalty and fidelity. We may suppose that the proliferating tournaments across the romance – twelve for instance, minutely described, in Book 3 alone – are simply local color, but they are not merely gratuitous ornament: in the author's view, they promote chivalric expertise, certainly, but also national harmony and diplomacy.[23] That said, the romance's exploration of kingship is usefully various: among the proliferating kings is an object lesson in calamitous kingship, and one that runs, interestingly, counter to genetic inheritance: Perceforest's own son, Betidés.[24] He is born, says his father in Book IV, under an unlucky star; he insists, in the teeth of an ominous comet and of strenuous opposition from Perceforest, on taking as his wife a traitorous and adulterous queen who allies herself with the Romans; deluded unthinkingly by her wiles, he neglects the paramount values of chivalry, allows his kingdom to slip into complacency, and finds his forces defeated, devastatingly, by the Romans under Julius Caesar. Kingship is not, in other words, a given:[25] it requires foresight, vigilance, a sense of personal responsibility – and avoidance of marital entanglements.

I have so far talked of "kingship," and this is misleading: this is an exploration of rulership, because the most remarkable, and powerful, of rulers in Perceforest's universe challenges the attitudes to gender which seem to mark earlier Arthuriana. *Perceforest* is remarkable in setting center stage a woman of power, the Reine Fée:[26] Lydoire, wife to Gadifer, king of Scotland. She is thrust into rulership when, during a hunt, her husband is crippled by a monstrous wild boar, and she becomes de facto ruler of Scotland. She is, it turns out, highly educated and well-read, having been taught astronomy, philosophy, and magic in her childhood by none other than Aristotle. She studies the heavens and can read the future; she becomes a tutelary genius of Britain. Extraordinarily, in Book IV, she is vouchsafed a vision of a young and beautiful Virgin and Child in a blaze of light: a vision of the Incarnation. Her learning and her increasing understanding of the One God make her a herald of Christianity – but also lend her unchallengeable authority:[27] the authority to govern, to direct a race of kings, and to shape the destiny of England and Scotland in the new world brought into being by the advent of Christianity. In Book VI, Christianity is brought to Britain, and although the kingdom thereafter returns to a state of anarchy, the seeds of a new, and Arthurian, peace and prosperity are sown.

But more than that: the Reine Fée, it might be said, is the most visible of a race of independent and powerful women who challenge gender expectations, and not only in *Perceforest*,[28] but also, for instance, in *Ysaïe le Triste*. When Tristan's son Ysaïe reaches adulthood, he falls in love with a certain Marte,[29] and they conceive a son, Marc. Ysaïe tires of domesticity and, like Chrétien's Yvain, departs in search of chivalric adventure. Marte, undaunted, sets off in pursuit, disguised as a male wandering minstrel; she is, it turns out, a considerable and sophisticated poet-musician, a mistress of complex versification.[30] Notably, she composes a long narrative *lai* recounting her love story with Ysaïe; this is relayed to Ysaïe by his faithful servant Tronc; Ysaïe recognizes Marte, and the two lovers are reunited. On the surface, a conventional enough romance trope – but what is remarkable is the way in which, as an active and expert poet, musician, and performer, Marte shapes her own destiny: her mastery of verse gives her choice and agency, and promotes her from mere prize in a chivalric culture to autonomous actor.

The Reine Fée and Marte are thus, perhaps, bearers, or forerunners, of a new gender politics which shows signs of transforming romance – but Renaissance readers at least, it seems, were happy with the currency of more conventional romance: throughout the sixteenth century[31] writers and publishers vied to provide the reading public with the new editions of canonical Arthuriana, and later to find means of renewing it. Early in the Renaissance, for instance, a certain Pierre Sala, a Lyonnais antiquarian who refused the lure of print and preferred manuscript, devoted himself to writing a new *Tristan* romance and to translating Chrétien's *Chevalier au Lion* into sober prose.[32] In 1530 or so, also in Lyon, an otherwise unknown writer, Claude Platin, cobbled together material from a series of previous romances to publish a hybrid romance he called the *Histoire de Giglan*.[33] The author borrows from a mish-mash of sources such tropes of Arthurian romance as the Pentecost challenge fulfilled by a young unknown, the discourtesies of Kay, the rash boon . . .[34] Later, in 1530, a consortium of publishers brought out a prose version of Chrétien's *Perceval* and part of its *Continuations*[35] – a "moralized" adaptation wary of the supernatural, and devoted to Perceval himself as the very image of perfect knighthood.

But in 1540 there was published in print in Paris, in French translation from the original Spanish, a romance which shows a nodding acquaintance with Arthuriana but which was radically to renew romance publishing in Europe: the extraordinary *Amadis de Gaule* and its avatars.[36] A gallimaufry of breathless adventure and operatic sensibility, *Amadis* was to become, by 1615, a series of twenty-four books, each having multiple editions. The immediate hero is Amadís, who was abandoned on a raft as a baby and washes up in Scotland, becoming a paragon of knighthood – but it embraces his heirs, their chivalric deeds, and turbulent loves; the romance has an exuberant capaciousness, reveling in monsters and enchanters, marvelous palaces and mysterious islands; it has multitudinous narrative strands, and a rhetorical exhibitionism which must have made romance as previously known seem lackluster – and which sparked a string of other sentimental romances. Some of these are avatars of *Amadis* – with the same multitudinous adventures and erotic sensibility: multivolumed Greco-Hispanic romances such as *Palmerin d'Olive* (from 1546; Palmerin is son to the king of Macedonia) and *Primaleon de Grece* (from 1572; Primaleon is Palmerin's son); some draw on the energetic expansiveness of *Amadis*, others echo its often lachrymose sentimentality.[37]

The impact of *Amadis* on the writing of romance in France can be traced, interestingly, through the career of a jobbing writer, Jean Maugin.[38] Very little is known of him; he flourished in the 1540s and 1550s. His first foray into the *Amadis* tradition is his translation from Castilian of the romance *Palmerin d'Olive*: Palmerin is in the *Amadis* mold, illegitimate grandson to the emperor of Constantinople, and distinguishes himself in battles against enchanters and Saracens in the exotic Middle East; Maugin's *editio princeps* appeared in 1549, and it enjoyed real success, with a string of further editions. His second attempt at exotic romance is his *Gérard d'Euphrate*, first published in 1549: once again, this is a medley of improbable chivalric exploits and exotic amours in the Orient; it enjoyed two further editions.[39] In 1554, Maugin published Book 1 of a *Nouveau Tristan*,[40] specializing in chivalric hyperbole and more particularly in emotional effusions: his account, for instance, of the drinking of the love potion is a model of determined hyperbole: Tristan and Iseut feel themselves to be two suns, two stars – comparable to Phoebus and Diana. Alas, his *Tristan*, intended to have two further volumes, was never completed – although this first volume was republished a number of times in the sixteenth century. Undaunted, and still perhaps thinking of *Amadis*'s strenuous sentimentality, Maugin was also, finally, author of a little romance seemingly of his own invention, with the tell-tale title *Melicello, discourant de ses Amours mal fortunées, la Fidélité abusée de l'Ingratitude* (1556); the young Melicello, passionately in love with the beautiful Varia, is finally rejected by her in favor of a wealthier suitor; cue extravagant grief and rhetorical outpourings. *Melicello*, alas, seems never to have been republished;[41] perhaps its mawkishness seemed, by now, out-dated. Maugin's career, in other words, in the years from 1549 to 1556, seems thus a determined effort to mirror, and capitalize on, *Amadis*'s wild success.

But it was another variety that was to carry romance across the Renaissance and into the Enlightenment. I have referred briefly, throughout this chapter, to *mise en prose*: the Burgundian prose versions of Chrétien de Troyes's romances, that of Chrétien's *Perceval*. But I left aside the most numerous and most popular of *mises en prose*: those of the "bourgeois" romances and much "romanticized" verse *chansons de geste*. If Arthurian romances attracted a perhaps nostalgic readership, if new romances, idyllic or marital, could be popular, then the *mises en prose* remained for far longer a staple of publishing.[42] Modern critics have treated them as distinctly inferior: Doutrepont himself, having devoted many years to a monumental study,[43] remains scathing: they deserve, he says, nothing but disparagement ("tout le mal qu'il *faut* dire"). Their number is, however, remarkable: the new *Nouveau répertoire* lists a total of eighty examples, some highly popular: there are twenty-four early editions of *Ogier le Danois*, twenty of *Robert le Diable*. Verse, say their authors, is now felt to be near-incomprehensible: readers want something brief and pleasurable ("abregee" and "plaisante").[44] Few have modern editions, but they repay reading: the authors are not mere slavish translators.[45] A *mise en prose* such as *Huon de Bordeaux*[46] began life as a *chanson de geste*, was first published in 1516, and by the end of the century is called a *roman*.[47] The *prosateur* lingers on the original's hints of the exotic. Huon forms a friendship with Auberon, the dwarf king *(nain fée)* of fairyland; they meet first in a mysterious forest where Auberon appears, says the original laconically, wearing a fine robe;[48] in prose and much extended, this becomes a costly and sumptuous garment thickly encrusted with jewels that gleam like the sun.[49] Auberon, says the original, is carrying an ivory horn fabricated, alluringly, by four nameless fairies on a mysterious island – around which our *prosateur* builds a little arsenal of circumstantial detail: the island is *Chifalonye*; the four fairies, exotically, are Gloriande, Transline, Margalie, and Lempatrix.[50] Embroideries like these are not merely translations; they are embellished, servants of their time.[51]

Accordingly, it is these versions in prose that survive beyond the Renaissance, and which attract a considerable readership. From the seventeenth century and well into the nineteenth, romanticized versions of medieval romances and *chansons de geste* were kept alive by the so-called *Bibliothèque Bleue*: a series of small, inexpensive chapbooks in heavy blue paper covers introduced from 1602 by the Troyes-based printer Nicolas Oudot and sold by itinerant peddlers. Books in the series offered a range of fictions, edifying treatises, and ephemera.[52] The series saw multiple editions of romance which sold abundantly into the nineteenth century.[53] A second publishing enterprise, in the face of distinct reservations as to the moral standing of romances, was the *Bibliothèque Universelle des Romans* (BUR):[54] a series published for subscribers, launched in 1775 and surviving until 1789, and providing no fewer than 224 volumes containing modernized, sometimes condensed, versions of medieval romances, with introductory notes:[55] an *Ogier*, for instance, in February 1778,[56] an *Huon de Bordeaux* in April of the same year, an *Olivier de Castille* in January 1781, and a *Jean de Saintré* in 1780.[57] The series allied erudition and popularization, and printed a remarkable 926 romances – not all, of course, medieval, and by no means all French; it enjoyed great success which carried forward into the nineteenth century, and it is perhaps as a result that medieval romance became, until quite recently, a surprising way of accessing a particular and pleasing vision of the medieval past: gallant knights, hapless fair maidens, magic, fantasy, adventure … After all, Edgar Quinet, in his *Merlin l'Enchanteur* published in

Figure 15.1 Antoine de la Sale's *Jehan de Saintré*: Saintré returns from a trip, greets the king, and meets Madame in a garden. MS Cotton Nero D ix, fol. 51r. © British Library Board. All Rights Reserved / Bridgeman Images.

1860, could capitalize on his readers' knowledge of Arthurian romance;[58] Proust, in his *Du côté de chez Swann* (1913), has his avatar Marcel remember the magic lantern in his childhood bedroom which showed the villainous Golo riding to persecute the beautiful Geneviève de Brabant, and was confident that his readers would recognize the romance to which the images refer.[59] And the romances remain emblematic of a medieval world which, even today perhaps, readers prefer: a dream Middle Ages of uncomplicated values, cloaked in mists of nostalgia, a dream of gallantry and love, and which persists unchallenged even today in popular historical romance.[60]

Notes

1. In the only complete manuscript, Paris, BnF, Arsenal, 3483–94. Whether early readers registered that this represented some 1,000 years of history is unclear.
2. *Valentin et Orson* was in all likelihood first composed as a *chanson de geste*, now lost, in the mid-fourteenth century. It is today known only in the prose adaptation produced at the end of the fifteenth: *Valentin et Orson*, ed. Schwam-Baird.

3. Roussineau's *Perceforest* is now complete in 13 volumes, published in Geneva from 1982 to 2014 by Droz.
4. Like the pioneering Georges Doutrepont, *Les mises en prose des épopées et des romans chevaleresques du XIVe au XVIe siècle* (Brussels: Palais des Académies, 1939), doggedly and dutifully reading tales he thought debased and sentimental.
5. What, for instance, might explain the remarkable longevity of certain romances? *Valentin et Orson* was adapted as a "romantic melo-drama" for the theater in London in 1804; *Jean de Saintré* was adapted for performance in Paris as a *comédie vaudeville* in 1820; *Huon de Bordeaux*, adapted by a certain Alexandre Arnoux, was performed at the Théâtre Pigalle in Paris in 1946.
6. By early editions, throughout, I mean those before 1600 or so; numbers of manuscripts and early editions are listed from the ARLIMA website (www.arlima.net/mp/ponthus_et_sidoine.html). See *Ponthus et Sidoine*, ed. de Crécy.
7. *Pierre de Provence*, ed. Colliot.
8. See Brown-Grant, *French Romance of the Later Middle Ages*, Introduction.
9. Pierre's original is edited in *Paris et Vienne*, ed. de Crécy and Brown-Grant.
10. See Rosalind Brown-Grant, "Adolescence, anxiety and amusement in versions of *Paris et Vienne*," *Cahiers de recherches médiévales et humanistes*, 20 (2010), 59–70 (here p. 65), and id., *French Romance of the Later Middle Ages*, ch. 2, pp. 79–128. The romance is edited by Babbi.
11. *Roman du Comte d'Artois*, ed. Seigneuret; it was produced at the Burgundian court and may perhaps have been composed by a certain Jean de Wavrin, best known as a chronicler.
12. *French Romance of the Later Middle Ages*, ch. 3
13. Brown-Grant, *French Romance of the Later Middle Ages*, p. 141. Brown-Grant marshals a surprisingly large number of contemporary treatises and sermons focusing on questions like the "loyaulté amoureuse" that married couples owe each other, and their spiritual bond.
14. *Jean de Paris*, ed. Wickersheimer.
15. Surviving in eleven mss and eleven early editions; see Antoine de La Sale, *Jehan de Saintré*, ed. Joel Blanchard and Michel Quereuil (Paris: Union Générale Française, 1995), and the translation by Krueger and Taylor, and cf. www.arlima.net/ad/antoine_de_la_sale.html. On La Sale and his *Saintré*, see most recently Michelle Szkilnik, *Jean de Saintré: une carrière chevaleresque au XVe siècle* (Geneva: Droz, 2003): Jean Froissart mentions an actual Jean de Saintré taken prisoner at Poitiers in 1356.
16. "Passage of arms": a ritualized form of joust during which a knight, or knights, would take up position at a bridge or gate and issue a general challenge.
17. See, for instance, Mary Beth Winn's *Anthoine Vérard, Parisian Publisher (1485–1512): Prologues, Poems, and Presentations* (Geneva: Droz, 1997).
18. *Erec*, ed. Colombo Timelli, and *Le Livre de Alixandre Empereur de Constentinoble et de Cligés son filz*, ed. Colombo Timelli. See also translations by Grimbert and Chase: *Chrétien de Troyes in Prose: The Burgundian* Erec *and* Cligès.
19. On all these, see Jane H. M. Taylor, "The Fourteenth Century: Context, Text and Intertext," in *The Legacy of Chrétien de Troyes*, ed. Norris Lacy, Douglas Kelly, and Keith Busby (Amsterdam: Rodopi, 1987), 267–332. Note, however, revised dates: Froissart's *Melyador* (ed. Bragantini-Maillard) now considered composed between 1362 and 1382; *Perceforest* as we now have it from fifteenth-century Burgundy

(revised from an earlier, lost version); *Ysaïe* from the early 1400s; *Papegau* from the end of the fifteenth century.

20. *Perceforest*, ed. Roussineau; *Ysaïe*, ed. Giacchetti; *Papegau*, with modern translation, ed. Charpentier and Victorin; Froissart, *Melyador*, ed. Bragantini-Maillard. Note that there are at least partial modern translations of these romances: see *Perceforest*, trans. Bryant and trans. Roussineau; *Ysaïe*, trans. Giacchetti; *The Knight of the Parrot*, trans. Vesce; *Melyador*, selected episodes trans. into modern French by Bouchet in *La légende arthurienne: le Graal et la Table Ronde*, ed. Régnier-Bohler.
21. Both of whom emerge more or less from the womb ready to fight for revenge and justice.
22. The starting point is the Alexander romances: see Noémie Chardonnens, "Broderies alexandrines: l'intégration des *Vœux du Paon* dans *le Roman de Perceforest*," in *Les Vœux du Paon de Jacques de Longuyon: originalité et rayonnement*, ed. Catherine Gaullier-Bougassas (Paris: Klincksieck, 2011), 171–87.
23. Tournaments were indeed historically important: see Michel Stanesco, *Jeux d'errance du chevalier médiéval: aspects ludiques de la fonction guerrière dans la littérature du Moyen Âge flamboyant* (Leiden: Brill, 1988), and Craig Taylor, *Chivalry and the Ideals of Knighthood in France during the Hundred Years' War* (Cambridge: University Press, 2013). Cf. also René, Duke of Anjou (1409–80), who made extensive use of tournaments for diplomatic purposes; see the essays in *René d'Anjou, écrivain et mécène (1409–1480)*, ed. Florence Bouchet (Turnhout: Brepols, 2011).
24. See Denyse Delcourt, "Ironie, magie, théâtre: le mauvais roi dans le *Roman de Perceforest*," *Le Moyen Français*, 54 (2004), 33–57.
25. Questions of kingship and governance were much debated in the later Middle Ages in France: see for instance Christine de Pizan's *Livre du corps de policie*, ed. Kennedy; on the wider historical context, see the issue of *Le Moyen Âge*, 3–4 (2010) entitled "Le prince en son 'miroir': littérature et politique sous les premiers Valois," and Joël Blanchard and Jean-Claude Mühlethaler, *Écriture et pouvoir à l'aube des temps modernes* (Paris: PUF, 2002).
26. On whom, see Jane H. M. Taylor, "The *Reine Fée* in the *Roman de Perceforest*: Rewriting, Rethinking," in *Arthurian Studies in Honour of P. J. Field*, ed. Bonnie Wheeler (Cambridge: D.S. Brewer, 2004), 81–91.
27. Her magic can be capricious: punishing two knights for encouraging the hunt during which her husband is wounded, she turns one into a bear, the other into a bull.
28. Note that *Perceforest* also provides readers with an abundance of benign enchantresses living in the forests: see Anne Berthelot, "Magiciennes et enchanteurs," in *Chant et enchantement au Moyen Âge* (Toulouse: Éditions Universitaires du Sud, 1999), 105–120.
29. See Michelle Szkilnik, "Des Femmes écrivains: Néronès dans le *Roman de Perceforest*, Marte dans *Ysaye le Triste*," *Romania*, 117 (1999), 474–506, and Brooke Findley, *Poet Heroines in Medieval French Narrative: Gender and Fictions of Literary Creation* (New York: Palgrave Macmillan, 2012).
30. *Perceforest*, interestingly, provides another poet heroine, Néronès: as gifted, if not quite as enterprising. Some women in *Melyador* are by contrast highly enterprising: Floree, Melyador's lady, personally organizes a tournament to locate him.
31. For all the romances cited in this section, see Jane H. M. Taylor, *Rewriting Arthurian Romance*, chs 5–7.

32. Sala, *Chevalier au lion*, ed. Servet, and Sala, *Tristan*, ed. Verchère. On adaptation techniques, see Jane H. M. Taylor, *Rewriting Arthurian Romance*, 11–37; on the former, see Olga Shcherbakova, "Le *Chevalier au lion* de Pierre Sala: du prologue aux enjeux d'une récriture," *Le Moyen Français*, 59 (2006), 125–37; on the latter, see Pierre Servet, "Le *Tristan* de Pierre Sala: entre roman chevaleresque et nouvelle," *Études françaises* 32 (1996), 57–69.
33. The publisher was the energetic Lyonnais Claude Nourry; at present, Nourry's *editio princeps* (Lyon, no date) can be accessed via Gallica; see https://gallica.bnf.fr/ark:/12148/btv1b8600083t. A modern edition is apparently imminent in the MHRA series, as *L'Ystoire de Giglan*, ed. C. A. Jewers. See, on this romance, Jane H. M. Taylor, *Rewriting Arthurian Romance*, 119–36; Sylvie Lefèvre, "La première aventure de Giglan: son écriture," in *Le roman de chevalerie au temps de la Renaissance*, ed. Marie -Thérèse Jones-Davies (Paris: Touzot, 1987), 49–66; and details in the *Nouveau répertoire*, pp. 401–9.
34. It is at Pentecost that Arthur draws the sword from the stone; Kay is already discourteous in Chrétien's romances, and remains so in, say, Malory's *Morte d'Arthur*; the "rash boon," a promise made before the consequences are understood, is a constant in Arthurian romances, as from Chrétien's *Charrette*.
35. A complete edition is in progress, edited by Maria Colombo Timelli and published in Paris by Classiques Garnier; as at November 2022, chapters 26–110 are available. See Pierre Servet, "D'un Perceval l'autre: la mise en prose du *Conte du Graal* (1530)," in *L'œuvre de Chrétien de Troyes: réminiscences, résurgences, et réécritures*, ed. Claude Lachet (Lyon: Université Jean Moulin, 1997), 197–210, and Jane H. M. Taylor, *Rewriting Arthurian Romance*, 136–46.
36. Published in Paris by Denis Janot. The immediate source is Garci Rodríguez de Montalvo's *Amadís de Gaula*, first known publication in Zaragoza in 1508, although there were certainly earlier printings; early books in the series were translated into French by Nicolas de Herberay, and later ones by others. For its publication history, see Hugues Vaganay, *Amadis en français. Essai de bibliographie et d'iconographie* (Florence: L. S. Olschki, 1906); for its impact, Luce Guillerm, *Sujet de l'écriture et traduction autour de 1540: la traduction française des quatre premiers livers de l'"Amadis de Gaulle: le discours sur la traduction en vulgaire* (Paris: ANRT, 1988) and Jane H. M. Taylor, *Rewriting Arthurian Romance*, 147–82; more generally, Marian Rothstein, *Reading in the Renaissance: Amadis de Gaule and the Lessons of Memory* (Newark: University of Delaware Press; London: Associated University Press, 1999).
37. *Palmerin,* as translated by Jean Maugin, is available on Gallica in an edition of 1572: https://gallica.bnf.fr/ark:/12148/bpt6k8728029t. *Primaleon* is also available on Gallica: see https://gallica.bnf.fr/ark:/12148/bpt6k8728029t
38. There is no overall study. Elsa Neuville's *L'espace paratextuel à la Renaissance: Jean Maugin et ses contemporains* is wider-ranging than its title suggests: see www.enssib.fr/bibliotheque-numerique/documents/48310-espace-paratextuel-a-la-renaissance-l-jean-maugin-et-ses-contemporains.pdf.
39. Richard Cooper, ed., *Le Premier Livre de l'histoire et ancienne cronique de Gérard d'Euphrate* (Paris: Classiques Garnier, 2012).
40. Paris: Veuve M. de La Porte; readable on Gallica https://gallica.bnf.fr/ark:/12148/bpt6k79318g?. See Laurence Harf-Lancner, "Tristan détristianisé," *Nouvelle Revue du Seizième Siècle* 2 (1964), 5–22.

41. Readable on Gallica in the 1556 *editio princeps*: see https://gallica.bnf.fr/ark:/12148/bpt6k1512224c
42. Here, the *Nouveau Répertoire* promises to transform our scholarly landscape.
43. Doutrepont, *Les mises en prose*, 652.
44. See typical remarks quoted by Catherine M. Jones, *Philippe de Vigneulles and the Art of Prose Translation* (Woodbridge: D. S. Brewer, 2008), 10–12.
45. See François Suard, "Les mises en prose épiques et romanesques: les enjeux littéraires," in *Mettre en prose*, ed. Colombo Timelli, 33–52.
46. *Huon de Bordeaux*, ed. M. J. Raby; for the decasyllabic original, see *Huon de Bordeaux*, ed. Kibler and Suard. On the movement from verse to prose, see Francis Gingras, "Quand la chanson devient roman: l'exemple de la transmission de *Huon de Bordeaux* du Moyen Âge à la Révolution," in *Accès aux textes médiévaux de la fin du Moyen Âge au XVIIIe siècle*, ed. Michèle Guéret-Laferté and Claudine Poulouin (Paris: Champion, 2012), 73–85.
47. See, on the transformation of *chanson de geste* into romance, C. Roussel, "Mise en prose ou mise en roman," *in Du roman courtois au roman baroque* (Paris: Les Belles Lettres, 2004), 339–52.
48. *Huon de Bordeaux*, ed. Kibler and Suard, ll. 1217–19.
49. *Huon de Bordeaux*, ed. Raby, 69–70.
50. See Jane H. M. Taylor, *Rewriting Arthurian Romance*, ch. 5.
51. *Ogier le Danois* in prose is edited in facsimile from Vérard's edition of 1496 by K. Togeby (Copenhagen: Munksgaard, 1967); it is also edited by Aurélia Dompierre, in an unpublished doctoral thesis: "Édition et étude littéraire de la version française en prose de la légende d'*Ogier le Danois*" (Université de Strasbourg, 1996). *Robert le Diable* is translated into modern French by Élisabeth Gaucher (Paris: Champion, 2006), and into English by Samuel N. Rosenberg (University Park: Pennsylvania State University Press, 2018).
52. See G. Bollème, *La Bibliothèque bleue: littérature populaire en France du XVII*[e] *au XIX*[e] *siècle* (Paris: Julliard, 1971), and Véronique Sigu, *Médiévisme et lumières: le Moyen Âge dans la "Bibliothèque universelle des romans"* (Oxford: Voltaire Foundation, 2013), 90–5.
53. See lists in Lise Andries, *La Bibliothèque bleue au dix-huitième siècle: une tradition éditoriale* (Oxford: Voltaire Foundation, 1989).
54. See R. Poirier, *La Bibliothèque universelle des romans: rédacteurs, textes, public* (Geneva: Droz 1977); the editors promised romance which would provide "une lecture diversifiée, instructive et amusante" (reading-matter which would be varied, instructive and amusing).
55. The *Prospectus* for the series promises "l'analyse raisonnée des romans anciens et modernes, anecdotes, notices critiques ..." (rigorous summaries of old and modern romances, anecdotes, full bibliographical information ...): see vol. 1, July 1775, p. 5.
56. See L. Saggiorato, "*Ogier le Danois* dans la Bibliothèque Universelle des romans: la matière épique au XVIIIe siècle," *Annali di Ca' Foscari. Serie occidentale*, 31 (1992), 265–80.
57. See Roberta L. Krueger's "Antoine de La Sale's *Petit Jean de Saintré* and the Comte de Tressan: libertinage, gallantry, and French identity in an eighteenth-century French adaptation," *Cahiers de recherches médiévales et humanistes*, 30 (2015), 329–51, which gives an excellent idea of the BUR's procedures.

58. For a wealth of other examples, see in particular Claudie Bernard, *Le passé recomposé: le roman historique français du dix-neuvième siècle* (Paris: Hachette supérieur, 1996).
59. Rightly so: the legend was to become one of the most popular medieval stories, the subject, across Europe, of novels, plays, and operas.
60. For the enduring attraction of historical romance more generally, see Brigitte Krulic, *Fascination du roman historique: intrigues, héros et femmes fatales* (Paris: Autrement, 2007); on the popularity of historical romance today, see Pamela Regis, *A Natural History of the Romance Novel* (Philadelphia: University of Pennsylvania Press, 2003), section IV.

Suggestions for Further Reading

Andries, Lise. *La Bibliothèque bleue au dix-huitième siècle: une tradition éditoriale.* Oxford: Voltaire Foundation, 1989.

Bernard, Claude. *Le Passé recomposé: le roman historique français du XIXe siècle.* Paris: Hachette Supérieur, 1996.

Brown-Grant, Rosalind. *French Romance of the Later Middle Ages: Gender, Morality and Desire.* Oxford: Oxford University Press, 2008.

Doutrepont, Georges. *La Littérature à la cour des ducs de Bourgogne: Philippe le Hardi, Jean sans Peur, Philippe le Bon, Charles le Téméraire.* Paris: Champion, 1909; accessible on Gallica: https://gallica.bnf.fr/ark:/12148/bpt6k6233731d.

Les mises en prose des épopées et des romans chevaleresques du XIVe au XVIe siècle. Brussels: Palais des Académies, 1939.

Durand-Leguern, Isabelle. *Le Moyen Âge des romantiques.* Rennes: Presses Universitaires, 2001.

Knight of the Parrot [Le Chevalier au Papegau], trans. Thomas E. Vesce. New York: Garland, 1986.

La Sale, Antoine de. *Jean de Saintré: A Late Medieval Education in Love and Chivalry*, trans. Roberta L. Krueger and Jane H. M. Taylor. Philadelphia: University of Pennsylvania Press, 2014.

Martin, Angus. *La Bibliothèque universelle des romans.* Oxford: The Voltaire Foundation, 1985.

Mettre en prose aux XIVe–XVIe siècles, ed. Marie Colombo Timelli, Barbara Ferrari, and Anne Schoysman. Turnhout: Brepols, 2010.

Nouveau répertoire de mises en prose (XIV–XVIe siècle), ed. Maria Colombo Timelli, Barbara Ferrari, Anne Schoysman, and François Suard. Paris: Classiques Garnier, 2014.

Perceforest: The Pre-History of King Arthur's Britain, trans. Nigel Bryant. Cambridge: D. S. Brewer, 2011.

Perceforest: Florilège de Perceforest, ed. Gilles Roussineau. Geneva: Droz, 2017.

Regis, Pamela. *A Natural History of the Romance Novel.* Philadelphia: University of Pennsylvania Press, 2003.

Taylor, Jane H. M. *Rewriting Arthurian Romance in Renaissance France: From Manuscript to Printed Book.* Cambridge: D. S. Brewer, 2014.

16

CRAIG TAYLOR

Romance in Historical Context

Literature and the Changing Values and Norms of Aristocratic Society

Literature is a product of its circumstances and therefore offers a valuable window into the past. Analyzing the evidence offered by any particular piece of writing is a complex process because no text offers a simple and straightforward view into the world in which it was created. Yet readers of chivalric romances once imagined that these narratives presented an honest portrait of medieval knightly values and assumed that their elegant depictions of aristocratic ideals and behavior encapsulated the historical reality of chivalric culture and society during the Middle Ages. This nostalgic celebration slowly gave way to disillusionment during the twentieth century as historians and literary scholars became dismayed at the gap between the lofty ideals encapsulated in romances and the toxic reality of medieval aristocratic behavior. Recent scholars have gone further in highlighting not just the darker side of romances but also the instability of the ieals and norms of chivalric society, and hence the anachronism of modern simplistic notions of what it meant to be chivalrous.

The crucial point is that any attempt to understand romance in its historical context must start by pushing aside simplistic modern assumptions about the culture of medieval aristocracies. There was no single age of chivalry that stretched from the eleventh or twelfth centuries to the fifteenth century and beyond, and there was no single code or ideal for how aristocrats should behave during that period. Society and culture changed over time, and there were also important geographical variations across the different regions and lands that today form Western Europe. This discussion will focus principally upon French and English texts from the fourteenth and fifteenth centuries, a period that has unfairly been downplayed as marking the decline of chivalry, though similar questions could and should be posed for romances written during the high Middle Ages or in other languages such as Italian, German, Spanish, and Portuguese.

* * * * *

On November 25, 1388, a famous chivalric author named Jean Froissart arrived at the court of Foix at Orthezin the province of Béarn, just north of the Pyrenees mountains. A few years later he gave a dramatic account of this visit in his great history of his times the *Chroniques*. Froissart recounted how he had remained at the court for twelve weeks, gathering stories for his chronicle and reading passages from his Arthurian romance *Méliador* to the famous count of Foix, Gaston Phébus. But in the *Chronique*s, Froissart transformed Orthez itself into the kind of magical place found in chivalric romances. He used the language traditionally employed in romances to describe knightly quests in order to transform his own journey across Béarn into an expedition into a strange and wondrous land full of marvels and dangers. He also recounted astonishing tales from the court of Foix, such as the stories of Gaston's brother Pierre, a sleepwalker who was haunted by a bear, and another baron who employed a demon to gather news from across Christendom.[1] In short, Froissart employed the language and tropes of romance to depict the court of Foix as something sprung from the pages of chivalric literature.

Froissart's use of the language and tropes of romance to describe his visit to Orthez in his chronicle is a reminder that chivalric texts were never simple mirrors of the medieval aristocratic societies in which they were read and consumed. The writer played with the wondrous elements of magic and fantasy found in romance in order to elevate Béarn in a way that transcended reality. And romances were rife with other elements and tropes that were also fantastical, not least heroes capable of performing such superhuman feats that excessively literal and unimaginative modern historians have insisted that no experienced medieval soldier could ever have taken them seriously.[2] These elements were essential to the genre and to the entertainment that it offered.

It should therefore come as no surprise that romances offer poor windows into the dramatic changes that were reshaping chivalric society during the course of the Middle Ages. To take one important example, substantial numbers of Englishmen who would have qualified for knighthood by birth began to shun that status during the late thirteenth century. That led in turn to a significant decline in the numbers of knights and the increased prominence of other social ranks such as squire and gentleman.[3] Yet late medieval romances continued to view squires merely as young knights in training, rarely acknowledging the expanding importance of that social status, while also continuing to celebrate and to focus upon the knight who still remains the archetype of the chivalric aristocrat in the modern imagination.

Indeed, romances were largely untouched by fundamental changes in warfare that significantly changed the military importance of the knight and of other mounted cavalry warriors, known collectively as men-at-arms. Superior equipment and training had given these men dominance on the medieval battlefield for centuries, but the relative importance of men-at-arms dramatically shifted during the fourteenth and fifteenth centuries because of an evolution in the effectiveness of infantry, including archers and crossbowmen. This was most evident when grand cavalry charges failed spectacularly at famous battles such as Crécy (1346), Poitiers (1356), Nicopolis (1396), and Agincourt (1415). And throughout the Middle Ages, great battles were far less common than the grind of siege warfare which offered far less opportunity for knights and mounted men-at-arms to shape military outcomes. The only opportunity for horsemen to fight during the brutal siege of Melun in 1420 was when Henry V jousted against Arnaud Guilhelm de Barbazan in the tunnels that sappers had dug under the walls. Developments in gunpowder and artillery during the late Middle Ages only accelerated changes in the military role and importance of knights. Yet few medieval romances provide insight into these dramatic changes in medieval warfare, termed infantry and artillery revolutions by the experts.[4]

The fact that chivalric romances were largely oblivious to social and military changes is an important starting point from which to engage with a more pressing problem. Modern discussions of chivalry have focused heavily upon the stark gap between the idealization and celebration of knighthood in chivalric narratives and the brutal reality of aristocratic violence during the Middle Ages. Anyone whose imagination has been fired by glorious tales of King Arthur will surely recoil with horror at the innumerable stories of violence and brutality perpetrated by knights and their retainers during the Middle Ages. Armies regularly raided throughout the countryside, deliberately targeting noncombatants. In 1346, 14,000 English soldiers cut through Normandy, ransacking and plundering along a corridor of destruction that was 15 or even 20 miles wide. Such brutality served important strategic goals, weakening the enemy, drawing them out onto the battlefield at Crécy, and also securing food and supplies to support an army so far from home. But it is telling that military commanders never really felt the need to justify such brutality toward noncombatants.[5] Furthermore, aristocratic violence was hardly confined to war. Throughout the Middle Ages, chivalric knights, families, retinues, and political parties repeatedly pursued brutal vendettas. So, for example, Bouchart de Vendôme, lord of Foullet and of Segré, exercised his right to prosecute his feud with Pierre lord of Loigny by attacking and plundering his rival's lands in a form of open warfare whose horrors were recounted in a royal pardon granted in 1361.[6] Supporters of Thomas Courtenay, Earl of Devon, escalated his feud with Sir William Bonville by stabbing Nicholas Radford outside of his home on October 23, 1455, before casting his corpse into a pit and throwing stones at it, then riding into Exeter with 1,000 men to force the dean and treasurer of the cathedral to hand over money and goods that had belonged to Radford; this disorder culminated in a pitched battle between the two sides at Clyst bridge on December 15, 1455.[7] Too often, women were the victims of knightly violence. In 1386, Marguerite de Thibouville bravely risked shame and humiliation by publicly accusing Jacques Le Gris of raping her when her husband, Jean de Carrouges, was away from their home. In 1393, a Parisian widow named Ysbalet des Champions was raped in the street by a group of servants of the Duke of Burgundy.[8]

Examples of violent and toxic behavior by medieval knights and aristocrats are legion and stand in stark contrast to the romantic fantasy of a chivalric culture that celebrated the protection of the weak and the innocent. This has inevitably led to modern disillusionment and disappointment at the reality of medieval aristocratic behavior. And that has only been compounded by the fact that the wanton destruction of the wars of the twentieth century and growing awareness of toxic masculinity have challenged the notion that our romantic ideals of chivalry can or should have any continued relevance in the modern world.

It is not surprising, then, that historical debates about medieval chivalry have been dominated by the dark side of knightly behavior. The most important and influential articulation of this criticism of medieval chivalry was offered by the great Dutch cultural historian Johan Huizinga, author of *Herfsttij der Middeleeuwen – Autumntide of the Middle Ages* (1919).[9] Huizinga praised and celebrated the beautiful, lofty ideals of knighthood as represented in medieval romances and other genres of chivalric writing but lamented the fact that such ideals had lost any practical value by the end of the Middle Ages. He highlighted not just the violent behavior of knights but also the decadence and hypocrisy of their courtly lifestyles which celebrated values and ideals that they themselves failed to uphold. For Huizinga, the central problem was that aristocratic life had been corrupted by the increasing decadence of the court as knights had moved away from the truth and purity of selfless service to the church embodied in crusading.

The challenges and concerns identified by Huizinga pose important questions about the relationship between romances and the historical context in which they were written and consumed. Taken to their extreme, they might suggest that romances and other chivalric literature were utterly disconnected from the reality of aristocratic society or, even worse, contributed to the problem by encouraging courtly decadence. But it is important to recognize that there were fundamental problems with Huizinga's approach to this subject. Firstly, there is no evidence that there had ever been a golden age when medieval knights had embodied the kind of ideals of knighthood imagined and celebrated by Huizinga. Medieval writers and commentators repeatedly complained that contemporary knights were falling short of the standards and ideals of their ancestors, who had embodied the true ideals of knighthood. But it would be naïve to take these nostalgic invocations of a lost golden age at face value. Such rhetoric had been voiced since medieval knighthood first emerged, usually to justify a specific agenda for reform. In fact, there had never been a perfect moment when medieval knights truly upheld and embodied an ideal standard of knighthood. As Sidney Painter observed, it is impossible to find any sustained moment "when knights refrained from rapine and casual manslaughter, protected the church and its clergy, and respected the rights of helpless non-combatants in war."[10]

Secondly, the ideals of knighthood against which Huzinga sought to test the behavior of late medieval aristocrats are also deeply problematic. His particular vision of those ideals was simplistic and anachronistic, owing far more to the work of modern romantic commentators like Sir Walter Scott than to medieval writers whose texts presented a much more complicated vision of knighthood. In the contemporary world, we often use the word "chivalry" to describe a romantic notion of men either treating warfare as an honorable game or seeking to impress and to romance ladies with their elevated and courtly manners. But it is very important to recognize that such modern notions of chivalry are a simplification and distortion of the surviving evidence. Indeed, medieval writers did not even use the term "chivalry" to mean the ideals of knighthood. When they spoke of chivalry, it was almost exclusively used as a collective noun for the order or class of knights that by the late Middle Ages was effectively synonymous with the aristocracy; very occasionally, the term was employed to refer to the deeds of arms performed by such men.[11]

When medieval writers did discuss knighthood, they did not focus solely upon the elevated ideals that so impressed Huizinga – that is to say, service to ladies, crusading, and the honorable treatment of enemy soldiers and of civilians. A closer reading of chivalric texts, including romances, reveals a much more complicated and sometimes darker truth. Richard Kaeuper has carefully and methodically demonstrated that male prowess, competition, and, above all, violence were consistently celebrated in chivalric literature.[12] His research has laid the groundwork for a more sophisticated understanding of the relationship between romances and historical context by challenging the authenticity of the modern romantic vision of chivalry as an eternal ideal of elegant and civilized masculinity. There were obvious tensions between the ideals of the courtly nobleman and the violent warrior, and this was just one area of debate within chivalric culture. For example, aristocratic society was founded upon the celebration of reputation and honor, but this sat uneasily alongside the Christian celebration of piety and humility and condemnation of vainglory. Similarly, chivalric culture frequently lionized the physicality and dynamism of young knights intent upon building their reputations through force of arms, but needed to reconcile this with the obvious value and importance of experience, leadership, and the wisdom of older men who could no longer be competitive in the lists or on a battlefield.

Such tensions reveal the dangers of assuming that there was a stable code for medieval knights or a simple checklist of ideal values and qualities. Once upon a time, modern writers published books setting out ten commandments of chivalry or attempting to offer simple surveys of the values and ideals that were required of medieval knights.[13] But such definitive lists represent an anachronistic simplification of medieval debates. In his prominent textbook on *Chivalry*, Maurice Keen did not attempt to offer a simple definition of the ideals of knighthood but instead carefully reviewed three attempts by medieval authors to debate this subject.[14] He chose the *Ordene de chevalerie* (ca. 1220), Ramon Llull's *Libre del ordre de cavayleria* (1274–6), and Geoffroi de Charny's *Livre de chevalerie* (ca. 1350). Taken together, these texts certainly paint a rich and complex picture of knighthood as encompassing qualities and virtues ranging from prowess, loyalty, largesse, and courtesy to moderation, magnanimity, prudence, and discipline. This served as starting point for Keen's investigations into chivalric culture, but this survey also underlined the difficulty of pinning down the ideals of knighthood into a simple code: each of these famous chivalric manuals offered subtle but important differences in their models for knightly behavior and values, and none of them can be seen as a definitive statement.

Medieval writers also debated the precise meanings of the various virtues and qualities associated with knighthood across all kinds of genres, from romance and chronicles to more didactic texts like chivalric manuals. So, for example, prowess was central to medieval knighthood, as Kaeuper has carefully demonstrated, but in practice warriors could perform deeds of arms in very different contexts, from tournaments and knightly games to great battles or military expeditions. There was therefore great scope for debate about the relative worthiness of these different kinds of deeds of arms, and hence the different criteria for assessing their value. How important for the evaluation of prowess was the challenge and danger presented by the opposition or the worthiness of different motivations for fighting, such as the desire to build one's reputation, to defend one's honor, to serve one's lord loyally, or even to protect Christendom itself as a crusader?

Above all, it would be wrong to imagine that being chivalrous in the Middle Ages was seen as a simple binary proposition. In the *Livre de chevalerie*, Geoffroi de Charny's central message was that knights and men-at-arms had an obligation to keep pushing themselves to do better, repeatedly proclaiming the motto that "he who does more is more worthy."[15] Charny did not set up a simple distinction between those who were worthy and those who were not, nor did he denounce anyone who only lived up to some of the criteria that he had identified; he merely argued that one should always strive to be better without ever realistically hoping to achieve perfection. This was consistent with the message of most chivalric writings, which were only too aware of the inherent tensions within the various ideals of knighthood. Such tales rarely presented any one individual as the embodiment of knightly perfection: heroes of chivalric narratives, such as the knights of the court of King Arthur in the romances of Chrétien de Troyes, often failed in different ways; this only made them more interesting figures, and encouraged debate and reflection upon human imperfection.

Of course, it really should not be surprising that the ideals of aristocratic masculinity were subject to change and to debate throughout the age of chivalry. It is inherently implausible that the ideals of knighthood would have remained stable across a period of time that is difficult to define but certainly lasted for well over 300 years, and which encompassed communities and societies in very diverse circumstances and geographical locations, spread across Western Europe and beyond.[16] Modern scholarship on gender and masculinities is increasingly aware of the complexity and cultural variability of both the male experience and the meanings of maleness.

Furthermore, the bulk of our sources for investigating and thinking about the ideals of knighthood in the Middle Ages were written by clerks and other outsiders on the fringes of aristocratic society who were not mere scientific observers of that world, but often sought to interpret and engage with ideals of knighthood driven by different agendas. Modern scholars use life-writings including letters, diaries, memoirs and autobiographies to great effect in their investigation of aristocratic and military cultures.[17] But such sources are rare for the Middle Ages when so few laymen were writers. It is therefore much more challenging to investigate the attitudes, values, and emotions of aristocratic elites during the Middle Ages, or indeed any members of the laity.

This has important consequences for thinking about the relationship between chivalric writings, including romances, and the historical context in which they were created and consumed. Chivalric texts occupy a complex space between being mirrors of the values and norms of the aristocratic audiences for whom they were created, and being active forces intended to shape those norms and pose questions about them. Most writers naturally aimed to entertain their aristocratic audiences, particularly through idealized representations of warfare and courtly life. But they also sought to explore points of debate within chivalric society and culture, such as the obvious tensions between a manly warrior and a courtly knight, not merely because these themes could provide energy and drama to their writings but also because there was an opportunity to shape the attitudes and ideas of their audiences. Many chivalric writers were actively seeking to influence and to educate, hoping to shape aristocratic attitudes by championing virtues and ideals drawn in particular from Christian moral philosophy.[18]

Rather than approach this complex problem with prior assumptions, each text or writer must be evaluated in its own right. The didactic function is most obvious in the chivalric manuals which were becoming an increasingly prominent genre by the late Middle Ages. So, for example, Geoffroi de Charny composed the *Livre de chevalerie* as part of a reform program initiated in 1351 by the French King Jean II, who was desperately trying to consolidate his control over his nobility and rally them against the English, who had enjoyed great successes in the first phase of the Hundred Years War.[19] Writers of other genres were also open about their didactic goals. Most chivalric biographers claimed that they were celebrating and commemorating the heroes of the recent past in order to provide models and inspirations for future generations, even when their real purposes were more mundane. So, for example, the *Livre des fais du bon messire Jehan le Maingre* (ca. 1409) was presented by its anonymous author as an attempt to inspire future generations through the example of Jean II Le Meingre, known as Boucicaut, even though the book was written during the lifetime of this controversial figure who did not die until 1421.[20] In truth, the *Livre des fais* offered a sophisticated defense of his career, not merely setting out his version of events but also arguing that Boucicaut was such a worthy individual that no one could regard any setback or misfortune that he might have endured as divine judgment against him. In the process, the *Livre des fais* presented another complicated and even contradictory model of knighthood, celebrating the traditional chivalric values such as prowess, courage, and loyalty embodied by Boucicaut, before culminating with a strange final section that lauded very different qualities such as piety, charity, chastity, discipline, justice, mercy, and eloquence. These courtly ideals sat awkwardly alongside the image painted of Boucicaut in the main narrative and may simply have been added in order to echo the more fashionable texts then in circulation at the French court, themselves reflecting classical sources and ideals.

Literary experts such as Stephen Jaeger have long drawn attention to the didactic impulse in medieval romance, for example through the impact of Latin clerical debates about courtliness.[21] These impulses became more overt toward the end of the Middle Ages, when writers with direct military experience turned to romance as a delivery system for the kind of practical advice on knighthood and warfare that was more commonly found in manuals and treatises. Antoine de La Sale was the illegitimate son of a mercenary captain and was himself an experienced tournamenter and soldier who later served as tutor for the sons of both Duke René d'Anjou and Louis de Luxembourg, Count of Saint-Pol. At the same time that he was providing practical martial and chivalric education for those young boys, Antoine composed two didactic manuals, *La salade* (1442–4) and *La Sale* (1451), before completing his great work *Le petit Jean de Saintré* (1456).[22] This was a romance set at the court of the fourteenth-century French King Jean II that presented a fictionalized biography of a real knight named Jean de Saintré. It also served as the perfect delivery system for chivalric advice and moral counsel, moving beyond the dry and encyclopedic forms of *La salade* and *La Sale* by blending lessons into the engaging and fascinating story of Saintré and his lover and mentor, the Dame des Belles Cousines.

Some ten years after La Sale had completed *Le petit Jean de Saintré*, another highly experienced soldier named Jean de Bueil wrote a "roman-à-clef" – that is to say, a romance that hid real history behind the façade of fiction. *Le Jouvencel* (late 1460s) recounted the military career of a young nobleman identified simply as Le Jouvencel (the young man) as he progressed through the ranks, learning how to lead soldiers and ultimately taking a great expedition to the kingdom of Amydoine, where he married a foreign princess and was appointed regent.[23] The didactic purpose of the book was even more overt than in *Le petit Jean de Saintré*, as the narrator compared the overall structure of his story to Aristotle's *Nicomachean Ethics* and characters in the story frequently paused to offer lengthy speeches on military leadership, discipline and the law of arms, the causes of war, the origins and purpose of nobility, and the tensions between the life of a courtier and that of a soldier. Furthermore, the notion that the people and places named in *Le Jouvencel* were fictional was revealed to be a lie shortly after the death of Jean de Bueil: one of his squires, Guillaume Tringant, added a commentary in which he explained that the romance had been heavily inspired by Bueil's own career and experiences, and Tringant carefully identified the real people, places, and events represented in the story.

Of course, the most difficult challenge is to assess the impact of chivalric writings upon the knights and men-at-arms themselves. This is a stiff challenge, even for the late Middle Ages where evidence is often more plentiful. In 1389,

Philippe de Mézières acknowledged the tremendous power of the stories of Alexander the Great, King Arthur, Godefroi de Bouillon, and Charlemagne, warning that they encouraged the hubris and vainglory of French knights, and therefore recommending instead stories of service to God in the Old Testament, as well as Roman histories such as those of Titus Livy and Valerius Maximus.[24] In 1415, Thomas Hoccleve advised Sir John Oldcastle to read stories that were suitable for a "manly knyght," including tales of Lancelot of the Lake and the sieges of Troy and Thebes.[25] And it is striking that there was a dramatic increase not just in the number of texts that were being written or translated in the late Middle Ages, but also in the sheer numbers of manuscripts circulating even before the advent of printing. Ironically, though, many of the most well-known and celebrated chivalric texts today, from Charny's *Livre de chevalerie* to *Sir Gawain and the Green Knight* and Malory's *Le Morte Darthur*, each survive in just one or two manuscripts, whereas other texts that were much more widely disseminated in their day have received far less modern attention.

Yet the fact that a book was owned by an individual is not automatic evidence either that they read it or that they automatically endorsed every idea that it contained. The examples of Antoine de La Sale and Jean de Bueil highlight the complexity of the problem. The Dame des Belles Cousines advised Saintré to read books for pleasure, to instruct his mind and to cultivate the knowledge and wisdom to counsel his lord. But, in practice, almost all of the chivalric knowledge and experience of both Saintré and La Sale were developed through practical action rather than through listening to the advice of others. In *Le Jouvencel*, the young hero was never reported to have read a book; he learned his craft in an even more traditional manner – that is to say, by actively practicing the art of warfare and by listening to the advice of experienced soldiers, just as the author, Jean de Bueil, had done. This is an important reminder that even the authors of chivalric texts recognized and acknowledged the fact that written sources played a marginal role in the practical education of knights and aristocrats. In the *Livre de chevalerie*, Geoffroi de Charny consistently emphasized the importance of practical experience acquired through a lifetime of activity without ever making a case for texts as part of a chivalric education, though he did insist that older knights who had achieved the most would be able to offer advice and criticism to the younger generation. The anonymous author of the *Livre des fais du bon messire Jehan le Maingre* opened the biography of Boucicaut with a famous defense of learning and books as the mechanism through which the deeds of past heroes could be remembered and thereby presented for emulation. But there was no suggestion in the biography that the marshal had ever benefited from the advice and counsel provided by books or learned men, and the author completely ignored any evidence that Boucicaut was himself a book owner and patron.

Ultimately, the best evidence for the impact of romance remains the clear effect that such tales had upon court culture. In the summer of 1446, Antoine de La Sale and Jean de Bueil took part in an elaborate *pas d'armes* at Saumur, where more than a hundred knights fought in jousts that re-enacted the Arthurian story of Sir Lancelot and the defense of the *perron* (pillar) at the Joyeuse Garde.[26] Such events had become commonplace in the fifteenth century and are one of the best indications of the influence of romance upon the wider aristocratic culture of the day. The elaborate literary themes that were performed at this great *pas d'armes* at Saumur reveal a court culture that was deeply engaged with chivalric romance, whilst the elaborate drama of the event served extremely important functions, most importantly highlighting the magnificence of the host, René d'Anjou, and of the French King Charles VII, who had organized a sequence of these great events in the 1440s to bring together his aristocracy as he pushed through major military reforms ahead of the reconquest of Normandy from the English. The playfulness of the combats at Saumur was a deliberate choice, designed to ensure that the jousts between the 101 combatants remained *à plaisance* and did not degenerate into outright hostility and murderous violence – a genuine risk given the significant rivalries between different individuals and factions grouped around the French King Charles VII. For Huizinga, these *pas d'armes* were signs of mounting decadence, but it is hard not to see them as a sign of an energetic chivalric society.

The *pas d'armes* at Saumur demonstrates the importance for historians of looking at chivalric activity on its own terms, without imposing prior assumptions or beliefs, and of developing more detailed and sophisticated interdisciplinary analysis of chronologically and geographically diverse chivalric cultures. That in turn will provide a richer context within which to historicize chivalric literature, reassessing its relationship with changing courtly and martial lifestyles, from tournaments, feasts, and chivalric orders to heraldry and knighting ceremonies – that is to say, the social practices and rituals of knights at court, the military activities of medieval knights and men-at-arms, and the values and ethos that informed and framed these practices.

Notes

1. Jean Froissart, *Voyage en Béarn*, ed. A. H. Diverres (Manchester: Manchester University Press, 1953), and Valerie Fasseur, *Froissart à la cour de Béarn. L'écrivain, les arts et le pouvoir* (Turnhout: Brepols, 2009).
2. See, for example, Bernard S. Bachrach, "Is the Song of Roland's Roncevalles a Military Satire?" in *Prowess, Piety, and Public Order in Medieval Society*

Studies in Honor of Richard W. Kaeuper, ed. Craig M. Nakashian and Daniel P. Franke (Turnhout: Brepols, 2017), pp. 13–35.

3. Peter R. Coss, *The Knight in Medieval England, 1000–1400* (Stroud: Alan Sutton, 1993), and *The Origins of the English Gentry* (Cambridge: Cambridge University Press, 2003); Maurice H. Keen, *The Origins of the English Gentleman. Heraldry, Gentility and Chivalry in Medieval England, c.1300-c.1500* (Stroud: Tempus, 2002).
4. Clifford J. Rogers, "The Military Revolutions of the Hundred Years War," *Journal of Military History*, 57 (1993), pp. 241–78, and Maurice H. Keen, "The Changing Scene: Guns, Gunpowder and Permanent Armies," in *Medieval Warfare: A History*, ed. Maurice H. Keen (Oxford: Oxford University Press, 1999), pp. 273–91.
5. Clifford J. Rogers, *War Cruel and Sharp. English Strategy Under Edward III, 1327–1360* (Woodbridge: Boydell Press, 2000); Andrew Ayton and Philip Preston (eds.), *The Battle of Crécy, 1346* (Woodbridge: Boydell Press, 2005); and Nicholas Wright, *Knights and Peasants. The Hundred Years War in the French Countryside* (Woodbridge: Boydell and Brewer, 1998).
6. Siméon Luce, *Histoire de la Jacquerie*, 2nd ed. (Paris: Honoré Champion, 1895), pp. 309–12, and Justine Firnhaber-Baker, *Violence and the State in Languedoc, 1250–1400* (Cambridge: Cambridge University Press, 2014).
7. Martin Cherry, "The Struggle for Power in Mid-Fifteenth Century Devonshire," in *Patronage, the Crown and the Provinces in Late Medieval England*, ed. R. A. Griffiths (Gloucester: Alan Sutton, 1981), pp. 123–44.
8. Eric Jager, *The Last Duel* (London: Arrow, 2004); Walter Prevenier, "Violence Against Women in a Medieval Metropolis: Paris Around 1400," in *Law, Custom and the Social Fabric in Medieval Europe*, ed. B. S. Bachrach and D. Nicholas (Kalamazoo: Western Institute Publications, 1990), pp. 263–84.
9. Johan Huizinga, *The Autumntide of the Middle Ages*, trans. D. Webb (Leiden: Leiden University Press, 2020).
10. Sidney Painter, *French Chivalry. Chivalric Ideas and Practices in Medieval France* (Baltimore: Johns Hopkins University Press, 1940), p. 92.
11. Craig Taylor, *Chivalry and the Ideals of Knighthood in France During the Hundred Years War* (Cambridge: Cambridge University Press, 2013).
12. Richard W. Kaeuper, *Chivalry and Violence in Medieval Europe* (Oxford: Oxford University Press, 1999); see also Kaeuper, *Holy Warriors. The Religious Ideology of Chivalry* (Philadelphia PA: University of Pennsylvania Press, 2009), and *Medieval Chivalry* (Cambridge: Cambridge University Press, 2016).
13. Leon Gautier, *Chivalry* (New York: Barnes and Noble, 1965).
14. Maurice H. Keen, *Chivalry* (New Haven: Yale University Press, 1984), pp. 6–17, discussing Keith Busby (ed.), *Raoul de Hodenc, "Le roman des eles"; the anonymous "Ordene de chevalerie"* (Amsterdam: John Benjamins, 1983), pp. 71–146; R. Llull, *The Book of the Order of Chivalry*, trans. Noel Fallows (Woodbridge: Boydell Press, 2013), G. de Charny, *The Book of Chivalry of Geoffroi de Charny: Text, Context and Translation*, ed. Richard W. Kaeuper and Elspeth Kennedy (Philadelphia: University of Pennsylvania Press, 1996).

15. See, for example, Charny, *The Book of Chivalry*, pp. 86, 92, 94, 96 and 98.
16. Derek G. Neal, *The Masculine Self in Late Medieval England* (Chicago: University of Chicago Press, 2008).
17. See, for example, Joanna Bourke, *An Intimate History of Killing. Face-to-Face Killing in Twentieth-Century Warfare* (London: Granta, 1999).
18. C. Stephen Jaeger, *The Origins of Courtliness. Civilizing Trends and the Formation of courtly ideals, 939–1210* (Philadelphia: University of Pennsylvania Press, 1985), and Jaeger, "Book-Burning at Don Quixote's. Thoughts on the Educating Force of Courtly Romance," in *Courtly Arts and the Art of Courtliness*, ed. Keith Busby and Christopher Kleinhenz (Cambridge: D. S. Brewer, 2006), pp. 3–28, together with Richard W. Kaeuper, "Chivalry and the 'Civilizing Process'", in *Violence in Medieval Society*, ed. Richard W. Kaeuper (Woodbridge: Boydell and Brewer, 2000), pp. 21–35.
19. Charny, *The Book of Chivalry*, pp. 18–22, and also see D'A. J. D. Boulton, *The Knights of the Crown: The Monarchical Orders in Later Medieval Europe, 1325–1520* (Woodbridge: Boydell Press), pp. 167–210.
20. Craig Taylor and Jane H.M. Taylor (trans.), *The Deeds of Arms of Jean II Le Meingre, dit Boucicaut* (Woodbridge: Boydell Press, 2016), and Craig Taylor, *A Virtuous Knight. Defending Marshal Boucicaut (Jean II Le Meingre, 1366–1421)* (York: York Medieval Press, 2019).
21. C. Stephen Jaeger, *The Origins of Courtliness*, and *Ennobling Love. In Search of a Lost Sensibility* (Philadelphia: University of Pennsylvania Press, 1999).
22. Anotoine de La Sale, *Oeuvres complètes d'Antoine de La Sale*, ed. Fernand Desonay, 2 vols. (Liège-Paris: Bibliothèque de la Faculté de Philosophie et Lettres de l'Université de Liége, 1935–41), and *Jean de Saintré. A Late Medieval Education in Love and Chivalry*, trans. Roberta L. Krueger and Jane H. M. Taylor (Philadelphia: University of Pennsylvania Press, 2014).
23. Jean de Bueil, *Le jouvencel*, trans. Craig Taylor and Jane H. M. Taylor (Woodbridge: Boydell Press, 2020).
24. Philippe de Mézières, *Le songe du vieil pelerin*, ed. G. W. Coopland, 2 vols. (Cambridge: Cambridge University Press, 1969), II, pp. 221, 379–80 and 383.
25. Thomas Hoccleve, *Hoccleve's Works. The Minor Poems*, ed. Frederick J. Furnival and Israel Gollancz, rev. J. Mitchell and A. I. Doyle (London: Early English Text Society, 1970), p. 14.
26. Christian de Mérindol, *Les fêtes de chevalerie à la cour du roi René. Emblématique, art et histoire (les joutes de Nancy, le Pas de Saumur et le Pas de Tarascon)* (Paris, 1993). I am currently writing an article about this important event.

Suggestions for Further Reading

Jones, Robert and Coss, Peter (eds.). *A Companion to Chivalry* (Woodbridge: Boydell Press, 2019).

Keen, Maurice H. *Chivalry* (New Haven: Yale University Press, 1984).

Taylor, Craig. *Chivalry and the Ideals of Knighthood in France During the Hundred Years War* (Cambridge: Cambridge University Press, 2013).

"English Writings on Chivalry and Warfare During the Hundred Years War," in *Soldiers, Nobles and Gentlemen. Essays in Honour of Maurice Keen*, ed. Peter Coss and Christoper Tyerman (Woodbridge: Boydell Press, 2009), pp. 64–84.

Vale, Malcolm G. A. *War and Chivalry. Warfare and Aristocratic Culture in England, France and Burgundy* (London: Duckworth & Co, 1981).

17

SUSAN ARONSTEIN

Romance in Twentieth- and Twenty-First-Century Popular Culture

At the end of Walt Disney's *The Sword in the Stone* (1963), Merlin returns from the "big modern mess" of the twentieth century to take his place at the side of young Arthur, promising the newly crowned king a long narrative future: "Boy, you'll become a great legend. They will be writing books about you for centuries to come. Why, they might even make a motion picture about you ... That's something like television," the wizard clarifies, "without commercials." Merlin's prediction here recognizes the chain of adaptation that lies at the heart of medieval romance's centuries-long vitality. The genre's ability to adapt – to, in the words of Linda Hutcheon, "be made suitable" in new cultural and historical contexts – has allowed authors, from Chrétien de Troyes, to Sir Thomas Malory to T. H. White to Disney, both to continually adjust and alter medieval narratives for a new generation of readers and to take advantage of changing media and technologies to reach new audiences. By so doing, these authors have assured the cultural sustainability of the genre's medieval tales and tropes: King Arthur, Robin Hood, the Knights of the Round Table, chivalric quests, fays, wizards, giants, dragons, castles, enchanted forests, Grails, magical swords ... the list could (and does) go on.[1]

This chapter begins with a brief examination of the unique intersection of genre, story world, and media that makes medieval romance so infinitely adaptable, leading to its long generic afterlife. This afterlife extends to multiple national traditions: French adaptations of *Tristan and Isolde* and Arthurian romances; Germany's continuing engagement, epitomized in Wagner's operas, with medieval materials; Italian novels, such as those written by Umberto Eco and Italo Calvino; Spanish adaptations of *Don Quixote* and *El Cid*; and the long Anglo-American love affair with the medieval past. Here, to illustrate the process by which the romance genre has sustained itself over time, I will focus my discussion on post-World War II Anglo-American adaptations. Even within this relatively narrow focus, however, the array of possible texts is impossibly vast; they range from whole traditions, such as the Arthurian and Robin Hood legends, through narratives such as *The Princess Bride*, *Dragonheart*, and *Stardust* that use the setting and memes of medieval romance – often filtered through the fairy tale – to tell new stories and retellings of specific romances such as *Sir Gawain and the Green Knight*, to tales such as *The Natural*, *Knightriders*, *The Fisher King*, and Steven Spielberg's original *Indiana Jones* trilogy that translate the narrative into a nonmedieval world, offering mundane modernity the enchantments of romance. I have chosen to further focus my discussion on the Arthurian tradition, selecting a series of literary and cinematic texts from moments when either cultural context or technological innovation particularly provided the impetus for a new Arthurian adaptation, which, in turn, attracted the attention of audiences and critics alike, bringing the narrative back into the cultural conversation, and inspiring other producers to seek also to capitalize on King Arthur's popularity, resulting in a further proliferation of medieval romance tales.

Romance invites proliferation. The genre, Matilda Tomaryn Bruckner observes, steps "outside of history," replacing a "linear march forward with ... spiraling designs ... open[ing] up the door to new and multiple departures: situations, materials, themes, and characters may now be explored and reinvented from a variety of angles."[2] Its characteristic interlaced structure, in which one tale is suspended to turn to the adventures of another knight, "expresses both the impetus to segment the narrative into separate units and the equally powerful compulsion to associate and continue the romance across such division" (Bruckner, p. 25); it begs for more stories: new episodes, new points of view, new characters. As it does so, romances encourage what we would now call fan fiction: stories, in Sheenagh Pugh's definition, "based on a situation or characters originally created by someone else," driven by the desire for more stories.[3] These stories, in turn, whet the "craving for further adventures," the desire "to explore new territories [and] develop characters and relationships" (Pugh, p. 9), and are set up to satisfy audiences who "never want [the] story to end," who want "to know what happened before, what happened after, what happened in between" (Pugh, pp. 9, 18).

Along with its generic structure, the story world of the romance – its festive courts and enchanted forests, its unknown seas and fairy kingdoms – beckons adaptors, providing infinite space for new stories; like fantasy and science fiction (both generic descendants), romances offer audiences an expansive invented world to explore.[4] While many spaces are marked on the map, from Camelot to Brocéliande, others are unnamed, and still others beckon beyond the borders of the imaginary map. New adventures glimmer on the horizon. Furthermore, no one owns the realms of medieval romance; no author has the final word. Instead, romance belongs to what J. R. R. Tolkien famously called the Cauldron of Story: that pot in which characters, motifs, settings, and tales simmer.[5] From the genre's very beginning, Bruckner notes, romance authors such as Chrétien de Troyes drew their narratives from this Cauldron of Story, "a network of shared forms and storymatter" (Bruckner, p. 13). Here, they found several motifs that, as Helen Cooper observes in *The English Romance in Time*, "prove[d] so useful, so infectious" that they "took on a life of [their] own." "There is a word for such things now," Cooper continues: "a 'meme', an idea that behaves like a gene in its ability to replicate faithfully and abundantly, but also on occasion to adapt, to mutate, and therefore survive in different forms and cultures."[6] Forms, storymatter (plot, characters, themes), and memes provide authors, medieval and modern, with a rich Cauldron of Story – King Arthur, Lancelot, Guinevere, Camelot, Avalon, Excalibur, dragons, chivalry, *fin amor* – from which to draw and to which they, in turn, can contribute new tales: *Le Morte D'Arthur*, *Sir Gawain and the Green Knight*, *Idylls of the King*, *The Sword in the Stone*, *The Mists of Avalon*.

As they do so, authors both satisfy their audiences' desire for more stories and provide them with the pleasures of recognition and repetition. Even medieval writers, as Bruckner observes, could assume that their audiences were "connoisseurs" of the genre; in much the same way that the writers and directors of the latest *Star Wars* films depend upon movie-goers' familiarity with George Lucas's trilogies, these authors expected their audiences to be "able to recognize the interplay of repetition and transformation" and participate in the pleasure to "be found in the play of resemblance spiced with difference" (Bruckner, pp. 14, 23). This dialogue between authors and audiences, however, extends beyond play. As authors adapt the stories to new contexts, they also, as Roberta L. Krueger notes, encourage audiences "to recognize and reflect on important contemporary issues," critiquing and replacing their sources as often as they replicate them.[7]

By offering audiences something *new* – a different take on plot or characters, a new perspective, an altered world, a different point of entry into the narrative – adaptors continue to extend the medieval tales' suitability and expand their audiences. However, narrative adaptation alone cannot not keep a genre sustainable. Genres must also engage in what Richard Bolter and David Grusin call "remediation"; they must adapt to new media platforms: manuscripts to printed books, books to film, film to television, television to video games.[8] Remediations, like adaptations, keep the story moving, offering what Linda Hutcheon calls "knowing" audiences a new and more immediate experience of the tale while also reaching audiences who may not normally consume products in the old media. Remediation as well as adaptation, Cooper argues, has been key to the sustainability of romance since the sixteenth century, when authors adapted their medieval material to new media and new technologies, moving both from page to stage and from "manuscript culture, with its primary appeal to a rich and leisured or educated elite ... to print, with its potential for mass-circulation." "Now available in cheap prints ..., medieval romances became the pulp fiction of the Tudor age" (Cooper, pp. 5, 3).

Cooper's analysis of the beginning of mass-market medievalism provides us with a fitting starting point for thinking about the sustainability of the romance genre and its narratives in the twentieth and twenty-first centuries. Just as the cheap print adaptations of medieval romances brought manuscript tales to extended audiences in the early modern period, so, in the mid-twentieth century, film and television adaptations of these narratives expanded the genre's reach while maintaining (perhaps even restoring) its public character and ensuring that the medieval narratives remained part of the cultural conversation. In fact, I would argue, cinematic remediation was as important to the genre's cultural sustainability as narrative adaptation. These remediations kept the narratives "current," offering new products to consume and ensuring that medieval romances escaped library and classroom shelves. In other words, they kept the stories marketable – and "marketability," as Hutcheon reminds us, "is key" to narrative sustainability (p. 5). Adaptation takes place within a context of producers, consumers, and medium. No story gets adapted, especially to expensive mediums such as film and television, unless there is something in it for the producers paying for that adaptation; as such, a tale must have the potential both to deliver a pre-existing audience and to attract a new one.

Marketability certainly played into Hollywood's post-World War II spate of Arthurian films and television shows. Medieval romances, particularly those based on the tales of King Arthur and his knights, already had a long history of popular adaptation, stretching from Malory's *Morte D'Arthur*, through the Victorian Arthurian craze inspired by Tennyson's *Idylls of the King* (1859), and parodied by Mark Twain in *A Connecticut Yankee in King Arthur's Court* (1889) and the film industry's early-twentieth-century *Connecticut Yankee* films (1921 and 1931) and modernized Grail narratives (*The Grail* [1915], *The Knights of the Square Table* [1917], and *The Light in the Dark* [1922]), to T. H. White's three Arthurian novellas, *The Sword in the Stone* (1938), *The Queen of Air and Darkness* (1939), and *The Ill-Made Knight* (1941). This cultural ubiquity meant that producers and publishers could be reasonably certain that the new Arthurian tales they brought to market would be successful. Arthurian legend had it all: cultural capital, high-name recognition, popularity, and, apart from White's work, public domain, which only increased its profit potential.

Beginning with 1949's *The Adventures of Sir Galahad* and concluding with 2021's *The Green Knight*, these texts mobilize the romance genre's adaptive potential: an expansive story world; multiple story lines, points of entry and conclusion; opportunities to introduce new characters and points of view; the "proclivity, as Simon Gaunt notes, for absorbing paradigms from other genres."[9] They also often deploy new media and technologies, both to provide knowing audiences with a new, more immediate experience of the story and to attract new audiences. These remediations also allow them to expand the tale's reach to new and increasingly niche market segments: movie-goers, family viewers, children, teenage girls, and adolescent boys, as well as to "fans" of other popular shows and genres. Each draws on an Arthurian archive that stretches back to the early medieval romances; each also deposits new material into that archive, making it available to later authors.

Columbia Studios' 1949 serial, *The Adventures of Sir Galahad*, premiered on December 22, 1949 – a little less than four months after the Soviets tested an atomic bomb. Standing at the beginning of the industry's post-World War II Arthuriana, *Sir Galahad* marks Hollywood's first foray into a non-*Connecticut Yankee* film set primarily in the Middle Ages. As they translated the Arthurian legend to the big-screen serial, producer Sam Katzman and director Spencer Bennett unwittingly returned the narrative to its medieval generic roots. The movie serial, which follows its erstwhile heroes through adventures, from peril to peril, often cutting between scenes to pick up another character's story as it does so, all within the framework of an overarching quest, directly descends from the episodic and interlaced structures of medieval romance; also like romance, it crosses generic borders, casting its trademark tale of "courageous heroes who valiantly struggled for justice, loyalty and the American Way" against "masked villains [who] strove for world domination with a vast array of diabolical devices" in "Westerns, Jungle Tales, Swashbucklers ... Superhero Tales, Science Fiction Adventures and Spy Thrillers."[10] Katzman and Bennett added Arthurian romance to this list. Their medievalized merry mix-and-match of genres – Western, science fiction, and the spy thriller, with an occasional nod to Superheroes – brought the tales of King Arthur and the Round Table to both the serial's target audience of eight- to fourteen-year-old boys and to adult viewers who fondly remembered the genre's pre-World War II golden age. It offered both the pleasures of recognition and something new: knights in shining armor, sword fights, wizards and magic – a cold-war narrative wrapped in Arthurian tropes.

The basic plot of the serial is relatively straightforward: Galahad arrives at Arthur's Court, seeking knighthood; Excalibur, the divinely given and all-powerful weapon that ensures peace in Camelot is stolen; the court accuses Galahad and the new knight spends several episodes seeking to clear his name, find Excalibur, and defend Arthur's kingdom from invasion and betrayal. After many perils, Galahad unmasks the enemy within, assures a skeptical Lady of the Lake that Excalibur – and its destructive power – are safe in the hands of a king who only seeks security, and restores the sword to Arthur and peace and prosperity to Camelot. Through Galahad's adventures, the serial transports America's Cold War atomic narrative to the Middle Ages, offering audiences a medieval version of a projected atomic utopia in which America's nuclear dominance ensures a global golden age. Here, in Camelot, an anxious nation received multiple assurances: Arthur possesses a divine mandate; he and his proto-American democracy, with its brotherhood of knights and leaders, can be trusted never to abuse their powerful weapon for destruction and conquest; such powerful secrets are safe from enemy hands; and, in the end, "right" will always prevail. As Hollywood's first hybrid Arthurian Western, it introduced many of the anti-communist themes that would pervade the better-known cinemascope Cold War Arthuriana of McCarthy-era films such as *Prince Valiant*, *The Black Knight*, and *Knights of The Round Table*: the worthy newcomer, the threat of invasion, and the unmasking the enemy within.

These popular technicolor events established – or added to – a horizon of Arthurian narrative and visual expectations. They provided the knowing audience, familiar with earlier Arthurian tales such as Malory, Tennyson, or *The Boy's King Arthur*, with an immersive, spectacular experience of Arthurian romance at the same time that they introduced the legend to an unknowing audience, acquainting them with both its main characters (Arthur; his wife, Guinevere; his best knight, Lancelot; his evil sister, Morgan; the wizard, Merlin; Arthur's son and Camelot's enemy, Mordred; and a variety of Round Table Knights: Gawain, Kay, Bors, Gereint, Gareth, Galahad) and some of the legend's persistent story lines (the love triangle between Arthur, Guinevere, and Lancelot; the Quest for the Holy Grail; Mordred's betrayal). However, by the time that T. H. White published 1958's *The Once and Future King* (an extended and revised version of his earlier Arthurian novellas), four years had passed since Joseph McCarthy had been censured and the House Un-American Activities Committee (HUAC) hearings discontinued. Additionally, Hollywood had adapted the Arthurian legend as an ideal showcase for CinemaScope and Technicolor;

when these were no longer new and exciting technologies, the industry turned to other narratives. Thus, had it not been for the success of White's novel, the narrative may well have lost its marketability and, with that, the interest of Hollywood's producers. But *The Once and Future King*, building on the market-base of White's earlier novellas – particularly *The Sword in the Stone*, which had crossed over to the *Reader's Digest* Book of the Month, been remediated to radio, and was purchased by Disney Studios – quickly achieved market and critical success on both sides of the Atlantic, inspiring Lerner and Loewe to adapt White's Arthurian retelling to the Broadway stage. *Camelot* ran from December 1960 to January 1963, enjoying public buzz, generating good box-office receipts, and garnering several awards. The show also reached beyond the Broadway audience: its cast recording held the number-one spot for sixty weeks and the cast itself appeared on *The Ed Sullivan Show*. After the show had closed, Jackie Kennedy's poignant *Life Magazine* interview (December 6, 1963), describing young Jack's fascination with the Arthurian legend and his love of the musical, cemented *Camelot*'s place in the cultural conversation. A few weeks later, the Christmas Day release of Disney's *The Sword in the Stone* offered audiences yet another White-inspired version of the Arthurian legend, followed by 1967's *Camelot*, which brought Lerner and Loewe's musical to the much-broader film audience. Taken together, these four versions of Arthurian romance revived Arthur's narrative for mid-twentieth-century audiences; as they adapted White's novel, however, they eliminated his central message. The antiwar, antinationalist sentiments that pervade *The Once and Future King* were clearly unsuited to midcentury American Arthuriana, which from *The Adventures of Sir Galahad* on had been resolutely tied to a national identity rooted in American exceptionalism. Instead, these adaptations deploy White's novelistic treatment of character and motivation, along with his use of irony and anachronism, to strengthen the equation between an idealized Camelot and American national identity, adding several characters and themes to the archive as they do so: a Merlin who moves backward through time, Arthur's magical education, a boyish, innocent Arthur, a conflicted Guinevere.

A bestselling novel, a Broadway musical, a political parallel, an animated film, a Hollywood extravaganza: for nearly a decade the Arthurian legend was in the cultural spotlight. Furthermore, by humorously connecting the medieval to the modern, providing audiences with developed characters complete with twentieth-century psychological motivations, and explicitly drawing a connection between Camelot and America, these versions made the medieval romances upon which they were based newly relevant to their audience. By offering their content across a range of media platforms, they reached a broad and varied audience: readers of popular fiction, Broadway audiences, Disney's cross-generational viewers and movie-goers. The disappointing reception of *Camelot* in 1967, as movie audiences turned away from Warner Brother's musical spectacle to films such as *The Graduate* and *Bonnie and Clyde*, however, suggested that, if the tales of Arthur and his knights, of chivalry and Camelot, were to remain vital, they needed to be more radically adapted, to come to terms with unfinished cultural business.

In 1975, *Monty Python and The Holy Grail* burst into the Arthurian cultural conversation and has at least hovered around the edges of it ever since. Filmed on a shoestring budget and aimed at a niche audience, the film takes apart both the Arthurian legend's central myths – the destined king, chivalry, Camelot, the Holy Grail – and the multiple genres that have sustained and disseminated the tale – interlaced romance, cinematic spectacles, Broadway musicals. In it, the Pythons take on some of the unfinished cultural business that caused *Camelot* to flounder at the box office – monarchy, corrupt (or inept) establishment authority, class – exposing Arthurian romance's complicity in, to quote Dennis' famous line "the violence inherent in the system." *MPHG*'s very existence, not to mention its popularity, suggested that the Arthurian legends had lost their cultural relevance. Parody and satire, as Hans Robert Jauss observes, signal that – unless something happens to breathe new life into them – narratives have reached the end of their cultural run.[11] Ironically, however, *Monty Python and The Holy Grail* has had quite the opposite effect; over the years, the film has inspired repeated and ritual viewing, continually introducing Arthurian memes and narratives to new audiences and adding a number of unexpected items to the archive – coconuts, swallows, shrubberies – as well as contributing several lines to everyday conversation: "I am not dead yet"; "I am being repressed"; "Go and change your armor." And, in 2004, Eric Idle adapted the film for Broadway; *Spamalot* was a runaway success with both audiences and critics, greenlighting a film version, currently in development at Paramount Studios.

But what the film did make abundantly clear was that the 1950s and early 1960s versions of Arthurian romance were no longer marketable; if the narrative was to remain sustainable, it needed to radically change. In a post-Watergate, post-Pentagon Papers, post-Vietnam America, old stories about benevolent patriarchy, the divine right of kings, and American exceptionalism had not only lost their relevance, they had also become part of the baggage of a past that must be left behind. In order for an Arthurian romance to flourish in these times, it needed either to be disguised – as it is in Spielberg's blockbuster *Indiana Jones* films, where Indy takes on the role of the Arthurian knight, rescuing maidens, finding Grails, restoring order, and revalorizing America – or it needed to be freed from its nationalist past – as it is John Boorman's 1981 film, *Excalibur*. Boorman's R-rated cinematic Arthur, replete with sex and violence, met with decidedly mixed critical reception, but it was a runaway box-office success. Artistically filmed adult fare, *Excalibur* made the legend serious again, appealing to audiences who had grown up on Disney's animated Arthur but whose sensibilities were now more in line with Boorman's earlier films, including *Point Blank* (1967), *Deliverance* (1972), and *Zardoz* (1974) – all hard-hitting explorations of violent masculinity and critiques of social norms and structures. As Boorman translated his vision to the Arthurian legend, he removed the narrative from the linear history of nations, setting the tale in a mythic prehistory and drawing from an all-but-forgotten corner of the Arthurian archive, exemplified by Jesse Weston's *From Ritual to Romance* and the work of late-nineteenth- and early-twentieth-century Arthurian mystics, to place Arthur's kingdom on the border between a lost, mystical past and linear history. In the tale of this transition from myth to history, Boorman rewrote Arthur's tale as a Jungian-inflected battle between true kingship and poisoned patriarchy, invoking Hollywood's traditional equation between America and Camelot to critique rather than valorize; his Camelot incorporates Monty Python's smug and privileged elite, oblivious to the death and destruction around them, happy to exploit the peasants and never adverse to violence; in it, Arthur's knights sip from golden goblets while the people starve in the wasteland. Boorman's Arthur may achieve the Grail, but Camelot loses its moral authority; it cannot stand; and Excalibur disappears into the lake, leaving the realm again in chaos.

While *Excalibur*'s turn to myth and mysticism profoundly influenced the trajectory of the Arthurian tradition, its attempt to address unfinished cultural business related to class and nationalism shied away from – in fact, perhaps, made worse – the Arthurian legend's gender trouble. In 1983, Marion Zimmer Bradley, also drawing from the more mystical side of the Arthurian archive, placed this gender trouble center stage. Her novel, *The Mists of Avalon*,[12] taking up romance's invitation to multiple points of view, allows the Arthurian women – particularly Morgan, who speaks in the first-person – to tell the familiar tale, replacing the story of the once and future king with that of the passing of the Goddess. As the narrative progresses, Christianity, with its priests, its laws, and its disdain for women, appropriates the holy relics of the Goddess – the sword, the cup, the spear – binding king and land to its rigid patriarchal order. The novel ends as Avalon fades into the mist, and, with it, the mysteries of the Goddess; but Avalon, Bradley promises, remains; it and its mysteries can still be found in Glastonbury where the veil between the worlds is thin.

Bradley's nearly 1,000-page mass-market novel was not only widely and favorably reviewed, it also topped the *New York Times'* bestseller list for 16 weeks. By bringing the Arthurian tale again to the popular reading public and making it newly suitable to a generation of women readers uninterested in tales of rescued maidens and faithless wives, it irrevocably changed the Arthurian archive. Not only did Bradley's novel inspire a new generation of would-be goddesses and mystic seekers to flock to Glastonbury, it also inflected future films, shows, and novels; after *The Mists of Avalon*, new Arthurian adaptations had to at least take Bradley's critique of Camelot's patriarchal and homosocial order into account – even if, in the end, they dismissed it.[13] Post-Bradley adaptations include more options for their female characters and more gestures toward a feminist perspective, while often repeating the novel's narrative trajectory in which Arthur and Christianity displace Morgan and the old religion. Bradley's influence is clear in the next two decades' big-screen Arthurian offerings: 1995's *First Knight* and 2004's *King Arthur*, even if these films' attempts to update their gender roles border on window dressing. *First Knight* introduces a spunky soccer-playing Guinevere, who may love Lancelot but stays true to Arthur – only to be handed over to Lancelot, along with the kingdom, by the dying king at the end of the film. *King Arthur* transforms her into a leather-bikini-clad warrior, battling alongside Arthur's knights, but, otherwise, does little to disrupt the legend's determinedly homosocial order. In spite of their feisty Guineveres, neither of these films did particularly well at the box office or with the critics; in many ways, both films, with their echoes of American exceptionalism, were, stylistically and ideologically, throwbacks to the technicolor epics of the 1950s and, as such, out of touch with the political and ethical systems of their cultural moment.

In 2017, director Guy Ritchie and producer Lionel Wigram sought to make Arthur relevant again, deploying Ritchie's signature "rapid-fire-wisecracks-gleeful-violence-flash-cutting-and-camera-moves" blokes-and-banter style to tell the story of Arthur, the bloke who becomes a king.[14] It was time, Wigram insisted, for a new franchisable Arthur, a definitive age-of-Marvel King striding through the Camelot-verse, poised for sequels. And Ritchie, who had helmed the wildly successful reboot of *Sherlock Holmes*, seemed to be just the man for the job. From the London brothel, through Kung Fu George, to snakes straight from *The Lair of the White Worm*, *The Legend of the Sword* reimagines the tale through Ritchie's sensibilities. The film cheerfully disregards both tradition and authenticity; it could care less about the historical Arthur, or Malory, or Geoffrey (in spite of borrowing a trope or two from the *Historia*) – or even Boorman's *Excalibur* (which Warner Brothers had bought the rights to nearly a decade before in a somewhat comic attempt to sew up the Arthurian brand. Instead, it shamelessly appeals to Ritchie's target audience of adolescent males, offering them what became known in medievalist circles as *Excalibro*. The film, however, also failed to achieve box-office success; in fact, it has yet fully to recoup its $175 million budget, and it seems unlikely that the planned sequels will ever see the big screen.

The fate of these three films poses a question: what needs to happen in order for Arthur to remain marketable, for the story to keep moving, to remain relevant in the twenty-first century? This question lies at the heart of 2019's family film *The Kid Who Would be King*, which begins with an Arthurian book, a tale told of a medieval past of brave and chivalrous knights, as the opening narrative intones "hearts were not hollow and hopeless" and the land "was not lost and leaderless." Its narrative, however, is set in the present; a bullied boy stumbles across Excalibur, pulls it from the stone, and – with the help of a Merlin living backward through time and his new knights – leads a multicultural and gender-diverse group of schoolkids to vanquish Morgana and save Britain. Produced after the far-right Brexit campaigns and the Charlottesville Unite the Right rally, *The Kid Who Would be King* is certainly aware of the dangers posed by nostalgia for the Middle Ages: it can either explicitly or implicitly buttress the centrality of a white European identity, asserting a view of national heritage as patrimony, passed down from one heir to the next, and providing a retreat from a racially complex present. But the film seeks to rewrite the Arthurian story to serve more progressive ends, seeking to counter these dangers by deliberately adapting the Arthurian stories to repudiate this ethical system. Its hero begins by thinking he is the true heir; the quest for his lost father, however, serves to disconnect the Arthurian obsession with genealogy, destiny, and racial identity from the magic associated with the legend itself. "The sword doesn't care who your parents are," Merlin insists. "It doesn't choose by birth or blood ... but by heart and mind." "Legends," the wizard continues, "are mere rumors whispered down the centuries, written and rewritten, told and retold, sometimes by the rich and powerful so they can hold onto power ... If your legends say different, then perhaps you must write them anew." The film ends with the Arthurian narrative written anew; Merlin presents his modern knights with the old book, reillustrated, now chronicling the adventures of this new Arthur and his multicultural (and multigendered) Round Table, writing over the medieval tale, dominated by white, European and male knights, with which the film began.

Netflix's 2020 series *Cursed* takes *The Kid Who Would be King*'s attempt to deal with the unfinished business of the Arthurian legend's masculinist white nationalist roots one step further. The series begins, in a surely deliberate reference to Boorman's *Excalibur*, as Gothic letters appear on the screen, recounting "a story lost to the mists of time of the Sword of Power and the young woman who wielded it. They called her a demon, sorceress, savior. Before Arthur the King, the Sword of Power chose a Queen." In addition to granting Arthurian women central and powerful positions within the story, the narrative that follows adapts Boorman's and Bradley's tales of the ending of an age to the series' cultural moment; the Red Paladins wage a relentless genocidal war against the fay, seeking to wipe the nonhuman races from the face of the earth, but the "sword of the first men," wielded by Nimue, stands in their way. As such, *Cursed* explicitly addresses issues of racial genocide, white hegemony, and the rise of far-right nationalist groups, reflecting its message in its casting: the Red Paladins are almost exclusively male and white, whereas the "fay kind" are played by a multicultural cast, including Devon Terrell's (who played the young Barack Obama in 2016's *Barry*) Arthur. In addition to redeploying Arthurian memes to critique its cultural moment, the series took advantage of Netflix's streaming platform to reach a broad audience of consumers used both to consuming media at their own convenience and binge-watching for narrative immersion. Full of references, including an effective visual adaptation of interlacement, to previous cinematic and narrative Arthuriana, *Cursed* offered knowing audiences the pleasures of recognition and surprise at the same time that its focus on powerful young women and its use of *Game of Thrones*-style cinematography attracted young adult audiences; the series quickly secured Netflix's number-one viewing slot, but the streaming service disappointed fans and critics alike by refusing to greenlight the show for a second season.

Instead, in August 2021, entertainment studio A24 offered viewers hungry for more Arthurian legend a "fantasy retelling of the medieval story of Sir Gawain and the Green Knight," written and directed by David Lowery and starring Dev Patel as Gawain. The trailers seemed to promise a film in the studio's trademark art-horror style, as established in 2015's *The Witch* and 2019's *Midsommar – Sir Gawain and the Green Knight* by way of *The Wickerman*, colored by the popular epic fantasy films and shows discussed earlier. The film itself, however, offers something very different. From its introduction of a decidedly nonheroic Gawain, through its portrayal of a joyless court presided over by an aging and bewildered king and queen and Gawain's baffled passivity as he travels to meet his destiny, to the film's ambiguously tragic ending, *The Green Knight* eschews Hollywood's determined Arthurian optimism. A film for a darker time, it did surprisingly well at the pandemic box office. As an adaptation about adaptation, Lowery's film also provides a fitting conclusion for this chapter. Continually calling our attention to earlier versions of the tale – texts, paintings, tapestries, performances – it explicitly asks us to think about the ways in which stories sustain themselves over time. The Lady (Alicia Vikander) sums it up in her reply to Gawain's enquiry as to whether she has read all of the books that line the shelves and spill off the tables in her elaborate library: "Some I've read; some I've copied; some I've written, and . . . where I see room for improvements, I make them." Stories, *The Green Knight* insists, shift, change, and survive through retelling.

The Arthurian adaptations discussed here are but a small fraction of the many retellings that both attest and contribute to the legend's survival across centuries, continents, and media. In addition to other more traditional remediations (Starz' *Camelot* or the BBC's *Merlin*, for instance), Arthur endlessly returns in modern settings such as *Avalon High* and the magical library of season 1 of *The Librarians* or the world of Guillermo del Toro's *Trollhunters* series. Guinevere Jones fights the forces of evil while dealing with the travails of high school; the mechanic, Mr. Merlin, finds a new apprentice when a boy pulls a crowbar out of a bucket of cement in 1980s San Francisco; and – if all goes as planned – Arthur Pendragon will soon be solving cold cases in twenty-first-century London. The Three Stooges, Mickey Mouse, Tom and Jerry, Sabrina the Teenage Witch, Dr. Who, Spongebob Square Pants, and Bugs Bunny are just a handful of the characters who have traveled to the Arthurian past; *Star Gate* and *Once Upon a Time* both offered Arthurian seasons. Arthurian fantasy novels aimed at multiple audiences are too numerous to name. And then there are the comic books, the board and video games, the theme parks and themed restaurants. Taken together, all of these artifacts attest to the legend's – and, by extension, medieval romance's – enduring place in Anglo-American culture. As one of our culture's enduring myths, authors, directors, producers, and marketers can draw on its characters and memes to create (and sell) new Arthurian products, ensuring that King Arthur remains, as Malory and T. H. White promised, and Disney's Merlin predicted, the once and future king.

Notes

1. See Linda Hutcheon, *A Theory of Adaptation* (New York: Routledge, 2012), for an extended discussion and definition of adaptation, including the assertion that to adapt is to make suitable.
2. Matilda Tomaryn Bruckner, "The Shape of Romance in Medieval France," in *The Cambridge Companion to Medieval Romance*, ed. Roberta L. Krueger (Cambridge: Cambridge University Press, 2000), 13–28, 25.
3. Sheenagh Pugh, *The Democratic Genre: Fan Fiction in a Literary Context* (Bridgend Wales: Seren, 2006), 9

4. For a discussion of the invented map and its evocation of continuing adventures, see Michael Chabon, *Maps and Legends: Reading and Writing along the Borderlands* (New York: Harper Collins, 2008), 56.
5. J. R. R. Tolkien, "On Faerie Tales," in J. R. R. Tolkien, *Tree and Leaf* (Boston: Houghton Mifflin, 1964), 3–73.
6. Helen Cooper, *The English Romance in Time: Transforming Motifs from Geoffrey of Monmouth to the Death of Shakespeare* (Oxford: Oxford University Press, 2004), 3.
7. Roberta L. Krueger, "Introduction," in *The Cambridge Companion to Medieval Romance*, ed. Roberta L. Krueger (Cambridge: Cambridge University Press, 2000), 1–9, 1.
8. David Bolter and Richard Grusin, *Remediation: Understanding New Media* (Boston: MIT Press, reprint ed., 2008).
9. Simon Gaunt, "Romance and other genres," in *The Cambridge Companion to Medieval Romance*, ed. Roberta L. Krueger (Cambridge: Cambridge University Press, 2000), 45–59, at 57.
10. Gary Johnson, "The Serials: An Introduction," *Images* 4 (July 1997): 1–5, 1.
11. Hans Robert Jauss, "Theory of Genres and Medieval Literature," in *Modern Genre Theory*. Ed. David Duff (New York: Longman, 2000).
12. Marion Zimmer Bradley, *The Mists of Avalon* (New York: Ballantine, 1984, 2001). Originally published by Michael Joseph Ltd, 1983.
13. For a colorful overview of Bradley's influence in Glastonbury's Goddess culture, see Arthur Pendragon and C. J. Stone, *The Trials of Arthur* (Rockport, MA: Elements Books Ltd, 2003). The Glastonbury Goddess Conference is an annual event; for a retrospective, see Kathy Jones, "21 Years of Glastonbury Goddess Conference," https://goddess-pages.co.uk/galive/21-years-of-glastonbury-goddess-conference/ (accessed April 7, 2021).
14. Andrea Gronvall, "King Arthur Legend of the Sword." *Chicago Reader*, May 10, 2017. https://chicagoreader.com/film/king-arthur-legend-of-the-sword/.

Suggestions for Further Reading

Archibald, Elizabeth, and Ad Putter, eds. *The Cambridge Companion to the Arthurian Legend*. Cambridge: Cambridge University Press, 2009.

Aronstein, Susan. *Hollywood Knights: Arthurian Cinema and the Politics of Nostalgia*. New York: Palgrave Macmillan, 2005.

D'Arcens, Louise, ed. *The Cambridge Companion to Medievalism*. Cambridge: CambridgeUniversity Press, 2016.

Elliot, Andrew B. R. *Remaking the Middle Ages: The Methods of Cinema and History in Portraying the Medieval World*. North Carolina: McFarland Publishing, 2010.

Finke, Laurie and Martin B. Shichtman. *Cinematic Illuminations: The Middle Ages on Film*. Baltimore: Johns Hopkins Press, 2009.

Fraser, John. *America and the Patterns of Chivalry*. New York: Cambridge University Press, 1982.

Harty, Kevin J., ed. *Cinema Arthuriana (revised edition)*. North Caroline: McFarland Publishing, 2002.

Lupack, Alan and Barbara Tepa Lupack. *King Arthur in America*. Suffolk: D. S. Brewer, 1999.

The Camelot Project. University of Rochester, https://d.lib.rochester.edu/camelot-project. Accessed April 6, 2021.

Rosenthal, Bernard and Paul Szarmach, eds. *Medievalism in American Culture*. New York: Medieval and Renaissance Texts and Studies, 1989.

Sullivan, Karen. *The Danger of Romance: Truth, Fantasy and Arthurian Fictions*. Chicago: University of Chicago Press, 2018.

Utz, Richard. *Medievalism: A Manifesto*. Kalamazoo, MI: Arc Humanities Press, 2017.

BIBLIOGRAPHY OF EDITIONS AND TRANSLATIONS

This bibliography provides editions of romances cited. For some works, we have listed several editions, which are based on different manuscripts or editorial policies, or which offer additional critical apparatus. Selected translations in English or a modern language are noted. **Indicates an edition with the original text and facing-page translation. *Indicates that the romance appears only in modern translation.

In addition to the many print editions listed here, an increasing number of libraries provide electronic access to the precious manuscripts and early printed books they hold. Since the digitization of texts is ongoing, it is impossible to provide a complete list of accessible manuscripts and books. Both the Bibliothèque Nationale de Paris, through the site Gallica, and the British Library, through its collection of Digitized Manuscripts, have extensive electronic holdings, for example. The French site ARLIMA (Archives de Littérature du Moyen Age) provides links for many manuscripts and early printed editions. The BnF and British Library catalogues proper list online versions of early printed material; in addition, university libraries provide electronic access to many of the printed editions and secondary sources referenced in these pages. Students seeking access to electronic resources in any of the subjects or languages of this volume should not hesitate to ask their professors or their college's or university's research librarians for assistance.

Old French Romances

Adenet le Roi. *Cleomadés*. In *Les Œuvres d'Adenet le Roi*. Ed. Albert Henry. Vol. 5. Brussels: Editions de l'Université de Bruxelles, 1971.

Aimon de Varennes. *Florimont: ein altfranzösischer Abenteuerroman*. Ed. Alphonse Hilka. Göttingen: Niemayer, 1932.

**Alexandre de Paris. *Le roman d'Alexandre*. Trans. Laurence Harf-Lancner (ed. E. C. Armstrong et al.). Lettres gothiques. Paris: Librairie générale française, 1994.

Li romans d'Athis et Procelias. Édition du manuscrit 940 de la bibliothèque municipale de Tours. Éd. Marie-Madeleine Castellani. Paris, Champion, 2006.

Le Roman d'Alexandre en prose du manuscrit Royal 15 E VI de la British Library. Ed. Philippe Ménard, Yorio Otakam Hideka Fukui and Christine Ferlampin-Acher. Osaka: C. Rech. Intercult. Univ. Otemae, 2003.

Antoine de la Sale. *Œuvres complètes*. Ed. Fernand Desonay. 2 vols. Liège: Faculté de philosophie et lettres. Paris: Droz, 1935–41.

**Jehan de Saintré*. Ed. Joël Blanchard; trans. Michel Quereuil. Lettres gothiques. Paris: Librairie générale française, 1995; *Jehan de Saintré*. Ed. Jean Misrahi and Charles A. Knudson. Geneva: Droz, 1965; **Jean de Saintré: A Late Medieval Education in Love and Chivalry*; trans. Roberta L. Krueger and Jane H. M. Taylor. Philadelphia: University of Pennsylvania Press, 2014.

L'Atre périlleux: roman de la table ronde. Ed. Brian Woledge. Paris: Champion, 1936.

***Aucassin et Nicolette: édition critique*. Ed. and trans. Jean Dufournet. Paris: Flammarion, 1984.

***Baudouin de Flandre*. Ed. and trans. Élisabeth Pinto-Mathieu. Lettres Gothiques. Paris: Librairie générale française, 2011.

Benoît de Sainte-Maure. *Le Roman de Troie*. Ed. Léopold Constans. 6 vols. SATF. Paris: Firmin-Didot, 1904–12; **The Roman de Troie*. Trans. Glyn S. Burgess and Douglas Kelly. Cambridge: D. S. Brewer, 2017.

**Béroul. *Le roman de Tristan*. In *Tristan et Iseut. Les poèmes français. La saga norroise*. Ed. and trans. Daniel Lacroix and Philippe Walter. Lettres gothiques. Paris: Librairie générale française, 1989.

Bueil, Jean de. *Le Jouvencel*. Ed. C. Favre, L. Lecestre, et al. 2 vols. Paris: Renouard, 1887–9. **Le Jouvencel*. Trans. Craig Taylor and Jane H. M. Taylor. Woodbridge: Boydell, 2020.

Der anglonormannische Boeve de Haumtone. Ed. Albert Stimming. Bibliotheca Normannica. Halle: Niemeyer, 1899; repr. Geneva: Slatkine, 1974; ***Beuve de Hamptone, chanson de geste anglo-normande de la fin du XIIe siècle*. Ed. and trans. Jean-Pierre Martin. Paris: Champion, 2014; *"*Boeve de Haumtone" and "Gui de Warewic": Two Anglo-Norman romances*. Trans. Judith Weiss. French of England Translation Series. Tempe: Arizona Center for Medieval and Renaissance Studies, 2008.

***La Châtelaine de Vergy: édition bilingue*. Ed. and trans. Jean Dufournet and Liliane Dulac. Folio. Paris: Gallimard: 1994.

Chrétien de Troyes. *Les Romans de Chrétien de Troyes. I: Erec et Enide*. Ed. Mario Roques. Paris: Champion, 1953. ***Erec et Enide*. Ed. and trans. Jean-Marie Fritz. Lettres gothiques. Paris: Librarie générale française, 1992; *Trans. Carleton W. Carroll in *Chrétien de Troyes: Arthurian Romances*. Ed. and trans. William W. Kibler and Carleton W. Carroll. London: Penguin, 2004.

Les Romans de Chrétien de Troyes. II: Cligès. Ed. Alexandre Micha. Paris: Champion,1957; **"*Cligès," suivi des chansons courtoises*. Trans. and notes, Charles Méla and Olivier Collet; introduction by Charles Méla (for the *Chansons courtoises*. Ed. and trans. Marie-Claire Gérard-Zaï). Lettres gothiques. Paris: Librairie générale française, 1994.

Le Chevalier de la Charrete. Les Romans de Chrétien de Troyes III. Ed. Mario Roques. Paris: H. Champion, 1983; *Le Le Chevalier de la Charrette (Lancelot)*. Ed. Jean Frappier. 2nd ed. rev. Paris: Champion, 1982; ***Le Chevalier de la Charrette ou le roman de Lancelot*. Ed. Charles Méla. Lettres gothiques. Paris: Librairie Générale Française, 1992; *Lancelot, ou, Le chevalier de la charrette*. Ed. Jean-Claude Aubailly. Paris: Flammarion, 1991. * *The Knight of the Cart (Lancelot)*. Trans. William. W. Kibler in *Chrétien de*

Troyes: Arthurian Romances. Ed. and trans. William W. Kibler and Carleton W. Carroll. London: Penguin, 2004.

Yvain, ou, Le chevalier au lion. Ed. Mario Roques. CFMA. Paris: Champion, 1963. *Yvain*. Ed. Jan Nelson, Carleton W. Carroll, and Douglas Kelly. New York: Appleton-Century-Crofts, 1968; ***Le chevalier au lion ou Le roman d'Yvain*. Ed. and trans. David F. Hult. Lettres gothiques. Paris: Librairie générale française, 1994. **Yvain*. Trans. William W. Kibler, in *Chrétien de Troyes: Arthurian Romances*.

Le Roman de Perceval ou Le Conte du Graal. Textes Littéraires Français. Ed. William Roach. Genève: Librairie Droz, 1959; *Le roman de Perceval, ou, Le conte du Graal. Edition critique d'après tous les manuscrits*. Ed. Keith Busby. Tübingen: Max Niemeyer, 1993. ** *Le conte du Graal, ou le roman de Perceval*. Ed. and trans. Charles Méla. Lettres Gothiques. Paris: Librairie Générale Française, 1990.

The Continuations of the Old French Perceval of Chretien de Troyes. Ed. William Roach. 5 vols. Philadelphia: The American Philosphical Society, 1949–83.

**Arthurian Romances*. Trans. William W. Kibler. New York: Penguin Books, 2004; *The Complete Romances of Chrétien de Troyes*. Trans. David Staines. Bloomington: Indiana University Press, 1990.

Philomena, conte raconté d'après Ovide. Ed. Cornelis de Boer. Paris: Librairie Paul Geuthner, 1909; ***Pyrame et Thisbé, Narcisse, Philomena*. Ed. and trans. Emmanuèle Baumgartner. Paris: Gallimard, 2000.

Cligès en prose.Le Livre de Alixandre empereur de Constentinoble et de Cligés son filz: roman en prose du XVe siècle. Ed. Maria Colombo Timelli. Genève:Droz, 2004. *Chrétien de Troyes in Prose: The Burgundian *Erec* and *Cligés*. Trans. Joan Grimbert and Carol Chase. Cambridge: D.S. Brewer, 2011.

Le Roman du Comte d'Artois (XVe siècle). Ed. Jean-Claude Seigneuret. Geneva: Droz, 1966.

Enéas. ***Le roman d'Enéas: édition critique d'après le manuscrit B.N. fr.60*. Ed. and trans. Aimé Petit. Lettres gothiques. Paris: Libraire générale française, 1997; **Eneas: A Twelfth-Century French Romance*. Trans. John A. Yunck. New York: Columbia University Press, 1974.

L'"*Histoire d'Erec" en prose roman du XV siècle*. Ed. Maria Colombo Timelli. Geneva: Droz, 2000.

La Fille du comte de Pontieu: nouvelle du XIIIe siècle. Ed. Clovis Félix Brunel. Paris: Champion, 1926. **La Fille du comte de Ponthieu: Nouvelle du XIIIe siècle, roman du XVe siècle*. Ed. and trans. Roger Dubuis. Paris: H. Champion, 2010.

***Floriant et Florete*. Ed. and trans. Annie Combes and Richard Trachsler. Paris: Honoré Champion, 2003.

Froissart, Jean. *Melyador: Roman en vers de la fin du XIVe siècle*. 2 vols. Ed. Nathalie Bragantini-Maillard. Geneva: Droz, 2012.

L'Espinette amoureuse. Ed. Anthime Fourrier. Paris: Klinksieck, 1962.

Voyage en Béarn. Ed. A. H. Diverres. Manchester: Machester University Press, 1953.

Dit du Florin, in *Dits et Débats*. Ed. Anthime Fourrier. Genève: Droz, 1979.

Chroniques de J. Froissart. Ed. Siméon Luce, Gaston Raynaud and Léon Mirot. Paris: Klincksieck, Librairie de la Société de l'Histoire de France, 1869–1975.

Gautier d'Arras. *Eracle*. Ed. Guy Raynaud de Lage. CFMA. Paris: Champion, 1976; **Eracle*. Ed and trans. Karen Pratt. London: King's College London Medieval Studies, 2007.

Ille et Galeron. Ed. Yves Lefèvre. CFMA. Paris: Champion, 1988. **Ille et Galeron*. Trans. Jean-Claude Delclos and Michel Quereuil. Paris: Champion, 1993.

Gerbert de Montreuil. *Le Roman de la Violette ou de Gerart de Nevers*. SATF. Ed. Douglas-Labaree Buffum. Paris: Honoré Champion, 1928. **Le Roman de la Violette*. Trans. Mireille Demaules. Paris: Stock, 1992.

La Continuation de Perceval. 3 vols. Ed. Mary Williams and Marguerite Oswald. Paris: Champion, 1922–75.

Gillion de Trazegnies. Ed. Stéphanie Vincent. Turnhout: Brepols, 2011.

**Gillion de Trazegnies. The adventures of Gillion de Trazegnies: Chivalry and Romance in the Medieval East*. Trans. Elizabeth Morrison and Zrinka Stahuljak. Los Angeles: The J. Paul Getty Museum, 2015. (Provides excerpts from the text in translation and full program of illuminations, in color.)

Gui de Warewic: roman du XIIIe siècle. Ed. A. Ewert, 2 vols. Paris: Champion, 1932–3.

**Boeve de Haumtone and Gui de Warewic: Two Anglo-Norman Romances*. Trans. Judith Weiss. Tempe, AZ: Arizona Center for Medieval and Renaissance Studies, 2008.

Guillaume de Lorris and Jean de Meun. *Le Roman de la Rose*. Ed. Armand Strubel. Lettres Gothiques. Paris: Librairie générale française, 1992. **The Romance of the Rose*. Trans. Charles Dahlberg. Princeton, NJ: Princeton University Press, 1971.

Guiron le Courtois: roman arthurien en prose du XIIIe siècle. Ed. Venceslas Bubenicek. Berlin: De Gruyter, 2015. *Il ciclo di Guiron le Courtois. Romanzi in prosa del secolo XIII*. Ed and critical discussion Lino Leonardi and Richard Trachsler, 4 vols. Firenze: Edizione del Galluzo, 2020–1, in Open Access.

Le lai d'Haveloc in *Le lai d'Haveloc and Gaimar's Haveloc episode*. Ed. Alexander Bell. Manchester: Manchester University Press, 1925; *Trans. Judith Weiss in *The Birth of Romance in England: Four Twelfth-Century Romances in the French of England*. Tempe, AZ: Arizona Center for Medieval and Renaissance Studies, 2009.

Heldris de Cornuailles. *Le Roman de Silence: A Thirteenth-Century Arthurian Verse Romance*. Ed. Lewis Thorpe. Cambridge: Heffer, 1972. **Le Roman de Silence*. Trans. F. Regina Psaki. New York: Garland, 1991; **Silence: A Thirteenth-Century French Romance*. Ed. and trans. Sarah Roche-Mahdi. East Lansing: Michigan State University Press, 1992.

Herbert. *Le roman de Dolopathos*.3 vols. Ed. Jean-Luc Leclanche. Paris: Champion, 1997.

Hue de Rotelande, *Ipomédon*. Ed. A. J. Holden. Paris: Klincksieck, 1979.

Protheselaus. Ed. A. J. Holden. 3 vols. London: Anglo-Norman Text Society, 1991–3.

Huon de Bordeaux, roman en prose du XVe siècle. Ed. Michel J. Raby. New York: Peter Lang, 1998. ***Huon de Bordeaux, chanson de geste du XIIIe siècle*, published from the manuscript of Paris BnF fr. 22555. Ed. and trans. William W. Kibler and François Suard: Paris: Champion, 2003.

The Romance of Hunbaut: An Arthurian Poem of the Thirteenth Century. Ed. Margaret E. Winters. Leiden: E. J. Brill, 1984.

L'istoire de la chastelaine du Vergier et de Tristan le chevalier In *La Châtelaine de Vergy* Ed. René Stuip. Paris: Union générale d'éditions, 1985.

Jean Renart *Le roman de la rose ou de Guillaume de Dole*. Ed. Félix Lecoy. CFMA. Paris: Champion, 1962; **Le Roman de la rose ou de Guillaume de Dole*. Ed. and trans. Jean Dufournet and Félix Lecoy. Paris: Champion, 2008; **The Romance of the Rose, or, Guillaume de Dole*. Trans. Patricia Terry and Nancy Vine Durling. Philadelphia: University of Pennsylvania Press, 1993.

L'Escoufle: roman d'aventures. Ed. Franklin Sweetser. Geneva: Droz, 1974.

Jehan de Paris, Le Roman de. Ed. Edith Wickersheimer. SATF. Paris: Champion, 1923. **Le roman de Jehan de Paris, roman anonyme du XVe siècle traduit en français moderne*. Trans. Roger Dubuis. Paris: Champion, 2002.

La légende Arthurienne: le Graal et la Table ronde. Ed. Danielle Régnier-Bohler. Bouquins. Paris: Laffont, 1991.

Lancelot, roman en prose du XIIIe siècle. Ed. Alexandre Micha. 9 vols. Genève: Droz, 1978–83; *The Vulgate Version of the Arthurian Romances edited from Manuscripts in the British Museum*. Ed. Oskar H. Sommer. 8 vols. Washington: Carnegie Institute, 1910; **Lancelot-Grail: The Old French Arthurian Vulgate and Post-Vulgate in Translation*. Trans. Norris J. Lacy et al. New York and London: Garland [now Routledge], 5 vols., 1993–6. Reissued in 10 vols., Cambridge: D. S. Brewer, 2010.

Lancelot do Lac: The Non-Cyclic Old French Prose Romance. Ed. Elspeth Kennedy. Oxford: Clarendon Press, 1980.

Manessier. ***La troisième continuation du Conte du Graal. Edition bilingue*. Ed. William Roach and Marie-Noëlle Toury. Paris: Champion, 2004.

Marie de France. *Les Lais de Marie de France*. Ed. Jean Rychner. Paris: Champion, 1966; ***Lais de Marie de France*. Ed. and trans. Laurence Harf-Lancner. Lettres Gothiques. Paris: Librairie générale française, 1990. "Chaitivel" in *Lais*. Ed. A. Ewert. Oxford: Blackwell, 1965; trans. Laura Ashe in *Early Fiction in England: From Geoffrey of Monmouth to Chaucer*. London: Penguin, 2015. Also translated (with the rest of the *Lais*) in **The Lais of Marie de France*. Ed. and trans. Glyn S. Burgess. 2nd ed. London: Penguin, 1999.

Maugin, Jean. *Melicello, discourant de ses Amours mal fortunées, la Fidélité abusée de l'Ingratitude*. Paris: Estienne Groulleau, 1556; see https://gallica.bnf.fr/ark:/12148/bpt6k1512224c.

Le premier livre du nouveau Tristan, prince de Leonnais, chevalier de la Table Ronde, et d'Yseulte, Princesse d'Yrlande, Royne de Cornouaille. Paris: Veuve M. de La Porte, 1554. https://gallica.bnf.fr/ark:/12148/btv1b86001761.

La Mort le roi Artu. Ed. Jean Frappier. Textes Littéraires Français. Geneva: Droz 1964; ***La Mort du Roi Arthur*. Ed. and trans. David Hult. Lettres Gothiques. Paris: Livre de Poche, 2009. **The Death of King Arthur*. Trans. James Cable. Harmondsworth: Penguin Books, 1971. Rprt. 1975; 1976; 1978; *The Death of Arthur*, trans. Norris J. Lacy in *Lancelot-Grail*. Ed Lacy, vol. 4.

***Papegau. Le Conte du Papegau*. Ed. and trans. Hélène Charpentier and Patricia Victorin. Paris: Champion, 2004; **The Knight of the Parrot*. Trans. Thomas E. Vesce. New York and London: Garland, 1986.

Paris et Vienne, romanzo cavalleresco del XV secolo, Parigi. Bibliothèque nationale ms. fr.20044. Ed. Anna Maria Babbi. Milan: Franco Angeli, 1992.

Partonopeu de Blois. Ed. Joseph Gildea. 2 vols. Villanova: Villanova University Press, 1967–70. ***Le roman de Partonopeu de Blois*. Ed. Olivier Collet and Pierre-Marie Joris. Lettres gothiques. Paris: Librairie générale française, 2005.

Perceforest. Ed. Gilles Roussineau. 13 vols. Geneva: Droz, 1982–2014. **Perceforest: florilège de Perceforest*. Ed. and trans. Gilles Roussineau. Geneva: Droz, 2017. **Perceforest: The Pre-History of King Arthur's Britain*. Trans. Nigel Bryant. Cambridge: D. S.Brewer, 2011.

Perlesvaus. ***Le Haut Livre du Graal (Perlesvaus)*. Ed. and trans. Armand Strubel. Lettres gothiques. Paris: Librairie générale française, 2007; **The High Book of The Grail: A Translation of the Thirteenth-Century Romance of "Perlesvaus."* Trans. Nigel Bryant. Ipswich: D. S. Brewer, 1978.

**Philippe de Rémi. *Le Roman de la Manekine*. Édition bilingue. Ed. and trans. Marie-Madeleine Castellani. Paris: Champion, 2012; ***Le Roman de la Manekine*. Ed. and trans. Barbara N. Sargent-Baur, with Allison Stones and Roger Middleton. Amsterdam: Rodopi, 1999.

***Jehan et Blonde, Poems, and Songs*. Ed. Barbara N. Sargent-Baur. Rodopoi: Amsterdamand Atlanta, 2001.

Pierre de la Cépède. *Paris et Vienne*. Ed. Marie-Claude de Crécy and Rosalind Brown-Grant. Paris: Classiques Garnier, 2015; **Paris and Vienne*. Ed. MacEdward Leach and trans. William Caxton. Early English Text Society. Oxford: Oxford University Press, 1957.

Pierre de Provence. Ed. Régine Colliot. Aix-en-Provence: CUER-MA, 1977.

Ponthus et Sidoine. Ed. Marie-Claude de Crécy. Geneva: Droz, 1997.

La Queste del saint Graal, roman du XIIIe siècle. Ed. Albert Pauphilet. Paris: Champion, 1923. **The Quest of the Holy Grail*. Trans. Pauline M. Matarasso. London: Penguin, 1969. See also **Lancelot-Grail*. Ed Lacy, vol. 4. *The Quest of the Holy Grail*. Trans. E. Jane Burns.

Raoul de Houdenc. *Meraugis de Portlesguez*. Ed. Michelle Szkilnik. Paris: Honoré Champion, 2004.

Renart. Le Roman de Renart. Ed. Jean Dufournet, Laurence Harf-Lancner, Marie-Thérèse de Medeiros and Jean Subrenat. 2 vols. Paris: Champion, 2013–15.

**René d'Anjou, *Le Cuer d'amour espris*. Ed. and trans. Gilles Roussineau. Geneva: Droz, 2020.

Le livre du coeur d'Amour épris. Ed. and trans. Florence Bouchet. Paris: LGF, 2003.

**The Book of the Love-Smitten Heart*. Ed. and trans. Stephanie Viereck Gibbs and Kathryn Karczewska. New York: Routledge, 2001.

Renaud de Beaujeu. *Le Bel Inconnu*. Ed. Perrie Williams. Paris: Champion, 1929; *Le bel inconnu*. Ed. Michèle Perret. Trans. Michèle Perret and Isabelle Weill. Paris: Champion, 2003. **Le Bel Inconnu. Li Biaus Descounëus. The Fair Unknown*. Ed. Karen Fresco, trans. Colleen P. Donagher. New York: Garland, 1992.

**Renaut. *Galeran de Bretagne*. Ed. and trans Jean Dufournet. Paris: Champion, 2000.

Robert de Boron. *Joseph d'Arimathie (also known as Le Roman de l'estoire dou Graal). Joseph d'Arimathie: A Critical Edition of the Verse and Prose Versions*. Ed. Richard O'Gorman. Toronto: Pontifical Institute of Medieval Studies, 1995.

Merlin. Suite du Merlin. Ed. Gaston Paris and Jacob Ulrich as *Merlin: Roman en prose du XIIIe siècle*, 2 vols. Paris: Société des Anciens Textes Français, 1886; *Merlin, roman en prose du XIIIe siècle*. Ed. Gaston Paris,and Jacob Ulrich. 2 vols. Paris: Firmin Didot, 1886; *Merlin: roman du XIIIe siècle*. Ed. Alexandre Micha. Geneva: Droz, 1979.

Robert le Diable, Édition bilingue. Ed. and trans. Élisabeth Gaucher. CFMA. Paris: Champion, 2006.

Sala, Pierre. *Le Chevalier au lion*. Ed. Pierre Servet. Paris: Champion, 1996.

Tristan: Roman d'aventure du XVe siècle. Ed Lynette Muir. Geneva: Droz, 1958; *Tristan*. Ed C. Verchère. Paris: Champion, 2008.

***Le roman de Thèbes*. Ed. and trans. Francine Mora-Lebrun. Lettres gothiques. Paris: Libraire générale française, 1995; **Le Roman de Thèbes: The Story of Thebes*. Trans. John Smartt Coley. New York: Garland, 1986. **The Romance of Thebes (Roman de Thebes)*. Trans. Joan M. Ferrante and Robert W. Hanning. The French of Italy Translation Series 11. Tempe: Arizona Center for Medieval and Renaissance Studies Press, 2018.

Thomas. *The Romance of Horn*. Ed. Mildred K. Pope and T. B. W. Reid. Oxford: Blackwell, 1955–64; *trans. Judith Weiss in *The Birth of Romance in England: Four Twelfth-Century Romances in the French of England*. Tempe: Arizona Center for Medieval and Renaissance Studies, 2009.

Thomas of Britain. *Tristan et Iseut. Les poèmes français. La saga norroise. Textes originaux et intégraux*. Ed. and trans. Daniel Lacroix and Philippe Walter. Lettres gothiques. Paris: Librairie générale française, 1989. *Tristan*. Ed. and trans. Stewart Gregory, in *Early French Tristan Poems: Vol. 2*. Ed. Norris J. Lacy. Cambridge: D. S. Brewer, 1998. *Trans. Laura Ashe in *Early Fiction in England: From Geoffrey of Monmouth to Chaucer*. London: Penguin, 2015.

**Thomas of Kent. *Le Roman d'Alexandre ou le Roman de Toute Chevalerie*. Ed. Brian Foster and Ian Short. Trans. Catherine Gaullier-Bougassas and Laurence Harf-Lancner. Champion Classiques du Moyen Age. Paris: Champion, 2003.

Thomas III de Saluces. *Le Livre du Chevalier errant*. Ed. Robert Fajen. Wiesbaden: Reichert Verlag, 2019.

Le roman de Tristan en prose. Version of manuscript 757 of the Bibliothèque Nationale de Paris. Ed. Joël Blanchard et al. Paris: Champion, 1997–2007; *Le roman de Tristan en prose*. Ed. Philippe Ménard et al. 9 vols. Geneva: Droz, 1987–97; **The Romance of Tristan: the thirteenth-century Old French "Prose Tristan."* Trans. Renée L. Curtis. Oxford: Oxford University Press, 1994.

**Ysaïe le Triste*. Trans. André Giacchetti. Rouen: Publications de l'Université de Rouen, 1993.

Valentin et Orson, An Edition and Translation of the Fifteenth-Century Romance Epic. Ed. and trans. Shira Schwam-Baird. Tempe: Arizona Center for Medieval and Renaissance Studies, 2011.

Wace. *Le roman de Brut de Wace*. Ed. Ivor Arnold. 2 vols. Paris: Société des anciens textes français, 1938–1940. ***Roman de Brut: A History of the British*. Ed. and trans. Judith Weiss, rev. edn. Exeter: Exeter University Press, 2002.

Wauchier de Denain. **La Deuxième continuation du Conte du Graal. Ed. Francis Gingras, trans. F. Gingras and M.-L. Ollier. Paris: H. Champion, 2021.

Wauquelin, Jean. *La belle Hélène de Constantinople, mise en prose d'une chanson de geste*. Ed. Marie-Claude de Crécy. Geneva: Droz, 2002.

Middle English Romances

Chaucer, Geoffrey. *The Riverside Chaucer*. Ed Larry D. Benson. New York: Houghton Mifflin, 1986.

Sir Thopas, The Complaint unto Pity, Troilus and Criseyde in The Riverside Chaucer, gen. ed. Larry D. Benson. Boston: Houghton Mifflin, 1987. *Sir Bevis of Hampton*. Ed. Jennifer Fellows. 2 vols., EEETS o.s. 349–50. Oxford: Oxford University Press, 2017.

Sir Gawain and the Green Knight and Pearl, in *The Works of the Gawain Poet*. Ed. Ad Putter and Myra Stokes. Harmondsworth: Penguin, 2014.

Havelok the Dane, in *Four Romances of England: King Horn, Havelok the Dane, Bevis of Hampton, Athelston*. Ed. Ronald B. Herzman, Graham Drake, and Eve Salisbury. Kalamazoo, MI: Medieval Institute Publications, 1999.

Lybeaus Desconus. Ed. Maldwyn Mills, EETS. Oxford: Oxford University Press, 1969.

Malory, Sir Thomas. *The Morte Darthur*. Ed. P. J. C. Field, 2 vols. Woodbridge: D. S. Brewer, 2013.

Richard Coer de Lyon. Ed. Peter Larkin. Kalamazoo, MI: Medieval Institute Publications, 2015. **Richard Coeur de Lion*. Ed. and trans. Katherine H. Terrell. Tonawanda, NY: Broadview Press, 2019.

The Romance of Guy of Warwick. Ed. Julius Zupitza. 3 vols. EETS e.s. 42, 49, 59. London, 1883–91.

Sir Gawain: Eleven Romances and Tales. Ed. Thomas Hahn. TEAMS. Kalamazoo: Western Michigan University, 1995.

Sir Gawain and the Green Knight, in *The Works of the Gawain Poet*. Ed Ad Putter and Myra Stokes. London: Penguin, 2014.

Stanzaic Guy of Warwick. Ed. Alison Wiggins. Kalamazoo, MI: Medieval Institute Publications, 2004.

Stanzaic Morte Arthur, in *King Arthur's Death*. Ed. L. D. Benson, rev. Edward Foster, TEAMS. Kalamazoo, MI: Medieval Institute Publications, 1994.

Ywain and Gawain. Ed. Albert B. Friedman and Norman T. Harrington. EETS, o. s.254. London: Oxford University Press, 1964.

Medieval German Romances

Der Altfranzösische Yderroman. Ed. Heinrich Gelzer. Dresden: Gesellschaft für romanische Literatur, 1913.

[Elisabeth von Nassau-Saarbrücken], *Herzog Herpin*. Ed. Bernd Bastert. Texte des späten Mittelalters und der frühen Neuzeit, 51. Berlin: Erich Schmidt Verlag, 2014.

Fleck, Konrad. *Flore und Blanscheflur: Text und Untersuchung*. Ed. Christine Putzo. Münchener Texte und Untersuchungen zur deutschen Literatur des Mittelalters, 143. Berlin and Boston: Walter de Gruyter, 2015.

Fortunatus, in Romane des 15. und 16. Jahrhunderts. Ed. Jan-Dirk Müller. Bibliothek derFrühen Neuzeit, 1. Frankfurt a. M.: Deutscher Klassiker Verlag, 1990.

Gottfried von Strassburg. *Tristan*. Ed. Karl Marold. Berlin and New York: Walter de Gruyter, 2004.

Tristan. Ed. Gertrud Utzmann and Werner Hoffman. Darmstadt: Wissenschafliche Buchgesellschaft, 1967.

Tristan, with the 'Tristran' of Thomas. Trans. by A. T. Hatto. Harmondsworth: Penguin, 1960.

Tristan. Ed. and trans. Rüdiger Krohn. Stuttgart: Philipp Reclam Jun., 1980.

Tristan and Isolde: With Ulrich von Türheim's Continuation. Trans. W.Whobrey. Indianapolis, IN: Hackett, 2018.

Hartmann von Aue. *Erec*. Ed. and trans. Manfred Günter Scholz and Susanne Held. Bibliothek deutscher Klassiker, 188. Frankfurt a. M.: Deutscher Klassiker Verlag, 2004; **Erec*. Trans. Michael Resler. The Middle Ages Series. Philadelphia: University of Pennsylvania Press, 1985.

Iwein. Ed. Thomas Cramer. 4th rev. ed. Berlin and New York: Walter de Gruyter, 1968; **Iwein*. Trans. Patrick M. McConeghy. Garland Library of Medieval Literature, 19. New York: Garland, 1984.

Heinrich von Veldeke. *Eneasroman: Mittelhochdeutsch/Neuhochdeutsch*. Ed. and trans. Dieter Kartschoke. Stuttgart: Philipp Reclam Jun., 2014;

Eneit. Trans. J. Thomas. Garland Library of Medieval Literature, 48. New York: Garland, 1985.

Herzog Ernst: Mittelhochdeutsch / Neuhochdeutsch. Version B with fragments A, B, and Kl published from the main manuscript, translated and commented on by M. Herweg. Stuttgart: Philipp Reclam Jun., 2019; *Herzog Ernst/The Legend of Duke Ernst*. Trans. J. W. Thomas. Lincoln: University of Nebraska Press, 1979.

Konrad von Würzburg. *Partonopier und Meliur*. Ed. Karl Bartsch. Deutsche Neudrucke: Reihe: Texte des Mittelalters. Berlin: Walter de Gruyter, 1970.

Mai und Beaflor. Ed. and trans. Albrecht Classen. Beihefte zur Mediaevistik, 6. Frankfurt a. M.: Peter Lang, 2006.

Maximilian I. *Theuerdank 1517*. Ed. Horst Appuhn. Dortmund: Harenberg Kommunikation, 1979.

Prosalancelot: nach der Heidelberger Handschrift Cod. Pal. germ. 147, [orig.] ed. Reinhold Kluge, *ergänzt durch die Handschrift Ms. allem. 8017 – 8020 der Bibliothèque de l' Arsenal Paris*. 3 vols. Berlin: Akademie-Verlag. 1948–74 (Deutsche Textes de Mitelalters, 42, 47, 63). Trans., commentary, and ed. Hans-Hugo Steinhoff. Bibliothek des Mittelalters, 15. Frankfurt a. M.: Deutscher Klassiker Verlag, 1995.

Reinfried von Braunschweig. Trans. and commentary Elisabeth Martschini. 3 vols. Kiel: Solivagus Verlag, 2017–19.

Rudolf von Ems. *Der guote Gêrhart*. Ed. J. A. Asher. Tübingen: Max Niemeyer Verlag, 1971. **An English Translation of Rudolf von Ems's* Der guote Gêrhart. Trans. Albrecht Classen. Newcastle upon Tyne: Cambridge Scholars Press, 2016.

Der Stricker. *Daniel von dem Blühenden Tal*. Ed. Michael Resler. 2nd ed. Altdeutsch Textbibliothek, 92. Tübingen: Max Niemeyer, 1995. *The Stricker. *Daniel of the Blossoming Valley*. Trans. Michael Resler. 2nd ed. Garland Library of Medieval Literature, 58. New York: Garland, 1990.

Thüring von Ringoltingen. *Melusine*, in *Romane des 15. und 16. Jahrhunderts*. Ed. Jan-Dirk Müller. Bibliothek der Frühen Neuzeit, 1. Frankfurt: Deutscher Klassiker Verlag, 1990.

**Titurel; and, the Songs*. Trans. Sidney M. Johnson and Marion E. Gibbs. Garland Library of Medieval Literature, 57. New York: Garland, 1988.

Ulrich von Zatzikhoven. *Lanzelet*. Trans. Thomas Kerth. Records of Western Civilization. New York: Columbia University Press, 2004.

Wirnt von Grafenberg. *Wigalois*. Ed. Sabine and Ulrich Seelbach. Berlin: Walter de Gruyter, 2005.

Wolfram von Eschenbach. *Parzival*. Ed. Bernard Schirok, trans. Peter Knecht. Berlin: Walter de Gruyter, 1998. **Parzival*. Trans. Cyril W. Edwards. Oxford World's Classics. Oxford: Oxford University Press, 2006.

Medieval Italian Romances

French/Franco-Italian

Les Prophesies de Merlin. Ed. Anne Berthelot. Geneva: Fondation Martin Bodmer, 1992.

Il romanzo arturiano di Rustichello da Pisa. Ed. Fabrizio Cigni. Pisa: Pacini Editore, 1994.

Italian

Ariosto, Ludovico. *Orlando Furioso*. 2 vols. Ed. Emilio Bigi. Milan: Rusconi, 1983; **Orlando Furioso: A New Verse Translation*. Trans. David R. Slavit. Cambridge, MA: Harvard University Press, 2009.

Boccaccio, Giovanni. *Teseida delle Nozze d'Emilia*. Ed. Edvige Agostinelli and William Coleman. Florence: Edizioni del Galluzzo for the Fondazione Ezio Franceschini, 2015.

**Theseid of the Nuptials of Emilia*. Trans. Vincenzo Traversa. New York: Peter Lang, 2002.

Boiardo, Matteo Maria. *Orlando Innamorato: L'inamoramento De Orlando*. Ed. Andrea Canova. Milan: RCS Libri S. p. A., 2011; *Orlando Innamorato: Orlando in Love.Trans. Charles Stanley Ross. West Lafayette, IN: Parlor Press, 2004.

Infurna, Marco. *La Inchiesta del San Gradale: Volgarizzamento toscano della Queste del Saint Graal*. Florence: Leon Olschki, 1995.

Pieri, Paulino. *La Storia di Merlino*. Ed. Mauro Cursietti. Rome: Zauli, 1997.

Pulci, Luigi. *Poeti, Volume 1: Il morgante maggiore*. Berlin: De Gruyter, 2021.

**Morgante: The Epic Adventures of Orlando and His Giant Friend Morgante*. Trans. Joseph Tusiani. Bloomington: Indiana University Press, 1998.

Il libro di messer Tristano ("Tristano Veneto"). Ed. Aulo Donadello. Venice: Marsilio, 1994.

La Tavola Ritonda. Ed. Marie-José Heijkant. Milan: Luni Editrice, 1997. **Tristan and the Round Table: A Translation of the Tavola Ritonda*. Trans. Ann Shaver. Binghampton, NY: Medieval and Renaissance Texts and Studies, 1983.

Tasso, Torquato. *Gerusalemme Liberata*. Ed. Ludovico Caretti. Turin: Einaudi, 1971; **The Liberation of Jerusalem*. Trans. Max Wickert. Oxford: Oxford University Press, 2009.

Tristano Corsinano. Ed. and trans. Gloria Allaire. Cambridge: D. S. Brewer, 2015.

Tristano Panciatichiano. Ed. and trans. Gloria Allaire. Cambridge: D. S. Brewer, 2002.

Tristano Riccardiano. Ed. Regina Psaki. Cambridge: D. S. Brewer, 2006.

Medieval Spanish and Iberian Peninsula Romances

Ben Elazar, Jacob. *The Love Stories of Jacob Ben Elazar (1170–1233?)* [Hebrew]. Ed Yonah David. Tel Aviv: Ramot Publishing, 1992.

Bohigas, Pere. *Los textos españoles y gallego-portugueses de la Demanda del santo grial*. Imprenta clásica española, (Madrid)1925.

Curial e Güelfa. Ed. R Aramon i Serra, Joan Santanach, Amadeu Soberanas, and Jaume Torró. Barcelona: Editorial Barcino, 2018; *Curial and Guelfa: a classic of the Crown of Aragon*. Trans. Max Wheeler. Amsterdam: John Benjamins Pub. Co., 2011.

Hadith Baya a-Riyad. In *Medieval Andalusian Courtly Culture in the Mediterranean*. Ed. and trans. Cynthia Robinson. London: Routledge, 2007.

King Artus: A Hebrew Arthurian Romance of 1279. Ed. Kurt Leviant. Assen: Van Gorcum & Co., 1969.

Kitab fihi hadith Ziyad ibn ʿAmir al-Kinani. Ed. Al-Shenawi Ali al-Gharib Muhammad. Cairo: Maktabat al-Adaab, 2009. **Zeyyad ben Amir el de Quinena*. Trans. Francisco Fernández y González. Madrid: Museo Español de Antigüedades, 1882.

Martorell, Joanot, and Martí Joan de Galba. *Tirant lo Blanc*. Ed. Martín de Riquer Barcelona: Ariel, 1982. **Tirant Lo Blanch*, trans. David H. Rosenthal Baltimore: Johns Hopkins University Press, 1984.

Medieval Iberia: Readings from Christian, Muslim, and Jewish Sources. Ed. Olivia Remie Constable. 2nd ed. Philadelphia: University of PennsylvaniaPress, 2011.

Rodríguez de Montalvo, Garci. *Amadís de Gaula*. Ed Juan Manuel Cacho Blecua. Madrid: Cátedra, 1996. **Amadis of Gaul: A Novel of Chivalry of the 14th Century Presumably First Written in Spanish*. Trans. Edwin B. Place and Herbert C. Behm. Lexington: University Press of Kentucky, 1974.

The Labors of the Very Brave Knight Esplandián, trans. William Thomas Little Binghamton, NY: Center for Medieval and Early Renaissance Studies, State University of New York at Binghamton, 1992.

Zeyyad ben Amir el de Quinena. Trans. Francisco Fernández y González. Madrid Museo Español de Antigüedades, 1882.

Romances from Other Traditions

"Culhwch and Olwen." *Mabinogion*. Trans. S. Davies. Oxford: Oxford University Press, 2007.

Digenis Akritis: The Grottaferrata and Escorial Versions. Ed. and trans. Elizabeth Jeffreys. Cambridge: Cambridge University Press, 1998.

Four Byzantine Novels. Trans. Elizabeth Jeffreys. Liverpool: Liverpool University Press, 2012.

Ganjavi, Nezami. *Layli and Majnun*. Trans. Dick Davies. London: Penguin, 2021.

Haft Paykar: A Medieval Persian Romance. Trans. Julie Scott Meisami. Indianapolis: Hackett, 2015.

Gorgānī, Fakhraddin. *Vis and Ramin*. Trans. Dick Davies. London: Penguin Books, 2009.

Llyfr Gwyn Rhydderch. Ed. R. M. Jones. Cardiff: University of Wales Press, 1973.

Other Primary Medieval and Early Modern Sources

Andreas Capellanus. *The Art of Courtly Love*. Trans. John Jay Parry. New York: Columbia University Press, 1990.

La Belle Hélène de Constantinople: chanson de geste du XIVe siècle. Ed. Claude Roussel. Geneva: Droz, 1995.

Boccaccio, Giovanni. *Decameron*, 2 vols. Ed. Vittore Branca. Turin: Einaudi, 1992; * *Decameron*. Trans. Wayne A. Rebhorn. New York: W. W. Norton, 2013.

Bodel, Jehan. *La Chanson des Saisnes*. Ed. Annette Brasseur. 2 vols. *Textes Littéraires Français* Geneva: Droz, 1989.

Boethius. *The Consolation of Philosophy*. Trans. David R. Slavitt. Cambridge: Harvard University Press, 2008.

Boucicaut. *Le livre des fais du bon messire Jehan le Maingre, dit Bouciquaut, mareschal deFrance et gouverneur de Jennes*. Ed. Denis Lalande. Paris: Droz, 1985.

**The Chivalric Biography of Boucicaut, Jean II le Meingre*. Trans. Craig Taylor and Jane H. M. Taylor. Woodbridge: Boydell, 2016.

***La Chanson de Roland*. Ed. and trans. Ian Short. Paris: LGF, 1990.

Le Charroi de Nîmes: Chanson de geste du Cycle de Guillaume d'Orange. Ed. and trans. Claude Lachet. Paris: Gallimard, 1999. *"The Convoy to Nimes," in *An Old French Trilogy: Texts from the William of Orange Cycle*. Trans. Catherine M. Jones, William W. Kibler, and Logan E. Whalen. Gainesville: University Press of Florida, 2020.

Christine de Pizan. *Le livre du corps de policie*. Ed. Angus J. Kennedy, Paris: Champion, 1998.

Dante, *De vulgari eloquentia*. Ed. and trans. Steven Botterill. Cambridge: Cambridge University Press, 1996.

Gaimar, Geffrei. *Estoire des Engleis: History of the English*. Ed. and trans. Ian Short. Oxford: Oxford University Press, 2009.

Geoffrey of Charny. *The Book of Chivalry of Geoffroi de Charny: text, context and translation*.Ed. Richard W. Kaeuper and Elspeth Kennedy. Philadelphia: University of Pennsylvania Press, 1996.

Geoffrey of Monmouth. *The History of the Kings of Britain: An Edition and Translation of Degestis Britonum (Historia Regum Britanniae)*. Ed. Michael D. Reeve, trans. Neil Wright. Woodbridge: Boydell Press, 2007.

Hoccleve, T. *Hoccleve's Works: The Minor Poems*. Ed. F. J. Furnival and I. Gollancz, rev. J. Mitchell and A. I. Doyle. London: Pub. for the Early English Text Society by K. Paul, Trench, Trübner, 1970.

Latini, Brunetto. *Livres dou Trésor*. Ed. Pietro Beltrami. Torino: Einaudi, 2007;

**The Book of the Treasure – Li Livres Dou Treasure*. Trans. Paul Barrette and Spurgeon Baldwin. London: Garland, 1993.

*Llull, Ramon. *A Contemporary Life*. Ed. and trans. Anthony Bonner. Barcelona: Barcino, 2010.

**The Book of the Order of Chivalry*. Trans. Noel Fallows. Woodbridge: The Boydell Press, 2013.

Philippe de Mézières. *Le songe du vieil pelerin*. Ed. G. W. Coopland. 2 vols. Cambridge: Cambridge University Press, 1969.

Torsello, Marino Sanudo. *The Book of the Secrets of the Faithful of the Cross*. Ed. and trans. Peter Lock. Burlington, VT: Ashgate, 2011.

Raoul de Hodenc. "*Le roman des eles*": *The anonymous "Ordene de chevalerie."* Ed. Keith Busby. Amsterdam: Benjamins, 1983.

Wauchier de Denain. *The Histoire ancienne jusqu'à César: A Digital Edition*. Ed Hannah Morcos, Simon Gaunt, Simone Ventura, et al. London: King's Digital Lab (The Values of French), 2021.

Wauchier de Denain. "*L'histoire des moines d'Égypte,*" *suivie de "La vie de saint Paul le simple*." Ed Michelle Szkilnik. Geneva: Droz, 1993.

William of Adam. *How to Defeat the Saracens*. Ed. and trans. Giles Constable. Washington, DC: Dumbarton Oaks Research Library and Collection, 2012.

Contemporary Arthurian Film and Fiction

The Adventures of Sir Galahad. Directed by Spencer Bennett. Columbia Pictures, 1949.

Bradley, Marion Zimmer. *The Mists of Avalon*. New York: Ballantine Books, 1984.

Camelot. Directed by Joshua Logan. Warner Brothers Studio, 1967.

Cursed. Created by Frank Miller and Tom Wheeler. Netflix Studios, 2020.

Excalibur. Directed by John Boorman. Orion Pictures, 1981.

First Knight. Directed by Jerry Zucker. Columbia Pictures, 1995.

The Green Knight. Directed by David Lowery. Les Line Entertainment, 2021.

The Kid Who Would be King. Directed by Joe Cornish. Twentieth Century Fox Studios, 2019.

King Arthur. Directed by Antoine Fuqua. Touchstone Pictures, 2004.

King Arthur: Legend of the Sword. Directed by Guy Ritchie. Warner Brothers Pictures, 2017.

Monty Python and The Holy Grail. Directed by Terry Jones and Terry Gilliam. Python (Monty) Pictures, 1975.

The Sword in the Stone. Directed by Wolfgang Reitherman. Walt Disney Productions, 1963.

White, T. H. *The Once and Future King*. New York: Ace Publishing, 2011.

INDEX

Cambridge Companions To . . .

AUTHORS

Edward Albee edited by Stephen J. Bottoms

Margaret Atwood edited by Coral Ann Howells (second edition)

W. H. Auden edited by Stan Smith

Jane Austen edited by Edward Copeland and Juliet McMaster (second edition)

Balzac edited by Owen Heathcote and Andrew Watts

Beckett edited by John Pilling

Bede edited by Scott DeGregorio

Aphra Behn edited by Derek Hughes and Janet Todd

Saul Bellow edited by Victoria Aarons

Walter Benjamin edited by David S. Ferris

William Blake edited by Morris Eaves

James Baldwin edited by Michele Elam

Boccaccio edited by Guyda Armstrong, Rhiannon Daniels, and Stephen J. Milner

Jorge Luis Borges edited by Edwin Williamson

Brecht edited by Peter Thomson and Glendyr Sacks (second edition)

The Brontës edited by Heather Glen

Bunyan edited by Anne Dunan-Page

Frances Burney edited by Peter Sabor

Byron edited by Drummond Bone

Albert Camus edited by Edward J. Hughes

Willa Cather edited by Marilee Lindemann

Catullus edited by Ian Du Quesnay and Tony Woodman

Cervantes edited by Anthony J. Cascardi

Chaucer edited by Piero Boitani and Jill Mann (second edition)

Chekhov edited by Vera Gottlieb and Paul Allain

Kate Chopin edited by Janet Beer

Caryl Churchill edited by Elaine Aston and Elin Diamond

Cicero edited by Catherine Steel

J. M. Coetzee edited by Jarad Zimbler

Coleridge edited by Lucy Newlyn

Coleridge edited by Tim Fulford (new edition)

Wilkie Collins edited by Jenny Bourne Taylor

Joseph Conrad edited by J. H. Stape

H. D. edited by Nephie J. Christodoulides and Polina Mackay

Dante edited by Rachel Jacoff (second edition)

Daniel Defoe edited by John Richetti

Don DeLillo edited by John N. Duvall

Charles Dickens edited by John O. Jordan

Emily Dickinson edited by Wendy Martin

John Donne edited by Achsah Guibbory

Dostoevskii edited by W. J. Leatherbarrow

Theodore Dreiser edited by Leonard Cassuto and Claire Virginia Eby

John Dryden edited by Steven N. Zwicker

W. E. B. Du Bois edited by Shamoon Zamir

George Eliot edited by George Levine and Nancy Henry (second edition)

T. S. Eliot edited by A. David Moody

Ralph Ellison edited by Ross Posnock

Ralph Waldo Emerson edited by Joel Porte and Saundra Morris

William Faulkner edited by Philip M. Weinstein

Henry Fielding edited by Claude Rawson

F. Scott Fitzgerald edited by Ruth Prigozy

Flaubert edited by Timothy Unwin

E. M. Forster edited by David Bradshaw

Benjamin Franklin edited by Carla Mulford

Brian Friel edited by Anthony Roche

Robert Frost edited by Robert Faggen

Gabriel García Márquez edited by Philip Swanson

Elizabeth Gaskell edited by Jill L. Matus

Edward Gibbon edited by Karen O'Brien and Brian Young

Goethe edited by Lesley Sharpe

Günter Grass edited by Stuart Taberner

Thomas Hardy edited by Dale Kramer

David Hare edited by Richard Boon

Nathaniel Hawthorne edited by Richard Millington

Seamus Heaney edited by Bernard O'Donoghue

Ernest Hemingway edited by Scott Donaldson

Hildegard of Bingen edited by Jennifer Bain

Homer edited by Robert Fowler

Horace edited by Stephen Harrison

Ted Hughes edited by Terry Gifford

Ibsen edited by James McFarlane

Henry James edited by Jonathan Freedman

Samuel Johnson edited by Greg Clingham

Ben Jonson edited by Richard Harp and Stanley Stewart

James Joyce edited by Derek Attridge (second edition)

Kafka edited by Julian Preece

Keats edited by Susan J. Wolfson

Rudyard Kipling edited by Howard J. Booth

Lacan edited by Jean-Michel Rabaté

D. H. Lawrence edited by Anne Fernihough

Primo Levi edited by Robert Gordon

Lucretius edited by Stuart Gillespie and Philip Hardie

Machiavelli edited by John M. Najemy

David Mamet edited by Christopher Bigsby

Thomas Mann edited by Ritchie Robertson

Christopher Marlowe edited by Patrick Cheney

Andrew Marvell edited by Derek Hirst and Steven N. Zwicker

Ian McEwan edited by Dominic Head

Herman Melville edited by Robert S. Levine

Arthur Miller edited by Christopher Bigsby (second edition)

Milton edited by Dennis Danielson (second edition)

Molière edited by David Bradby and Andrew Calder

Toni Morrison edited by Justine Tally

Alice Munro edited by David Staines

Nabokov edited by Julian W. Connolly

Eugene O'Neill edited by Michael Manheim

George Orwell edited by John Rodden

Ovid edited by Philip Hardie

Petrarch edited by Albert Russell Ascoli and Unn Falkeid

Harold Pinter edited by Peter Raby (second edition)

Sylvia Plath edited by Jo Gill

Plutarch edited by Frances B. Titchener and Alexei Zadorojnyi

Edgar Allan Poe edited by Kevin J. Hayes

Alexander Pope edited by Pat Rogers

Ezra Pound edited by Ira B. Nadel

Proust edited by Richard Bales

Pushkin edited by Andrew Kahn

Thomas Pynchon edited by Inger H. Dalsgaard, Luc Herman and Brian McHale

Rabelais edited by John O'Brien

Rilke edited by Karen Leeder and Robert Vilain

Philip Roth edited by Timothy Parrish

Salman Rushdie edited by Abdulrazak Gurnah

John Ruskin edited by Francis O'Gorman

Sappho edited by P. J. Finglass and Adrian Kelly

Seneca edited by Shadi Bartsch and Alessandro Schiesaro

Shakespeare edited by Margareta de Grazia and Stanley Wells (second edition)

George Bernard Shaw edited by Christopher Innes

Shelley edited by Timothy Morton

Mary Shelley edited by Esther Schor

Sam Shepard edited by Matthew C. Roudané

Spenser edited by Andrew Hadfield

Laurence Sterne edited by Thomas Keymer

Wallace Stevens edited by John N. Serio

Tom Stoppard edited by Katherine E. Kelly

Harriet Beecher Stowe edited by Cindy Weinstein

August Strindberg edited by Michael Robinson

Jonathan Swift edited by Christopher Fox

J. M. Synge edited by P. J. Mathews

Tacitus edited by A. J. Woodman

Henry David Thoreau edited by Joel Myerson

Thucydides edited by Polly Low

Tolstoy edited by Donna Tussing Orwin

Anthony Trollope edited by Carolyn Dever and Lisa Niles

Mark Twain edited by Forrest G. Robinson

John Updike edited by Stacey Olster

Mario Vargas Llosa edited by Efrain Kristal and John King

Virgil edited by Fiachra Mac Góráin and Charles Martindale (second edition)

Voltaire edited by Nicholas Cronk

David Foster Wallace edited by Ralph Clare

Edith Wharton edited by Millicent Bell

Walt Whitman edited by Ezra Greenspan

Oscar Wilde edited by Peter Raby

Tennessee Williams edited by Matthew C. Roudané

William Carlos Williams edited by Christopher MacGowan

August Wilson edited by Christopher Bigsby

Mary Wollstonecraft edited by Claudia L. Johnson

Virginia Woolf edited by Susan Sellers (second edition)

Wordsworth edited by Stephen Gill

Richard Wright edited by Glenda R. Carpio

W. B. Yeats edited by Marjorie Howes and John Kelly

Xenophon edited by Michael A. Flower

Zola edited by Brian Nelson

TOPICS

The Actress edited by Maggie B. Gale and John Stokes

The African American Novel edited by Maryemma Graham

The African American Slave Narrative edited by Audrey A. Fisch

African American Theatre edited by Harvey Young

Allegory edited by Rita Copeland and Peter Struck

American Crime Fiction edited by Catherine Ross Nickerson

American Gothic edited by Jeffrey Andrew Weinstock

American Horror edited by Stephen Shapiro and Mark Storey

American Literature and the Body by Travis M. Foster

American Literature and the Environment edited by Sarah Ensor and Susan Scott Parrish

American Literature of the 1930s edited by William Solomon

American Modernism edited by Walter Kalaidjian

American Poetry since 1945 edited by Jennifer Ashton

American Realism and Naturalism edited by Donald Pizer

American Travel Writing edited by Alfred Bendixen and Judith Hamera

American Women Playwrights edited by Brenda Murphy

Ancient Rhetoric edited by Erik Gunderson

Arthurian Legend edited by Elizabeth Archibald and Ad Putter

Australian Literature edited by Elizabeth Webby

The Australian Novel edited by Nicholas Birns and Louis Klee

The Beats edited by Stephen Belletto

Boxing edited by Gerald Early

British Black and Asian Literature (1945–2010) edited by Deirdre Osborne

British Fiction: 1980–2018 edited by Peter Boxall

British Fiction since 1945 edited by David James

British Literature of the 1930s edited by James Smith

British Literature of the French Revolution edited by Pamela Clemit

British Romantic Poetry edited by James Chandler and Maureen N. McLane

British Romanticism edited by Stuart Curran (second edition)

British Romanticism and Religion edited by Jeffrey Barbeau

British Theatre, 1730–1830 edited by Jane Moody and Daniel O'Quinn

Canadian Literature edited by Eva-Marie Kröller (second edition)

The Canterbury Tales edited by Frank Grady

Children's Literature edited by M. O. Grenby and Andrea Immel

The Classic Russian Novel edited by Malcolm V. Jones and Robin Feuer Miller

Contemporary Irish Poetry edited by Matthew Campbell

Creative Writing edited by David Morley and Philip Neilsen

Crime Fiction edited by Martin Priestman

Dante's 'Commedia' edited by Zygmunt G. Barański and Simon Gilson

Dracula edited by Roger Luckhurst

Early American Literature edited by Bryce Traister

Early Modern Women's Writing edited by Laura Lunger Knoppers

The Eighteenth-Century Novel edited by John Richetti

Eighteenth-Century Poetry edited by John Sitter

Eighteenth-Century Thought edited by Frans De Bruyn

Emma edited by Peter Sabor

English Dictionaries edited by Sarah Ogilvie

English Literature, 1500–1600 edited by Arthur F. Kinney

English Literature, 1650–1740 edited by Steven N. Zwicker

English Literature, 1740–1830 edited by Thomas Keymer and Jon Mee

English Literature, 1830–1914 edited by Joanne Shattock

English Melodrama edited by Carolyn Williams

English Novelists edited by Adrian Poole

English Poetry, Donne to Marvell edited by Thomas N. Corns

English Poets edited by Claude Rawson

English Renaissance Drama edited by A. R. Braunmuller and Michael Hattaway, (second edition)

English Renaissance Tragedy edited by Emma Smith and Garrett A. Sullivan Jr.

English Restoration Theatre edited by Deborah C. Payne Fisk

Environmental Humanities edited by Jeffrey Cohen and Stephanie Foote

The Epic edited by Catherine Bates

Erotic Literature edited by Bradford Mudge

The Essay edited by Kara Wittman and Evan Kindley

European Modernism edited by Pericles Lewis

European Novelists edited by Michael Bell

Fairy Tales edited by Maria Tatar

Fantasy Literature edited by Edward James and Farah Mendlesohn

Feminist Literary Theory edited by Ellen Rooney

Fiction in the Romantic Period edited by Richard Maxwell and Katie Trumpener

The Fin de Siècle edited by Gail Marshall

Frankenstein edited by Andrew Smith

The French Enlightenment edited by Daniel Brewer

French Literature edited by John D. Lyons

The French Novel: from 1800 to the Present edited by Timothy Unwin

Gay and Lesbian Writing edited by Hugh Stevens

German Romanticism edited by Nicholas Saul

Global Literature and Slavery edited by Laura T. Murphy

Gothic Fiction edited by Jerrold E. Hogle

The Graphic Novel edited by Stephen Tabachnick

The Greek and Roman Novel edited by Tim Whitmarsh

Greek and Roman Theatre edited by Marianne McDonald and J. Michael Walton

Greek Comedy edited by Martin Revermann

Greek Lyric edited by Felix Budelmann

Greek Mythology edited by Roger D. Woodard

Greek Tragedy edited by P. E. Easterling

The Harlem Renaissance edited by George Hutchinson

The History of the Book edited by Leslie Howsam

Human Rights and Literature edited by Crystal Parikh

The Irish Novel edited by John Wilson Foster

Irish Poets edited by Gerald Dawe

The Italian Novel edited by Peter Bondanella and Andrea Ciccarelli

The Italian Renaissance edited by Michael Wyatt

Jewish American Literature edited by Hana Wirth-Nesher and Michael P. Kramer

The Latin American Novel edited by Efraín Kristal

Latin American Poetry edited by Stephen Hart

Latina/o American Literature edited by John Morán González

Latin Love Elegy edited by Thea S. Thorsen

Literature and the Anthropocene edited by John Parham

Literature and Climate edited by Adeline Johns-Putra and Kelly Sultzbach

Literature and Disability edited by Clare Barker and Stuart Murray

Literature and Food edited by J. Michelle Coghlan

Literature and the Posthuman edited by Bruce Clarke and Manuela Rossini

Literature and Religion edited by Susan M. Felch

Literature and Science edited by Steven Meyer

The Literature of the American Civil War and Reconstruction edited by Kathleen Diffley and Coleman Hutchison

The Literature of the American Renaissance edited by Christopher N. Phillips

The Literature of Berlin edited by Andrew J. Webber

The Literature of the Crusades edited by Anthony Bale

The Literature of the First World War edited b Vincent Sherry

The Literature of London edited by Lawrence Manley

The Literature of Los Angeles edited by Kevin R. McNamara

The Literature of New York edited by Cyrus Patell and Bryan Waterman

The Literature of Paris edited by Anna-Louise Milne

The Literature of World War II edited by Marina MacKay

Literature on Screen edited by Deborah Cartme and Imelda Whelehan

Lyrical Ballads edited by Sally Bushell

Medieval British Manuscripts edited by Orietta Da Rold and Elaine Treharne

Medieval English Culture edited by Andrew Galloway

Medieval English Law and Literature edited by Candace Barrington and Sebastian Sobecki

Medieval English Literature edited by Larry Scanlon

Medieval English Mysticism edited by Samuel Fanous and Vincent Gillespie

Medieval English Theatre edited by Richard Beadle and Alan J. Fletcher (second edition)

Medieval French Literature edited by Simon Gaunt and Sarah Kay

Medieval Romance edited by Roberta L. Krueger

Medieval Romance edited by Roberta L. Krueger (new edition)

Medieval Women's Writing edited by Carolyn Dinshaw and David Wallace

Modern American Culture edited by Christopher Bigsby

Modern British Women Playwrights edited by Elaine Aston and Janelle Reinelt

Modern French Culture edited by Nicholas Hewitt

Modern German Culture edited by Eva Kolinsky and Wilfried van der Will

The Modern German Novel edited by Graham Bartram

The Modern Gothic edited by Jerrold E. Hogle

Modern Irish Culture edited by Joe Cleary and Claire Connolly

Modern Italian Culture edited by Zygmunt G. Baranski and Rebecca J. West

Modern Latin American Culture edited by John King

Modern Russian Culture edited by Nicholas Rzhevsky

Modern Spanish Culture edited by David T. Gies

Modernism edited by Michael Levenson (second edition)

The Modernist Novel edited by Morag Shiach

Modernist Poetry edited by Alex Davis and Lee M. Jenkins

Modernist Women Writers edited by Maren Tova Linett

Narrative edited by David Herman

Narrative Theory edited by Matthew Garrett

Native American Literature edited by Joy Porter and Kenneth M. Roemer

Nineteen Eighty-Four edited by Nathan Waddell

Nineteenth-Century American Poetry edited by Kerry Larson

Nineteenth-Century American Women's Writing edited by Dale M. Bauer and Philip Gould

Nineteenth-Century Thought edited by Gregory Claeys

The Novel edited by Eric Bulson

Old English Literature edited by Malcolm Godden and Michael Lapidge (second edition)

Performance Studies edited by Tracy C. Davis

Piers Plowman edited by Andrew Cole and Andrew Galloway

The Poetry of the First World War edited by Santanu Das

Popular Fiction edited by David Glover and Scott McCracken

Postcolonial Literary Studies edited by Neil Lazarus

Postcolonial Poetry edited by Jahan Ramazani

Postcolonial Travel Writing edited by Robert Clarke

Postmodern American Fiction edited by Paula Geyh

Postmodernism edited by Steven Connor

Prose edited by Daniel Tyler

The Pre-Raphaelites edited by Elizabeth Prettejohn

Pride and Prejudice edited by Janet Todd

Queer Studies edited by Siobhan B. Somerville

Renaissance Humanism edited by Jill Kraye

Robinson Crusoe edited by John Richetti

Roman Comedy edited by Martin T. Dinter

The Roman Historians edited by Andrew Feldherr

Roman Satire edited by Kirk Freudenburg

Science Fiction edited by Edward James and Farah Mendlesohn

Scottish Literature edited by Gerald Carruthers and Liam McIlvanney

Sensation Fiction edited by Andrew Mangham

Shakespeare and Contemporary Dramatists edited by Ton Hoenselaars

Shakespeare and Popular Culture edited by Robert Shaughnessy

Shakespeare and Race edited by Ayanna Thompson

Shakespeare and Religion edited by Hannibal Hamlin

Shakespeare and War edited by David Loewenstein and Paul Stevens

Shakespeare on Film edited by Russell Jackson (second edition)

Shakespeare on Screen edited by Russell Jackson

Shakespeare on Stage edited by Stanley Wells and Sarah Stanton

Shakespearean Comedy edited by Alexander Leggatt

Shakespearean Tragedy edited by Claire McEachern (second edition)

Shakespeare's First Folio edited by Emma Smith

Shakespeare's History Plays edited by Michael Hattaway

Shakespeare's Language edited by Lynne Magnusson with David Schalkwyk

Shakespeare's Last Plays edited by Catherine M. S. Alexander

Shakespeare's Poetry edited by Patrick Cheney

Sherlock Holmes edited by Janice M. Allan and Christopher Pittard

The Sonnet edited by A. D. Cousins and Peter Howarth

The Spanish Novel: from 1600 to the Present edited by Harriet Turner and Adelaida López de Martínez

Textual Scholarship edited by Neil Fraistat and Julia Flanders

Theatre and Science edited by Kristen E. Shepherd-Barr

Theatre History edited by David Wiles and Christine Dymkowski

Transnational American Literature edited by Yogita Goyal

Travel Writing edited by Peter Hulme and Tim Youngs

Twentieth-Century British and Irish Women's Poetry edited by Jane Dowson

The Twentieth-Century English Novel edited by Robert L. Caserio

Twentieth-Century English Poetry edited by Neil Corcoran

Twentieth-Century Irish Drama edited by Shaun Richards

Twentieth-Century Literature and Politics edited by Christos Hadjiyiannis and Rachel Potter

Twentieth-Century Russian Literature edited by Marina Balina and Evgeny Dobrenko

Utopian Literature edited by Gregory Claeys

Victorian and Edwardian Theatre edited by Kerry Powell

The Victorian Novel edited by Deirdre David (second edition)

Victorian Poetry edited by Joseph Bristow

Victorian Women's Poetry edited by Linda K. Hughes

Victorian Women's Writing edited by Linda H. Peterson

War Writing edited by Kate McLoughlin

Women's Writing in Britain, 1660–1789 edited by Catherine Ingrassia

Women's Writing in the Romantic Period edited by Devoney Looser

World Literature edited by Ben Etherington and Jarad Zimbler

World Crime Fiction edited by Jesper Gulddal, Stewart King and Alistair Rolls

Writing of the English Revolution edited by N. H. Keeble

The Writings of Julius Caesar edited by Christopher Krebs and Luca Grillo

Printed by Printforce, United Kingdom